A Theologico-Political Treatise
and
A Political Treatise

Benedict de Spinoza

Translated with an Introduction by
R. H. M. Elwes

Dover Publications, Inc.
Mineola, New York

DOVER PHILOSOPHICAL CLASSICS

Bibliographical Note

This Dover edition, first published in 2004, is an unabridged republication of the work originally published as Volume 1 of *The Chief Works of Benedict de Spinoza* by G. Bell and Sons, London, in 1883–1884, and republished under the present title (with an added bibliographical note by Francesco Cordasco) by Dover Publications, Inc., in 1951. Letters referred to in the Introduction to this volume can be found in Volume 2 of the Bell edition—reprinted by Dover as *On the Improvement of the Understanding; the Ethics; Correspondence* (ISBN 0-486-20250-X).

International Standard Book Number: 0-486-43722-1

Manufactured in the United States of America
Dover Publications, Inc., 31 East 2nd Street, Mineola, N.Y. 11501

CONTENTS

	PAGE
INTRODUCTION	v

Original unpopularity of Spinoza's writings, their gradually
   increasing influence in Germany, France, Holland, and
   England   v

Authorities for the life of Spinoza : Colerus, &c. . . . ix

Birth, 1634, and education of Spinoza x

His breach with the synagogue, 1656 xii

Life near Amsterdam and at Rhijnsburg xiii

Friendship with Simon de Vries xiv

Removal to Voorburg and the Hague xv

Correspondence with Oldenburg, Leibnitz, Tschirnhausen, and
   others. Publication of Tractatus Theologico-Politicus, 1670.   xvi

Massacre of the De Witts, 1672. Indignation and danger of
   Spinoza xvii

Completion of the Ethics, 1674 xviii

Later life of Spinoza xviii

Death and burial, February, 1677 xx

Opera Posthuma published 1677 xxi

Sketch of Spinoza's philosophy xxi

Scope of the present work xxxii

THEOLOGICO-POLITICAL TREATISE 1

Preface 3

Origin and consequences of superstition 3

Causes that have led the author to write . . . 6

Course of his investigation 8

For what readers the treatise is designed. Submission of
   author to the rulers of his country 11

Chap. I.—*Of Prophecy* 13

Definition of prophecy 13

Distinction between revelation to Moses and to the other
   prophets 15

Between Christ and all other recipients of revelation . . 19

Ambiguity of the word " Spirit " 19

The different senses in which things may be referred to God. 20

Different senses of " Spirit of God " 22

Prophets perceived revelation by imagination . . . 24

CONTENTS.

PAGE

Chap. II.—*Of Prophets* 27
   A mistake to suppose that prophecy can give knowledge of
     phenomena 27
   Certainty of prophecy based on (1) Vividness of Imagination,
     (2) A Sign, (3) Goodness of the Prophet 29
   Variation of prophecy with the temperament and opinions of
     the individual 30

Chap. III.—*Of the Vocation of the Hebrews, and whether the
    Gift of Prophecy was peculiar to them* 43
   Happiness of Hebrews did not consist in the inferiority of the
     Gentiles 43
   Nor in philosophic knowledge or virtue 45
   But in their conduct of affairs of state and escape from poli-
     tical dangers 46
   Even this distinction did not exist in the time of Abraham . 48
   Testimony from the Old Testament itself to the share of the
     Gentiles in the law and favour of God 49
   Explanation of apparent discrepancy of the Epistle to the
     Romans 53
   Answer to the arguments for the eternal election of the Jews. 54

Chap. IV.—*Of the Divine Law* 57
   Laws either depend on natural necessity or on human decree.
     The existence of the latter not inconsistent with the former
     class of laws 57
   Divine law a kind of law founded on human decree : called
     Divine from its object 59
   Divine law (1) universal; (2) independent of the truth of any
     historical narrative; (3) independent of rites and ceremonies;
     (4) its own reward 61
   Reason does not present God as a law-giver for men . . 62
   Such a conception a proof of ignorance—in Adam—in the
     Israelites—in Christians 63
   Testimony of the Scriptures in favour of reason and the
     rational view of the Divine law 65

Chap. V.—*Of the Ceremonial Law* 69
   Ceremonial law of the Old Testament no part of the Divine
     universal law, but partial and temporary. Testimony of
     the prophets themselves to this 69
   Testimony of the New Testament 72
   How the ceremonial law tended to preserve the Hebrew kingdom 73
   Christian rites on a similar footing 76
   What part of the Scripture narratives is one bound to believe? 76

Chap. VI.—*Of Miracles* 81
   Confused ideas of the vulgar on the subject 81
   A miracle in the sense of a contravention of natural laws an
     absurdity 82
   In the sense of an event, whose cause is unknown, less edify-
     ing than an event better understood 84

CONTENTS.

	PAGE
God's providence identical with the course of nature	89
How Scripture miracles may be interpreted	92

Chap. VII.—*Of the Interpretation of Scripture.* . . . 98
Current systems of interpretation erroneous	98
Only true system to interpret it by itself	100
Reasons why this system cannot now be carried out in its entirety	108
Yet these difficulties do not interfere with our understanding the plainest and most important passages	113
Rival systems examined—that of a supernatural faculty being necessary—refuted	114
That of Maimonides	114
Refuted	116
Traditions of the Pharisees and the Papists rejected	118

Chap. VIII.—*Of the authorship of the Pentateuch, and the other historical books of the Old Testament* . . . 120
The Pentateuch not written by Moses	120
His actual writings distinct	124
Traces of late authorship in the other historical books	127
All the historical books the work of one man	129
Probably Ezra	130
Who compiled first the book of Deuteronomy	131
And then a history, distinguishing the books by the names of their subjects	132

Chap. IX.—*Other questions about these books* . . . 133
That these books have not been thoroughly revised and made to agree	133
That there are many doubtful readings	139
That the existing marginal notes are often such	140
The other explanations of these notes refuted	141
The hiatus	145

Chap. X.—*An Examination of the remaining books of the Old Testament according to the preceding method* . . . 146
Chronicles, Psalms, Proverbs	146
Isaiah, Jeremiah	147
Ezekiel, Hosea	148
Other prophets, Jonah, Job	149
Daniel, Ezra, Nehemiah, Esther	150
The author declines to undertake a similar detailed examination of the New Testament	156

Chap. XI.—*An Inquiry whether the Apostles wrote their Epistles as Apostles and Prophets, or merely as Teachers, and an Explanation of what is meant by an Apostle* . . . 157
The epistles not in the prophetic style	157
The Apostles not commanded to write nor to preach in particular places	159
Different methods of teaching adopted by the Apostles	163

CONTENTS.

PAGE

Chap. XII.—*Of the true Original of the Divine Law, and where-fore Scripture is called Sacred, and the Word of God. How that, in so far as it contains the Word of God, it has come down to us uncorrupted* 165

Chap. XIII.—*It is shown, that Scripture teaches only very Simple Doctrines, such as suffice for right conduct* 175

Error in speculative doctrine not impious—nor knowledge pious. Piety consists in obedience 180

Chap. XIV.—*Definitions of Faith, the True Faith, and the Foundations of Faith, which is once for all separated from Philosophy* 182

Danger resulting from the vulgar idea of faith . . . 182

The only test of faith obedience and good works . . . 184

As different men are disposed to obedience by different opinions, universal faith can contain only the simplest doctrines 186

Fundamental distinction between faith and philosophy—the key-stone of the present treatise 189

Chap. XV.—*Theology is shown not to be subservient to Reason, nor Reason to Theology: a Definition of the reason which enables us to accept the Authority of the Bible* . . . 190

Theory that Scripture must be accommodated to Reason—maintained by Maimonides—already refuted in Chapter VII. 190

Theory that Reason must be accommodated to Scripture—maintained by Alpakhar—examined . . . 191

And refuted 194

Scripture and Reason independent of one another . . 195

Certainty of fundamental faith not mathematical but moral . 196

Great utility of Revelation 198

Chap. XVI.—*Of the Foundations of a State; of the Natural and Civil Rights of Individuals; and of the Rights of the Sovereign Power* 200

In Nature right co-extensive with power 200

This principle applies to mankind in the state of Nature . 201

How a transition from this state to a civil state is possible . 203

Subjects not slaves 206

Definition of private civil right—and wrong . . . 207

Of alliance 208

Of treason 209

In what sense sovereigns are bound by Divine law . . 210

Civil government not inconsistent with religion . . . 211

Chap. XVII.— *It is shown, that no one can or need transfer all his Rights to the Sovereign Power. Of the Hebrew Republic, as it was during the lifetime of Moses, and after his death till the foundation of the Monarchy; and of its Excellence. Lastly, of the Causes why the Theocratic Republic fell, and why it could hardly have continued without Dissension* . . 214

PAGE

The absolute theory of Sovereignty ideal—No one can in
fact transfer all his rights to the Sovereign power. Evi-
dence of this 214
The greatest danger in all States from within, not without . 216
Original independence of the Jews after the Exodus . . 218
Changed first to a pure democratic Theocracy . . . 219
Then to subjection to Moses. 220
Then to a Theocracy with the power divided between the
high priest and the captains 221
The tribes confederate States 224
Restraints on the civil power 226
Restraints on the people 228
Causes of decay involved in the constitution of the Levitical
priesthood 232

Chap. XVIII.—*From the Commonwealth of the Hebrews and their
History certain Lessons are deduced* 237
The Hebrew constitution no longer possible or desirable, yet
lessons may be derived from its history 237
As the danger of entrusting any authority in politics to
ecclesiastics — the danger of identifying religion with
dogma 241
The necessity of keeping all judicial power with the sovereign
—the danger of changes in the form of a State . . . 242
This last danger illustrated from the history of England—of
Rome 243
And of Holland 244

Chap. XIX. *It is shown that the Right over Matters Spiritual lies
wholly with the Sovereign, and that the Outward Forms of
Religion should be in accordance with Public Peace, if we
would worship God aright* 245
Difference between external and inward religion . . . 245
Positive law established only by agreement 246
Piety furthered by peace and obedience 249
Position of the Apostles exceptional 250
Why Christian States, unlike the Hebrew, suffer from dis-
putes between the civil and ecclesiastical powers . . 254
Absolute power in things spiritual of modern rulers . . 256

Chap. XX. *That in a Free State every man may Think what
he Likes, and Say what he Thinks* 257
The mind not subject to State authority 257
Therefore in general language should not be 258
A man who disapproving of a law, submits his adverse opinion
to the judgment of the authorities, while acting in accor-
dance with the law, deserves well of the State . . . 259
That liberty of opinion is beneficial, shown from the history
of Amsterdam 264
Danger to the State of withholding it.—Submission of the
Author to the judgment of his country's rulers . . 265

CONTENTS.

	PAGE
AUTHOR'S NOTES TO THE TREATISE	267
A POLITICAL TREATISE	279
Extract from the Preface to Opera Posthuma	281
Contents	283
Chap. I. Introduction	287
II. Of Natural Right	291
III. Of the Right of Supreme Authorities	301
IV. Of the Functions of Supreme Authorities	309
V. Of the Best State of a Dominion	313
VI. Of Monarchy	316
VII. Of Monarchy. *Continuation*	327
VIII. Of Aristocracy	345
IX. Of Aristocracy. *Continuation*	370
X. Of Aristocracy. *Conclusion*	378
XI. Of Democracy	385
BIBLIOGRAPHICAL NOTE	389

INTRODUCTION.

"Konstatiert ist es, das der Lebenswandel des Spinoza frei von allem Tadel war, und rein und makellos wie das Leben seines göttlichen Vetters, Jesu Christi. Auch wie Dieser litt er für seine Lehre wie Dieser trug er die Dornenkrone. Ueberall, wo ein grosser Geist seine Gedenken ausspricht, ist Golgotha."—HEINE.

A VERY few years ago the writings of Spinoza were almost unknown in this country. The only authorities to which the English reader could be referred were the brilliant essays of Mr. Froude[1] and Mr. Matthew Arnold,[2] the graphic but somewhat misleading sketch in Lewes's "History of Philosophy," and the unsatisfactory volume of Dr. R. Willis.[3] But in 1880 Mr. Pollock brought out his most valuable "Spinoza, his Life and Philosophy,"[4] likely long to remain the standard work on the subject; Dr. Martineau has followed with a sympathetic and gracefully written "Study of Spinoza;" Professor Knight has edited a volume of Spinozistic Essays by Continental Philoso-

[1] "Short Studies in Great Subjects," first series, art. "Spinoza."
[2] "Essays in Criticism," art. "Spinoza and the Bible."
[3] "Benedict de Spinoza; his Life, Correspondence, and Ethics." 1870.
[4] I take this early opportunity of recording my deep obligations to Mr. Pollock's book. I have made free use of it, together with Dr. Martineau's, in compiling this introduction. In the passages which Mr. Pollock has incidentally translated, I have been glad to be able to refer to the versions of so distinguished a scholar.

phers; Auerbach's biographical novel[1] has been translated, and many writers have made contributions to the subject in magazines and reviews.

At first sight this stir of tardy recognition may seem less surprising than the preceding apathy, for history can show few figures more remarkable than the solitary thinker of Amsterdam. But the causes which kept Spinoza in comparative obscurity are not very far to seek. Personally he shrank with almost womanly sensitiveness from anything like notoriety: his chief work was withheld till after his death, and then published anonymously; his treatise on Religion was also put forth in secret, and he disclaims with evident sincerity all desire to found a school, or give his name to a sect.

Again, the form in which his principal work is cast is such as to repel those dilettante readers, whose suffrage is necessary for a widely-extended reputation; none but genuine students would care to grapple with the serried array of definitions, axioms, and propositions, of which the Ethics is composed, while the display of geometric accuracy flatters the careless into supposing, that the whole structure is interdependent, and that, when a single breach has been effected, the entire fabric has been demolished.

The matter, no less than the manner, of Spinoza's writings was such as to preclude popularity. He genuinely shocked his contemporaries. Advances in thought are tolerated in proportion as they respond to and, as it were, kindle into flame ideas which are already smouldering obscurely in many minds. A teacher may deepen, modify, transfigure what he finds, but he must not attempt radical reconstruction. In the seventeenth century all men's deepest convictions were inseparably bound up with anthropomorphic notions of the Deity; Spinoza, in attacking these latter and endeavouring to substitute the conception

---

[1] "Spinoza: ein Denkerleben." 1855.

of eternal and necessary law, seemed to be striking at the very roots of moral order: hence with curious irony his works, which few read and still fewer understood, became associated with notions of monstrous impiety, and their author, who loved virtue with single-hearted and saintly devotion, was branded as a railer against God and a subverter of morality, whom it was a shame even to speak of. Those from whom juster views might have been expected swelled the popular cry. The Cartesians sought to confirm their own precarious reputation for orthodoxy by emphatic disavowals of their more daring associate. Leibnitz, who had known Spinoza personally, speaks of him, whether from jealousy or some more avowable motive, in tones of consistent depreciation.

The torrent of abuse, which poured forth from the theologians and their allies, served to overwhelm the ethical and metaphysical aspect of Spinoza's teaching. The philosopher was hidden behind the arch-heretic. Throughout almost the whole of the century following his death, he is spoken of in terms displaying complete misapprehension of his importance and scope. The grossly inaccurate account given by Bayle in the "Dictionnaire Philosophique" was accepted as sufficient. The only symptom of a following is found in the religious sect of Hattemists, which based some of its doctrines on an imperfect understanding of the so-called mystic passages in the Ethics. The first real recognition came from Lessing, who found in Spinoza a strength and solace he sought in vain elsewhere, though he never accepted the system as a whole. His conversation with Jacobi (1780), a diligent though hostile student of the Ethics, may be said to mark the beginning of a new epoch in the history of Spinozism. Attention once attracted was never again withdrawn, and received a powerful impulse from Goethe, who more than once confessed his indebtedness to the Ethics, which indeed is abundantly evident throughout his writings. Schleiermacher paid an eloquent tribute to "the holy, the rejected Spinoza." Novalis celebrated him as "the man intoxicated with Deity" (*der Gottvertrunkene Mann*), and Heine for once forgot to sneer, as he recounted his life. The brilliant novelist, Auerbach, has not only translated his complete works, but has also made his history the subject of a biographical romance. Among German philosophers Kant is, perhaps, the last, who shows no traces of Spinozism. Hegel has declared, that "to be a philosopher one must first be a Spinozist." In recent years a new impulse has been given to the study of the Ethics by their curious harmony with the last results of physiological research.

In France Spinoza has till lately been viewed as a disciple and perverter of Descartes. M. Emile Saisset prefixed to his translation of the philosopher's chief works a critical introduction written from this standpoint. Since the scientific study of philosophic systems has begun among the French, M. Paul Janet has written on Spinoza as a link in the chain of the history of thought; a new translation of his complete works has been started, and M. Renan has delivered a discourse on him at the bicentenary of his death celebrated at the Hague.

In Holland there has also been a revival of interest in the illustrious Dutch thinker. Professors Van Vloten and Land were mainly instrumental in procuring the erection of a statue to his memory, and are now engaged in a fine edition of his works, of which the first volume has appeared.[1] In England, as before said, the interest in Spinoza has till recently been slight. The controversialists of the eighteenth century, with the exception of Toland, passed him by as unworthy of serious study. The first recognition of his true character came probably from Germany through Coleridge, who in his desultory way expressed enthusiastic admiration,

[1] "B. de Spinoza, Opera. I." The Hague, 1882.

and recorded his opinion (in a pencil note to a passage in Schelling), that the Ethics, the Novum Organum, and the Critique of Pure Reason were the three greatest works written since the introduction of Christianity. The influence of Spinoza has been traced by Mr. Pollock in Wordsworth, and it is on record that Shelley not only contemplated but began a translation of the Tractatus Theologico-Politicus, to be published with a preface by Lord Byron, but the project was cut short by his death. It is said that George Eliot left behind her at her decease a MS. translation of the Ethics.

It may strike those who are strangers to Spinoza as curious, that, notwithstanding the severely abstract nature of his method, so many poets and imaginative writers should be found among his adherents. Lessing, Goethe, Heine, Auerbach, Coleridge, Shelley, George Eliot; most of these not only admired him, but studied him deeply. On closer approach the apparent anomaly vanishes. There is about Spinoza a power and a charm, which appeals strongly to the poetic sense. He seems to dwell among heights, which most men see only in far off, momentary glimpses. The world of men is spread out before him, the workings of the human heart lie bared to his gaze, but he does not fall to weeping, or to laughter, or to reviling: his thoughts are ever with the eternal, and something of the beauty and calm of eternal things has passed into his teaching. If we may, as he himself was wont to do, interpret spiritually a Bible legend, we may say of him that, like Moses returning from Sinai, he bears in his presence the witness that he has held communion with the Most High.

The main authority for the facts of Spinoza's life is a short biography by Johannes Colerus [1] (Köhler), Lutheran

[1] Originally written in Dutch (1706). Translated the same year into

pastor at the Hague, who occupied the lodgings formerly
tenanted by the philosopher. The orthodox Christian felt
a genuine abhorrence for the doctrines, which he regarded as
atheistic, but was honest enough to recognize the stainless
purity of their author's character. He sets forth what he
has to say with a quaint directness in admirable keeping
with the outward simplicity of the life he depicts.

Further authentic information is obtainable from passing
notices in the works of Leibnitz, and from Spinoza's published correspondence, though the editors of the latter have
suppressed all that appeared to them of merely personal
interest. There is also a biography attributed to Lucas,
physician at the Hague (1712), but this is merely a confused panegyric, and is often at variance with more trustworthy records. Additional details may be gleaned from
Bayle's hostile and inaccurate article in the "Dictionnaire
Philosophique;" from S. Kortholt's preface to the second
edition (1700) of his father's book "De tribus impostoribus
magnis:" and, lastly, from the recollections of Colonel
Stoupe (1673), an officer in the Swiss service, who had met
the philosopher at Utrecht, but does not contribute much
to our knowledge.

Baruch de Spinoza was born in Amsterdam Nov. 24.
1634. His parents were Portuguese, or possibly Spanish
Jews, who had sought a refuge in the Netherlands from
the rigours of the Inquisition in the Peninsula. Though
nothing positive is known of them, they appear to have
been in easy circumstances, and certainly bestowed on their
only son—their other two children being girls—a thorough
education according to the notions of their time and sect.
At the Jewish High School, under the guidance of Mor-
teira, a learned Talmudist, and possibly of the brilliant

French and English, and afterwards (1723) into German. The English
version is reprinted in Mr. Pollock's book as an appendix.

Manasseh Ben Israel, who afterwards (1655) was employed to petition from Cromwell the re-admission of the Jews to England, the young Spinoza was instructed in the learning of the Hebrews, the mysteries of the Talmud and the Cabbala, the text of the Old Testament, and the commentaries of Ibn Ezra and Maimonides. Readers of the *Tractatus Theologico-Politicus* will be able to appreciate the use made of this early training. Besides such severer studies, Spinoza was, in obedience to Rabbinical tradition, made acquainted with a manual trade, that of lens polishing, and gained a knowledge of French, Italian, and German; Spanish, Portuguese, and Hebrew were almost his native tongues, but curiously enough, as we learn from one of his lately discovered letters,[1] he wrote Dutch with difficulty. Latin was not included in the Jewish curriculum, being tainted with the suspicion of heterodoxy, but Spinoza, feeling probably that it was the key to much of the world's best knowledge, set himself to learn it;[2] first, with the aid of a German master, afterwards at the house of Francis Van den Ende, a physician. It is probably from the latter that he gained the sound knowledge of physical science, which so largely leavened his philosophy; and, no doubt, he at this time began the study of Descartes, whose reputation towered above the learned world of the period.

Colerus relates that Van den Ende had a daughter, Clara Maria, who instructed her father's pupils in Latin and music during his absence. "She was none of the

---

[1] Letter XXXII. See vol. ii.

[2] A translator has special opportunities for observing the extent of Spinoza's knowledge of Latin. His sentences are grammatical and his meaning almost always clear. But his vocabulary is restricted; his style is wanting in flexibility, and seldom idiomatic; in fact, the niceties of scholarship are wanting. He reminds one of a clever workman who accomplishes much with simple tools.

most beautiful, but she had a great deal of wit," and as the story runs displayed her sagacity by rejecting the proffered love of Spinoza for the sake of his fellow-pupil Kerkering, who was able to enhance his attractions by the gift of a costly pearl necklace. It is certain that Van den Ende's daughter and Kerkering were married in 1671, but the tradition of the previous love affair accords ill with ascertained dates. Clara Maria was only seven years old when Spinoza left her father's house, and sixteen when he left the neighbourhood.

Meanwhile the brilliant Jewish student was overtaken by that mental crisis, which has come over so many lesser men before and since. The creed of his fathers was found unequal to the strain of his own wider knowledge and changed spiritual needs. The Hebrew faith with its immemorial antiquity, its unbroken traditions, its myriads of martyrs, could appeal to an authority which no other religion has equalled, and Spinoza, as we know from a passage in one of his letters,[1] felt the claim to the full. We may be sure that the gentle and reserved youth was in no haste to obtrude his altered views, but the time arrived when they could no longer be with honesty concealed. The Jewish doctors were exasperated at the defection of their most promising pupil, and endeavoured to retain him in their communion by the offer of a yearly pension of 1,000 florins. Such overtures were of course rejected. Sterner measures were then resorted to. It is even related, on excellent authority, that Spinoza's life was attempted as he was coming out of the Portuguese synagogue. Be this as it may, he fled from Amsterdam, and was (1656) formally excommunicated and anathematized according to the rites of the Jewish church.

Thus isolated from his kindred, he sought more congenial society among the dissenting community of Colle-

[1] Letter LXXIV.

giants, a body of men who without priests or set forms of worship carried out the precepts of simple piety. He passed some time in the house of one of that body, not far from Amsterdam, on the Ouwerkerk road, and in 1660 or the following year removed with his friend to the headquarters of the sect at Rhijnsburg, near Leyden, where the memory of his sojourn is still preserved in the name "Spinoza Lane." His separation from Judaism was marked by his substituting for his name Baruch the Latin equivalent Benedict, but he never received baptism or formally joined any Christian sect. Only once again does his family come into the record of his life. On the death of his father, his sisters endeavoured to deprive him of his share of the inheritance on the ground that he was an outcast and heretic. Spinoza resisted their claim by law, but on gaining his suit yielded up to them all they had demanded except one bed.

Skill in polishing lenses gave him sufficient money for his scanty needs, and he acquired a reputation as an optician before he became known as a philosopher. It was in this capacity that he was consulted by Leibnitz.[1] His only contribution to the science was a short treatise on the rainbow, printed posthumously in 1687. This was long regarded as lost, but has, in our own time, been recovered and reprinted by Dr. Van Vloten.

Spinoza also drew, for amusement, portraits of his friends with ink or charcoal. Colerus possessed "a whole book of such draughts, amongst which there were some heads of several considerable persons, who were known to him, or had occasion to visit him," and also a portrait of the philosopher himself in the costume of Masaniello.

So remarkable a man could hardly remain obscure, and we have no reason to suppose that Spinoza shrank from social intercourse. Though in the last years of his life his

[1] Letters LI., LII.

habits were somewhat solitary, this may be set down to
failing health, poverty, and the pressure of uncompleted
work. He was never a professed ascetic, and probably, in
the earlier years of his separation from Judaism, was the
centre of an admiring and affectionate circle of friends. In
his letters he frequently states that visitors leave him no
time for correspondence, and the tone, in which he was addressed by comparative strangers, shows that he enjoyed
considerable reputation and respect. Before the appearance
of the Tractatus Theologico-Politicus, he had published
nothing which could shock the susceptibilities of Christians,
and he was known to be a complete master of Cartesianism,
then regarded as the consummation and crown of learning.
It is recorded that a society of young men used to hold
meetings in Amsterdam for the discussion of philosophical
problems, and that Spinoza contributed papers as material
for their debates.[1] Possibly the MS. treatise "On God,
Man, and his Blessedness," which has been re-discovered in
two Dutch copies during our own time, may be referred
to this period. It is of no philosophic value compared
with the Ethics, but is interesting historically as throwing
light on the growth of Spinoza's mind and his early relations to Cartesianism.

Oblivion has long since settled down over this little band
of questioners, but a touching record has been preserved
of one of their number, Simon de Vries, who figures in
Spinoza's correspondence. He had often, we are told,
wished to bestow gifts of money on his friend and master,
but these had always been declined. During the illness
which preceded his early death, he expressed a desire to
make the philosopher his heir. This again was declined,
and he was prevailed on by Spinoza to reduce the bequest
to a small annuity, and to leave the bulk of his property

---

[1] Letters XXVI., XXVII., according to the corrected text of Dr.
Van Vloten, herein adopted.

to his family. When he had passed away his brother fixed the pension at 500 florins, but Spinoza declared the sum excessive, and refused to accept more than 300 florins, which were punctually paid him till his death.

Besides this instruction by correspondence, for which he seems to have demanded no payment ("mischief," as one of his biographers puts it, "could be had from him for nothing"), Spinoza at least in one instance received into his house a private pupil,[1] generally identified with one Albert Burgh, who became a convert to Rome in 1675, and took that occasion to admonish his ex-tutor in a strain of contemptuous pity.[2] Probably to this youth were dictated "The principles of Cartesianism geometrically demonstrated," which Spinoza was induced by his friends to publish, with the addition of some metaphysical reflections, in 1663.[3] Lewis Meyer, a physician of Amsterdam, and one of Spinoza's intimates, saw the book through the press, and supplied a preface. Its author does not appear to have attached any importance to the treatise, which he regarded merely as likely to pave the way for the reception of more original work. It is interesting as an example of the method afterwards employed in the Ethics, used to support propositions not accepted by their expounder. It also shows that Spinoza thoroughly understood the system he rejected.

In the same year the philosopher removed from Rhijnsburg to Voorburg, a suburb of the Hague, and in 1670 to the Hague itself, where he lived till his death in 1677, lodging first in the house (afterwards tenanted by Colerus) of the widow Van Velden, and subsequently with Van der

---

[1] Letters XXVI., XXVII.   [2] Letter LXXIII.

[3] The full title is, "Renati des Cartes Principiorum partes I. et II. more geometrico demonstratæ per Benedictum de Spinoza Amstelodamensem. Accesserunt ejusdem cogitata metaphysica. Amsterdam, 1663."

Spijk, a painter. He was very likely led to leave Rhijnsburg by his increasing reputation and a desire for educated
society. By this time he was well known in Holland, and
counted among his friends, John de Witt, who is said to
have consulted him on affairs of state. Nor was his fame
confined to his native country. Henry Oldenburg, the first
secretary of the newly-established Royal Society of England, had visited him at Rhijnsburg, introduced possibly
by Huyghens, and had invited him to carry on a correspondence,[1] in terms of affectionate intimacy. Oldenburg
was rather active-minded than able, never really understood
or sympathized with Spinoza's standpoint, and was
thoroughly shocked[2] at the appearance of the Tractatus
Theologico-Politicus, but he was the intimate friend of
Robert Boyle, and kept his correspondent acquainted with
the progress of science in England. Later on (1671),
Leibnitz consulted Spinoza on a question of practical optics,[3]
and in 1676, Ludwig von Tschirnhausen, a Bohemian
nobleman, known in the history of mathematical science,
contribuced some pertinent criticisms on the Ethics, then
circulated in MS.[4]

Amusing testimonies to Spinoza's reputation are afforded
by the volunteered effusions of Blyenbergh,[5] and the artless
questionings of the believer in ghosts.[6]

In 1670, the Tractatus Theologico-Politicus was published anonymously, with the name of a fictitious printer at
Hamburg. It naturally produced a storm of angry controversy. It was, in 1674, formally prohibited by the States-
General, and, as a matter of course, was placed on the Index
by the Romish Church. Perhaps few books have been

---

[1] Letter I., *sqq.*

[2] But Tschirnhausen seems to have brought Oldenburg and Boyle to
a better mind. Letter LXV.

[3] Letter LI.

[4] Letter LXI. *sqq.*

[5] Letter XXXI. *sqq.*

[6] Letter LV. *sqq.*

more often "refuted," or less seriously damaged by the
ordeal. Its author displayed his disinclination to disturb
the faith of the unlearned by preventing during his lifetime
the appearance of the book in the vernacular.

In 1672, men's thoughts were for a time diverted from
theological controversy by the French invasion of the
Netherlands, and the consequent outbreak of domestic
faction. The shameful massacre of the brothers De Witt
by an infatuated mob brought Spinoza into close and pain-
ful contact with the passions seething round him. For
once his philosophic calm was broken: he was only by
force prevented from rushing forth into the streets at the
peril of his life, and proclaiming his abhorrence of the
crime.

Shortly afterwards, when the head-quarters of the French
army were at Utrecht, Spinoza was sent for by the Prince
de Condé, who wished to make his acquaintance. On his
arrival at the camp, however, he found that the Prince was
absent; and, after waiting a few days, returned home
without having seen him. The philosopher's French enter-
tainers held out hopes of a pension from Louis XIV., if a
book were dedicated to that monarch; but these overtures
were declined.

On his arrival at the Hague, Spinoza was exposed to
considerable danger from the excited populace, who suspected him of being a spy. The calm, which had failed him
on the murder of his friend, remained unruffled by the
peril threatening himself. He told his landlord, who was
in dread of the house being sacked, that, if the mob showed
any signs of violence, he would go out and speak to them
in person, though they should serve him as they had served
the unhappy De Witts. "I am a good republican," he
added, "and have never had any aim but the welfare and
good of the State."

In 1673, Spinoza was offered by the Elector Palatine,

Charles Lewis,[1] a professorship of philosophy at Heidelberg, but declined it,[2] on the plea that teaching would interfere with his original work, and that doctrinal restrictions, however slight, would prove irksome.

In the following year, the Ethics were finished and circulated in MS. among their author's friends. Spinoza made a journey to Amsterdam for the purpose of publishing them, but changed his intention on learning that they would probably meet with a stormy reception. Perhaps failing health strengthened his natural desire for peace, and considerations of personal renown never had any weight with him.

To this closing period belong the details as to Spinoza's manner of life collected by Colerus. They are best given in the biographer's simple words, as rendered in the contemporary English version: "It is scarce credible how sober and frugal he was. Not that he was reduced to so great a poverty, as not to be able to spend more, if he had been willing. He had friends enough, who offered him their purses, and all manner of assistance; but he was naturally very sober, and would be satisfied with little." His food apparently cost him but a few pence a day, and he drank hardly any wine. "He was often invited to eat with his friends, but chose rather to live upon what he had at home, though it were never so little, than to sit down to a good table at the expense of another man. . . . He was very careful to cast up his accounts every quarter; which he did, that he might spend neither more nor less than what he could spend every year. And he would say sometimes to the people of the house, that he was like the serpent, who forms a circle with his tail in his mouth, to denote that he had nothing left at the year's end. He added, that he designed to lay up no more money than what would be necessary for him to have a decent burying. . . .

[1] Letter LIII.   [2] Letter LIV.

He was of a middle size; he had good features in his face, the skin somewhat black; black curled hair; long eye-brows, and of the same colour, so that one might easily know by his looks that he was descended from Portuguese Jews. . . . If he was very frugal in his way of living, his conversation was also very sweet and easy. He knew admirably well how to be master of his passions: he was never seen very melancholy, nor very merry. . . . He was besides very courteous and obliging. He would very often discourse with his landlady, especially when she lay in, and with the people of the house, when they happened to be sick or afflicted: he never failed, then, to comfort them, and exhort them to bear with patience those evils which God assigned to them as a lot. He put the children in mind of going often to church, and taught them to be obedient and dutiful to their parents. When the people of the house came from church, he would often ask them what they had learned, and what they remembered of the sermon. He had a great esteem for Dr. Cordes, my predecessor, who was a learned and good-natured man, and of an exemplary life, which gave occasion to Spinoza to praise him very often: nay, he went sometimes to hear him preach. . . . It happened one day that his landlady asked him whether he believed she could be saved in the religion she professed. He answered: *Your religion is a very good one; you need not look for another, nor doubt that you may be saved in it, provided, whilst you apply yourself to piety, you live at the same time a peaceable and quiet life.*"

His amusements were very simple: talking on ordinary matters with the people of the house; smoking now and again a pipe of tobacco; watching the habits and quarrels of insects; making observations with a microscope—such were his pastimes in the hours which he could spare from his philosophy. But the greater part of his day was taken up with severe mental work in his own room. Sometimes he would become so absorbed, that he would remain alone for two or three days together, his meals being carried up to him.

Spinoza had never been robust, and had for more than twenty years been suffering from phthisis, a malady which, at any rate in those days, never allowed its victims to escape. The end came quite suddenly and quietly, in February, 1677. On Saturday, the 20th, after the landlord and his wife had returned from church, Spinoza spent some time with them in conversation, and smoked a pipe of tobacco, but went to bed early. Apparently, he had previously sent for his friend and physician, Lewis Meyer, who arrived on Sunday morning. On the 21st, Spinoza came down as usual, and partook of some food at the midday meal. In the afternoon, the physician stayed alone with his patient, the rest going to church. But when the landlord and his wife returned, they were startled with the news that the philosopher had expired about three o'clock. Lewis Meyer returned to Amsterdam that same evening.

Thus passed away all that was mortal of Spinoza. If we have read his character aright, his last hours were comforted with the thought, not so much that he had raised for himself an imperishable monument, as that he had pointed out to mankind a sure path to happiness and peace. Perhaps, with this glorious vision, there mingled the more tender feeling, that, among the simple folk with whom he lived, his memory would for a few brief years be cherished with reverence and love.

The funeral took place on the 25th February, "being attended by many illustrious persons, and followed by six coaches." The estate left behind him by the philosopher was very scanty. Rebekah de Spinoza, sister of the deceased, put in a claim as his heir; but abandoned it on finding that, after the payment of expenses, little or nothing would remain.

The MSS., which were found in Spinoza's desk, were, in accordance with his wishes, forwarded to John Rieuwertz, a publisher of Amsterdam, and were that same year brought out by Lewis Meyer, and another of the philosopher's friends, under the title, "B. D. S. Opera Posthuma." They consisted of the Ethics, a selection of letters, a compendium of Hebrew grammar, and two uncompleted treatises, one on politics, the other (styled "An Essay on the Improvement of the Understanding") on logical method. The last-named had been begun several years previously, but had apparently been added to from time to time. It develops some of the doctrines indicated in the Ethics, and serves in some sort as an introduction to the larger work.

In considering Spinoza's system of philosophy, it must not be forgotten that the problem of the universe seemed much simpler in his day, than it does in our own. Men had not then recognized, that knowledge is " a world whose margin fades for ever and for ever as we move." They believed that truth was something definite, which might be grasped by the aid of a clear head, diligence, and a sound method. Hence a tone of confidence breathed through their inquiries, which has since died away, and a completeness was aimed at, which is now seen to be unattainable. But the products of human thought are often valuable in ways undreamt of by those who fashioned them, and long after their original use has become obsolete. A system, obviously inadequate and defective as a whole, may yet enshrine ideas which the world is the richer for possessing.

This distinction between the framework and the central thoughts is especially necessary in the study of Spinoza; for the form in which his work is cast would seem to lay stress on their interdependence. It has often been said, that the geometrical method was adopted, because it was

believed to insure absolute freedom from error. But examination shows this to be a misconception. Spinoza, who
had purged his mind of so many illusions, can hardly have
succumbed to the notion, that his Ethics was a flawless
mass of irrefragable truth. He adopted his method because he believed, that he thus reduced argument to its
simplest terms, and laid himself least open to the seduc-
tions of rhetoric or passion. "It is the part of a wise
man," he says, "not to bewail nor to deride, but to understand." Human nature obeys fixed laws no less than do
the figures of geometry. "I will, therefore, write about
human beings, as though I were concerned with lines, and
planes, and solids."

As no system is entirely true, so also no system is entirely original. Each must in great measure be the recom-
bination of elements supplied by its predecessors. Spinozism
forms no exception to this rule; many of its leading conceptions may be traced in the writings of Jewish Rabbis
and of Descartes.

The biography of the philosopher supplies us in some
sort with the genesis of his system. His youth had been
passed in the study of Hebrew learning, of metaphysical
speculations on the nature of the Deity. He was then
confronted with the scientific aspect of the world as revealed by Descartes. At first the two visions seemed
antagonistic, but, as he gazed, their outlines blended and
commingled, he found himself in the presence not of two,
but of one; the universe unfolded itself to him as the
necessary result of the Perfect and Eternal God.

Other influences, no doubt, played a part in shaping his
convictions; we know, for instance, that he was a student
of Bacon and of Hobbes, and almost certainly of Giordano
Bruno, but these two elements, the Jewish and the Carte-
sian, are the main sources of his system, though it cannot
properly be called the mere development of either. From

Descartes, as Mr. Pollock points out, he derived his notions of physical science and his doctrine of the conservation of motion.

In the fragment on the Improvement of the Understanding, Spinoza sets forth the causes which prompted him to turn to philosophy.[1] It is worthy of note that they are not speculative but practical. He did not seek, like Descartes, "to walk with certainty," but to find a happiness beyond the reach of change for himself and his fellow-men. With a fervour that reminds one of Christian fleeing from the City of Destruction, he dilates on the vanity of men's ordinary ambitions, riches, fame, and the pleasures of sense, and on the necessity of looking for some more worthy object for their desires. Such an object he finds in the knowledge of truth, as obtainable through clear and distinct ideas, bearing in themselves the evidence of their own veracity.

Spinoza conceived as a vast unity all existence actual and possible; indeed, between actual and possible he recognizes no distinction, for, if a thing does not exist, there must be some cause which prevents its existing, or in other words renders it impossible. This unity he terms indifferently Substance or God, and the first part of the Ethics is devoted to expounding its nature.

Being the sum of existence, it is necessarily infinite (for there is nothing external to itself to make it finite), and it can be the cause of an infinite number of results. It must necessarily operate in absolute freedom, for there is nothing by which it can be controlled; but none the less necessarily it must operate in accordance with eternal and immutable laws, fulfilling the perfection of its own nature.

Substance consists in, or rather displays itself through an infinite number of Attributes, but of these only two,

---

[1] These observations are not offered as a complete exposition of Spinozism, but merely as an indication of its general drift.

Extension and Thought, are knowable by us; therefore, the rest may be left out of account in our inquiries. These Attributes are not different things, but different aspects of the same thing (Spinoza does not make it clear, whether the difference is intrinsic or due to the percipient); thus Extension and Thought are not parallel and interacting, but identical, and both acting in one order and connection. Hence all questions of the dependence of mind on body, or body on mind, are done away with at a stroke. Every manifestation of either is but a manifestation of the other, seen under a different aspect.

Attributes are again subdivided, or rather display themselves through an infinite number of Modes; some eternal and universal in respect of each Attribute (such as motion and the sum of all psychical facts); others having no eternal and necessary existence, but acting and reacting on one another in ceaseless flux, according to fixed and definite laws. These latter have been compared in relation to their Attributes to waves in relation to the sea; or again they may be likened to the myriad hues which play over the iridescent surface of a bubble; each is the necessary result of that which went before, and is the necessary precursor of that which will come after; all are modifications of the underlying film. The phenomenal world is made up of an infinite number of these Modes. It is manifest that the Modes of one Attribute cannot be acted upon by the Modes of another Attribute, for each may be expressed in terms of the other; within the limits of each Attribute the variation in the Modes follows an absolutely necessary order. When the first is given, the rest follow as inevitably, as from the nature of a triangle it follows, that its three angles are equal to two right angles. Nature is uniform, and no infringement of her laws is conceivable without a reduction to chaos.

Hence it follows, that a thing can only be called contingent in relation to our knowledge. To an infinite intelligence such a term would be unmeaning.

Hence also it follows, that the world cannot have been created for any purpose other than that which it fulfils by being what it is. To say that it has been created for the good of man, or for any similar end, is to indulge in grotesque anthropomorphism.

Among the Modes of thought may be reckoned the human mind, among the Modes of extension may be reckoned the human body; taken together they constitute the Mode man.

The nature of mind forms the subject of the second part of the Ethics. Man's mind is the idea of man's body, the consciousness of bodily states. Now bodily states are the result, not only of the body itself, but also of all things affecting the body; hence the human mind takes cognizance, not only of the human body, but also of the external world, in so far as it affects the human body. Its capacity for varied perceptions is in proportion to the body's capacity for receiving impressions.

The succession of ideas of bodily states cannot be arbitrarily controlled by the mind taken as a power apart, though the mind, as the aggregate of past states, may be a more or less important factor in the direction of its course. We can, in popular phrase, direct our thoughts at will, but the will, which we speak of as spontaneous, is really determined by laws as fixed and necessary, as those which regulate the properties of a triangle or a circle. The illusion of freedom, in the sense of uncaused volition, results from the fact, that men are conscious of their actions, but unconscious of the causes whereby those actions have been determined. The chain of causes becomes, so to speak, incandescent at a particular point, and men assume that only at that point does it start into existence. They ignore the links which still remain in obscurity.

If mind be simply the mirror of bodily states, how can we account for memory ? When the mind has been affected by two things in close conjunction, the recurrence of one re-awakens into life the idea of the other. To take an illustration, mind is like a traveller revisiting his former home, for whom each feature of the landscape recalls associations of the past. From the interplay of associations are woven memory and imagination.

Ideas may be either adequate or inadequate, in other words either distinct or confused ; both kinds are subject to the law of causation. Falsity is merely a negative conception. All adequate ideas are necessarily true, and bear in themselves the evidence of their own veracity. The mind accurately reflects existence, and if an idea be due to the mental association of two different factors, the joining, so to speak, may, with due care, be discerned. General notions and abstract terms arise from the incapacity of the mind to retain in completeness more than a certain number of mental images ; it therefore groups together points of resemblance, and considers the abstractions thus formed as units.

There are three kinds of knowledge : opinion, rational knowledge, and intuitive knowledge. The first alone is the cause of error ; the second consists in adequate ideas of particular properties of things, and in general notions ; the third proceeds from an adequate idea of some attribute of God to the adequate knowledge of particular things.

The reason does not regard things as contingent, but as necessary, considering them under the form of eternity, as part of the nature of God. The will has no existence apart from particular acts of volition, and since acts of volition are ideas, the will is identical with the understanding.

The third part of the Ethics is devoted to the consideration of the emotions.

In so far as it has adequate ideas, *i.e.*, is purely rational, the mind may be said to be active; in so far as it has inadequate ideas, it is passive, and therefore subject to emotions.

Nothing can be destroyed from within, for all change must come from without. In other words, everything endeavours to persist in its own being. This endeavour must not be associated with the "struggle for existence" familiar to students of evolutionary theories, though the suggestion is tempting; it is simply the result of a thing being what it is. When it is spoken of in reference to the human mind only, it is equivalent to the will; in reference to the whole man, it may be called appetite. Appetite is thus identified with life; desire is defined as appetite, with consciousness thereof. All objects of our desire owe their choiceworthiness simply to the fact that we desire them: we do not desire a thing, because it is intrinsically good, but we deem a thing good, because we desire it. Everything which adds to the bodily or mental powers of activity is pleasure; everything which detracts from them is pain.

From these three fundamentals—desire, pleasure, pain—Spinoza deduces the entire list of human emotions. Love is pleasure, accompanied by the idea of an external cause; hatred is pain, accompanied by the idea of an external cause. Pleasure or pain may be excited by anything, incidentally, if not directly. There is no need to proceed further with the working out of the theory, but we may remark, in passing, the extraordinary fineness of perception and sureness of touch, with which it is accomplished; here, if nowhere else, Spinoza remains unsurpassed.[1] Almost

---

[1] It may be worth while to cite the often-quoted testimony of the distinguished physiologist, Johannes Muller:—"With regard to the relations of the passions to one another apart from their physiological conditions, it is impossible to give any better account than that which Spinoza has laid down with unsurpassed mastery."—*Physiologie des Menschen*, ii. 543. He follows up this praise by quoting the propositions in question *in extenso*.

all the emotions arise from the passive condition of the mind, but there is also a pleasure arising from the mind's contemplation of its own power. This is the source of virtue, and is purely active.

In the fourth part of the Ethics, Spinoza treats of man in so far as he is subject to the emotions, prefixing a few remarks on the meaning of the terms perfect and imperfect, good and evil. A thing can only be called perfect in reference to the known intention of its author. We style "good" that which we know with certainty to be useful to us: we style "evil" that which we know will hinder us in the attainment of good. By "useful," we mean that which will aid us to approach gradually the ideal we have set before ourselves. Man, being a part only of nature, must be subject to emotions, because he must encounter circumstances of which he is not the sole and sufficient cause. Emotion can only be conquered by another emotion stronger than itself, hence knowledge will only lift us above the sway of passions, in so far as it is itself "touched with emotion." Every man necessarily, and therefore rightly, seeks his own interest, which is thus identical with virtue; but his own interest does not lie in selfishness, for man is always in need of external help, and nothing is more useful to him than his fellow-men; hence individual well-being is best promoted by harmonious social effort. The reasonable man will desire nothing for himself, which he does not desire for other men; therefore he will be just, faithful, and honourable.

The code of morals worked out on these lines bears many resemblances to Stoicism, though it is improbable that Spinoza was consciously imitating. The doctrine that rational emotion, rather than pure reason, is necessary for subduing the evil passions, is entirely his own.

The means whereby man may gain mastery over his passions, are set forth in the first portion of the fifth part

of the Ethics. They depend on the definition of passion
as a confused idea. As soon as we form a clear and distinct idea of a passion, it changes its character, and ceases
to be a passion. Now it is possible, with due care, to form
a distinct idea of every bodily state; hence a true knowledge of the passions is the best remedy against them.
While we contemplate the world as a necessary result of
the perfect nature of God, a feeling of joy will arise in our
hearts, accompanied by the idea of God as its cause. This
is the intellectual love of God, which is the highest happiness man can know. It seeks for no special love from God
in return, for such would imply a change in the nature of
the Deity. It rises above all fear of change through envy
or jealousy, and increases in proportion as it is seen to be
participated in by our fellow-men.

The concluding propositions of the Ethics have given
rise to more controversy than any other part of the system. Some critics have maintained that Spinoza is indulging in vague generalities without any definite meaning, others have supposed that the language is intentionally obscure. Others, again, see in them a doctrine of
personal immortality, and, taking them in conjunction with
the somewhat transcendental form of the expressions concerning the love of God, have claimed the author of the
Ethics as a Mystic. All these suggestions are reductions
to the absurd, the last not least so. Spinoza may have
been not unwilling to show that his creed could be expressed
in exalted language as well as the current theology, but his
"intellectual love" has no more in common with the ecstatic
enthusiasm of cloistered saints, than his "God" has in
common with the Divinity of Romanist peasants, or his
"eternity" with the paradise of Mahomet. But to return
to the doctrine in dispute.[1] "The human mind," says
Spinoza, "cannot be wholly destroyed with the body, but

[1] The explanation here indicated is based on that given by Mr.

somewhat of it remains, which is eternal." The eternity thus predicated cannot mean indefinite persistence in time, for eternity is not commensurable with time. It must mean some special kind of existence; it is, in fact, defined as a mode of thinking. Now, the mind consists of adequate and inadequate ideas; in so far as it is composed of the former, it is part of the infinite mind of God, which broods, as it were, over the extended universe as its expression in terms of thought. As such, it is necessarily eternal, and, since knowledge implies self-consciousness, it knows that it is so. Inadequate ideas will pass away with the body, because they are the result of conditions, which are merely temporary, and inseparably connected with the body, but adequate ideas will not pass away, inasmuch as they are part of the mind of the Eternal. Knowledge of the third or intuitive kind is the source of our highest perfection and blessedness; even as it forms part of the infinite mind of God, so also does the joy with which it is accompanied—the intellectual love of God—form part of the infinite intellectual love, wherewith God regards Himself.

Spinoza concludes with the admonition, that morality rests on a basis quite independent of the acceptance of the mind's Eternity. Virtue is its own reward, and needs no other. This doctrine, which appears, as it were, perfunctorily in so many systems of morals, is by Spinoza insisted on with almost passionate earnestness; few things seem to have moved him to more scornful denial than the popular creed, that supernatural rewards and punishments are necessary as incentives to virtue. "I see in what mud this man sticks," he exclaims in answer to some such statement. "He is one of those who would follow after his own lusts, if he were not restrained by the fear of hell. He ab-

Pollock, "Spinoza," &c., ch. ix., to which the reader is referred for a masterly exposition of the question.

stains from evil actions and fulfils God's commands like a slave against his will, and for his bondage he expects to be rewarded by God with gifts far more to his taste than Divine love, and great in proportion to his original dislike of virtue."[1]   Again, at the close of the Ethics, he draws an ironical picture of the pious coming before God at the Judgment, and looking to be endowed with incalculable blessings in recompense for the grievous burden of their piety.   For him, who is truly wise, Blessedness is not the reward of virtue, but virtue itself.   "And though the way thereto be steep, yet it may be found—all things excellent are as difficult, as they are rare."

Such, in rough outline, is the philosophy of Spinoza; few systems have been more variously interpreted.   Its author has been reviled or exalted as Atheist, Pantheist, Mono-theist, Materialist, Mystic, in fact, under almost every name in the philosophic vocabulary.   But such off-hand classifi-cation is based on hasty reading of isolated passages, rather than on sound knowledge of the whole.   We shall act more wisely, and more in the spirit of the master, if, as Professor Land advises, "we call him simply Spinoza, and endeavour to learn from himself what he sought and what he found."

The two remaining works, translated in these volumes, may be yet more briefly considered.   They present no special difficulties, and are easily read in their entirety.

The Tractatus Theologico-Politicus is an eloquent plea for religious liberty.   True religion is shown to consist in the practice of simple piety, and to be quite independent of philosophical speculations.   The elaborate systems of dog-mas framed by theologians are based on superstition, result-ing from fear.

The Bible is examined by a method, which anticipates in great measure the procedure of modern rationalists, and

[1] Letter XLIX.

the theory of its verbal inspiration is shown to be un-
tenable. The Hebrew prophets were distinguished not by
superior wisdom, but by superior virtue, and they set forth
their higher moral ideals in language, which they thought
would best commend it to the multitude whom they addressed. For anthropomorphic notions of the Deity as a
heavenly King and Judge, who displays His power by
miraculous interventions, is substituted the conception set
forth in the Ethics of an Infinite Being, fulfilling in the
uniformity of natural law the perfection of His own
Nature. Men's thoughts cannot really be constrained by
commands ; therefore, it is wisest, so long as their actions
conform to morality, to allow them absolute liberty to
think what they like, and say what they think.

The Political Treatise was the latest work of Spinoza's
life, and remains unfinished. Though it bears abundant
evidence of the influence of Hobbes, it differs from him in
several important points. The theory of sovereignty is the
same in both writers, but Spinoza introduces considerable
qualifications. Supreme power is ideally absolute, but its
rights must, in practice, be limited by the endurance of its
subjects. Thus governments are founded on the common
consent, and for the convenience of the governed, who
are, in the last resort, the arbiters of their continuance.

Spinoza, like Hobbes, peremptorily sets aside all claims
of religious organizations to act independently of, or as
superior to the civil power. Both reject as outside the
sphere of practical politics the case of a special revelation
to an individual. In all matters affecting conduct the State
must be supreme.

It remains to say a few words about the present version.
I alone am responsible for the contents of these volumes,
with the exception of the Political Treatise, which has
been translated for me by my friend Mr. A. H. Gosset,

Fellow of New College, Oxford, who has also, in my absence from England, kindly seen the work through the press. I have throughout followed Bruder's text,[1] correcting a few obvious misprints. The additional letters given in Professor Van Vloten's Supplement,[2] have been inserted in their due order.

This may claim to be the first version[3] of Spinoza's works offered to the English reader; for, though Dr. R. Willis has gone over most of the ground before, he laboured under the disadvantages of a very imperfect acquaintance with Latin, and very loose notions of accuracy. The Tractatus Theologico-Politicus had been previously translated in 1689. Mr. Pollock describes this early version as "pretty accurate, but of no great literary merit."

Whatever my own shortcomings, I have never consciously eluded a difficulty by a paraphrase. Clearness has throughout been aimed at in preference to elegance. Though the precise meaning of some of the philosophical terms (*e.g. idea*) varies in different passages, I have, as far as possible, given a uniform rendering, not venturing to attempt greater subtlety than I found. I have abstained from notes; for, if given on an adequate scale, they would have unduly swelled the bulk of the work. Moreover, excellent commentaries are readily accessible.

R. H. M. ELWES.

[1] "B. de Spinosa Opera quæ Supersunt Omnia," ed. C. H. Bruder. *Leipzig (Tauchnitz)*, 1843.

[2] "Ad B. D. S. Opera quæ Supersunt Omnia Supplementum." Amsterdam, 1862.

[3] While these volumes were passing through the press, a translation of the Ethics appeared by Mr. Hale White (Trübner and Co.). The Tractatus Politicus was translated in 1854 by W. Maccall, but the book has become so rare as to be practically inaccessible.

A THEOLOGICO-
POLITICAL TREATISE
—— *and* ——
A POLITICAL TREATISE

PREFACE.

MEN would never be superstitious, if they could govern all their circumstances by set rules, or if they were always favoured by fortune: but being frequently driven into straits where rules are useless, and being often kept fluctuating pitiably between hope and fear by the uncertainty of fortune's greedily coveted favours, they are consequently, for the most part, very prone to credulity. The human mind is readily swayed this way or that in times of doubt, especially when hope and fear are struggling for the mastery, though usually it is boastful, over-confident, and vain.

This as a general fact I suppose everyone knows, though few, I believe, know their own nature; no one can have lived in the world without observing that most people, when in prosperity, are so over-brimming with wisdom (however inexperienced they may be), that they take every offer of advice as a personal insult, whereas in adversity they know not where to turn, but beg and pray for counsel from every passer-by. No plan is then too futile, too absurd, or too fatuous for their adoption; the most frivolous causes will raise them to hope, or plunge them into despair—if anything happens during their fright which reminds them of some past good or ill, they think it portends a happy or unhappy issue, and therefore (though it may have proved abortive a hundred times before) style it a lucky or unlucky omen. Anything which excites their astonishment they believe to be a portent signifying the anger of the gods or of the Supreme Being, and, mistaking superstition for religion, account it impious not to avert the evil with prayer and sacrifice. Signs and wonders

4 A THEOLOGICO-POLITICAL TREATISE.

of this sort they conjure up perpetually, till one might think Nature as mad as themselves, they interpret her so fantastically.

Thus it is brought prominently before us, that super-stition's chief victims are those persons who greedily covet temporal advantages; they it is, who (especially when they are in danger, and cannot help themselves) are wont with prayers and womanish tears to implore help from God: upbraiding Reason as blind, because she cannot show a sure path to the shadows they pursue, and rejecting human wisdom as vain; but believing the phantoms of imagination, dreams, and other childish absurdities, to be the very oracles of Heaven. As though God had turned away from the wise, and written His decrees, not in the mind of man but in the entrails of beasts, or left them to be proclaimed by the inspiration and instinct of fools, madmen, and birds. Such is the unreason to which terror can drive mankind!

Superstition, then, is engendered, preserved, and fostered by fear. If anyone desire an example, let him take Alex-ander, who only began superstitiously to seek guidance from seers, when he first learnt to fear fortune in the passes of Sysis (Curtius, v. 4); whereas after he had conquered Darius he consulted prophets no more, till a second time frightened by reverses. When the Scythians were pro-voking a battle, the Bactrians had deserted, and he him-self was lying sick of his wounds, "he once more turned to superstition, the mockery of human wisdom, and bade Aristander, to whom he confided his credulity, inquire the issue of affairs with sacrificed victims." Very numerous examples of a like nature might be cited, clearly showing the fact, that only while under the dominion of fear do men fall a prey to superstition; that all the portents ever invested with the reverence of misguided religion are mere phantoms of dejected and fearful minds; and lastly, that prophets have most power among the people, and are most formidable to rulers, precisely at those times when the state is in most peril. I think this is sufficiently plain to all, and will therefore say no more on the subject.

The origin of superstition above given affords us a clear reason for the fact, that it comes to all men naturally, though some refer its rise to a dim notion of God, universal to mankind, and also tends to show, that it is no less inconsistent and variable than other mental hallucinations and emotional impulses, and further that it can only be maintained by hope, hatred, anger, and deceit; since it springs, not from reason, but solely from the more powerful phases of emotion. Furthermore, we may readily understand how difficult it is, to maintain in the same course men prone to every form of credulity. For, as the mass of mankind remains always at about the same pitch of misery, it never assents long to any one remedy, but is always best pleased by a novelty which has not yet proved illusive.

This element of inconsistency has been the cause of many terrible wars and revolutions; for, as Curtius well says (lib. iv. chap. 10): "The mob has no ruler more potent than superstition," and is easily led, on the plea of religion, at one moment to adore its kings as gods, and anon to execrate and abjure them as humanity's common bane. Immense pains have therefore been taken to counteract this evil by investing religion, whether true or false, with such pomp and ceremony, that it may rise superior to every shock, and be always observed with studious reverence by the whole people—a system which has been brought to great perfection by the Turks, for they consider even controversy impious, and so clog men's minds with dogmatic formulas, that they leave no room for sound reason, not even enough to doubt with.

But if, in despotic statecraft, the supreme and essential mystery be to hoodwink the subjects, and to mask the fear, which keeps them down, with the specious garb of religion, so that men may fight as bravely for slavery as for safety, and count it not shame but highest honour to risk their blood and their lives for the vainglory of a tyrant; yet in a free state no more mischievous expedient could be planned or attempted. Wholly repugnant to the general freedom are such devices as enthralling men's minds with prejudices, forcing their judgment, or employing any of the weapons of quasi-religious sedition; indeed, such seditions only spring up, when law enters the domain of speculative thought, and opinions are put on trial and condemned on the same footing as crimes, while those who defend and follow them are sacrificed, not to public safety, but to their

opponents' hatred and cruelty. If deeds only could be
made the grounds of criminal charges, and words were
always allowed to pass free, such seditions would be divested
of every semblance of justification, and would be separated
from mere controversies by a hard and fast line.

Now, seeing that we have the rare happiness of living in a
republic, where everyone's judgment is free and unshackled,
where each may worship God as his conscience dictates,
and where freedom is esteemed before all things dear and
precious, I have believed that I should be undertaking no
ungrateful or unprofitable task, in demonstrating that not
only can such freedom be granted without prejudice to the
public peace, but also, that without such freedom, piety
cannot flourish nor the public peace be secure.

Such is the chief conclusion I seek to establish in this
treatise; but, in order to reach it, I must first point out
the misconceptions which, like scars of our former bondage,
still disfigure our notion of religion, and must expose the
false views about the civil authority which many have
most impudently advocated, endeavouring to turn the mind
of the people, still prone to heathen superstition, away from
its legitimate rulers, and so bring us again into slavery.
As to the order of my treatise I will speak presently, but
first I will recount the causes which led me to write.

I have often wondered, that persons who make a boast of
professing the Christian religion, namely, love, joy, peace,
temperance, and charity to all men, should quarrel with
such rancorous animosity, and display daily towards one
another such bitter hatred, that this, rather than the virtues they claim, is the readiest criterion of their faith.
Matters have long since come to such a pass, that one can
only pronounce a man Christian, Turk, Jew, or Heathen, by
his general appearance and attire, by his frequenting this
or that place of worship, or employing the phraseology of
a particular sect—as for manner of life, it is in all cases
the same. Inquiry into the cause of this anomaly leads
me unhesitatingly to ascribe it to the fact, that the minis-
tries of the Church are regarded by the masses merely as dig-
nities, her offices as posts of emolument—in short, popular
religion may be summed up as respect for ecclesiastics.
The spread of this misconception inflamed every worthless

fellow with an intense desire to enter holy orders, and thus the love of diffusing God's religion degenerated into sordid avarice and ambition. Every church became a theatre, where orators, instead of church teachers, harangued, caring not to instruct the people, but striving to attract admiration, to bring opponents to public scorn, and to preach only novelties and paradoxes, such as would tickle the ears of their congregation. This state of things necessarily stirred up an amount of controversy, envy, and hatred, which no lapse of time could appease; so that we can scarcely wonder that of the old religion nothing survives but its outward forms (even these, in the mouth of the multitude, seem rather adulation than adoration of the Deity), and that faith has become a mere compound of credulity and prejudices—aye, prejudices too, which degrade man from rational being to beast, which completely stifle the power of judgment between true and false, which seem, in fact, carefully fostered for the purpose of extinguishing the last spark of reason! Piety, great God! and religion are become a tissue of ridiculous mysteries; men, who flatly despise reason, who reject and turn away from understanding as naturally corrupt, these, I say, these of all men, are thought, O lie most horrible! to possess light from on High. Verily, if they had but one spark of light from on High, they would not insolently rave, but would learn to worship God more wisely, and would be as marked among their fellows for mercy as they now are for malice; if they were concerned for their opponents' souls, instead of for their own reputations, they would no longer fiercely persecute, but rather be filled with pity and compassion.

Furthermore, if any Divine light were in them, it would appear from their doctrine. I grant that they are never tired of professing their wonder at the profound mysteries of Holy Writ; still I cannot discover that they teach anything but speculations of Platonists and Aristotelians, to which (in order to save their credit for Christianity) they have made Holy Writ conform; not content to rave with the Greeks themselves, they want to make the prophets rave also; showing conclusively, that never even in sleep have they caught a glimpse of Scripture's Divine nature. The very vehemence of their admiration for the mysteries plainly attests, that their belief in the Bible is a formal assent rather than a living faith: and the fact is made still more apparent by their laying down beforehand, as a foundation for the study and true interpretation of Scripture, the principle that it is in every passage true and divine. Such a doctrine should be reached only after strict scrutiny and thorough comprehension of the Sacred Books (which would teach it much better, for they stand in need of no human fictions), and not be set up on the threshold, as it were, of inquiry.

As I pondered over the facts that the light of reason is not only despised, but by many even execrated as a source of impiety, that human commentaries are accepted as divine records, and that credulity is extolled as faith; as I marked the fierce controversies of philosophers raging in Church and State, the source of bitter hatred and dissension, the ready instruments of sedition and other ills innumerable, I determined to examine the Bible afresh in a careful, impartial, and unfettered spirit, making no assumptions concerning it, and attributing to it no doctrines, which I do not find clearly therein set down. With these precautions I constructed a method of Scriptural interpretation, and thus equipped proceeded to inquire—What is prophecy? in what sense did God reveal Himself to the prophets, and why were these particular men chosen by Him? Was it on account of the sublimity of their thoughts about the Deity and nature, or was it solely on account of their piety? These questions being answered, I was easily able to conclude, that the authority of the prophets has weight only in matters of morality, and that their speculative doctrines affect us little.

Next I inquired, why the Hebrews were called God's chosen people, and discovering that it was only because God had chosen for them a certain strip of territory, where they might live peaceably and at ease, I learnt that the Law revealed by God to Moses was merely the law of the individual Hebrew state, therefore that it was binding on none but Hebrews, and not even on Hebrews after the downfall of their nation. Further, in order to ascertain, whether it could be concluded from Scripture, that the human understanding is naturally corrupt, I inquired whether the Universal Religion, the Divine Law revealed through the Prophets and Apostles to the whole human race, differs from that which is taught by the light of natural reason, whether miracles can take place in violation of the laws of nature, and if so, whether they imply the existence of God more surely and clearly than events, which we understand plainly and distinctly through their immediate natural causes.

Now, as in the whole course of my investigation I found nothing taught expressly by Scripture, which does not agree with our understanding, or which is repugnant thereto, and as I saw that the prophets taught nothing, which is not very simple and easily to be grasped by all, and further, that they clothed their teaching in the style, and confirmed it with the reasons, which would most deeply move the mind of the masses to devotion towards God, I became thoroughly convinced, that the Bible leaves reason absolutely free, that it has nothing in common with philosophy, in fact, that Revelation and Philosophy stand on totally different footings. In order to set this forth categorically and exhaust the whole question, I point out the way in which the Bible should be interpreted, and show that all knowledge of spiritual questions should be sought from it alone, and not from the objects of ordinary knowledge. Thence I pass on to indicate the false notions, which have arisen from the fact that the multitude—ever prone to superstition, and caring more for the shreds of antiquity than for eternal truths—pays homage to the Books of the Bible, rather than to the Word of God. I show that the Word of God has not been revealed as a certain number of books, but was displayed to the prophets as a simple idea of the Divine mind, namely, obedience to God in singleness of heart, and in the practice of justice and charity; and I further point out, that this doctrine is set forth in Scripture in accordance with the opinions and understandings of those, among whom the Apostles and Prophets preached, to the end that men might receive it willingly, and with their whole heart.

Having thus laid bare the bases of belief, I draw the conclusion that Revelation has obedience for its sole object, and therefore, in purpose no less than in foundation and

method, stands entirely aloof from ordinary knowledge;
each has its separate province, neither can be called the
handmaid of the other.

Furthermore, as men's habits of mind differ, so that
some more readily embrace one form of faith, some another,
for what moves one to pray may move another only to scoff,
I conclude, in accordance with what has gone before, that
everyone should be free to choose for himself the foundations of his creed, and that faith should be judged only by
its fruits; each would then obey God freely with his whole
heart, while nothing would be publicly honoured save
justice and charity.

Having thus drawn attention to the liberty conceded to
everyone by the revealed law of God, I pass on to another
part of my subject, and prove that this same liberty can and
should be accorded with safety to the state and the magisterial authority—in fact, that it cannot be withheld without
great danger to peace and detriment to the community.

In order to establish my point, I start from the natural
rights of the individual, which are co-extensive with his
desires and power, and from the fact that no one is bound
to live as another pleases, but is the guardian of his own
liberty. I show that these rights can only be transferred
to those whom we depute to defend us, who acquire with
the duties of defence the power of ordering our lives, and
I thence infer that rulers possess rights only limited by
their power, that they are the sole guardians of justice and
liberty, and that their subjects should act in all things as
they dictate: nevertheless, since no one can so utterly
abdicate his own power of self-defence as to cease to be a
man, I conclude that no one can be deprived of his natural
rights absolutely, but that subjects, either by tacit agreement, or by social contract, retain a certain number, which
cannot be taken from them without great danger to the state.

From these considerations I pass on to the Hebrew State,
which I describe at some length, in order to trace the
manner in which Religion acquired the force of law, and
to touch on other noteworthy points. I then prove, that
the holders of sovereign power are the depositaries and
interpreters of religious no less than of civil ordinances,
and that they alone have the right to decide what is just or

unjust, pious or impious; lastly, I conclude by showing, that they best retain this right and secure safety to their state by allowing every man to think what he likes, and say what he thinks.

Such, Philosophical Reader, are the questions I submit to your notice, counting on your approval, for the subject matter of the whole book and of the several chapters is important and profitable. I would say more, but I do not want my preface to extend to a volume, especially as I know that its leading propositions are to Philosophers but commonplaces. To the rest of mankind I care not to commend my treatise, for I cannot expect that it contains anything to please them: I know how deeply rooted are the prejudices embraced under the name of religion; I am aware that in the mind of the masses superstition is no less deeply rooted than fear; I recognize that their constancy is mere obstinacy, and that they are led to praise or blame by impulse rather than reason. Therefore the multitude, and those of like passions with the multitude, I ask not to read my book; nay, I would rather that they should utterly neglect it, than that they should misinterpret it after their wont. They would gain no good themselves, and might prove a stumbling-block to others, whose philosophy is hampered by the belief that Reason is a mere handmaid to Theology, and whom I seek in this work especially to benefit. But as there will be many who have neither the leisure, nor, perhaps, the inclination to read through all I have written, I feel bound here, as at the end of my treatise, to declare that I have written nothing, which I do not most willingly submit to the examination and judgment of my country's rulers, and that I am ready to retract anything, which they shall decide to be repugnant to the laws or prejudicial to the public good. I know that I am a man and, as a man, liable to error, but against error I have taken scrupulous care, and striven to keep in entire accordance with the laws of my country, with loyalty, and with morality.

THEOLOGICO-POLITICAL TREATISE.

CHAPTER I.

OF PROPHECY.

PROPHECY, or revelation, is sure knowledge revealed by God to man. A prophet is one who interprets the revelations of God to those who are unable to attain to sure knowledge of the matters revealed, and therefore can only apprehend them by simple faith.

The Hebrew word for prophet is "*nabi*,"[1] *i.e.* speaker or interpreter, but in Scripture its meaning is restricted to interpreter of God, as we may learn from Exodus vii. 1, where God says to Moses, "See, I have made thee a god to Pharaoh, and Aaron thy brother shall be thy prophet;" implying that, since in interpreting Moses' words to Pharaoh, Aaron acted the part of a prophet, Moses would be to Pharaoh as a god, or in the attitude of a god.

Prophets I will treat of in the next chapter, and at present consider prophecy.

Now it is evident, from the definition above given, that prophecy really includes ordinary knowledge; for the knowledge which we acquire by our natural faculties depends on our knowledge of God and His eternal laws; but ordinary knowledge is common to all men as men, and rests on foundations which all share, whereas the multitude always strains after rarities and exceptions, and thinks little of the gifts of nature; so that, when prophecy is talked of, ordinary knowledge is not supposed to be included. Neverthe-

[1] See Notes, p. 269, Note 1.

less it has as much right as any other to be called Divine, for God's nature, in so far as we share therein, and God's laws, dictate it to us; nor does it suffer from that to which we give the pre-eminence, except in so far as the latter transcends its limits and cannot be accounted for by natural laws taken in themselves. In respect to the certainty it involves, and the source from which it is derived, *i.e.* God, ordinary knowledge is no whit inferior to prophetic, unless indeed we believe, or rather dream, that the prophets had human bodies but superhuman minds, and therefore that their sensations and consciousness were entirely different from our own.

But, although ordinary knowledge is Divine, its professors cannot be called prophets,[1] for they teach what the rest of mankind could perceive and apprehend, not merely by simple faith, but as surely and honourably as themselves.

Seeing then that our mind subjectively contains in itself and partakes of the nature of God, and solely from this cause is enabled to form notions explaining natural phenomena and inculcating morality, it follows that we may rightly assert the nature of the human mind (in so far as it is thus conceived) to be a primary cause of Divine revelation. All that we clearly and distinctly understand is dictated to us, as I have just pointed out, by the idea and nature of God; not indeed through words, but in a way far more excellent and agreeing perfectly with the nature of the mind, as all who have enjoyed intellectual certainty will doubtless attest. Here, however, my chief purpose is to speak of matters having reference to Scripture, so these few words on the light of reason will suffice.

I will now pass on to, and treat more fully, the other ways and means by which God makes revelations to mankind, both of that which transcends ordinary knowledge, and of that within its scope; for there is no reason why God should not employ other means to communicate what we know already by the power of reason.

Our conclusions on the subject must be drawn solely from Scripture; for what can we affirm about matters transcending our knowledge except what is told us by the words or writings of prophets? And since there are, so far as I know, no prophets now alive, we have no alternative but

[1] See Note 2.

to read the books of prophets departed, taking care the
while not to reason from metaphor or to ascribe anything
to our authors which they do not themselves distinctly state.
I must further premise that the Jews never make any mention or account of secondary, or particular causes, but in a
spirit of religion, piety, and what is commonly called godli-
ness, refer all things directly to the Deity. For instance,
if they make money by a transaction, they say God gave it
to them; if they desire anything, they say God has disposed
their hearts towards it; if they think anything, they say
God told them. Hence we must not suppose that everything is prophecy or revelation which is described in
Scripture as told by God to anyone, but only such things
as are expressly announced as prophecy or revelation, or are
plainly pointed to as such by the context.

A perusal of the sacred books will show us that all God's
revelations to the prophets were made through words or
appearances, or a combination of the two. These words
and appearances were of two kinds; (1) *real* when external
to the mind of the prophet who heard or saw them, (2)
imaginary when the imagination of the prophet was in a
state which led him distinctly to suppose that he heard or
saw them.

With a real voice God revealed to Moses the laws which
He wished to be transmitted to the Hebrews, as we may
see from Exodus xxv. 22, where God says, "And there I
will meet with thee and I will commune with thee from the
mercy seat which is between the Cherubim." Some sort of
real voice must necessarily have been employed, for Moses
found God ready to commune with him at any time. This,
as I shall shortly show, is the only instance of a real voice.

We might, perhaps, suppose that the voice with which
God called Samuel was real, for in 1 Sam. iii. 21, we read,
"And the Lord appeared again in Shiloh, for the Lord re-
vealed Himself to Samuel in Shiloh by the word of the
Lord;" implying that the appearance of the Lord consisted in
His making Himself known to Samuel through a voice; in
other words, that Samuel heard the Lord speaking. But
we are compelled to distinguish between the prophecies of
Moses and those of other prophets, and therefore must de-
cide that this voice was imaginary, a conclusion further

supported by the voice's resemblance to the voice of Eli, which Samuel was in the habit of hearing, and therefore might easily imagine; when thrice called by the Lord, Samuel supposed it to have been Eli.

The voice which Abimelech heard was imaginary, for it is written, Gen. xx. 6, "And God said unto him in a dream." So that the will of God was manifest to him, not in waking, but only in sleep, that is, when the imagination is most active and uncontrolled. Some of the Jews believe that the actual words of the Decalogue were not spoken by God, but that the Israelites heard a noise only, without any distinct words, and during its continuance apprehended the Ten Commandments by pure intuition; to this opinion I myself once inclined, seeing that the words of the Decalogue in Exodus are different from the words of the Decalogue in Deuteronomy, for the discrepancy seemed to imply (since God only spoke once) that the Ten Commandments were not intended to convey the actual words of the Lord, but only His meaning. However, unless we would do violence to Scripture, we must certainly admit that the Israelites heard a real voice, for Scripture expressly says, Deut. v. 4, "God spake with you face to face," i.e. as two men ordinarily interchange ideas through the instrumentality of their two bodies; and therefore it seems more consonant with Holy Writ to suppose that God really did create a voice of some kind with which the Decalogue was revealed. The discrepancy of the two versions is treated of in Chap. VIII.

Yet not even thus is all difficulty removed, for it seems scarcely reasonable to affirm that a created thing, depending on God in the same manner as other created things, would be able to express or explain the nature of God either verbally or really by means of its individual organism: for instance, by declaring in the first person, "I am the Lord your God."

Certainly when anyone says with his mouth, "I understand," we do not attribute the understanding to the mouth, but to the mind of the speaker; yet this is because the mouth is the natural organ of a man speaking, and the hearer, knowing what understanding is, easily comprehends, by a comparison with himself, that the speaker's mind is meant; but if we knew nothing of God beyond the mere

name and wished to commune with Him, and be assured of
His existence, I fail to see how our wish would be satisfied
by the declaration of a created thing (depending on God
neither more nor less than ourselves), "I am the Lord."
If God contorted the lips of Moses, or, I will not say Moses,
but some beast, till they pronounced the words, "I am the
Lord," should we apprehend the Lord's existence therefrom?

Scripture seems clearly to point to the belief that God
spoke Himself, having descended from heaven to Mount
Sinai for the purpose—and not only that the Israelites
heard Him speaking, but that their chief men beheld Him
(Ex. xxiv.) Further the law of Moses, which might neither
be added to nor curtailed, and which was set up as a national
standard of right, nowhere prescribed the belief that God
is without body, or even without form or figure, but only
ordained that the Jews should believe in His existence and
worship Him alone: it forbade them to invent or fashion
any likeness of the Deity, but this was to insure purity of
service; because, never having seen God, they could not by
means of images recall the likeness of God, but only the
likeness of some created thing which might thus gradually
take the place of God as the object of their adoration.
Nevertheless, the Bible clearly implies that God has a form,
and that Moses when he heard God speaking was permitted
to behold it, or at least its hinder parts.

Doubtless some mystery lurks in this question which we
will discuss more fully below. For the present I will call
attention to the passages in Scripture indicating the means
by which God has revealed His laws to man.

Revelation may be through figures only, as in 1 Chron.
xxii., where God displays his anger to David by means of
an angel bearing a sword, and also in the story of Balaam.

Maimonides and others do indeed maintain that these and
every other instance of angelic apparitions (e.g. to Manoah
and to Abraham offering up Isaac) occurred during sleep,
for that no one with his eyes open ever could see an angel,
but this is mere nonsense. The sole object of such commentators seems to be to extort from Scripture confirmations
of Aristotelian quibbles and their own inventions, a proceeding which I regard as the acme of absurdity.

In figures, not real but existing only in the prophet's

imagination, God revealed to Joseph his future lordship,
and in words and figures He revealed to Joshua that He
would fight for the Hebrews, causing to appear an angel, as
it were the Captain of the Lord's host, bearing a sword,
and by this means communicating verbally. The forsaking
of Israel by Providence was portrayed to Isaiah by a vision
of the Lord, the thrice Holy, sitting on a very lofty throne,
and the Hebrews, stained with the mire of their sins, sunk
as it were in uncleanness, and thus as far as possible distant from God. The wretchedness of the people at the time
was thus revealed, while future calamities were foretold in
words. I could cite from Holy Writ many similar examples,
but I think they are sufficiently well known already.

However, we get a still more clear confirmation of our
position in Num. xii. 6, 7, as follows: "If there be any
prophet among you, I the Lord will make myself known
unto him in a vision" (*i.e.* by appearances and signs, for God
says of the prophecy of Moses that it was a vision without
signs), "and will speak unto him in a dream" (*i.e.* not with
actual words and an actual voice). "My servant Moses is
not so; with him will I speak mouth to mouth, even
apparently, and not in dark speeches, and the similitude of
the Lord he shall behold," *i.e.* looking on me as a friend
and not afraid, he speaks with me (cf. Ex. xxxiii. 17).

This makes it indisputable that the other prophets did
not hear a real voice, and we gather as much from Deut.
xxiv. 10: "And there arose not a prophet since in Israel
like unto Moses whom the Lord knew face to face," which
must mean that the Lord spoke with none other; for not
even Moses saw the Lord's face. These are the only media
of communication between God and man which I find
mentioned in Scripture, and therefore the only ones which
may be supposed or invented. We may be able quite to
comprehend that God can communicate immediately with
man, for without the intervention of bodily means He com-
municates to our minds His essence; still, a man who can by
pure intuition comprehend ideas which are neither contained
in nor deducible from the foundations of our natural knowledge, must necessarily possess a mind far superior to those
of his fellow men, nor do I believe that any have been so
endowed save Christ. To Him the ordinances of God lead-

ing men to salvation were revealed directly without words or visions, so that God manifested Himself to the Apostles through the mind of Christ as He formerly did to Moses through the supernatural voice. In this sense the voice of Christ, like the voice which Moses heard, may be called the voice of God, and it may be said that the wisdom of God (*i.e.* wisdom more than human) took upon itself in Christ human nature, and that Christ was the way of salvation. I must at this juncture declare that those doctrines which certain churches put forward concerning Christ, I neither affirm nor deny, for I freely confess that I do not understand them. What I have just stated I gather from Scripture, where I never read that God appeared to Christ, or spoke to Christ, but that God was revealed to the Apostles through Christ; that Christ was the Way of Life, and that the old law was given through an angel, and not immediately by God; whence it follows that if Moses spoke with God face to face as a man speaks with his friend (*i.e.* by means of their two bodies) Christ communed with God mind to mind.

Thus we may conclude that no one except Christ received the revelations of God without the aid of imagination, whether in words or vision. Therefore the power of prophecy implies not a peculiarly perfect mind, but a peculiarly vivid imagination, as I will show more clearly in the next chapter. We will now inquire what is meant in the Bible by the Spirit of God breathed into the prophets, or by the prophets speaking with the Spirit of God; to that end we must determine the exact signification of the Hebrew word *ruagh*, commonly translated spirit.

The word *ruagh* literally means a wind, *e.g.* the south wind, but it is frequently employed in other derivative significations. It is used as equivalent to,

(1.) Breath: "Neither is there any spirit in his mouth," Ps. cxxxv. 17.

(2.) Life, or breathing: "And his spirit returned to him," 1 Sam. xxx. 12; *i.e.* he breathed again.

(3.) Courage and strength: "Neither did there remain any more spirit in any man," Josh. ii. 11; "And the spirit entered into me, and made me stand on my feet," Ezek. ii. 2.

(4.) Virtue and fitness: "Days should speak, and multi-

tudes of years should teach wisdom; but there is a spirit
in man," Job xxxii. 7 ; *i.e.* wisdom is not always found among
old men, for I now discover that it depends on individual
virtue and capacity. So, " A man in whom is the Spirit,"
Numbers xxvii. 18.

(5.) Habit of mind : " Because he had another spirit with
him," Numbers xiv. 24; *i.e.* another habit of mind. "Behold I will pour out My Spirit unto you," Prov. i. 23.

(6.) Will, purpose, desire, impulse : " Whither the spirit
was to go, they went," Ezek. i. 12; "That cover with a
covering, but not of My Spirit," Is. xxx. 1 ; " For the Lord
hath poured out on you the spirit of deep sleep," Is. xxix.
10 ; "Then was their spirit softened," Judges viii. 3 ; "He
that ruleth his spirit, is better than he that taketh a city,"
Prov. xvi. 32 ; "He that hath no rule over his own spirit,"
Prov. xxv. 28 ; "Your spirit as fire shall devour you,"
Isaiah xxxiii. 1.

From the meaning of disposition we get—

(7.) Passions and faculties. A lofty spirit means pride,
a lowly spirit humility, an evil spirit hatred and melancholy. So, too, the expressions spirits of jealousy, fornica-
tion, wisdom, counsel, bravery, stand for a jealous, lascivious, wise, prudent, or brave mind (for we Hebrews use
substantives in preference to adjectives), or these various
qualities.

(8.) The mind itself, or the life : " Yea, they have all one
spirit," Eccles. iii. 19 ; " The spirit shall return to God Who
gave it."

(9.) The quarters of the world (from the winds which
blow thence), or even the side of anything turned towards
a particular quarter—Ezek. xxxvii. 9 ; xlii. 16, 17, 18,
19, &c.

I have already alluded to the way in which things are
referred to God, and said to be of God.

(1.) As belonging to His nature, and being, as it were,
part of Him ; *e.g.* the power of God, the eyes of God.

(2.) As under His dominion, and depending on His
pleasure ; thus the heavens are called the heavens of the
Lord, as being His chariot and habitation. So Nebuchadnezzar is called the servant of God, Assyria the scourge of
God, &c.

(3.) As dedicated to Him, *e.g.* the Temple of God, a Nazarene of God, the Bread of God.

(4.) As revealed through the prophets and not through our natural faculties. In this sense the Mosaic law is called the law of God.

(5.) As being in the superlative degree. Very high mountains are styled the mountains of God, a very deep sleep, the sleep of God, &c. In this sense we must explain Amos iv. 11: "I have overthrown you as the overthrow of the Lord came upon Sodom and Gomorrah," *i.e.* that memorable overthrow, for since God Himself is the Speaker, the passage cannot well be taken otherwise. The wisdom of Solomon is called the wisdom of God, or extraordinary. The size of the cedars of Lebanon is alluded to in the Psalmist's expression, "the cedars of the Lord."

Similarly, if the Jews were at a loss to understand any phenomenon, or were ignorant of its cause, they referred it to God. Thus a storm was termed the chiding of God, thunder and lightning the arrows of God, for it was thought that God kept the winds confined in caves, His treasuries; thus differing merely in name from the Greek wind-god Eolus. In like manner miracles were called works of God, as being especially marvellous; though in reality, of course, all natural events are the works of God, and take place solely by His power. The Psalmist calls the miracles in Egypt the works of God, because the Hebrews found in them a way of safety which they had not looked for, and therefore especially marvelled at.

As, then, unusual natural phenomena are called works of God, and trees of unusual size are called trees of God, we cannot wonder that very strong and tall men, though impious robbers and whoremongers, are in Genesis called sons of God.

This reference of things wonderful to God was not peculiar to the Jews. Pharaoh, on hearing the interpretation of his dream, exclaimed that the mind of the gods was in Joseph. Nebuchadnezzar told Daniel that he possessed the mind of the holy gods; so also in Latin anything well made is often said to be wrought with Divine hands, which is equivalent to the Hebrew phrase, wrought with the hand of God.

We can now very easily understand and explain those passages of Scripture which speak of the Spirit of God. In some places the expression merely means a very strong, dry, and deadly wind, as in Isaiah xl. 7, "The grass withereth, the flower fadeth, because the Spirit of the Lord bloweth upon it." Similarly in Gen. i. 2: "The Spirit of the Lord moved over the face of the waters." At other times it is used as equivalent to a high courage, thus the spirit of Gideon and of Samson is called the Spirit of the Lord, as being very bold, and prepared for any emergency. Any unusual virtue or power is called the Spirit or Virtue of the Lord, Ex. xxxi. 3: "I will fill him (Bezaleel) with the Spirit of the Lord," *i.e.*, as the Bible itself explains, with talent above man's usual endowment. So Isa. xi. 2: "And the Spirit of the Lord shall rest upon him," is explained afterwards in the text to mean the spirit of wisdom and understanding, of counsel and might.

The melancholy of Saul is called the melancholy of the Lord, or a very deep melancholy, the persons who applied the term showing that they understood by it nothing supernatural, in that they sent for a musician to assuage it by harp-playing. Again, the "Spirit of the Lord" is used as equivalent to the mind of man, for instance, Job xxvii. 3: "And the Spirit of the Lord in my nostrils," the allusion being to Gen. ii. 7: "And God breathed into man's nostrils the breath of life." Ezekiel also, prophesying to the dead, says (xxvii. 14), "And I will give to you My Spirit, and ye shall live;" *i.e.* I will restore you to life. In Job xxxiv. 14, we read: "If He gather unto Himself His Spirit and breath;" in Gen. vi. 3: "My Spirit shall not always strive with man, for that he also is flesh," *i.e.* since man acts on the dictates of his body, and not the spirit which I gave him to discern the good, I will let him alone. So, too, Ps. li. 12: "Create in me a clean heart, O God, and renew a right spirit within me; cast me not away from Thy presence, and take not Thy Holy Spirit from me." It was supposed that sin originated only from the body, and that good impulses come from the mind; therefore the Psalmist invokes the aid of God against the bodily appetites, but prays that the spirit which the Lord, the Holy One, had given him might be renewed. Again, inasmuch as the Bible, in concession to popular ignorance, describes God as having a mind, a heart, emotions—nay, even a body and breath—the expression Spirit of the Lord is used for God's mind, disposition, emotion, strength, or breath. Thus, Isa. xl. 13: "Who hath disposed the Spirit of the Lord?" *i.e.* who, save Himself, hath caused the mind of the Lord to will anything? and Isa. lxiii. 10: "But they rebelled, and vexed the Holy Spirit."

The phrase comes to be used of the law of Moses, which in a sense expounds God's will, Is. lxiii. 11, "Where is He that put His Holy Spirit within him?" meaning, as we clearly gather from the context, the law of Moses. Nehemiah, speaking of the giving of the law, says, i. 20, "Thou gavest also thy good Spirit to instruct them." This is referred to in Deut. iv. 6, "This is your wisdom and understanding," and in Ps. cxliii. 10, "Thy good Spirit will lead me into the land of uprightness." The Spirit of the Lord may mean the breath of the Lord, for breath, no less than a mind, a heart, and a body are attributed to God in Scripture, as in Ps. xxxiii. 6. Hence it gets to mean the power, strength, or faculty of God, as in Job xxxiii. 4, "The Spirit of the Lord made me," *i.e.* the power, or, if you prefer, the decree of the Lord. So the Psalmist in poetic language declares, xxxiii. 6, "By the word of the Lord were the heavens made, and all the host of them by the breath of His mouth," *i.e.* by a mandate issued, as it were, in one breath. Also Ps. cxxxix. 7, "Whither shall I go from Thy Spirit, or whither shall I flee from Thy presence?" *i.e.* whither shall I go so as to be beyond Thy power and Thy presence?

Lastly, the Spirit of the Lord is used in Scripture to express the emotions of God, *e.g.* His kindness and mercy, Micah ii. 7, "Is the Spirit [*i.e.* the mercy] of the Lord straitened? Are these cruelties His doings?" Zech. iv. 6, "Not by might or by power, but My Spirit [*i.e.* mercy], saith the Lord of hosts." The twelfth verse of the seventh chapter of the same prophet must, I think, be interpreted in like manner: "Yea, they made their hearts as an adamant stone, lest they should hear the law, and the words which the Lord of hosts hath sent in His Spirit [*i.e.* in His mercy] by the former prophets." So also

Haggai ii. 5: "So My Spirit remaineth among you: fear ye not."

The passage in Isaiah xlviii. 16, "And now the Lord God and His Spirit hath sent me," may be taken to refer either to God's mercy or His revealed law; for the prophet says, "From the beginning" (*i.e.* from the time when I first came to you, to preach God's anger and His sentence gone forth against you) "I spoke not in secret; from the time that it was, there am I," and now I am sent by the mercy of God as a joyful messenger to preach your restoration. Or we may understand him to mean by the revealed law that he had before come to warn them by the command of the law (Levit. xix. 17) in the same manner and under the same conditions as Moses had warned them, and that now, like Moses, he ends by preaching their restoration. But the first explanation seems to me the best.

Returning, then, to the main object of our discussion, we find that the Scriptural phrases, "The Spirit of the Lord was upon a prophet," "The Lord breathed His Spirit into men," "Men were filled with the Spirit of God, with the Holy Spirit," &c., are quite clear to us, and mean that the prophets were endowed with a peculiar and extraordinary power, and devoted themselves to piety with especial constancy;[1] that thus they perceived the mind or the thought of God, for we have shown that God's Spirit signifies in Hebrew God's mind or thought, and that the law which shows His mind and thought is called His Spirit; hence that the imagination of the prophets, inasmuch as through it were revealed the decrees of God, may equally be called the mind of God, and the prophets be said to have possessed the mind of God. On our minds also the mind of God and His eternal thoughts are impressed; but this being the same for all men is less taken into account, especially by the Hebrews, who claimed a pre-eminence, and despised other men and other men's knowledge.

Lastly, the prophets were said to possess the Spirit of God because men knew not the cause of prophetic knowledge, and in their wonder referred it with other marvels directly to the Deity, styling it Divine knowledge.

We need no longer scruple to affirm that the prophets

[1] See Note 3.

only perceived God's revelation by the aid of imagination, that is, by words and figures either real or imaginary. We find no other means mentioned in Scripture, and therefore must not invent any. As to the particular law of Nature by which the communications took place, I confess my ignorance. I might, indeed, say as others do, that they took place by the power of God; but this would be mere trifling, and no better than explaining some unique specimen by a transcendental term. Everything takes place by the power of God. Nature herself is the power of God under another name, and our ignorance of the power of God is co-extensive with our ignorance of Nature. It is absolute folly, therefore, to ascribe an event to the power of God when we know not its natural cause, which is the power of God.

However, we are not now inquiring into the causes of prophetic knowledge. We are only attempting, as I have said, to examine the Scriptural documents, and to draw our conclusions from them as from ultimate natural facts; the causes of the documents do not concern us.

As the prophets perceived the revelations of God by the aid of imagination, they could indisputably perceive much that is beyond the boundary of the intellect, for many more ideas can be constructed from words and figures than from the principles and notions on which the whole fabric of reasoned knowledge is reared.

Thus we have a clue to the fact that the prophets perceived nearly everything in parables and allegories, and clothed spiritual truths in bodily forms, for such is the usual method of imagination. We need no longer wonder that Scripture and the prophets speak so strangely and obscurely of God's Spirit or Mind (cf. Numbers xi. 17, 1 Kings xxii. 21, &c.), that the Lord was seen by Micah as sitting, by Daniel as an old man clothed in white, by Ezekiel as a fire, that the Holy Spirit appeared to those with Christ as a descending dove, to the apostles as fiery tongues, to Paul on his conversion as a great light. All these expressions are plainly in harmony with the current ideas of God and spirits.

Inasmuch as imagination is fleeting and inconstant, we find that the power of prophecy did not remain with a prophet for long, nor manifest itself frequently, but was very rare; manifesting itself only in a few men, and in them not often.

We must necessarily inquire how the prophets became assured of the truth of what they perceived by imagination, and not by sure mental laws; but our investigation must be confined to Scripture, for the subject is one on which we cannot acquire certain knowledge, and which we cannot explain by the immediate causes. Scripture teaching about the assurance of prophets I will treat of in the next chapter.

CHAPTER II.

OF PROPHETS.

IT follows from the last chapter that, as I have said, the prophets were endowed with unusually vivid imaginations, and not with unusually perfect minds. This conclusion is amply sustained by Scripture, for we are told that Solomon was the wisest of men, but had no special faculty of prophecy. Heman, Calcol, and Dara, though men of great talent, were not prophets, whereas uneducated countrymen, nay, even women, such as Hagar, Abraham's handmaid, were thus gifted. Nor is this contrary to ordinary experience and reason. Men of great imaginative power are less fitted for abstract reasoning, whereas those who excel in intellect and its use keep their imagination more restrained and controlled, holding it in subjection, so to speak, lest it should usurp the place of reason.

Thus to suppose that knowledge of natural and spiritual phenomena can be gained from the prophetic books, is an utter mistake, which I shall endeavour to expose, as I think philosophy, the age, and the question itself demand. I care not for the girdings of superstition, for superstition is the bitter enemy of all true knowledge and true morality. Yes; it has come to this! Men who openly confess that they can form no idea of God, and only know Him through created things, of which they know not the causes, can unblushingly accuse philosophers of Atheism.

Treating the question methodically, I will show that prophecies varied, not only according to the imagination and physical temperament of the prophet, but also according to his particular opinions; and further that prophecy never rendered the prophet wiser than he was before. But I will first discuss the assurance of truth which the prophets received, for this is akin to the subject-matter of the chapter, and will serve to elucidate somewhat our present point.

Imagination does not, in its own nature, involve any certainty of truth, such as is implied in every clear and distinct idea, but requires some extrinsic reason to assure us of its objective reality: hence prophecy cannot afford certainty, and the prophets were assured of God's revelation by some sign, and not by the fact of revelation, as we may see from Abraham, who, when he had heard the promise of God, demanded a sign, not because he did not believe in God, but because he wished to be sure that it was God Who made the promise. The fact is still more evident in the case of Gideon: "Show me," he says to God, "show me a sign, that I may know that it is Thou that talkest with me." God also says to Moses: "And let this be a sign that I have sent thee." Hezekiah, though he had long known Isaiah to be a prophet, none the less demanded a sign of the cure which he predicted. It is thus quite evident that the prophets always received some sign to certify them of their prophetic imaginings; and for this reason Moses bids the Jews (Deut. xviii.) ask of the prophets a sign, namely, the prediction of some coming event. In this respect, prophetic knowledge is inferior to natural knowledge, which needs no sign, and in itself implies certitude. Moreover, Scripture warrants the statement that the certitude of the prophets was not mathematical, but moral. Moses lays down the punishment of death for the prophet who preaches new gods, even though he confirm his doctrine by signs and wonders (Deut. xiii.); "For," he says, "the Lord also worketh signs and wonders to try His people." And Jesus Christ warns His disciples of the same thing (Matt. xxiv. 24). Furthermore, Ezekiel (xiv. 9) plainly states that God sometimes deceives men with false revelations; and Micaiah bears like witness in the case of the prophets of Ahab.

Although these instances go to prove that revelation is open to doubt, it nevertheless contains, as we have said, a considerable element of certainty, for God never deceives the good, nor His chosen, but (according to the ancient proverb, and as appears in the history of Abigail and her speech), God uses the good as instruments of goodness, and the wicked as means to execute His wrath. This may be seen from the case of Micaiah above quoted; for although

God had determined to deceive Ahab, through prophets, He made use of lying prophets; to the good prophet He revealed the truth, and did not forbid his proclaiming it.

Still the certitude of prophecy remains, as I have said, merely moral; for no one can justify himself before God, nor boast that he is an instrument for God's goodness. Scripture itself teaches and shows that God led away David to number the people, though it bears ample witness to David's piety.

The whole question of the certitude of prophecy was based on these three considerations :—

1. That the things revealed were imagined very vividly, affecting the prophets in the same way as things seen when awake;

2. The presence of a sign;

3. Lastly and chiefly, that the mind of the prophet was given wholly to what was right and good.

Although Scripture does not always make mention of a sign, we must nevertheless suppose that a sign was always vouchsafed; for Scripture does not always relate every condition and circumstance (as many have remarked), but rather takes them for granted. We may, however, admit that no sign was needed when the prophecy declared nothing that was not already contained in the law of Moses, because it was confirmed by that law. For instance, Jeremiah's prophecy of the destruction of Jerusalem was confirmed by the prophecies of other prophets, and by the threats in the law, and, therefore, it needed no sign; whereas Hananiah, who, contrary to all the prophets, foretold the speedy restoration of the state, stood in need of a sign, or he would have been in doubt as to the truth of his prophecy, until it was confirmed by facts. "The prophet which prophesieth of peace, when the word of the prophet shall come to pass, then shall the prophet be known that the Lord hath truly sent him."

As, then, the certitude afforded to the prophet by signs was not mathematical (*i.e.* did not necessarily follow from the perception of the thing perceived or seen), but only moral, and as the signs were only given to convince the prophet, it follows that such signs were given according to the opinions and capacity of each prophet, so that a sign which would

convince one prophet would fall far short of convincing
another who was imbued with different opinions.   Therefore the signs varied according to the individual prophet.

So also did the revelation vary, as we have stated,
according to individual disposition and temperament, and
according to the opinions previously held.

It varied according to disposition, in this way: if a
prophet was cheerful, victories, peace, and events which
make men glad, were revealed to him; in that he was
naturally more likely to imagine such things.   If, on the
contrary, he was melancholy, wars, massacres, and calamities were revealed; and so, according as a prophet was
merciful, gentle, quick to anger, or severe, he was more
fitted for one kind of revelation than another.   It varied
according to the temper of imagination in this way: if a
prophet was cultivated he perceived the mind of God in a
cultivated way, if he was confused he perceived it confusedly.   And so with revelations perceived through visions.
If a prophet was a countryman he saw visions of oxen, cows,
and the like; if he was a soldier, he saw generals and
armies; if a courtier, a royal throne, and so on.

Lastly, prophecy varied according to the opinions held
by the prophets; for instance, to the Magi, who believed
in the follies of astrology, the birth of Christ was revealed
through the vision of a star in the East.   To the augurs of
Nebuchadnezzar the destruction of Jerusalem was revealed
through entrails, whereas the king himself inferred it from
oracles and the direction of arrows which he shot into the
air.   To prophets who believed that man acts from free
choice and by his own power, God was revealed as standing
apart from and ignorant of future human actions.   All of
which we will illustrate from Scripture.

The first point is proved from the case of Elisha, who, in
order to prophecy to Jehoram, asked for a harp, and was
unable to perceive the Divine purpose till he had been re-
created by its music; then, indeed, he prophesied to Jehoram and to his allies glad tidings, which previously he had
been unable to attain to because he was angry with the
king, and these who are angry with anyone can imagine
evil of him, but not good.   The theory that God does not
reveal Himself to the angry or the sad, is a mere dream:

contumacy — def: refusal to obey authority

for God revealed to Moses while angry, the terrible
slaughter of the firstborn, and did so without the intervention of a harp. To Cain in his rage, God was revealed, and to
Ezekiel, impatient with anger, was revealed the contumacy
and wretchedness of the Jews. Jeremiah, miserable and
weary of life, prophesied the disasters of the Hebrews, so
that Josiah would not consult him, but inquired of a
woman, inasmuch as it was more in accordance with
womanly nature that God should reveal His mercy thereto.
So, Micaiah never prophesied good to Ahab, though other
true prophets had done so, but invariably evil. Thus we
see that individual prophets were by temperament more
fitted for one sort of revelation than another.

The style of the prophecy also varied according to the
eloquence of the individual prophet. The prophecies of
Ezekiel and Amos are not written in a cultivated style like
those of Isaiah and Nahum, but more rudely. Any Hebrew
scholar who wishes to inquire into this point more closely,
and compares chapters of the different prophets treating of
the same subject, will find great dissimilarity of style.
Compare, for instance, chap. i. of the courtly Isaiah, verse
11 to verse 20, with chap. v. of the countryman Amos,
verses 21-24. Compare also the order and reasoning of
the prophecies of Jeremiah, written in Idumæa (chap. xlix.),
with the order and reasoning of Obadiah. Compare, lastly,
Isa. xl. 19, 20, and xliv. 8, with Hosea viii. 6, and xiii. 2.
And so on.

A due consideration of these passage will clearly show us
that God has no particular style in speaking, but, according to the learning and capacity of the prophet, is cultivated,
compressed, severe, untutored, prolix, or obscure.

There was, moreover, a certain variation in the visions
vouchsafed to the prophets, and in the symbols by which
they expressed them, for Isaiah saw the glory of the Lord
departing from the Temple in a different form from that
presented to Ezekiel. The Rabbis, indeed, maintain that
both visions were really the same, but that Ezekiel, being
a countryman, was above measure impressed by it, and
therefore set it forth in full detail; but unless there is a
trustworthy tradition on the subject, which I do not for a
moment believe, this theory is plainly an invention. Isaiah

saw seraphim with six wings, Ezekiel beasts with four
wings; Isaiah saw God clothed and sitting on a royal
throne, Ezekiel saw Him in the likeness of a fire; each
doubtless saw God under the form in which he usually
imagined Him.

Further, the visions varied in clearness as well as in details; for the revelations of Zechariah were too obscure to
be understood by the prophet without explanation, as appears from his narration of them; the visions of Daniel
could not be understood by him even after they had been
explained, and this obscurity did not arise from the difficulty of the matter revealed (for being merely human
affairs, these only transcended human capacity in being
future), but solely in the fact that Daniel's imagination was
not so capable for prophecy while he was awake as while
he was asleep; and this is further evident from the fact
that at the very beginning of the vision he was so terrified
that he almost despaired of his strength. Thus, on account
of the inadequacy of his imagination and his strength, the
things revealed were so obscure to him that he could not
understand them even after they had been explained.
Here we may note that the words heard by Daniel, were,
as we have shown above, simply imaginary, so that it is
hardly wonderful that in his frightened state he imagined
them so confusedly and obscurely that afterwards he could
make nothing of them. Those who say that God did not
wish to make a clear revelation, do not seem to have read
the words of the angel, who expressly says that he came to
make the prophet understand what should befall his people
in the latter days (Dan. x. 14).

The revelation remained obscure because no one was
found, at that time, with imagination sufficiently strong to
conceive it more clearly.

Lastly, the prophets, to whom it was revealed that God
would take away Elijah, wished to persuade Elisha that he
had been taken somewhere where they would find him;
showing sufficiently clearly that they had not understood
God's revelation aright.

There is no need to set this out more amply, for nothing
is more plain in the Bible than that God endowed some
prophets with far greater gifts of prophecy than others.

But I will show in greater detail and length, for I consider the point more important, that the prophecies varied according to the opinions previously embraced by the prophets, and that the prophets held diverse and even contrary opinions and prejudices. (I speak, be it understood, solely of matters speculative, for in regard to uprightness and morality the case is widely different.) From thence I shall conclude that prophecy never rendered the prophets more learned, but left them with their former opinions, and that we are, therefore, not at all bound to trust them in matters of intellect.

Everyone has been strangely hasty in affirming that the prophets knew everything within the scope of human intellect; and, although certain passages of Scripture plainly affirm that the prophets were in certain respects ignorant, such persons would rather say that they do not understand the passages than admit that there was anything which the prophets did not know; or else they try to wrest the Scriptural words away from their evident meaning.

If either of these proceedings is allowable we may as well shut our Bibles, for vainly shall we attempt to prove anything from them if their plainest passages may be classed among obscure and impenetrable mysteries, or if we may put any interpretation on them which we fancy. For instance, nothing is more clear in the Bible than that Joshua, and perhaps also the author who wrote his history, thought that the sun revolves round the earth, and that the earth is fixed, and further that the sun for a certain period remained still. Many, who will not admit any movement in the heavenly bodies, explain away the passage till it seems to mean something quite different; others, who have learned to philosophize more correctly, and understand that the earth moves while the sun is still, or at any rate does not revolve round the earth, try with all their might to wrest this meaning from Scripture, though plainly nothing of the sort is intended. Such quibblers excite my wonder! Are we, forsooth, bound to believe that Joshua the soldier was a learned astronomer? or that a miracle could not be revealed to him, or that the light of the sun could not remain longer than usual above the horizon, without his knowing the cause? To me both alternatives appear ridiculous, and

PARHELIA — atmospheric phenomenon causing of light in the sky like sun. Gen. 5—5

34 A THEOLOGICO-POLITICAL TREATISE. [CHAP. II.

therefore I would rather say that Joshua was ignorant of the true cause of the lengthened day, and that he and the whole host with him thought that the sun moved round the earth every day, and that on that particular occasion it stood still for a time, thus causing the light to remain longer; and I would say that they did not conjecture that, from the amount of snow in the air (see Josh. x. 11), the refraction may have been greater than usual, or that there may have been some other cause which we will not now inquire into.

So also the sign of the shadow going back was revealed to Isaiah according to his understanding; that is, as proceeding from a going backwards of the sun; for he, too, thought that the sun moves and that the earth is still; of parhelia he perhaps never even dreamed. We may arrive at this conclusion without any scruple, for the sign could really have come to pass, and have been predicted by Isaiah to the king, without the prophet being aware of the real cause.

With regard to the building of the Temple by Solomon, if it was really dictated by God we must maintain the same doctrine: namely, that all the measurements were revealed according to the opinions and understanding of the king; for as we are not bound to believe that Solomon was a mathematician, we may affirm that he was ignorant of the true ratio between the circumference and the diameter of a circle, and that, like the generality of workmen, he thought that it was as three to one. But if it is allowable to declare that we do not understand the passage, in good sooth I know nothing in the Bible that we can understand; for the process of building is there narrated simply and as a mere matter of history. If, again, it is permitted to pretend that the passage has another meaning, and was written as it is from some reason unknown to us, this is no less than a complete subversal of the Bible; for every absurd and evil invention of human perversity could thus, without detriment to Scriptural authority, be defended and fostered. Our conclusion is in no wise impious, for though Solomon, Isaiah, Joshua, &c. were prophets, they were none the less men, and as such not exempt from human shortcomings.

According to the understanding of Noah it was revealed

to him that God was about to destroy the whole human race, for Noah thought that beyond the limits of Palestine the world was not inhabited.

Not only in matters of this kind, but in others more important, the prophets could be, and in fact were, ignorant; for they taught nothing special about the Divine attributes, but held quite ordinary notions about God, and to these notions their revelations were adapted, as I will demonstrate by ample Scriptural testimony; from all which one may easily see that they were praised and commended, not so much for the sublimity and eminence of their intellect as for their piety and faithfulness.

Adam, the first man to whom God was revealed, did not know that He is omnipotent and omniscient; for he hid himself from Him, and attempted to make excuses for his fault before God, as though he had had to do with a man; therefore to him also was God revealed according to his understanding—that is, as being unaware of his situation or his sin, for Adam heard, or seemed to hear, the Lord walking in the garden, calling him and asking him where he was; and then, on seeing his shamefacedness, asking him whether he had eaten of the forbidden fruit. Adam evidently only knew the Deity as the Creator of all things. To Cain also God was revealed, according to his understanding, as ignorant of human affairs, nor was a higher conception of the Deity required for repentance of his sin.

To Laban the Lord revealed Himself as the God of Abraham, because Laban believed that each nation had its own special divinity (see Gen. xxxi. 29). Abraham also knew not that God is omnipresent, and has foreknowledge of all things; for when he heard the sentence against the inhabitants of Sodom, he prayed that the Lord should not execute it till He had ascertained whether they all merited such punishment; for he said (see Gen. xviii. 24), "Peradventure there be fifty righteous within the city," and in accordance with this belief God was revealed to him; as Abraham imagined, He spake thus: "I will go down now, and see whether they have done altogether according to the cry of it which is come unto Me; and, if not, I will know." Further, the Divine testimony concerning Abraham asserts nothing but that he was obedient, and that he " commanded

his household after him that they should keep the way of
the Lord" (Gen. xviii. 19); it does not state that he held
sublime conceptions of the Deity.

Moses, also, was not sufficiently aware that God is omniscient, and directs human actions by His sole decree, for
although God Himself says that the Israelites should
hearken to Him, Moses still considered the matter doubtful
and repeated, "But if they will not believe me, nor hearken
unto my voice." To him in like manner God was revealed
as taking no part in, and as being ignorant of, future human
actions: the Lord gave him two signs and said, "And it
shall come to pass that if they will not believe thee, neither
hearken to the voice of the first sign, that they will believe
the voice of the latter sign; but if not, thou shalt take of
the water of the river," &c. Indeed, if any one considers
without prejudice the recorded opinions of Moses, he will
plainly see that Moses conceived the Deity as a Being Who
has always existed, does exist, and always will exist, and
for this cause he calls Him by the name Jehovah, which
in Hebrew signifies these three phases of existence: as to
His nature, Moses only taught that He is merciful, gracious,
and exceeding jealous, as appears from many passages in
the Pentateuch. Lastly, he believed and taught that this
Being was so different from all other beings, that He could
not be expressed by the image of any visible thing; also,
that He could not be looked upon, and that not so much
from inherent impossibility as from human infirmity;
further, that by reason of His power He was without equal
and unique. Moses admitted, indeed, that there were
beings (doubtless by the plan and command of the Lord)
who acted as God's vicegerents—that is, beings to whom
God had given the right, authority, and power to direct
nations, and to provide and care for them; but he taught
that this Being Whom they were bound to obey was the
highest and Supreme God, or (to use the Hebrew phrase)
God of gods, and thus in the song (Exod. xv. 11) he exclaims, "Who is like unto Thee, O Lord, among the gods?"
and Jethro says (Exod. xviii. 11), "Now I know that the
Lord is greater than all gods." That is to say, "I am at
length compelled to admit to Moses that Jehovah is greater
than all gods, and that His power is unrivalled." We must

remain in doubt whether Moses thought that these beings who acted as God's vicegerents were created by Him, for he has stated nothing, so far as we know, about their creation and origin. He further taught that this Being had brought the visible world into order from Chaos, and had given Nature her germs, and therefore that He possesses supreme right and power over all things; further, that by reason of this supreme right and power He had chosen for Himself alone the Hebrew nation and a certain strip of territory, and had handed over to the care of other gods substituted by Himself the rest of the nations and territories, and that therefore He was called the God of Israel and the God of Jerusalem, whereas the other gods were called the gods of the Gentiles. For this reason the Jews believed that the strip of territory which God had chosen for Himself, demanded a Divine worship quite apart and different from the worship which obtained elsewhere, and that the Lord would not suffer the worship of other gods adapted to other countries. Thus they thought that the people whom the king of Assyria had brought into Judæa were torn in pieces by lions because they knew not the worship of the National Divinity (2 Kings xvii. 25).

Jacob, according to Aben Ezra's opinion, therefore admonished his sons when he wished them to seek out a new country, that they should prepare themselves for a new worship, and lay aside the worship of strange gods—that is, of the gods of the land where they were (Gen. xxxv. 2, 3).

David, in telling Saul that he was compelled by the king's persecution to live away from his country, said that he was driven out from the heritage of the Lord, and sent to worship other gods (1 Sam. xxvi. 19). Lastly, he believed that this Being or Deity had His habitation in the heavens (Deut. xxxiii. 27), an opinion very common among the Gentiles.

If we now examine the revelations to Moses, we shall find that they were accommodated to these opinions; as he believed that the Divine Nature was subject to the conditions of mercy, graciousness, &c., so God was revealed to him in accordance with his idea and under these attributes (see Exodus xxxiv. 6, 7, and the second commandment). Further it is related (Ex. xxxiii. 18) that Moses asked of God that he might behold Him, but as Moses (as

we have said) had formed no mental image of God, and
God (as I have shown) only revealed Himself to the prophets in accordance with the disposition of their imagination, He did not reveal Himself in any form. This, I
repeat, was because the imagination of Moses was unsuit-
able, for other prophets bear witness that they saw the
Lord; for instance, Isaiah, Ezekiel, Daniel, &c.   For this
reason God answered Moses, "Thou canst not see My
face;" and inasmuch as Moses believed that God can be
looked upon—that is, that no contradiction of the Divine
nature is therein involved (for otherwise he would never
have preferred his request)—it is added, "For no one shall
look on Me and live," thus giving a reason in accordance
with Moses' idea, for it is not stated that a contradiction
of the Divine nature would be involved, as was really the
case, but that the thing would not come to pass because
of human infirmity.

When God would reveal to Moses that the Israelites,
because they worshipped the calf, were to be placed in the
same category as other nations, He said (ch. xxxiii. 2, 3),
that He would send an angel (that is, a being who should
have charge of the Israelites, instead of the Supreme Being),
and that He Himself would no longer remain among them;
thus leaving Moses no ground for supposing that the
Israelites were more beloved by God than the other nations
whose guardianship He had entrusted to other beings or
angels (vide verse 16).

Lastly, as Moses believed that God dwelt in the heavens,
God was revealed to him as coming down from heaven
on to a mountain, and in order to talk with the Lord
Moses went up the mountain, which he certainly need
not have done if he could have conceived of God as omnipresent.

The Israelites knew scarcely anything of God, although
He was revealed to them; and this is abundantly evident
from their transferring, a few days afterwards, the honour
and worship due to Him to a calf, which they believed to
be the god who had brought them out of Egypt.   In
truth, it is hardly likely that men accustomed to the super-
stitions of Egypt, uncultivated and sunk in most abject
slavery, should have held any sound notions about the

Deity, or that Moses should have taught them anything beyond a rule of right living; inculcating it not like a philosopher, as the result of freedom, but like a lawgiver compelling them to be moral by legal authority. Thus the rule of right living, the worship and love of God, was to them rather a bondage than the true liberty, the gift and grace of the Deity. Moses bid them love God and keep His law, because they had in the past received benefits from Him (such as the deliverance from slavery in Egypt), and further terrified them with threats if they transgressed His commands, holding out many promises of good if they should observe them; thus treating them as parents treat irrational children. It is, therefore, certain that they knew not the excellence of virtue and the true happiness.

Jonah thought that he was fleeing from the sight of God, which seems to show that he too held that God had entrusted the care of the nations outside Judæa to other substituted powers. No one in the whole of the Old Testament speaks more rationally of God than Solomon, who in fact surpassed all the men of his time in natural ability. Yet he considered himself above the law (esteeming it only to have been given for men without reasonable and intellectual grounds for their actions), and made small account of the laws concerning kings, which are mainly three: nay, he openly violated them (in this he did wrong, and acted in a manner unworthy of a philosopher, by indulging in sensual pleasure), and taught that all Fortune's favours to mankind are vanity, that humanity has no nobler gift than wisdom, and no greater punishment than folly. See Proverbs xvi. 22, 23.

But let us return to the prophets whose conflicting opinions we have undertaken to note.

The expressed ideas of Ezekiel seemed so diverse from those of Moses to the Rabbis who have left us the extant prophetic books (as is told in the treatise of Sabbathus, i. 13, 2), that they had serious thoughts of omitting his prophecy from the canon, and would doubtless have thus excluded it if a certain Hananiah had not undertaken to explain it; a task which (as is there narrated) he with great zeal and labour accomplished. How he did so does not sufficiently appear, whether it was by writing a commentary which has now perished, or by altering Ezekiel's words and audaciously striking out phrases according to his fancy.   However this may be, chapter xviii. certainly does not seem to agree with Exodus xxxiv. 7, Jeremiah xxxii. 18, &c.

Samuel believed that the Lord never repented of anything He had decreed (1 Sam. xv. 29), for when Saul was sorry for his sin, and wished to worship God and ask for forgiveness, Samuel said that the Lord would not go back from his decree.

To Jeremiah, on the other hand, it was revealed that, "If that nation against whom I (the Lord) have pronounced, turn from their evil, I will repent of the evil that I thought to do unto them.   If it do evil in my sight, that it obey not my voice, then I will repent of the good wherewith I said I would benefit them" (Jer. xviii. 8-10).   Joel (ii. 13) taught that the Lord repented Him only of evil. Lastly, it is clear from Gen. iv. 7 that a man can overcome the temptations of sin, and act righteously; for this doctrine is told to Cain, though, as we learn from Josephus and the Scriptures, he never did so overcome them.   And this agrees with the chapter of Jeremiah just cited, for it is there said that the Lord repents of the good or the evil pronounced, if the men in question change their ways and manner of life.   But, on the other hand, Paul (Rom. ix. 10) teaches as plainly as possible that men have no control over the temptations of the flesh save by the special vocation and grace of God.   And when (Rom. iii. 5 and vi. 19) he attributes righteousness to man, he corrects himself as speaking merely humanly and through the infirmity of the flesh.

We have now more than sufficiently proved our point, that God adapted revelations to the understanding and opinions of the prophets, and that in matters of theory without bearing on charity or morality the prophets could be, and, in fact, were, ignorant, and held conflicting opinions. It therefore follows that we must by no means go to the prophets for knowledge, either of natural or of spiritual phenomena.

We have determined, then, that we are only bound to believe in the prophetic writings, the object and substance of the revelation; with regard to the details, every one may believe or not, as he likes.

For instance, the revelation to Cain only teaches us that God admonished him to lead the true life, for such alone is the object and substance of the revelation, not doctrines concerning free will and philosophy. Hence, though the freedom of the will is clearly implied in the words of the admonition, we are at liberty to hold a contrary opinion, since the words and reasons were adapted to the understanding of Cain.

So, too, the revelation to Micaiah would only teach that God revealed to him the true issue of the battle between Ahab and Aram; and this is all we are bound to believe. Whatever else is contained in the revelation concerning the true and the false Spirit of God, the army of heaven standing on the right hand and on the left, and all the other details, does not affect us at all. Every one may believe as much of it as his reason allows.

The reasonings by which the Lord displayed His power to Job (if they really were a revelation, and the author of the history is narrating, and not merely, as some suppose, rhetorically adorning his own conceptions), would come under the same category—that is, they were adapted to Job's understanding, for the purpose of convincing him, and are not universal, or for the convincing of all men.

We can come to no different conclusion with respect to the reasonings of Christ, by which He convicted the Pharisees of pride and ignorance, and exhorted His disciples to lead the true life. He adapted them to each man's opinions and principles. For instance, when He said to the Pharisees (Matt. xii. 26), "And if Satan cast out devils, his house is divided against itself, how then shall his kingdom stand?" He only wished to convince the Pharisees according to their own principles, not to teach that there are devils, or any kingdom of devils. So, too, when He said to His disciples (Matt. viii. 10), "See that ye despise not one of these little ones, for I say unto you that their angels," &c., He merely desired to warn them against pride and despising any of their fellows, not to insist on the actual reason given, which was simply adopted in order to persuade them more easily.

Lastly, we should say exactly the same of the apostolic signs and reasonings, but there is no need to go further into the subject.   If I were to enumerate all the passages of Scripture addressed only to individuals, or to a particular man's understanding, and which cannot, without great danger to philosophy, be defended as Divine doctrines, I should go far beyond the brevity at which I aim.   Let it suffice, then, to have indicated a few instances of general application, and let the curious reader consider others by himself.   Although the points we have just raised concerning prophets and prophecy are the only ones which have any direct bearing on the end in view, namely, the separation of Philosophy from Theology, still, as I have touched on the general question, I may here inquire whether the gift of prophecy was peculiar to the Hebrews, or whether it was common to all nations.   I must then come to a conclusion about the vocation of the Hebrews, all of which I shall do in the ensuing chapter.

CHAPTER III.

OF THE VOCATION OF THE HEBREWS, AND WHETHER THE
GIFT OF PROPHECY WAS PECULIAR TO THEM.

EVERY man's true happiness and blessedness consist solely in the enjoyment of what is good, not in the pride that he alone is enjoying it, to the exclusion of others. He who thinks himself the more blessed because he is enjoying benefits which others are not, or because he is more blessed or more fortunate than his fellows, is ignorant of true happiness and blessedness, and the joy which he feels is either childish or envious and malicious. For instance, a man's true happiness consists only in wisdom, and the knowledge of the truth, not at all in the fact that he is wiser than others, or that others lack such knowledge : such considerations do not increase his wisdom or true happiness.

Whoever, therefore, rejoices for such reasons, rejoices in another's misfortune, and is, so far, malicious and bad, knowing neither true happiness nor the peace of the true life.

When Scripture, therefore, in exhorting the Hebrews to obey the law, says that the Lord has chosen them for Himself before other nations (Deut. x. 15); that He is near them, but not near others (Deut. iv. 7); that to them alone He has given just laws (Deut. iv. 8); and, lastly, that He has marked them out before others (Deut. iv. 32); it speaks only according to the understanding of its hearers, who, as we have shown in the last chapter, and as Moses also testifies (Deut. ix. 6, 7), knew not true blessedness. For in good sooth they would have been no less blessed if God had called all men equally to salvation, nor would God have been less present to them for being equally present to others; their laws would have been no less just if they had been ordained for all, and they themselves would have been no less wise. The miracles would have shown

God's power no less by being wrought for other nations
also; lastly, the Hebrews would have been just as much
bound to worship God if He had bestowed all these gifts
equally on all men.

When God tells Solomon (1 Kings iii. 12) that no one
shall be as wise as he in time to come, it seems to be only
a manner of expressing surpassing wisdom; it is little
to be believed that God would have promised Solomon, for
his greater happiness, that He would never endow anyone
with so much wisdom in time to come; this would in no
wise have increased Solomon's intellect, and the wise king
would have given equal thanks to the Lord if everyone had
been gifted with the same faculties.

Still, though we assert that Moses, in the passages of the
Pentateuch just cited, spoke only according to the understanding of the Hebrews, we have no wish to deny that
God ordained the Mosaic law for them alone, nor that He
spoke to them alone, nor that they witnessed marvels
beyond those which happened to any other nation; but we
wish to emphasize that Moses desired to admonish the
Hebrews in such a manner, and with such reasonings as
would appeal most forcibly to their childish understanding,
and constrain them to worship the Deity.   Further, we
wished to show that the Hebrews did not surpass other
nations in knowledge, or in piety, but evidently in some
attribute different from these; or (to speak like the Scriptures, according to their understanding), that the Hebrews
were not chosen by God before others for the sake of the
true life and sublime ideas, though they were often thereto
admonished, but with some other object.   What that object
was, I will duly show.

But before I begin, I wish in a few words to explain
what I mean by the guidance of God, by the help of God,
external and inward, and, lastly, what I understand by
fortune.

By the help of God, I mean the fixed and unchangeable
order of nature or the chain of natural events: for I have
said before and shown elsewhere that the universal laws of
nature, according to which all things exist and are determined, are only another name for the eternal decrees of
God, which always involve eternal truth and necessity.

So that to say that everything happens according to natural laws, and to say that everything is ordained by the decree and ordinance of God, is the same thing. Now since the power in nature is identical with the power of God, by which alone all things happen and are determined, it follows that whatsoever man, as a part of nature, provides himself with to aid and preserve his existence, or whatsoever nature affords him without his help, is given to him solely by the Divine power, acting either through human nature or through external circumstance. So whatever human nature can furnish itself with by its own efforts to preserve its existence, may be fitly called the inward aid of God, whereas whatever else accrues to man's profit from outward causes may be called the external aid of God.

We can now easily understand what is meant by the election of God. For since no one can do anything save by the predetermined order of nature, that is by God's eternal ordinance and decree, it follows that no one can choose a plan of life for himself, or accomplish any work save by God's vocation choosing him for the work or the plan of life in question, rather than any other. Lastly, by fortune, I mean the ordinance of God in so far as it directs human life through external and unexpected means. With these preliminaries I return to my purpose of discovering the reason why the Hebrews were said to be elected by God before other nations, and with the demonstration I thus proceed.

All objects of legitimate desire fall, generally speaking, under one of these three categories:—

1. The knowledge of things through their primary causes.

2. The government of the passions, or the acquirement of the habit of virtue.

3. Secure and healthy life.

The means which most directly conduce towards the first two of these ends, and which may be considered their proximate and efficient causes are contained in human nature itself, so that their acquisition hinges only on our own power, and on the laws of human nature. It may be concluded that these gifts are not peculiar to any nation, but have always been shared by the whole human race, unless, indeed, we would indulge the dream that nature formerly

created men of different kinds. But the means which conduce
to security and health are chiefly in external circumstance,
and are called the gifts of fortune because they depend
chiefly on objective causes of which we are ignorant; for a
fool may be almost as liable to happiness or unhappiness
as a wise man.   Nevertheless, human management and
watchfulness can greatly assist towards living in security
and warding off the injuries of our fellow-men, and even of
beasts. Reason and experience show no more certain means
of attaining this object than the formation of a society with
fixed laws, the occupation of a strip of territory, and the
concentration of all forces, as it were, into one body, that is
the social body. Now for forming and preserving a society,
no ordinary ability and care is required : that society will
be most secure, most stable, and least liable to reverses,
which is founded and directed by far-seeing and careful
men; while, on the other hand, a society constituted by
men without trained skill, depends in a great measure on
fortune, and is less constant. If, in spite of all, such a
society lasts a long time, it is owing to some other directing
influence than its own ; if it overcomes great perils and its
affairs prosper, it will perforce marvel at and adore the
guiding Spirit of God (in so far, that is, as God works
through hidden means, and not through the nature and
mind of man), for everything happens to it unexpectedly
and contrary to anticipation, it may even be said and
thought to be by miracle. Nations, then, are distinguished
from one another in respect to the social organization and
the laws under which they live and are governed; the Hebrew nation was not chosen by God in respect to its wisdom
nor its tranquillity of mind, but in respect to its social organization and the good fortune with which it obtained
supremacy and kept it so many years.   This is abundantly
clear from Scripture.   Even a cursory perusal will show
us that the only respects in which the Hebrews surpassed
other nations, are in their successful conduct of matters relating to government, and in their surmounting great perils
solely by God's external aid; in other ways they were on a
par with their fellows, and God was equally gracious to all.
For in respect to intellect (as we have shown in the last
chapter) they held very ordinary ideas about God and

nature, so that they cannot have been God's chosen in this respect; nor were they so chosen in respect of virtue and the true life, for here again they, with the exception of a very few elect, were on an equality with other nations: therefore their choice and vocation consisted only in the temporal happiness and advantages of independent rule. In fact, we do not see that God promised anything beyond this to the patriarchs[1] or their successors; in the law no other reward is offered for obedience than the continual happiness of an independent commonwealth and other goods of this life; while, on the other hand, against contumacy and the breaking of the covenant is threatened the downfall of the commonwealth and great hardships. Nor is this to be wondered at; for the ends of every social organization and commonwealth are (as appears from what we have said, and as we will explain more at length hereafter) security and comfort; a commonwealth can only exist by the laws being binding on all. If all the members of a state wish to disregard the law, by that very fact they dissolve the state and destroy the commonwealth. Thus, the only reward which could be promised to the Hebrews for continued obedience to the law was security[2] and its attendant advantages, while no surer punishment could be threatened for disobedience, than the ruin of the state and the evils which generally follow therefrom, in addition to such further consequences as might accrue to the Jews in particular from the ruin of their especial state. But there is no need here to go into this point at more length. I will only add that the laws of the Old Testament were revealed and ordained to the Jews only, for as God chose them in respect to the special constitution of their society and government, they must, of course, have had special laws. Whether God ordained special laws for other nations also, and revealed Himself to their lawgivers prophetically, that is, under the attributes by which the latter were accustomed to imagine Him, I cannot sufficiently determine. It is evident from Scripture itself that other nations acquired supremacy and particular laws by the external aid of God; witness only the two following passages:—

In Genesis xiv. 18, 19, 20, it is related that Melchisedek was king of Jerusalem and priest of the Most High God,

[1] See Note 4.   [2] See Note 5.

that in exercise of his priestly functions he blessed Abraham, and that Abraham the beloved of the Lord gave to this priest of God a tithe of all his spoils. This sufficiently shows that before He founded the Israelitish nation God constituted kings and priests in Jerusalem, and ordained for them rites and laws. Whether He did so prophetically is, as I have said, not sufficiently clear; but I am sure of this, that Abraham, whilst he sojourned in the city, lived scrupulously according to these laws, for Abraham had received no special rites from God; and yet it is stated (Gen. xxvi. 5), that he observed the worship, the precepts, the statutes, and the laws of God, which must be interpreted to mean the worship, the statutes, the precepts, and the laws of king Melchisedek. Malachi chides the Jews as follows (i. 10-11.):—"Who is there among you that will shut the doors? [of the Temple]; neither do ye kindle fire on mine altar for nought. I have no pleasure in you, saith the Lord of Hosts. For from the rising of the sun, even until the going down of the same My Name shall be great among the Gentiles; and in every place incense shall be offered in My Name, and a pure offering; for My Name is great among the heathen, saith the Lord of Hosts." These words, which, unless we do violence to them, could only refer to the current period, abundantly testify that the Jews of that time were not more beloved by God than other nations, that God then favoured other nations with more miracles than He vouchsafed to the Jews, who had then partly recovered their empire without miraculous aid; and, lastly, that the Gentiles possessed rites and ceremonies acceptable to God. But I pass over these points lightly: it is enough for my purpose to have shown that the election of the Jews had regard to nothing but temporal physical happiness and freedom, in other words, autonomous government, and to the manner and means by which they obtained it; consequently to the laws in so far as they were necessary to the preservation of that special government; and, lastly, to the manner in which they were revealed. In regard to other matters, wherein man's true happiness consists, they were on a par with the rest of the nations.

When, therefore, it is said in Scripture (Deut. iv. 7) that the Lord is not so nigh to any other nation as He is to the

Jews, reference is only made to their government, and to the period when so many miracles happened to them, for in respect of intellect and virtue—that is, in respect of blessedness—God was, as we have said already, and are now demonstrating, equally gracious to all. Scripture itself bears testimony to this fact, for the Psalmist says (cxlv. 18), "The Lord is near unto all them that call upon Him, to all that call upon Him in truth." So in the same Psalm, verse 9, "The Lord is good to all, and His tender mercies are over all His works." In Ps. xxxiii. 15, it is clearly stated that God has granted to all men the same intellect, in these words, "He fashioneth their hearts alike." The heart was considered by the Hebrews, as I suppose everyone knows, to be the seat of the soul and the intellect.

Lastly, from Job xxxviii. 28, it is plain that God had ordained for the whole human race the law to reverence God, to keep from evil doing, or to do well, and that Job, although a Gentile, was of all men most acceptable to God, because he excelled all in piety and religion. Lastly, from Jonah iv. 2, it is very evident that, not only to the Jews but to all men, God was gracious, merciful, long-suffering, and of great goodness, and repented Him of the evil, for Jonah says: "Therefore I determined to flee before unto Tarshish, for I know that Thou art a gracious God, and merciful, slow to anger, and of great kindness," &c., and that, therefore, God would pardon the Ninevites. We conclude, therefore (inasmuch as God is to all men equally gracious, and the Hebrews were only chosen by Him in respect to their social organization and government), that the individual Jew, taken apart from his social organization and government, possessed no gift of God above other men, and that there was no difference between Jew and Gentile. As it is a fact that God is equally gracious, merciful, and the rest, to all men; and as the function of the prophet was to teach men not so much the laws of their country, as true virtue, and to exhort them thereto, it is not to be doubted that all nations possessed prophets, and that the prophetic gift was not peculiar to the Jews. Indeed, history, both profane and sacred, bears witness to the fact. Although, from the sacred histories of the Old Testament, it is not evident that the other nations had as many pro-

phets as the Hebrews, or that any Gentile prophet was expressly sent by God to the nations, this does not affect the
question, for the Hebrews were careful to record their own
affairs, not those of other nations.   It suffices, then, that
we find in the Old Testament Gentiles, and uncircumcised,
as Noah, Enoch, Abimelech, Balaam, &c., exercising prophetic gifts; further, that Hebrew prophets were sent by
God, not only to their own nation but to many others also.
Ezekiel prophesied to all the nations then known; Obadiah
to none, that we are aware of, save the Idumeans; and
Jonah was chiefly the prophet to the Ninevites.   Isaiah
bewails and predicts the calamities, and hails the restoration not only of the Jews but also of other nations, for he
says (chap. xvi. 9), "Therefore I will bewail Jazer with
weeping;" and in chap. xix. he foretells first the calamities
and then the restoration of the Egyptians (see verses 19,
20, 21, 25), saying that God shall send them a Saviour to
free them, that the Lord shall be known in Egypt, and,
further, that the Egyptians shall worship God with sacrifice and oblation; and, at last, he calls that nation the
blessed Egyptian people of God; all of which particulars
are specially noteworthy.

Jeremiah is called, not the prophet of the Hebrew nation,
but simply the prophet of the nations (see Jer. i. 5).   He
also mournfully foretells the calamities of the nations, and
predicts their restoration, for he says (xlviii. 31) of the
Moabites, "Therefore will I howl for Moab, and I will cry
out for all Moab" (verse 36), "and therefore mine heart shall
sound for Moab like pipes;" in the end he prophesies their
restoration, as also the restoration of the Egyptians, Am-
monites, and Elamites.   Wherefore it is beyond doubt that
other nations also, like the Jews, had their prophets, who
prophesied to them.

Although Scripture only makes mention of one man,
Balaam, to whom the future of the Jews and the other
nations was revealed, we must not suppose that Balaam
prophesied only that once, for from the narrative itself it is
abundantly clear that he had long previously been famous
for prophecy and other Divine gifts.   For when Balak bade
him come to him, he said (Num. xxii. 6), "For I wot that
he whom thou blessest is blessed, and he whom thou cursest

is cursed." Thus we see that he possessed the gift which God had bestowed on Abraham. Further, as accustomed to prophesy, Balaam bade the messengers wait for him till the will of the Lord was revealed to him. When he prophesied, that is, when he interpreted the true mind of God, he was wont to say this of himself: "He hath said, which heard the words of God and knew the knowledge of the Most High, which saw the vision of the Almighty falling into a trance, but having his eyes open." Further, after he had blessed the Hebrews by the command of God, he began (as was his custom) to prophesy to other nations, and to predict their future; all of which abundantly shows that he had always been a prophet, or had often prophesied, and (as we may also remark here) possessed that which afforded the chief certainty to prophets of the truth of their prophecy, namely, a mind turned wholly to what is right and good, for he did not bless those whom he wished to bless, nor curse those whom he wished to curse, as Balak supposed, but only those whom God wished to be blessed or cursed. Thus he answered Balak: "If Balak should give me his house full of silver and gold, I cannot go beyond the commandment of the Lord to do either good or bad of my own mind; but what the Lord saith, that will I speak." As for God being angry with him in the way, the same happened to Moses when he set out to Egypt by the command of the Lord; and as to his receiving money for prophesying, Samuel did the same (1 Sam. ix. 7,8); if in any way he sinned, "there is not a just man upon earth that doeth good and sinneth not," Eccles. vii. 20. (*Vide* 2 Epist. Peter ii. 15, 16, and Jude 5, 11.)

His speeches must certainly have had much weight with God, and His power for cursing must assuredly have been very great from the number of times that we find stated in Scripture, in proof of God's great mercy to the Jews, that God would not hear Balaam, and that He changed the cursing to blessing (see Deut. xxiii. 6, Josh. xxiv. 10, Neh. xiii. 2). Wherefore he was without doubt most acceptable to God, for the speeches and cursings of the wicked move God not at all. As then he was a true prophet, and nevertheless Joshua calls him a soothsayer or augur, it is certain that this title had an honourable signification, and that

those whom the Gentiles called augurs and soothsayers
were true prophets, while those whom Scripture often
accuses and condemns were false soothsayers, who deceived
the Gentiles as false prophets deceived the Jews; indeed,
this is made evident from other passages in the Bible,
whence we conclude that the gift of prophecy was not
peculiar to the Jews, but common to all nations. The
Pharisees, however, vehemently contend that this Divine
gift was peculiar to their nation, and that the other nations
foretold the future (what will superstition invent next?)
by some unexplained diabolical faculty. The principal passage of Scripture which they cite, by way of confirming
their theory with its authority, is Exodus xxxiii. 16, where
Moses says to God, "For wherein shall it be known here
that I and Thy people have found grace in Thy sight? is
it not in that Thou goest with us? so shall we be separated,
I and Thy people, from all the people that are upon the
face of the earth." From this they would infer that Moses
asked of God that He should be present to the Jews, and
should reveal Himself to them prophetically; further, that
He should grant this favour to no other nation. It is
surely absurd that Moses should have been jealous of
God's presence among the Gentiles, or that he should have
dared to ask any such thing. The fact is, as Moses knew
that the disposition and spirit of his nation was rebellious,
he clearly saw that they could not carry out what they had
begun without very great miracles and special external aid
from God; nay, that without such aid they must necessarily
perish: as it was evident that God wished them to be preserved, He asked for this special external aid. Thus he
says (Ex. xxxiv. 9), "If now I have found grace in Thy
sight, O Lord, let my Lord, I pray Thee, go among us; for
it is a stiffnecked people." The reason, therefore, for his
seeking special external aid from God was the stiffnecked-
ness of the people, and it is made still more plain, that he
asked for nothing beyond this special external aid by God's
answer—for God answered at once (verse 10 of the same
chapter)—"Behold, I make a covenant: before all Thy people
I will do marvels, such as have not been done in all the
earth, nor in any nation." Therefore Moses had in view
nothing beyond the special election of the Jews, as I have

explained it, and made no other request to God. I confess
that in Paul's Epistle to the Romans, I find another text
which carries more weight, namely, where Paul seems to
teach a different doctrine from that here set down, for he
there says (Rom. iii. 1): "What advantage then hath the
Jew? or what profit is there of circumcision? Much every
way: chiefly, because that unto them were committed the
oracles of God."

But if we look to the doctrine which Paul especially
desired to teach, we shall find nothing repugnant to our
present contention; on the contrary, his doctrine is the same
as ours, for he says (Rom. iii. 29) "that God is the God
of the Jews and of the Gentiles, and" (ch. ii. 25, 26)
"But, if thou be a breaker of the law, thy circumcision is
made uncircumcision. Therefore if the uncircumcision keep
the righteousness of the law, shall not his uncircumcision
be counted for circumcision?" Further, in chap. iv. verse 9,
he says that all alike, Jew and Gentile, were under sin,
and that without commandment and law there is no sin.
Wherefore it is most evident that to all men absolutely
was revealed the law under which all lived—namely, the
law which has regard only to true virtue, not the law
established in respect to, and in the formation of, a particular state and adapted to the disposition of a particular
people. Lastly, Paul concludes that since God is the God
of all nations, that is, is equally gracious to all, and since
all men equally live under the law and under sin, so also
to all nations did God send His Christ, to free all men
equally from the bondage of the law, that they should no
more do right by the command of the law, but by the constant determination of their hearts. So that Paul teaches
exactly the same as ourselves. When, therefore, he says,
"To the Jews only were entrusted the oracles of God,"
we must either understand that to them only were the
laws entrusted in writing, while they were given to other
nations merely in revelation and conception, or else (as
none but Jews would object to the doctrine he desired to
advance) that Paul was answering only in accordance with
the understanding and current ideas of the Jews, for in
respect to teaching things which he had partly seen, partly
heard, he was to the Greeks a Greek, and to the Jews a Jew.

It now only remains to us to answer the arguments of those who would persuade themselves that the election of the Jews was not temporal, and merely in respect of their commonwealth, but eternal; for, they say, we see the Jews after the loss of their commonwealth, and after being scattered so many years and separated from all other nations, still surviving, which is without parallel among other peoples, and further the Scriptures seem to teach that God has chosen for Himself the Jews for ever, so that though they have lost their commonwealth, they still nevertheless remain God's elect.

The passages which they think teach most clearly this eternal election, are chiefly:—

(1.) Jer. xxxi. 36, where the prophet testifies that the seed of Israel shall for ever remain the nation of God, comparing them with the stability of the heavens and nature;

(2.) Ezek. xx. 32, where the prophet seems to intend that though the Jews wanted after the help afforded them to turn their backs on the worship of the Lord, that God would nevertheless gather them together again from all the lands in which they were dispersed, and lead them to the wilderness of the peoples—as He had led their fathers to the wilderness of the land of Egypt—and would at length, after purging out from among them the rebels and transgressors, bring them thence to his Holy mountain, where the whole house of Israel should worship Him. Other passages are also cited, especially by the Pharisees, but I think I shall satisfy everyone if I answer these two, and this I shall easily accomplish after showing from Scripture itself that God chose not the Hebrews for ever, but only on the condition under which He had formerly chosen the Canaanites, for these last, as we have shown, had priests who religiously worshipped God, and whom God at length rejected because of their luxury, pride, and corrupt worship.

Moses (Lev. xviii. 27) warned the Israelites that they be not polluted with whoredoms, lest the land spue them out as it had spued out the nations who had dwelt there before, and in Deut. viii. 19, 20, in the plainest terms He threatens their total ruin, for He says, "I testify against you that ye shall surely perish. As the nations which the Lord destroyeth before your face, so shall ye perish." In like manner many other passages are found in the law which expressly show that God chose the Hebrews neither absolutely nor for ever. If, then, the prophets foretold for them a new covenant of the knowledge of God, love, and grace, such a promise is easily proved to be only made to the elect, for Ezekiel in the chapter which we have just quoted expressly says that God will separate from them the rebellious and transgressors, and Zephaniah (iii. 12, 13), says that "God will take away the proud from the midst of them, and leave the poor." Now, inasmuch as their election has regard to true virtue, it is not to be thought that it was promised to the Jews alone to the exclusion of others, but we must evidently believe that the true Gentile prophets (and every nation, as we have shown, possessed such) promised the same to the faithful of their own people, who were thereby comforted. Wherefore this eternal covenant of the knowledge of God and love is universal, as is clear, moreover, from Zeph. iii. 10, 11 : no difference in this respect can be admitted between Jew and Gentile, nor did the former enjoy any special election beyond that which we have pointed out.

When the prophets, in speaking of this election which regards only true virtue, mixed up much concerning sacrifices and ceremonies, and the rebuilding of the temple and city, they wished by such figurative expressions, after the manner and nature of prophecy, to expound matters spiritual, so as at the same time to show to the Jews, whose prophets they were, the true restoration of the state and of the temple to be expected about the time of Cyrus.

At the present time, therefore, there is absolutely nothing which the Jews can arrogate to themselves beyond other people.

As to their continuance so long after dispersion and the loss of empire, there is nothing marvellous in it, for they so separated themselves from every other nation as to draw down upon themselves universal hate, not only by their outward rites, rites conflicting with those of other nations, but also by the sign of circumcision which they most scrupulously observe.

That they have been preserved in great measure by Gentile hatred, experience demonstrates. When the king

of Spain formerly compelled the Jews to embrace the State
religion or to go into exile, a large number of Jews accepted
Catholicism.   Now, as these renegades were admitted to all
the native privileges of Spaniards, and deemed worthy of
filling all honourable offices, it came to pass that they
straightway became so intermingled with the Spaniards as
to leave of themselves no relic or remembrance.   But
exactly the opposite happened to those whom the king of
Portugal compelled to become Christians, for they always,
though converted, lived apart, inasmuch as they were considered unworthy of any civic honours.

The sign of circumcision is, as I think, so important,
that I could persuade myself that it alone would preserve
the nation for ever.   Nay, I would go so far as to believe
that if the foundations of their religion have not emascu-
lated their minds they may even, if occasion offers, so
changeable are human affairs, raise up their empire afresh,
and that God may a second time elect them.

Of such a possibility we have a very famous example in
the Chinese.   They, too, have some distinctive mark on
their heads which they most scrupulously observe, and by
which they keep themselves apart from everyone else, and
have thus kept themselves during so many thousand years
that they far surpass all other nations in antiquity.   They
have not always retained empire, but they have recovered
it when lost, and doubtless will do so again after the spirit
of the Tartars becomes relaxed through the luxury of
riches and pride.

Lastly, if any one wishes to maintain that the Jews, from
this or from any other cause, have been chosen by God for
ever, I will not gainsay him if he will admit that this choice,
whether temporary or eternal, has no regard, in so far as it
is peculiar to the Jews, to aught but dominion and physical
advantages (for by such alone can one nation be distinguished from another), whereas in regard to intellect and
true virtue, every nation is on a par with the rest, and God
has not in these respects chosen one people rather than
another.

CHAPTER IV.

OF THE DIVINE LAW.

THE word law, taken in the abstract, means that by which an individual, or all things, or as many things as belong to a particular species, act in one and the same fixed and definite manner, which manner depends either on natural necessity or on human decree. A law which depends on natural necessity is one which necessarily follows from the nature, or from the definition of the thing in question; a law which depends on human decree, and which is more correctly called an ordinance, is one which men have laid down for themselves and others in order to live more safely or conveniently, or from some similar reason.

For example, the law that all bodies impinging on lesser bodies, lose as much of their own motion as they communicate to the latter is a universal law of all bodies, and depends on natural necessity. So, too, the law that a man in remembering one thing, straightway remembers another either like it, or which he had perceived simultaneously with it, is a law which necessarily follows from the nature of man. But the law that men must yield, or be compelled to yield, somewhat of their natural right, and that they bind themselves to live in a certain way, depends on human decree. Now, though I freely admit that all things are predetermined by universal natural laws to exist and operate in a given, fixed, and definite manner, I still assert that the laws I have just mentioned depend on human decree.

(1.) Because man, in so far as he is a part of nature, constitutes a part of the power of nature. Whatever, therefore, follows necessarily from the necessity of human nature (that is, from nature herself, in so far as we conceive of her as acting through man) follows, even though it be necessarily, from human power. Hence the sanction of such laws may very well be said to depend on man's decree, for it principally depends on the power of the human mind; so

Concatenation

that the human mind in respect to its perception of things
as true and false, can readily be conceived as without such
laws, but not without necessary law as we have just defined it.

(2.) I have stated that these laws depend on human decree
because it is well to define and explain things by their proximate causes.   The general consideration of fate and the
concatenation of causes would aid us very little in forming
and arranging our ideas concerning particular questions.
Let us add that as to the actual co-ordination and concatenation of things, that is how things are ordained and linked
together, we are obviously ignorant; therefore, it is more
profitable for right living, nay, it is necessary for us to consider things as contingent.   So much about law in the
abstract.

Now the word law seems to be only applied to natural
phenomena by analogy, and is commonly taken to signify
a command which men can either obey or neglect, inasmuch
as it restrains human nature within certain originally ex-
ceeded limits, and therefore lays down no rule beyond human
strength.   Thus it is expedient to define law more particularly as a plan of life laid down by man for himself or
others with a certain object.

However, as the true object of legislation is only perceived by a few, and most men are almost incapable of
grasping it, though they live under its conditions, legis-
lators, with a view to exacting general obedience, have wisely
put forward another object, very different from that which
necessarily follows from the nature of law : they promise to
the observers of the law that which the masses chiefly desire, and threaten its violators with that which they chiefly
fear : thus endeavouring to restrain the masses, as far as
may be, like a horse with a curb; whence it follows that
the word law is chiefly applied to the modes of life enjoined
on men by the sway of others; hence those who obey the
law are said to live under it and to be under compulsion.
In truth, a man who renders everyone their due because
he fears the gallows, acts under the sway and compulsion
of others, and cannot be called just.   But a man who does
the same from a knowledge of the true reason for laws and
their necessity, acts from a firm purpose and of his own
accord, and is therefore properly called just.   This, I take

it, is Paul's meaning when he says, that those who live
under the law cannot be justified through the law, for justice, as commonly defined, is the constant and perpetual
will to render every man his due.   Thus Solomon says
(Prov. xxi. 15), "It is a joy to the just to do judgment,"
but the wicked fear.

Law, then, being a plan of living which men have for a
certain object laid down for themselves or others, may, as
it seems, be divided into human law and Divine law.

By human law I mean a plan of living which serves only
to render life and the state secure.

By Divine law I mean that which only regards the highest
good, in other words, the true knowledge of God and love.

I call this law Divine because of the nature of the highest
good, which I will here shortly explain as clearly as I can.

Inasmuch as the intellect is the best part of our being, it
is evident that we should make every effort to perfect it as
far as possible if we desire to search for what is really profitable to us.   For in intellectual perfection the highest
good should consist.   Now, since all our knowledge, and the
certainty which removes every doubt, depend solely on the
knowledge of God;—firstly, because without God nothing
can exist or be conceived; secondly, because so long as we
have no clear and distinct idea of God we may remain in
universal doubt—it follows that our highest good and perfection also depend solely on the knowledge of God.   Further, since without God nothing can exist or be conceived, it is evident that all natural phenomena involve
and express the conception of God as far as their essence
and perfection extend, so that we have greater and more
perfect knowledge of God in proportion to our knowledge
of natural phenomena: conversely (since the knowledge of
an effect through its cause is the same thing as the knowledge of a particular property of a cause) the greater our
knowledge of natural phenomena, the more perfect is our
knowledge of the essence of God (which is the cause of all
things).   So, then, our highest good not only depends on
the knowledge of God, but wholly consists therein; and it
further follows that man is perfect or the reverse in proportion to the nature and perfection of the object of his special
desire; hence the most perfect and the chief sharer in the

highest blessedness is he who prizes above all else, and takes especial delight in, the intellectual knowledge of God, the most perfect Being.

Hither, then, our highest good and our highest blessedness aim—namely, to the knowledge and love of God; therefore the means demanded by this aim of all human actions, that is, by God in so far as the idea of him is in us, may be called the commands of God, because they proceed, as it were, from God Himself, inasmuch as He exists in our minds, and the plan of life which has regard to this aim may be fitly called the law of God.

The nature of the means, and the plan of life which this aim demands, how the foundations of the best states follow its lines, and how men's life is conducted, are questions pertaining to general ethics. Here I only proceed to treat of the Divine law in a particular application.

As the love of God is man's highest happiness and blessedness, and the ultimate end and aim of all human actions, it follows that he alone lives by the Divine law who loves God not from fear of punishment, or from love of any other object, such as sensual pleasure, fame, or the like; but solely because he has knowledge of God, or is convinced that the knowledge and love of God is the highest good. The sum and chief precept, then, of the Divine law is to love God as the highest good, namely, as we have said, not from fear of any pains and penalties, or from the love of any other object in which we desire to take pleasure. The idea of God lays down the rule that God is our highest good—in other words, that the knowledge and love of God is the ultimate aim to which all our actions should be directed. The worldling cannot understand these things, they appear foolishness to him, because he has too meagre a knowledge of God, and also because in this highest good he can discover nothing which he can handle or eat, or which affects the fleshly appetites wherein he chiefly delights, for it consists solely in thought and the pure reason. They, on the other hand, who know that they possess no greater gift than intellect and sound reason, will doubtless accept what I have said without question.

We have now explained that wherein the Divine law chiefly consists, and what are human laws, namely, all those which have a different aim unless they have been ratified by revelation, for in this respect also things are referred to God (as we have shown above) and in this sense the law of Moses, although it was not universal, but entirely adapted to the disposition and particular preservation of a single people, may yet be called a law of God or Divine law, inasmuch as we believe that it was ratified by prophetic insight. If we consider the nature of natural Divine law as we have just explained it, we shall see

I. That it is universal or common to all men, for we have deduced it from universal human nature.

II. That it does not depend on the truth of any historical narrative whatsoever, for inasmuch as this natural Divine law is comprehended solely by the consideration of human nature, it is plain that we can conceive it as existing as well in Adam as in any other man, as well in a man living among his fellows, as in a man who lives by himself.

The truth of a historical narrative, however assured, cannot give us the knowledge nor consequently the love of God, for love of God springs from knowledge of Him, and knowledge of Him should be derived from general ideas, in themselves certain and known, so that the truth of a historical narrative is very far from being a necessary requisite for our attaining our highest good.

Still, though the truth of histories cannot give us the knowledge and love of God, I do not deny that reading them is very useful with a view to life in the world, for the more we have observed and known of men's customs and circumstances, which are best revealed by their actions, the more warily we shall be able to order our lives among them, and so far as reason dictates to adapt our actions to their dispositions.

III. We see that this natural Divine law does not demand the performance of ceremonies—that is, actions in themselves indifferent, which are called good from the fact of their institution, or actions symbolizing something profitable for salvation, or (if one prefers this definition) actions of which the meaning surpasses human understanding. The natural light of reason does not demand anything which it is itself unable to supply, but only such as it can very clearly show to be good, or a means to our blessedness. Such things as

are good simply because they have been commanded or
instituted, or as being symbols of something good, are mere
shadows which cannot be reckoned among actions that are
the offspring, as it were, or fruit of a sound mind and
of intellect.   There is no need for me to go into this now
in more detail.

IV. Lastly, we see that the highest reward of the Divine
law is the law itself, namely, to know God and to love
Him of our free choice, and with an undivided and fruitful
spirit; while its penalty is the absence of these things, and
being in bondage to the flesh—that is, having an inconstant
and wavering spirit.

These points being noted, I must now inquire

I. Whether by the natural light of reason we can conceive of God as a law-giver or potentate ordaining laws for
men?

II. What is the teaching of Holy Writ concerning this
natural light of reason and natural law?

III. With what objects were ceremonies formerly instituted?

IV. Lastly, what is the good gained by knowing the
sacred histories and believing them?

Of the first two I will treat in this chapter, of the remaining two in the following one.

Our conclusion about the first is easily deduced from the
nature of God's will, which is only distinguished from His
understanding in relation to our intellect—that is, the will
and the understanding of God are in reality one and the
same, and are only distinguished in relation to our thoughts
which we form concerning God's understanding.   For
instance, if we are only looking to the fact that the nature
of a triangle is from eternity contained in the Divine
nature as an eternal verity, we say that God possesses the
idea of a triangle, or that He understands the nature of a
triangle; but if afterwards we look to the fact that the
nature of a triangle is thus contained in the Divine nature,
solely by the necessity of the Divine nature, and not by the
necessity of the nature and essence of a triangle—in fact,
that the necessity of a triangle's essence and nature, in so
far as they are conceived of as eternal verities, depends
solely on the necessity of the Divine nature and intellect,

we then style God's will or decree, that which before we styled His intellect. Wherefore we make one and the same affirmation concerning God when we say that He has from eternity decreed that three angles of a triangle are equal to two right angles, as when we say that He has understood it.

Hence the affirmations and the negations of God always involve necessity or truth; so that, for example, if God said to Adam that He did not wish him to eat of the tree of knowledge of good and evil, it would have involved a contradiction that Adam should have been able to eat of it, and would therefore have been impossible that he should have so eaten, for the Divine command would have involved an eternal necessity and truth. But since Scripture nevertheless narrates that God did give this command to Adam, and yet that none the less Adam ate of the tree, we must perforce say that God revealed to Adam the evil which would surely follow if he should eat of the tree, but did not disclose that such evil would of necessity come to pass. Thus it was that Adam took the revelation to be not an eternal and necessary truth, but a law—that is, an ordinance followed by gain or loss, not depending necessarily on the nature of the act performed, but solely on the will and absolute power of some potentate, so that the revelation in question was solely in relation to Adam, and solely through his lack of knowledge a law, and God was, as it were, a lawgiver and potentate. From the same cause, namely, from lack of knowledge, the Decalogue in relation to the Hebrews was a law, for since they knew not the existence of God as an eternal truth, they must have taken as a law that which was revealed to them in the Decalogue, namely, that God exists, and that God only should be worshipped. But if God had spoken to them without the intervention of any bodily means, immediately they would have perceived it not as a law, but as an eternal truth.

What we have said about the Israelites and Adam, applies also to all the prophets who wrote laws in God's name—they did not adequately conceive God's decrees as eternal truths. For instance, we must say of Moses that from revelation, from the basis of what was revealed to him, he perceived the method by which the Israelitish nation

could best be united in a particular territory, and could
form a body politic or state, and further that he perceived
the method by which that nation could best be constrained
to obedience; but he did not perceive, nor was it revealed
to him, that this method was absolutely the best, nor that
the obedience of the people in a certain strip of territory
would necessarily imply the end he had in view.   Wherefore he perceived these things not as eternal truths, but as
precepts and ordinances, and he ordained them as laws of
God, and thus it came to be that he conceived God as a
ruler, a legislator, a king, as merciful, just, &c., whereas
such qualities are simply attributes of human nature, and
utterly alien from the nature of the Deity.   Thus much
we may affirm of the prophets who wrote laws in the name
of God; but we must not affirm it of Christ, for Christ,
although He too seems to have written laws in the name of
God, must be taken to have had a clear and adequate perception, for Christ was not so much a prophet as the
mouthpiece of God.   For God made revelations to mankind
through Christ as He had before done through angels—that
is, a created voice, visions, &c.   It would be as unreasonable
to say that God had accommodated his revelations to the
opinions of Christ as that He had before accommodated them
to the opinions of angels (that is, of a created voice or visions)
as matters to be revealed to the prophets, a wholly absurd
hypothesis.   Moreover, Christ was sent to teach not only
the Jews but the whole human race, and therefore it was
not enough that His mind should be accommodated to the
opinions of the Jews alone, but also to the opinion and
fundamental teaching common to the whole human race—
in other words, to ideas universal and true.   Inasmuch as
God revealed Himself to Christ, or to Christ's mind immediately, and not as to the prophets through words and
symbols, we must needs suppose that Christ perceived truly
what was revealed, in other words, He understood it, for a
matter is understood when it is perceived simply by the
mind without words or symbols.

Christ, then, perceived (truly and adequately) what was
revealed, and if He ever proclaimed such revelations as
laws, He did so because of the ignorance and obstinacy of
the people, acting in this respect the part of God; inas-

much as He accommodated Himself to the comprehension of the people, and though He spoke somewhat more clearly than the other prophets, yet He taught what was revealed obscurely, and generally through parables, especially when He was speaking to those to whom it was not yet given to understand the kingdom of heaven. (See Matt. xiii. 10, &c.) To those to whom it was given to understand the mysteries of heaven, He doubtless taught His doctrines as eternal truths, and did not lay them down as laws, thus freeing the minds of His hearers from the bondage of that law which He further confirmed and established. Paul apparently points to this more than once (*e.g.* Rom. vii. 6, and iii. 28), though he never himself seems to wish to speak openly, but, to quote his own words (Rom. iii. 5, and vi. 19), "merely humanly." This he expressly states when he calls God just, and it was doubtless in concession to human weakness that he attributes mercy, grace, anger, and similar qualities to God, adapting his language to the popular mind, or, as he puts it (1 Cor. iii. 1, 2), to carnal men. In Rom. ix. 18, he teaches undisguisedly that God's anger and mercy depend not on the actions of men, but on God's own nature or will; further, that no one is justified by the works of the law, but only by faith, which he seems to identify with the full assent of the soul; lastly, that no one is blessed unless he have in him the mind of Christ (Rom. viii. 9), whereby he perceives the laws of God as eternal truths. We conclude, therefore, that God is described as a lawgiver or prince, and styled just, merciful, &c., merely in concession to popular understanding, and the imperfection of popular knowledge; that in reality God acts and directs all things simply by the necessity of His nature and perfection, and that His decrees and volitions are eternal truths, and always involve necessity. So much for the first point which I wished to explain and demonstrate.

Passing on to the second point, let us search the sacred pages for their teaching concerning the light of nature and this Divine law. The first doctrine we find in the history of the first man, where it is narrated that God commanded Adam not to eat of the fruit of the tree of the knowledge of good and evil; this seems to mean that God commanded

Adam to do and to seek after righteousness because it was
good, not because the contrary was evil: that is, to seek the
good for its own sake, not from fear of evil. We have seen
that he who acts rightly from the true knowledge and love
of right, acts with freedom and constancy, whereas he who
acts from fear of evil, is under the constraint of evil, and
acts in bondage under external control. So that this commandment of God to Adam comprehends the whole Divine
natural law, and absolutely agrees with the dictates of the
light of nature; nay, it would be easy to explain on this
basis the whole history or allegory of the first man. But I
prefer to pass over the subject in silence, because, in the
first place, I cannot be absolutely certain that my explanation would be in accordance with the intention of the
sacred writer; and, secondly, because many do not admit
that this history is an allegory, maintaining it to be a
simple narrative of facts. It will be better, therefore, to
adduce other passages of Scripture, especially such as were
written by him, who speaks with all the strength of his
natural understanding, in which he surpassed all his contemporaries, and whose sayings are accepted by the people
as of equal weight with those of the prophets. I mean Solomon, whose prudence and wisdom are commended in Scripture rather than his piety and gift of prophecy. He, in
his proverbs calls the human intellect the well-spring of
true life, and declares that misfortune is made up of folly.
"Understanding is a well-spring of life to him that hath it;
but the instruction of fools is folly," Prov. xvi. 22. Life
being taken to mean the true life (as is evident from
Deut. xxx. 19), the fruit of the understanding consists
only in the true life, and its absence constitutes punishment. All this absolutely agrees with what was set out in
our fourth point concerning natural law. Moreover our
position that it is the well-spring of life, and that the intellect alone lays down laws for the wise, is plainly taught
by the sage, for he says (Prov. xiii. 14): "The law of the
wise is a fountain of life"—that is, as we gather from the
preceding text, the understanding. In chap. iii. 13, he expressly teaches that the understanding renders man blessed
and happy, and gives him true peace of mind. "Happy is
the man that findeth wisdom, and the man that getteth

understanding," for "Wisdom gives length of days, and riches and honour; her ways are ways of pleasantness, and all her paths peace" (xiii. 16, 17). According to Solomon, therefore, it is only the wise who live in peace and equanimity, not like the wicked whose minds drift hither and thither, and (as Isaiah says, chap. lvii. 20) "are like the troubled sea, for them there is no peace."

Lastly, we should especially note the passage in chap. ii. of Solomon's proverbs which most clearly confirms our contention: "If thou criest after knowledge, and liftest up thy voice for understanding . . . then shalt thou understand the fear of the Lord, and find the knowledge of God; for the Lord giveth wisdom; out of His mouth cometh knowledge and understanding." These words clearly enunciate (1), that wisdom or intellect alone teaches us to fear God wisely —that is, to worship Him truly; (2), that wisdom and knowledge flow from God's mouth, and that God bestows on us this gift; this we have already shown in proving that our understanding and our knowledge depend on, spring from, and are perfected by the idea or knowledge of God, and nothing else. Solomon goes on to say in so many words that this knowledge contains and involves the true principles of ethics and politics: "When wisdom entereth into thy heart, and knowledge is pleasant to thy soul, discretion shall preserve thee, understanding shall keep thee, then shalt thou understand righteousness, and judgment, and equity, yea every good path." All of which is in obvious agreement with natural knowledge: for after we have come to the understanding of things, and have tasted the excellence of knowledge, she teaches us ethics and true virtue.

Thus the happiness and the peace of him who cultivates his natural understanding lies, according to Solomon also, not so much under the dominion of fortune (or God's external aid) as in inward personal virtue (or God's internal aid), for the latter can to a great extent be preserved by vigilance, right action, and thought.

Lastly, we must by no means pass over the passage in Paul's Epistle to the Romans, i. 20, in which he says: "For the invisible things of God from the creation of the world are clearly seen, being understood by the things that are made, even His eternal power and Godhead; so that they are without excuse, because, when they knew God, they glorified Him not as God, neither were they thankful." These words clearly show that everyone can by the light of nature clearly understand the goodness and the eternal divinity of God, and can thence know and deduce what they should seek for and what avoid ; wherefore the Apostle says that they are without excuse and cannot plead ignorance, as they certainly might if it were a question of supernatural light and the incarnation, passion, and resurrection of Christ. "Wherefore," he goes on to say (*ib.* 24), "God gave them up to uncleanness through the lusts of their own hearts;" and so on, through the rest of the chapter, he describes the vices of ignorance, and sets them forth as the punishment of ignorance. This obviously agrees with the verse of Solomon, already quoted, "The instruction of fools is folly," so that it is easy to understand why Paul says that the wicked are without excuse. As every man sows so shall he reap : out of evil, evils necessarily spring, unless they be wisely counteracted.

Thus we see that Scripture literally approves of the light of natural reason and the natural Divine law, and I have fulfilled the promises made at the beginning of this chapter.

CHAPTER V.

OF THE CEREMONIAL LAW.

IN the foregoing chapter we have shown that the Divine law, which renders men truly blessed, and teaches them the true life, is universal to all men; nay, we have so intimately deduced it from human nature that it must be esteemed innate, and, as it were, ingrained in the human mind.

But with regard to the ceremonial observances which were ordained in the Old Testament for the Hebrews only, and were so adapted to their state that they could for the most part only be observed by the society as a whole and not by each individual, it is evident that they formed no part of the Divine law, and had nothing to do with blessedness and virtue, but had reference only to the election of the Hebrews, that is (as I have shown in Chap. III.), to their temporal bodily happiness and the tranquillity of their kingdom, and that therefore they were only valid while that kingdom lasted. If in the Old Testament they are spoken of as the law of God, it is only because they were founded on revelation, or a basis of revelation. Still as reason, however sound, has little weight with ordinary theologians, I will adduce the authority of Scripture for what I here assert, and will further show, for the sake of greater clearness, why and how these ceremonials served to establish and preserve the Jewish kingdom. Isaiah teaches most plainly that the Divine law in its strict sense signifies that universal law which consists in a true manner of life, and does not signify ceremonial observances. In chapter i., verse 10, the prophet calls on his countrymen to hearken to the Divine law as he delivers it, and first excluding all kinds of sacrifices and all feasts, he at length sums up the law in these few words, "Cease to do evil, learn to do well: seek judgment, relieve the oppressed."

Not less striking testimony is given in Psalm xl. 7-9, where the Psalmist addresses God: "Sacrifice and offering Thou didst not desire; mine ears hast Thou opened; burnt offering and sin-offering hast Thou not required; I delight to do Thy will, O my God; yea, Thy law is within my heart." Here the Psalmist reckons as the law of God only that which is inscribed in his heart, and excludes ceremonies therefrom, for the latter are good and inscribed on the heart only from the fact of their institution, and not because of their intrinsic value.

Other passages of Scripture testify to the same truth, but these two will suffice. We may also learn from the Bible that ceremonies are no aid to blessedness, but only have reference to the temporal prosperity of the kingdom; for the rewards promised for their observance are merely temporal advantages and delights, blessedness being reserved for the universal Divine law. In all the five books commonly attributed to Moses nothing is promised, as I have said, beyond temporal benefits, such as honours, fame, victories, riches, enjoyments, and health. Though many moral precepts besides ceremonies are contained in these five books, they appear not as moral doctrines universal to all men, but as commands especially adapted to the understanding and character of the Hebrew people, and as having reference only to the welfare of the kingdom. For instance, Moses does not teach the Jews as a prophet not to kill or to steal, but gives these commandments solely as a lawgiver and judge; he does not reason out the doctrine, but affixes for its non-observance a penalty which may and very properly does vary in different nations. So, too, the command not to commit adultery is given merely with reference to the welfare of the state; for if the moral doctrine had been intended, with reference not only to the welfare of the state, but also to the tranquillity and blessedness of the individual, Moses would have condemned not merely the outward act, but also the mental acquiescence, as is done by Christ, Who taught only universal moral precepts, and for this cause promises a spiritual instead of a temporal reward. Christ, as I have said, was sent into the world, not to preserve the state nor to lay down laws, but solely to teach the universal moral law, so we can easily understand that He wished in nowise to do away with the law of Moses, inasmuch as He introduced no new laws of His own—His sole care was to teach moral doctrines, and distinguish them from the laws of the state; for the Pharisees, in their ignorance, thought that the observance of the state law and the Mosaic law was the sum total of morality; whereas such laws merely had reference to the public welfare, and aimed not so much at instructing the Jews as at keeping them under constraint. But let us return to our subject, and cite other passages of Scripture which set forth temporal benefits as rewards for observing the ceremonial law, and blessedness as reward for the universal law.

None of the prophets puts the point more clearly than Isaiah. After condemning hypocrisy, he commends liberty and charity towards one's self and one's neighbours, and promises as a reward: "Then shall thy light break forth as the morning, and thy health shall spring forth speedily, thy righteousness shall go before thee, and the glory of the Lord shall be thy rereward" (chap. lviii. 8). Shortly afterwards he commends the Sabbath, and for a due observance of it, promises: "Then shalt thou delight thyself in the Lord, and I will cause thee to ride upon the high places of the earth, and feed thee with the heritage of Jacob thy father: for the mouth of the Lord has spoken it." Thus the prophet for liberty bestowed, and charitable works, promises a healthy mind in a healthy body, and the glory of the Lord even after death; whereas, for ceremonial exactitude, he only promises security of rule, prosperity, and temporal happiness.

In Psalms xv. and xxiv. no mention is made of ceremonies, but only of moral doctrines, inasmuch as there is no question of anything but blessedness, and blessedness is symbolically promised: it is quite certain that the expressions, "the hill of God," and "His tents and the dwellers therein," refer to blessedness and security of soul, not to the actual mount of Jerusalem and the tabernacle of Moses, for these latter were not dwelt in by anyone, and only the sons of Levi ministered there. Further, all those sentences of Solomon to which I referred in the last chapter, for the cultivation of the intellect and wisdom, promise true blessedness, for by wisdom is the fear of God at length understood, and the knowledge of God found.

That the Jews themselves were not bound to practise their ceremonial observances after the destruction of their kingdom is evident from Jeremiah. For when the prophet saw and foretold that the desolation of the city was at hand, he said that God only delights in those who know and understand that He exercises loving-kindness, judgment, and righteousness in the earth, and that such persons only are worthy of praise. (Jer. ix. 23.) As though God had said that, after the desolation of the city, He would require nothing special from the Jews beyond the natural law by which all men are bound.

The New Testament also confirms this view, for only moral doctrines are therein taught, and the kingdom of heaven is promised as a reward, whereas ceremonial observances are not touched on by the Apostles, after they began to preach the Gospel to the Gentiles. The Pharisees certainly continued to practise these rites after the destruction of the kingdom, but more with a view of opposing the Christians than of pleasing God: for after the first destruction of the city, when they were led captive to Babylon, not being then, so far as I am aware, split up into sects, they straightway neglected their rites, bid farewell to the Mosaic law, buried their national customs in oblivion as being plainly superfluous, and began to mingle with other nations, as we may abundantly learn from Ezra and Nehemiah. We cannot, therefore, doubt that they were no more bound by the law of Moses, after the destruction of their kingdom, than they had been before it had been begun, while they were still living among other peoples before the exodus from Egypt, and were subject to no special law beyond the natural law, and also, doubtless, the law of the state in which they were living, in so far as it was consonant with the Divine natural law.

As to the fact that the patriarchs offered sacrifices, I think they did so for the purpose of stimulating their piety, for their minds had been accustomed from childhood to the idea of sacrifice, which we know had been universal from the time of Enoch; and thus they found in sacrifice their most powerful incentive.

The patriarchs, then, did not sacrifice to God at the bidding of a Divine right, or as taught by the basis of the Divine law, but simply in accordance with the custom of the time; and, if in so doing they followed any ordinance, it was simply the ordinance of the country they were living in, by which (as we have seen before in the case of Melchisedek) they were bound.

I think that I have now given Scriptural authority for my view: it remains to show why and how the ceremonial observances tended to preserve and confirm the Hebrew kingdom; and this I can very briefly do on grounds universally accepted.

The formation of society serves not only for defensive purposes, but is also very useful, and, indeed, absolutely necessary, as rendering possible the division of labour. If men did not render mutual assistance to each other, no one would have either the skill or the time to provide for his own sustenance and preservation: for all men are not equally apt for all work, and no one would be capable of preparing all that he individually stood in need of. Strength and time, I repeat, would fail, if every one had in person to plough, to sow, to reap, to grind corn, to cook, to weave, to stitch, and perform the other numerous functions required to keep life going; to say nothing of the arts and sciences which are also entirely necessary to the perfection and blessedness of human nature. We see that peoples living in uncivilized barbarism lead a wretched and almost animal life, and even they would not be able to acquire their few rude necessaries without assisting one another to a certain extent.

Now if men were so constituted by nature that they desired nothing but what is designated by true reason, society would obviously have no need of laws: it would be sufficient to inculcate true moral doctrines; and men would freely, without hesitation, act in accordance with their true interests. But human nature is framed in a different fashion: every one, indeed, seeks his own interest, but does not do so in accordance with the dictates of sound reason, for most men's ideas of desirability and usefulness are guided by their fleshly instincts and emotions, which take no thought beyond the present and the immediate object.

Therefore, no society can exist without government, and force, and laws to restrain and repress men's desires and immoderate impulses. Still human nature will not submit to absolute repression. Violent governments, as Seneca says, never last long; the moderate governments endure.

So long as men act simply from fear they act contrary to their inclinations, taking no thought for the advantages or necessity of their actions, but simply endeavouring to escape punishment or loss of life. They must needs rejoice in any evil which befalls their ruler, even if it should involve themselves; and must long for and bring about such evil by every means in their power. Again, men are especially intolerant of serving and being ruled by their equals. Lastly, it is exceedingly difficult to revoke liberties once granted.

From these considerations it follows, firstly, that authority should either be vested in the hands of the whole state in common, so that everyone should be bound to serve, and yet not be in subjection to his equals; or else, if power be in the hands of a few, or one man, that one man should be something above average humanity, or should strive to get himself accepted as such. Secondly, laws should in every government be so arranged that people should be kept in bounds by the hope of some greatly-desired good, rather than by fear, for then everyone will do his duty willingly.

Lastly, as obedience consists in acting at the bidding of external authority, it would have no place in a state where the government is vested in the whole people, and where laws are made by common consent. In such a society the people would remain free, whether the laws were added to or diminished, inasmuch as it would not be done on external authority, but their own free consent. The reverse happens when the sovereign power is vested in one man, for all act at his bidding; and, therefore, unless they had been trained from the first to depend on the words of their ruler, the latter would find it difficult, in case of need, to abrogate liberties once conceded, and impose new laws.

From these universal considerations, let us pass on to the kingdom of the Jews. The Jews when they first came out of Egypt were not bound by any national laws, and were therefore free to ratify any laws they liked, or to make new ones, and were at liberty to set up a government and occupy a territory wherever they chose. However, they were entirely unfit to frame a wise code of laws and to keep the sovereign power vested in the community; they were all uncultivated and sunk in a wretched slavery, therefore the sovereignty was bound to remain vested in the hands of one man who would rule the rest and keep them under constraint, make laws and interpret them. This sovereignty was easily retained by Moses, because he surpassed the rest in virtue and persuaded the people of the fact, proving it by many testimonies (see Exod. chap. xiv., last verse, and chap. xix., verse 9). He then, by the Divine virtue he possessed, made laws and ordained them for the people, taking the greatest care that they should be obeyed willingly and not through fear, being specially induced to adopt this course by the obstinate nature of the Jews, who would not have submitted to be ruled solely by constraint; and also by the imminence of war, for it is always better to inspire soldiers with a thirst for glory than to terrify them with threats; each man will then strive to distinguish himself by valour and courage, instead of merely trying to escape punishment. Moses, therefore, by his virtue and the Divine command, introduced a religion, so that the people might do their duty from devotion rather than fear. Further, he bound them over by benefits, and prophesied many advantages in the future; nor were his laws very severe, as anyone may see for himself, especially if he remarks the number of circumstances necessary in order to procure the conviction of an accused person.

Lastly, in order that the people which could not govern itself should be entirely dependent on its ruler, he left nothing to the free choice of individuals (who had hitherto been slaves); the people could do nothing but remember the law, and follow the ordinances laid down at the good pleasure of their ruler; they were not allowed to plough, to sow, to reap, nor even to eat; to clothe themselves, to shave, to rejoice, or in fact to do anything whatever as they liked, but were bound to follow the directions given in the law; and not only this, but they were obliged to have marks on

their door-posts, on their hands, and between their eyes to
admonish them to perpetual obedience.

This, then, was the object of the ceremonial law, that
men should do nothing of their own free will, but should
always act under external authority, and should continually
confess by their actions and thoughts that they were not
their own masters, but were entirely under the control of
others.

From all these considerations it is clearer than day that
ceremonies have nothing to do with a state of blessedness,
and that those mentioned in the Old Testament, *i.e.* the
whole Mosaic Law, had reference merely to the government
of the Jews, and merely temporal advantages.

As for the Christian rites, such as baptism, the Lord's
Supper, festivals, public prayers, and any other observances
which are, and always have been, common to all Christen-
dom, if they were instituted by Christ or His Apostles
(which is open to doubt), they were instituted as external
signs of the universal church, and not as having anything
to do with blessedness, or possessing any sanctity in themselves. Therefore, though such ceremonies were not ordained for the sake of upholding a government, they were
ordained for the preservation of a society, and accordingly he
who lives alone is not bound by them: nay, those who live
in a country where the Christian religion is forbidden, are
bound to abstain from such rites, and can none the less
live in a state of blessedness. We have an example of this
in Japan, where the Christian religion is forbidden, and the
Dutch who live there are enjoined by their East India
Company not to practise any outward rites of religion. I
need not cite other examples, though it would be easy to
prove my point from the fundamental principles of the New
Testament, and to adduce many confirmatory instances;
but I pass on the more willingly, as I am anxious to proceed to my next proposition. I will now, therefore, pass on
to what I proposed to treat of in the second part of this
chapter, namely, what persons are bound to believe in the
narratives contained in Scripture, and how far they are so
bound. Examining this question by the aid of natural
reason, I will proceed as follows.

If anyone wishes to persuade his fellows for or against

anything which is not self-evident, he must deduce his contention from their admissions, and convince them either by
experience or by ratiocination; either by appealing to facts
of natural experience, or to self-evident intellectual axioms.
Now unless the experience be of such a kind as to be
clearly and distinctly understood, though it may convince a
man, it will not have the same effect on his mind and dis-
perse the clouds of his doubt so completely as when the
doctrine taught is deduced entirely from intellectual axioms
—that is, by the mere power of the understanding and logical
order, and this is especially the case in spiritual matters
which have nothing to do with the senses.

But the deduction of conclusions from general truths
à priori, usually requires a long chain of arguments, and,
moreover, very great caution, acuteness, and self-restraint—
qualities which are not often met with; therefore people
prefer to be taught by experience rather than deduce their
conclusion from a few axioms, and set them out in logical
order.   Whence it follows, that if anyone wishes to teach a
doctrine to a whole nation (not to speak of the whole human
race), and to be understood by all men in every particular,
he will seek to support his teaching with experience, and
will endeavour to suit his reasonings and the definitions of
his doctrines as far as possible to the understanding of the
common people, who form the majority of mankind, and
he will not set them forth in logical sequence nor adduce the
definitions which serve to establish them.   Otherwise he
writes only for the learned—that is, he will be understood
by only a small proportion of the human race.

All Scripture was written primarily for an entire people,
and secondarily for the whole human race; therefore its
contents must necessarily be adapted as far as possible to
the understanding of the masses, and proved only by examples drawn from experience.   We will explain ourselves
more clearly.   The chief speculative doctrines taught in
Scripture are the existence of God, or a Being Who made
all things, and Who directs and sustains the world with
consummate wisdom; furthermore, that God takes the
greatest thought for men, or such of them as live piously
and honourably, while He punishes, with various penalties,
those who do evil, separating them from the good.   All

this is proved in Scripture entirely through experience—that is, through the narratives there related. No definitions of doctrine are given, but all the sayings and reasonings are adapted to the understanding of the masses. Although experience can give no clear knowledge of these things, nor explain the nature of God, nor how He directs and sustains all things, it can nevertheless teach and enlighten men sufficiently to impress obedience and devotion on their minds.

It is now, I think, sufficiently clear what persons are bound to believe in the Scripture narratives, and in what degree they are so bound, for it evidently follows from what has been said that the knowledge of and belief in them is particularly necessary to the masses whose intellect is not capable of perceiving things clearly and distinctly. Further, he who denies them because he does not believe that God exists or takes thought for men and the world, may be accounted impious; but a man who is ignorant of them, and nevertheless knows by natural reason that God exists, as we have said, and has a true plan of life, is altogether blessed—yes, more blessed than the common herd of believers, because besides true opinions he possesses also a true and distinct conception. Lastly, he who is ignorant of the Scriptures and knows nothing by the light of reason, though he may not be impious or rebellious, is yet less than human and almost brutal, having none of God's gifts.

We must here remark that when we say that the knowledge of the sacred narrative is particularly necessary to the masses, we do not mean the knowledge of absolutely all the narratives in the Bible, but only of the principal ones, those which, taken by themselves, plainly display the doctrine we have just stated, and have most effect over men's minds.

If all the narratives in Scripture were necessary for the proof of this doctrine, and if no conclusion could be drawn without the general consideration of every one of the histories contained in the sacred writings, truly the conclusion and demonstration of such doctrine would overtask the understanding and strength not only of the masses, but of humanity; who is there who could give attention to all the narratives at once, and to all the circumstances, and all the scraps of doctrine to be elicited from such a host of diverse histories? I cannot believe that the men who have left us the Bible as we have it were so abounding in talent that they attempted setting about such a method of demonstration, still less can I suppose that we cannot understand Scriptural doctrine till we have given heed to the quarrels of Isaac, the advice of Achitophel to Absalom, the civil war between Jews and Israelites, and other similar chronicles; nor can I think that it was more difficult to teach such doctrine by means of history to the Jews of early times, the contemporaries of Moses, than it was to the contemporaries of Esdras. But more will be said on this point hereafter, we may now only note that the masses are only bound to know those histories which can most powerfully dispose their mind to obedience and devotion. However, the masses are not sufficiently skilled to draw conclusions from what they read, they take more delight in the actual stories, and in the strange and unlooked-for issues of events than in the doctrines implied; therefore, besides reading these narratives, they are always in need of pastors or church ministers to explain them to their feeble intelligence.

But not to wander from our point, let us conclude with what has been our principal object—namely, that the truth of narratives, be they what they may, has nothing to do with the Divine law, and serves for nothing except in respect of doctrine, the sole element which makes one history better than another. The narratives in the Old and New Testaments surpass profane history, and differ among themselves in merit simply by reason of the salutary doctrines which they inculcate. Therefore, if a man were to read the Scripture narratives believing the whole of them, but were to give no heed to the doctrines they contain, and make no amendment in his life, he might employ himself just as profitably in reading the Koran or the poetic drama, or ordinary chronicles, with the attention usually given to such writings; on the other hand, if a man is absolutely ignorant of the Scriptures, and none the less has right opinions and a true plan of life, he is absolutely blessed and truly possesses in himself the spirit of Christ.

The Jews are of a directly contrary way of thinking, for they hold that true opinions and a true plan of life are of no service in attaining blessedness, if their possessors have arrived at them by the light of reason only, and not like the documents prophetically revealed to Moses. Maimonides ventures openly to make this assertion : "Every man who takes to heart the seven precepts and diligently follows them, is counted with the pious among the nations, and an heir of the world to come; that is to say, if he takes to heart and follows them because God ordained them in the law, and revealed them to us by Moses, because they were of aforetime precepts to the sons of Noah: but he who follows them as led thereto by reason, is not counted as a dweller among the pious, nor among the wise of the nations." Such are the words of Maimonides, to which R. Joseph, the son of Shem Job, adds in his book which he calls "Kebod Elohim, or God's Glory," that although Aristotle (whom he considers to have written the best ethics and to be above everyone else) has not omitted anything that concerns true ethics, and which he has adopted in his own book, carefully following the lines laid down, yet this was not able to suffice for his salvation, inasmuch as he embraced his doctrines in accordance with the dictates of reason and not as Divine documents prophetically revealed.

However, that these are mere figments, and are not supported by Scriptural authority will, I think, be sufficiently evident to the attentive reader, so that an examination of the theory will be sufficient for its refutation. It is not my purpose here to refute the assertions of those who assert that the natural light of reason can teach nothing of any value concerning the true way of salvation. People who lay no claims to reason for themselves, are not able to prove by reason this their assertion; and if they hawk about something superior to reason, it is a mere figment, and far below reason, as their general method of life sufficiently shows. But there is no need to dwell upon such persons. I will merely add that we can only judge of a man by his works. If a man abounds in the fruits of the Spirit, charity, joy, peace, long-suffering, kindness, goodness, faith, gentleness, chastity, against which, as Paul says (Gal. v. 22), there is no law, such an one, whether he be taught by reason only or by the Scripture only, has been in very truth taught by God, and is altogether blessed. Thus have I said all that I undertook to say concerning Divine law.

CHAPTER VI.

OF MIRACLES.

AS men are accustomed to call Divine the knowledge which transcends human understanding, so also do they style Divine, or the work of God, anything of which the cause is not generally known: for the masses think that the power and providence of God are most clearly displayed by events that are extraordinary and contrary to the conception they have formed of nature, especially if such events bring them any profit or convenience: they think that the clearest possible proof of God's existence is afforded when nature, as they suppose, breaks her accustomed order, and consequently they believe that those who explain or endeavour to understand phenomena or miracles through their natural causes are doing away with God and His providence. They suppose, forsooth, that God is inactive so long as nature works in her accustomed order, and *vice versâ*, that the power of nature and natural causes are idle so long as God is acting: thus they imagine two powers distinct one from the other, the power of God and the power of nature, though the latter is in a sense determined by God, or (as most people believe now) created by Him. What they mean by either, and what they understand by God and nature they do not know, except that they imagine the power of God to be like that of some royal potentate, and nature's power to consist in force and energy.

The masses then style unusual phenomena "miracles," and partly from piety, partly for the sake of opposing the students of science, prefer to remain in ignorance of natural causes, and only to hear of those things which they know least, and consequently admire most. In fact, the common people can only adore God, and refer all things to His power by removing natural causes, and conceiving things happening out of their due course, and only admires the power of God when the power of nature is conceived of as in subjection to it.

This idea seems to have taken its rise among the early Jews who saw the Gentiles round them worshipping visible gods such as the sun, the moon, the earth, water, air, &c., and in order to inspire the conviction that such divinities were weak and inconstant, or changeable, told how they themselves were under the sway of an invisible God, and narrated their miracles, trying further to show that the God whom they worshipped arranged the whole of nature for their sole benefit: this idea was so pleasing to humanity that men go on to this day imagining miracles, so that they may believe themselves God's favourites, and the final cause for which God created and directs all things.

What pretension will not people in their folly advance! They have no single sound idea concerning either God or nature, they confound God's decrees with human decrees, they conceive nature as so limited that they believe man to be its chief part! I have spent enough space in setting forth these common ideas and prejudices concerning nature and miracles, but in order to afford a regular demonstration I will show—

I. That nature cannot be contravened, but that she preserves a fixed and immutable order, and at the same time I will explain what is meant by a miracle.

II. That God's nature and existence, and consequently His providence cannot be known from miracles, but that they can all be much better perceived from the fixed and immutable order of nature.

III. That by the decrees and volitions, and consequently the providence of God, Scripture (as I will prove by Scriptural examples) means nothing but nature's order following necessarily from her eternal laws.

IV. Lastly, I will treat of the method of interpreting Scriptural miracles, and the chief points to be noted concerning the narratives of them.

Such are the principal subjects which will be discussed in this chapter, and which will serve, I think, not a little to further the object of this treatise.

Our first point is easily proved from what we showed in Chap. IV. about Divine law—namely, that all that God

wishes or determines involves eternal necessity and truth,
for we demonstrated that God's understanding is identical
with His will, and that it is the same thing to say that
God wills a thing, as to say that He understands it; hence,
as it follows necessarily from the Divine nature and perfection that God understands a thing as it is, it follows no
less necessarily that He wills it as it is.   Now, as nothing
is necessarily true save only by Divine decree, it is plain
that the universal laws of nature are decrees of God following from the necessity and perfection of the Divine nature.
Hence, any event happening in nature which contravened
nature's universal laws, would necessarily also contravene
the Divine decree, nature, and understanding; or if anyone asserted that God acts in contravention to the laws of
nature, he, *ipso facto*, would be compelled to assert that
God acted against His own nature—an evident absurdity.
One might easily show from the same premises that the
power and efficiency of nature are in themselves the Divine
power and efficiency, and that the Divine power is the very
essence of God, but this I gladly pass over for the present.
   Nothing, then, comes to pass in nature [1] in contravention to her universal laws, nay, everything agrees with
them and follows from them, for whatsoever comes to
pass, comes to pass by the will and eternal decree of God;
that is, as we have just pointed out, whatever comes to pass,
comes to pass according to laws and rules which involve
eternal necessity and truth; nature, therefore, always observes laws and rules which involve eternal necessity and
truth, although they may not all be known to us, and
therefore she keeps a fixed and immutable order.   Nor is
there any sound reason for limiting the power and efficacy
of nature, and asserting that her laws are fit for certain
purposes, but not for all; for as the efficacy and power of
nature, are the very efficacy and power of God, and as the
laws and rules of nature are the decrees of God, it is in every
way to be believed that the power of nature is infinite, and
that her laws are broad enough to embrace everything conceived by the Divine intellect; the only alternative is to
assert that God has created nature so weak, and has

---

[1] N.B. I do not mean here by "nature," merely matter and its modifications, but infinite other things besides matter.

ordained for her laws so barren, that He is repeatedly compelled to come afresh to her aid if He wishes that she should be preserved, and that things should happen as He desires: a conclusion, in my opinion, very far removed from reason.   Further, as nothing happens in nature which does not follow from her laws, and as her laws embrace everything conceived by the Divine intellect, and lastly, as nature preserves a fixed and immutable order; it most clearly follows that miracles are only intelligible as in relation to human opinions, and merely mean events of which the natural cause cannot be explained by a reference to any ordinary occurrence, either by us, or at any rate, by the writer and narrator of the miracle.

We may, in fact, say that a miracle is an event of which the causes cannot be explained by the natural reason through a reference to ascertained workings of nature; but since miracles were wrought according to the understanding of the masses, who are wholly ignorant of the workings of nature, it is certain that the ancients took for a miracle whatever they could not explain by the method adopted by the unlearned in such cases, namely, an appeal to the memory, a recalling of something similar, which is ordinarily regarded without wonder; for most people think they sufficiently understand a thing when they have ceased to wonder at it.   The ancients, then, and indeed most men up to the present day, had no other criterion for a miracle; hence we cannot doubt that many things are narrated in Scripture as miracles of which the causes could easily be explained by reference to ascertained workings of nature. We have hinted as much in Chap. II., in speaking of the sun standing still in the time of Joshua, and going backwards in the time of Ahaz; but we shall soon have more to say on the subject when we come to treat of the interpretation of miracles later on in this chapter.

It is now time to pass on to the second point, and show that we cannot gain an understanding of God's essence, existence, or providence by means of miracles, but that these truths are much better perceived through the fixed and immutable order of nature.

I thus proceed with the demonstration.   As God's existence is not self-evident,[1] it must necessarily be inferred from

---

[1] See Note 6.

ideas so firmly and incontrovertibly true, that no power can be postulated or conceived sufficient to impugn them. They ought certainly so to appear to us when we infer from them God's existence, if we wish to place our conclusion beyond the reach of doubt; for if we could conceive that such ideas could be impugned by any power whatsoever, we should doubt of their truth, we should doubt of our conclusion, namely, of God's existence, and should never be able to be certain of anything. Further, we know that nothing either agrees with or is contrary to nature, unless it agrees with or is contrary to these primary ideas; wherefore if we would conceive that anything could be done in nature by any power whatsoever which would be contrary to the laws of nature, it would also be contrary to our primary ideas, and we should have either to reject it as absurd, or else to cast doubt (as just shown) on our primary ideas, and consequently on the existence of God, and on everything howsoever perceived. Therefore miracles, in the sense of events contrary to the laws of nature, so far from demonstrating to us the existence of God, would, on the contrary, lead us to doubt it, where, otherwise, we might have been absolutely certain of it, as knowing that nature follows a fixed and immutable order.

Let us take miracle as meaning that which cannot be explained through natural causes. This may be interpreted in two senses: either as that which has natural causes, but cannot be examined by the human intellect; or as that which has no cause save God and God's will. But as all things which come to pass through natural causes, come to pass also solely through the will and power of God, it comes to this, that a miracle, whether it has natural causes or not, is a result which cannot be explained by its cause, that is a phenomenon which surpasses human understanding; but from such a phenomenon, and certainly from a result surpassing our understanding, we can gain no knowledge. For whatsoever we understand clearly and distinctly should be plain to us either in itself or by means of something else clearly and distinctly understood; wherefore from a miracle or a phenomenon which we cannot understand, we can gain no knowledge of God's essence, or existence, or indeed anything about God or nature; whereas when we know that

all things are ordained and ratified by God, that the opera-
tions of nature follow from the essence of God, and that
the laws of nature are eternal decrees and volitions of God,
we must perforce conclude that our knowledge of God and
of God's will increases in proportion to our knowledge and
clear understanding of nature, as we see how she depends
on her primal cause, and how she works according to eternal law. Wherefore so far as our understanding goes,
those phenomena which we clearly and distinctly understand have much better right to be called works of God,
and to be referred to the will of God than those about
which we are entirely ignorant, although they appeal powerfully to the imagination, and compel men's admiration.

It is only phenomena that we clearly and distinctly understand, which heighten our knowledge of God, and most
clearly indicate His will and decrees. Plainly, they are
but triflers who, when they cannot explain a thing, run
back to the will of God; this is, truly, a ridiculous way of
expressing ignorance. Again, even supposing that some
conclusion could be drawn from miracles, we could not
possibly infer from them the existence of God: for a
miracle being an event under limitations is the expression
of a fixed and limited power; therefore we could not possibly
infer from an effect of this kind the existence of a cause
whose power is infinite, but at the utmost only of a cause
whose power is greater than that of the said effect. I say
at the utmost, for a phenomenon may be the result of many
concurrent causes, and its power may be less than the power
of the sum of such causes, but far greater than that of any
one of them taken individually. On the other hand, the
laws of nature, as we have shown, extend over infinity, and
are conceived by us as, after a fashion, eternal, and nature
works in accordance with them in a fixed and immutable
order; therefore, such laws indicate to us in a certain degree
the infinity, the eternity, and the immutability of God.

We may conclude, then, that we cannot gain knowledge
of the existence and providence of God by means of miracles, but that we can far better infer them from the fixed
and immutable order of nature. By miracle, I here mean
an event which surpasses, or is thought to surpass, human
comprehension: for in so far as it is supposed to destroy or

interrupt the order of nature or her laws, it not only can give us no knowledge of God, but, contrariwise, takes away that which we naturally have, and makes us doubt of God and everything else.

Neither do I recognize any difference between an event against the laws of nature and an event beyond the laws of nature (that is, according to some, an event which does not contravene nature, though she is inadequate to produce or effect it)—for a miracle is wrought in, and not beyond nature, though it may be said in itself to be above nature, and, therefore, must necessarily interrupt the order of nature, which otherwise we conceive of as fixed and unchangeable, according to God's decrees. If, therefore, anything should come to pass in nature which does not follow from her laws, it would also be in contravention to the order which God has established in nature for ever through universal natural laws: it would, therefore, be in contravention to God's nature and laws, and, consequently, belief in it would throw doubt upon everything, and lead to Atheism.

I think I have now sufficiently established my second point, so that we can again conclude that a miracle, whether in contravention to, or beyond, nature, is a mere absurdity; and, therefore, that what is meant in Scripture by a miracle can only be a work of nature, which surpasses, or is believed to surpass, human comprehension. Before passing on to my third point, I will adduce Scriptural authority for my assertion that God cannot be known from miracles. Scripture nowhere states the doctrine openly, but it can readily be inferred from several passages. Firstly, that in which Moses commands (Deut. xiii.) that a false prophet should be put to death, even though he work miracles: "If there arise a prophet among you, and giveth thee a sign or wonder, and the sign or wonder come to pass, saying, Let us go after other gods . . . thou shalt not hearken unto the voice of that prophet; for the Lord your God proveth you, and that prophet shall be put to death." From this it clearly follows that miracles could be wrought even by false prophets; and that, unless men are honestly endowed with the true knowledge and love of God, they may be as easily led by miracles to follow false gods as to follow the true God; for these words are added: "For the

Lord your God tempts you, that He may know whether you love Him with all your heart and with all your mind."

Further, the Israelites, from all their miracles, were unable to form a sound conception of God, as their experience testified: for when they had persuaded themselves that Moses had departed from among them, they petitioned Aaron to give them visible gods; and the idea of God they had formed as the result of all their miracles was—a calf!

Asaph, though he had heard of so many miracles, yet doubted of the providence of God, and would have turned himself from the true way, if he had not at last come to understand true blessedness. (See Ps. lxxxiii.) Solomon, too, at a time when the Jewish nation was at the height of its prosperity, suspects that all things happen by chance. (See Eccles. iii. 19, 20, 21; and chap. ix. 2, 3, &c.)

Lastly, nearly all the prophets found it very hard to reconcile the order of nature and human affairs with the conception they had formed of God's providence, whereas philosophers who endeavour to understand things by clear conceptions of them, rather than by miracles, have always found the task extremely easy—at least, such of them as place true happiness solely in virtue and peace of mind, and who aim at obeying nature, rather than being obeyed by her. Such persons rest assured that God directs nature according to the requirements of universal laws, not according to the requirements of the particular laws of human nature, and that, therefore, God's scheme comprehends, not only the human race, but the whole of nature.

It is plain, then, from Scripture itself, that miracles can give no knowledge of God, nor clearly teach us the providence of God. As to the frequent statements in Scripture, that God wrought miracles to make Himself plain to man —as in Exodus x. 2, where He deceived the Egyptians, and gave signs of Himself, that the Israelites might know that He was God,—it does not, therefore, follow that miracles really taught this truth, but only that the Jews held opinions which laid them easily open to conviction by miracles. We have shown in Chap. II. that the reasons assigned by the prophets, or those which are formed from revelation, are not assigned in accordance with ideas universal and common to all, but in accordance with the accepted

doctrines, however absurd, and with the opinions of those
to whom the revelation was given, or those whom the Holy
Spirit wished to convince.

This we have illustrated by many Scriptural instances,
and can further cite Paul, who to the Greeks was a Greek,
and to the Jews a Jew. But although these miracles could
convince the Egyptians and Jews from their standpoint,
they could not give a true idea and knowledge of God, but
only cause them to admit that there was a Deity more
powerful than anything known to them, and that this Deity
took special care of the Jews, who had just then an unexpectedly happy issue of all their affairs. They could not
teach them that God cares equally for all, for this can be
taught only by philosophy: the Jews, and all who took
their knowledge of God's providence from the dissimilarity
of human conditions of life and the inequalities of fortune,
persuaded themselves that God loved the Jews above all
men, though they did not surpass their fellows in true
human perfection.

I now go on to my *third* point, and show from Scripture
that the decrees and mandates of God, and consequently
His providence, are merely the order of nature—that is,
when Scripture describes an event as accomplished by God
or God's will, we must understand merely that it was in
accordance with the law and order of nature, not, as most
people believe, that nature had for a season ceased to act,
or that her order was temporarily interrupted. But Scripture does not directly teach matters unconnected with its
doctrine, wherefore it has no care to explain things by their
natural causes, nor to expound matters merely speculative.
Wherefore our conclusion must be gathered by inference
from those Scriptural narratives which happen to be written
more at length and circumstantially than usual. Of these
I will cite a few.

In the first book of Samuel, ix. 15, 16, it is related that
God revealed to Samuel that He would send Saul to him,
yet God did not send Saul to Samuel as people are wont
to send one man to another. His " sending " was merely
the ordinary course of nature. Saul was looking for the
asses he had lost, and was meditating a return home without them, when, at the suggestion of his servant, he went

to the prophet Samuel, to learn from him where he might find them. From no part of the narrative does it appear that Saul had any command from God to visit Samuel beyond this natural motive.

In Psalm cv. 24 it is said that God changed the hearts of the Egyptians, so that they hated the Israelites. This was evidently a natural change, as appears from Exodus, chap. i., where we find no slight reason for the Egyptians reducing the Israelites to slavery.

In Genesis ix. 13, God tells Noah that He will set His bow in the cloud; this action of God's is but another way of expressing the refraction and reflection which the rays of the sun are subjected to in drops of water.

In Psalm cxlvii. 18, the natural action and warmth of the wind, by which hoar frost and snow are melted, are styled the word of the Lord, and in verse 15 wind and cold are called the commandment and word of God.

In Psalm civ. 4, wind and fire are called the angels and ministers of God, and various other passages of the same sort are found in Scripture, clearly showing that the decree, commandment, fiat, and word of God are merely expressions for the action and order of nature.

Thus it is plain that all the events narrated in Scripture came to pass naturally, and are referred directly to God because Scripture, as we have shown, does not aim at explaining things by their natural causes, but only at narrating what appeals to the popular imagination, and doing so in the manner best calculated to excite wonder, and consequently to impress the minds of the masses with devotion. If, therefore, events are found in the Bible which we cannot refer to their causes, nay, which seem entirely to contradict the order of nature, we must not come to a stand, but assuredly believe that whatever did really happen happened naturally. This view is confirmed by the fact that in the case of every miracle there were many attendant circumstances, though these were not always related, especially where the narrative was of a poetic character.

The circumstances of the miracles clearly show, I maintain, that natural causes were needed. For instance, in order to infect the Egyptians with blains, it was necessary that Moses should scatter ashes in the air (Exod. ix. 10); the locusts also came upon the land of Egypt by a command of God in accordance with nature, namely, by an east wind blowing for a whole day and night; and they departed by a very strong west wind (Exod. x. 14, 19). By a similar Divine mandate the sea opened a way for the Jews (Exod. xiv. 21), namely, by an east wind which blew very strongly all night.

So, too, when Elisha would revive the boy who was believed to be dead, he was obliged to bend over him several times until the flesh of the child waxed warm, and at last he opened his eyes (2 Kings iv. 34, 35).

Again, in John's Gospel (chap. ix.) certain acts are mentioned as performed by Christ preparatory to healing the blind man, and there are numerous other instances showing that something further than the absolute fiat of God is required for working a miracle.

Wherefore we may believe that, although the circumstances attending miracles are not related always or in full detail, yet a miracle was never performed without them.

This is confirmed by Exodus xiv. 27, where it is simply stated that "Moses stretched forth his hand, and the waters of the sea returned to their strength in the morning," no mention being made of a wind; but in the song of Moses (Exod. xv. 10) we read, "Thou didst blow with Thy wind (*i.e.* with a very strong wind),. and the sea covered them." Thus the attendant circumstance is omitted in the history, and the miracle is thereby enhanced.

But perhaps someone will insist that we find many things in Scripture which seem in nowise explicable by natural causes, as for instance, that the sins of men and their prayers can be the cause of rain and of the earth's fertility, or that faith can heal the blind, and so on. But I think I have already made sufficient answer: I have shown that Scripture does not explain things by their secondary causes, but only narrates them in the order and the style which has most power to move men, and especially uneducated men, to devotion; and therefore it speaks inaccurately of God and of events, seeing that its object is not to convince the reason, but to attract and lay hold of the imagination. If the Bible were to describe the destruction of an empire in the style of political historians, the masses would remain unstirred, whereas the contrary is the case when it adopts the method of poetic description, and refers all things immediately to God. When, therefore, the Bible says that the earth is barren because of men's sins, or that the blind were healed by faith, we ought to take no more notice than when it says that God is angry at men's sins, that He is sad, that He repents of the good He has promised and done ; or that on seeing a sign he remembers something He had promised, and other similar expressions, which are either thrown out poetically or related according to the opinion and prejudices of the writer.

We may, then, be absolutely certain that every event which is truly described in Scripture necessarily happened, like everything else, according to natural laws ; and if anything is there set down which can be proved in set terms to contravene the order of nature, or not to be deducible therefrom, we must believe it to have been foisted into the sacred writings by irreligious hands ; for whatsoever is contrary to nature is also contrary to reason, and whatsoever is contrary to reason is absurd, and, *ipso facto*, to be rejected.

There remain some points concerning the interpretation of miracles to be noted, or rather to be recapitulated, for most of them have been already stated. These I proceed to discuss in the fourth division of my subject, and I am led to do so lest anyone should, by wrongly interpreting a miracle, rashly suspect that he has found something in Scripture contrary to human reason.

It is very rare for men to relate an event simply as it happened, without adding any element of their own judgment. When they see or hear anything new, they are, unless strictly on their guard, so occupied with their own preconceived opinions that they perceive something quite different from the plain facts seen or heard, especially if such facts surpass the comprehension of the beholder or hearer, and, most of all, if he is interested in their happening in a given way.

Thus men relate in chronicles and histories their own opinions rather than actual events, so that one and the same event is so differently related by two men of different opinions, that it seems like two separate occurrences; and, further, it is very easy from historical chronicles to gather the personal opinions of the historian.

I could cite many instances in proof of this from the writings both of natural philosophers and historians, but I will content myself with one only from Scripture, and leave the reader to judge of the rest.

In the time of Joshua the Hebrews held the ordinary opinion that the sun moves with a daily motion, and that the earth remains at rest; to this preconceived opinion they adapted the miracle which occurred during their battle with the five kings. They did not simply relate that that day was longer than usual, but asserted that the sun and moon stood still, or ceased from their motion—a statement which would be of great service to them at that time in convincing and proving by experience to the Gentiles, who worshipped the sun, that the sun was under the control of another deity who could compel it to change its daily course. Thus, partly through religious motives, partly through preconceived opinions, they conceived of and related the occurrence as something quite different from what really happened.

Thus in order to interpret the Scriptural miracles and understand from the narration of them how they really happened, it is necessary to know the opinions of those who first related them, and have recorded them for us in writing, and to distinguish such opinions from the actual impression made upon their senses, otherwise we shall confound opinions and judgments with the actual miracle as it really occurred: nay, further, we shall confound actual events with symbolical and imaginary ones. For many things are narrated in Scripture as real, and were believed to be real, which were in fact only symbolical and imaginary. As, for instance, that God came down from heaven (Exod. xix. 28, Deut. v. 28), and that Mount Sinai smoked because God descended upon it surrounded with fire; or, again, that Elijah ascended into heaven in a chariot of fire, with horses of fire; all these things were assuredly merely symbols adapted to the opinions of those who have handed them down to us as they were represented to them, namely, as real. All who have any education know that God has no right hand nor left; that He is not moved nor at rest, nor in a particular place, but that He is absolutely infinite and contains in Himself all perfections.

These things, I repeat, are known to whoever judges of things by the perception of pure reason, and not according as his imagination is affected by his outward senses. Following the example of the masses who imagine a bodily Deity, holding a royal court with a throne on the convexity of heaven, above the stars, which are believed to be not very far off from the earth.

To these and similar opinions very many narrations in Scripture are adapted, and should not, therefore, be mistaken by philosophers for realities.

Lastly, in order to understand, in the case of miracles, what actually took place, we ought to be familiar with Jewish phrases and metaphors; anyone who did not make sufficient allowance for these, would be continually seeing miracles in Scripture where nothing of the kind is intended by the writer; he would thus miss the knowledge not only of what actually happened, but also of the mind of the writers of the sacred text. For instance, Zechariah speaking of some future war says (chap. xiv. verse 7): "It shall be one day which shall be known to the Lord, not day nor night; but at even time it shall be light." In these words he seems to predict a great miracle, yet he only means that the battle will be doubtful the whole day, that the issue will be known only to God, but that in the evening they will gain the victory: the prophets frequently used to predict victories and defeats of the nations in similar phrases. Thus Isaiah, describing the destruction of Babylon, says (chap. xiii.): "The stars of heaven, and the constellations thereof, shall not give their light; the sun shall be darkened in his going forth, and the moon shall not cause her light to shine." Now I suppose no one imagines that at the destruction of Babylon these phenomena actually occurred any more than that which the prophet adds, "For I will make the heavens to tremble, and remove the earth out of her place."

So, too, Isaiah in foretelling to the Jews that they would return from Babylon to Jerusalem in safety, and would not suffer from thirst on their journey, says: "And they thirsted not when He led them through the deserts; He caused the waters to flow out of the rocks for them; He clave the rocks, and the waters gushed out." These words merely mean that the Jews, like other people, found springs in the desert, at which they quenched their thirst; for when the Jews returned to Jerusalem with the consent of Cyrus, it is admitted that no similar miracles befell them.

In this way many occurrences in the Bible are to be regarded merely as Jewish expressions. There is no need for me to go through them in detail; but I will call attention generally to the fact that the Jews employed such phrases not only rhetorically, but also, and indeed chiefly, from devotional motives. Such is the reason for the substitution of "bless God" for "curse God" in 1 Kings xxi. 10, and Job ii. 9, and for all things being referred to God, whence it appears that the Bible seems to relate nothing but miracles, even when speaking of the most ordinary occurrences, as in the examples given above.

Hence we must believe that when the Bible says that the Lord hardened Pharaoh's heart, it only means that Pharaoh was obstinate; when it says that God opened the windows of heaven, it only means that it rained very hard, and so on. When we reflect on these peculiarities, and also on the fact that most things are related very shortly, with very little detail, and almost in abridgments, we shall see that there is hardly anything in Scripture which can be proved contrary to natural reason, while, on the other hand, many things which before seemed obscure, will after a little consideration be understood and easily explained.

I think I have now very clearly explained all that I proposed to explain, but before I finish this chapter I would call attention to the fact that I have adopted a different method in speaking of miracles to that which I employed in treating of prophecy. Of prophecy I have asserted nothing which could not be inferred from promises revealed in Scripture, whereas in this chapter I have deduced my conclusions solely from the principles ascertained by the natural light of reason. I have proceeded in this way advisedly, for prophecy, in that it surpasses human knowledge, is a purely theological question; therefore, I knew that I could not make any assertions about it, nor learn

wherein it consists, except through deductions from premises that have been revealed; therefore I was compelled
to collate the history of prophecy, and to draw therefrom
certain conclusions which would teach me, in so far as such
teaching is possible, the nature and properties of the gift.
But in the case of miracles, as our inquiry is a question
purely philosophical (namely, whether anything can happen
which contravenes, or does not follow from the laws of
nature), I was not under any such necessity: I therefore
thought it wiser to unravel the difficulty through premises
ascertained and thoroughly known by the natural light of
reason.   I say I thought it wiser, for I could also easily
have solved the problem merely from the doctrines and
fundamental principles of Scripture: in order that everyone may acknowledge this, I will briefly show how it could
be done.

Scripture makes the general assertion in several passages
that nature's course is fixed and unchangeable.   In Ps.
cxlviii. 6, for instance, and Jer. xxxi. 35.   The wise man
also, in Eccles. i. 10, distinctly teaches that "there is nothing new under the sun," and in verses 11, 12, illustrating
the same idea, he adds that although something occasionally
happens which seems new, it is not really new, but "hath
been already of old time, which was before us, whereof there
is no remembrance, neither shall there be any remembrance
of things that are to come with those that come after."
Again in chap. iii. 11, he says, "God hath made everything
beautiful in his time," and immediately afterwards adds,
"I know that whatsoever God doeth, it shall be for ever;
nothing can be put to it, nor anything taken from it."

Now all these texts teach most distinctly that nature
preserves a fixed and unchangeable order, and that God in
all ages, known and unknown, has been the same; further,
that the laws of nature are so perfect, that nothing can be
added thereto nor taken therefrom; and, lastly, that miracles
only appear as something new because of man's ignorance.

Such is the express teaching of Scripture: nowhere does
Scripture assert that anything happens which contradicts,
or cannot follow from the laws of nature; and, therefore,
we should not attribute to it such a doctrine.

To these considerations we must add, that miracles require causes and attendant circumstances, and that they follow, not from some mysterious royal power which the masses attribute to God, but from the Divine rule and decree, that is (as we have shown from Scripture itself) from the laws and order of nature; lastly, that miracles can be wrought even by false prophets, as is proved from Deut. xiii. and Matt. xxiv. 24.

The conclusion, then, that is most plainly put before us is, that miracles were natural occurrences, and must therefore be so explained as to appear neither new (in the words of Solomon) nor contrary to nature, but, as far as possible, in complete agreement with ordinary events. This can easily be done by anyone, now that I have set forth the rules drawn from Scripture. Nevertheless, though I maintain that Scripture teaches this doctrine, I do not assert that it teaches it as a truth necessary to salvation, but only that the prophets were in agreement with ourselves on the point; therefore everyone is free to think on the subject as he likes, according as he thinks it best for himself, and most likely to conduce to the worship of God and to single-hearted religion.

This is also the opinion of Josephus, for at the conclusion of the second book of his "Antiquities," he writes: "Let no man think this story incredible of the sea's dividing to save these people, for we find it in ancient records that this hath been seen before, whether by God's extraordinary will or by the course of nature it is indifferent. The same thing happened one time to the *Macedonians,* under the command of *Alexander,* when for want of another passage the *Pamphylian* Sea divided to make them way; God's Providence making use of *Alexander* at that time as His instrument for destroying the *Persian* Empire. This is attested by all the historians who have pretended to write the Life of that Prince. But people are at liberty to think what they please."

Such are the words of Josephus, and such is his opinion on faith in miracles.

CHAPTER VII.

OF THE INTERPRETATION OF SCRIPTURE.

WHEN people declare, as all are ready to do, that the Bible is the Word of God teaching man true blessedness and the way of salvation, they evidently do not mean what they say; for the masses take no pains at all to live according to Scripture, and we see most people endeavouring to hawk about their own commentaries as the word of God, and giving their best efforts, under the guise of religion, to compelling others to think as they do: we generally see, I say, theologians anxious to learn how to wring their inventions and sayings out of the sacred text, and to fortify them with Divine authority. Such persons never display less scruple or more zeal than when they are interpreting Scripture or the mind of the Holy Ghost; if we ever see them perturbed, it is not that they fear to attribute some error to the Holy Spirit, and to stray from the right path, but that they are afraid to be convicted of error by others, and thus to overthrow and bring into contempt their own authority. But if men really believed what they verbally testify of Scripture, they would adopt quite a different plan of life: their minds would not be agitated by so many contentions, nor so many hatreds, and they would cease to be excited by such a blind and rash passion for interpreting the sacred writings, and excogitating novelties in religion. On the contrary, they would not dare to adopt, as the teaching of Scripture, anything which they could not plainly deduce therefrom: lastly, those sacrilegious persons who have dared, in several passages, to interpolate the Bible, would have shrunk from so great a crime, and would have stayed their sacrilegious hands.

Ambition and unscrupulousness have waxed so powerful, that religion is thought to consist, not so much in respecting the writings of the Holy Ghost, as in defending commentaries, so that religion is no longer identified with charity, but with spreading discord and propagating insensate hatred disguised under the name of zeal for the Lord, and eager ardour.

To these evils we must add superstition, which teaches men to despise reason and nature, and only to admire and venerate that which is repugnant to both: whence it is not wonderful that for the sake of increasing the admiration and veneration felt for Scripture, men strive to explain it so as to make it appear to contradict, as far as possible, both one and the other: thus they dream that most profound mysteries lie hid in the Bible, and weary themselves out in the investigation of these absurdities, to the neglect of what is useful. Every result of their diseased imagination they attribute to the Holy Ghost, and strive to defend with the utmost zeal and passion; for it is an observed fact that men employ their reason to defend conclusions arrived at by reason, but conclusions arrived at by the passions are defended by the passions.

If we would separate ourselves from the crowd and escape from theological prejudices, instead of rashly accepting human commentaries for Divine documents, we must consider the true method of interpreting Scripture and dwell upon it at some length: for if we remain in ignorance of this we cannot know, certainly, what the Bible and the Holy Spirit wish to teach.

I may sum up the matter by saying that the method of interpreting Scripture does not widely differ from the method of interpreting nature—in fact, it is almost the same. For as the interpretation of nature consists in the examination of the history of nature, and therefrom deducing definitions of natural phenomena on certain fixed axioms, so Scriptural interpretation proceeds by the examination of Scripture, and inferring the intention of its authors as a legitimate conclusion from its fundamental principles. By working in this manner everyone will always advance without danger of error—that is, if they admit no principles for interpreting Scripture, and discussing its contents save such as they find in Scripture itself—and will be able with equal security to discuss what surpasses our understanding, and what is known by the natural light of reason.

In order to make clear that such a method is not only correct, but is also the only one advisable, and that it agrees with that employed in interpreting nature, I must remark that Scripture very often treats of matters which cannot be deduced from principles known to reason: for it is chiefly made up of narratives and revelation: the narratives generally contain miracles—that is, as we have shown in the last chapter, relations of extraordinary natural occurrences adapted to the opinions and judgment of the historians who recorded them: the revelations also were adapted to the opinions of the prophets, as we showed in Chap. II., and in themselves surpassed human comprehension. Therefore the knowledge of all these—that is, of nearly the whole contents of Scripture, must be sought from Scripture alone, even as the knowledge of nature is sought from nature. As for the moral doctrines which are also contained in the Bible, they may be demonstrated from received axioms, but we cannot prove in the same manner that Scripture intended to teach them, this can only be learned from Scripture itself.

If we would bear unprejudiced witness to the Divine origin of Scripture, we must prove solely on its own authority that it teaches true moral doctrines, for by such means alone can its Divine origin be demonstrated: we have shown that the certitude of the prophets depended chiefly on their having minds turned towards what is just and good, therefore we ought to have proof of their possessing this quality before we repose faith in them. From miracles God's divinity cannot be proved, as I have already shown, and need not now repeat, for miracles could be wrought by false prophets. Wherefore the Divine origin of Scripture must consist solely in its teaching true virtue. But we must come to our conclusion simply on Scriptural grounds, for if we were unable to do so we could not, unless strongly prejudiced, accept the Bible and bear witness to its Divine origin.

Our knowledge of Scripture must then be looked for in Scripture only.

Lastly, Scripture does not give us definitions of things

any more than nature does: therefore, such definitions must be sought in the latter case from the diverse workings of nature; in the former case, from the various narratives about the given subject which occur in the Bible.

The universal rule, then, in interpreting Scripture is to accept nothing as an authoritative Scriptural statement which we do not perceive very clearly when we examine it in the light of its history. What I mean by its history, and what should be the chief points elucidated, I will now explain.

The history of a Scriptural statement comprises—

I. The nature and properties of the language in which the books of the Bible were written, and in which their authors were accustomed to speak. We shall thus be able to investigate every expression by comparison with common conversational usages.

Now all the writers both of the Old Testament and the New were Hebrews: therefore, a knowledge of the Hebrew language is before all things necessary, not only for the comprehension of the Old Testament, which was written in that tongue, but also of the New: for although the latter was published in other languages, yet its characteristics are Hebrew.

II. An analysis of each book and arrangement of its contents under heads; so that we may have at hand the various texts which treat of a given subject. Lastly, a note of all the passages which are ambiguous or obscure, or which seem mutually contradictory.

I call passages clear or obscure according as their meaning is inferred easily or with difficulty in relation to the context, not according as their truth is perceived easily or the reverse by reason. We are at work not on the truth of passages, but solely on their meaning. We must take especial care, when we are in search of the meaning of a text, not to be led away by our reason in so far as it is founded on principles of natural knowledge (to say nothing of prejudices): in order not to confound the meaning of a passage with its truth, we must examine it solely by means of the signification of the words, or by a reason acknowledging no foundation but Scripture.

I will illustrate my meaning by an example. The words

of Moses, "God is a fire" and "God is jealous," are perfectly clear so long as we regard merely the signification of
the words, and I therefore reckon them among the clear
passages, though in relation to reason and truth they are
most obscure: still, although the literal meaning is repugnant to the natural light of reason, nevertheless, if it cannot
be clearly overruled on grounds and principles derived
from its Scriptural "history," it, that is, the literal meaning,
must be the one retained: and contrariwise if these passages literally interpreted are found to clash with principles
derived from Scripture, though such literal interpretation
were in absolute harmony with reason, they must be interpreted in a different manner, i.e. metaphorically.

If we would know whether Moses believed God to be a
fire or not, we must on no account decide the question on
grounds of the reasonableness or the reverse of such an
opinion, but must judge solely by the other opinions of
Moses which are on record.

In the present instance, as Moses says in several other
passages that God has no likeness to any visible thing,
whether in heaven or in earth, or in the water, either all
such passages must be taken metaphorically, or else the
one before us must be so explained. However, as we should
depart as little as possible from the literal sense, we must
first ask whether this text, God is a fire, admits of any but
the literal meaning—that is, whether the word fire ever
means anything besides ordinary natural fire. If no such
second meaning can be found, the text must be taken
literally, however repugnant to reason it may be: and all
the other passages, though in complete accordance with
reason, must be brought into harmony with it. If the
verbal expressions would not admit of being thus har-
monized, we should have to set them down as irreconcilable,
and suspend our judgment concerning them. However, as
we find the name fire applied to anger and jealousy (see
Job xxxi. 12) we can thus easily reconcile the words of
Moses, and legitimately conclude that the two propositions
God is a fire, and God is jealous, are in meaning identical.

Further, as Moses clearly teaches that God is jealous,
and nowhere states that God is without passions or
emotions, we must evidently infer that Moses held this

doctrine himself, or at any rate, that he wished to teach it, nor must we refrain because such a belief seems contrary to reason: for as we have shown, we cannot wrest the meaning of texts to suit the dictates of our reason, or our preconceived opinions.   The whole knowledge of the Bible must be sought solely from itself.

III.   Lastly, such a history should relate the environment of all the prophetic books extant; that is, the life, the conduct, and the studies of the author of each book, who he was, what was the occasion, and the epoch of his writing, whom did he write for, and in what language.   Further, it should inquire into the fate of each book: how it was first received, into whose hands it fell, how many different versions there were of it, by whose advice was it received into the Bible, and, lastly, how all the books now universally accepted as sacred, were united into a single whole.

All such information should, as I have said, be contained in the "history" of Scripture.   For, in order to know what statements are set forth as laws, and what as moral precepts, it is important to be acquainted with the life, the conduct, and the pursuits of their author: moreover, it becomes easier to explain a man's writings in proportion as we have more intimate knowledge of his genius and temperament.

Further, that we may not confound precepts which are eternal with those which served only a temporary purpose, or were only meant for a few, we should know what was the occasion, the time, the age, in which each book was written, and to what nation it was addressed.

Lastly, we should have knowledge on the other points I have mentioned, in order to be sure, in addition to the authenticity of the work, that it has not been tampered with by sacrilegious hands, or whether errors can have crept in, and, if so, whether they have been corrected by men sufficiently skilled and worthy of credence.   All these things should be known, that we may not be led away by blind impulse to accept whatever is thrust on our notice, instead of only that which is sure and indisputable.

Now, when we are in possession of this history of Scripture, and have finally decided that we assert nothing as prophetic doctrine which does not directly follow from such

history, or which is not clearly deducible from it, then, I
say, it will be time to gird ourselves for the task of investigating the mind of the prophets and of the Holy Spirit.
But in this further arguing, also, we shall require a method
very like that employed in interpreting nature from her
history.   As in the examination of natural phenomena we
try first to investigate what is most universal and common
to all nature—such, for instance, as motion and rest, and
their laws and rules, which nature always observes, and
through which she continually works—and then we proceed
to what is less universal; so, too, in the history of Scripture, we seek first for that which is most universal, and
serves for the basis and foundation of all Scripture, a doctrine, in fact, that is commended by all the prophets as
eternal and most profitable to all men.   For example, that
God is one, and that He is omnipotent, that He alone
should be worshipped, that He has a care for all men, and
that He especially loves those who adore Him and love
their neighbour as themselves, &c. These and similar doctrines, I repeat, Scripture everywhere so clearly and expressly teaches, that no one was ever in doubt of its meaning concerning them.

The nature of God, His manner of regarding and providing for things, and similar doctrines, Scripture nowhere
teaches professedly, and as eternal doctrine; on the contrary, we have shown that the prophets themselves did not
agree on the subject; therefore, we must not lay down any
doctrine as Scriptural on such subjects, though it may
appear perfectly clear on rational grounds.

From a proper knowledge of this universal doctrine of
Scripture, we must then proceed to other doctrines less
universal, but which, nevertheless, have regard to the
general conduct of life, and flow from the universal doctrine like rivulets from a source; such are all particular
external manifestations of true virtue, which need a given
occasion for their exercise; whatever is obscure or ambiguous on such points in Scripture must be explained and
defined by its universal doctrine; with regard to contradictory instances, we must observe the occasion and the time
in which they were written. For instance, when Christ
says, "Blessed are they that mourn, for they shall be com-

forted," we do not know, from the actual passage, what sort of mourners are meant; as, however, Christ afterwards teaches that we should have care for nothing, save only for the kingdom of God and His righteousness, which is commended as the highest good (see Matt. vi. 33), it follows that by mourners He only meant those who mourn for the kingdom of God and righteousness neglected by man: for this would be the only cause of mourning to those who love nothing but the Divine kingdom and justice, and who evidently despise the gifts of fortune. So, too, when Christ says: "But if a man strike you on the right cheek, turn to him the left also," and the words which follow.

If He had given such a command, as a lawgiver, to judges, He would thereby have abrogated the law of Moses, but this He expressly says He did not do (Matt. v. 17). Wherefore we must consider who was the speaker, what was the occasion, and to whom were the words addressed. Now Christ said that He did not ordain laws as a legislator, but inculcated precepts as a teacher: inasmuch as He did not aim at correcting outward actions so much as the frame of mind. Further, these words were spoken to men who were oppressed, who lived in a corrupt commonwealth on the brink of ruin, where justice was utterly neglected. The very doctrine inculcated here by Christ just before the destruction of the city was also taught by Jeremiah before the first destruction of Jerusalem, that is, in similar circumstances, as we see from Lamentations iii. 25-30.

Now as such teaching was only set forth by the prophets in times of oppression, and was even then never laid down as a law; and as, on the other hand, Moses (who did not write in times of oppression, but—mark this—strove to found a well-ordered commonwealth), while condemning envy and hatred of one's neighbour, yet ordained that an eye should be given for an eye, it follows most clearly from these purely Scriptural grounds that this precept of Christ and Jeremiah concerning submission to injuries was only valid in places where justice is neglected, and in a time of oppression, but does not hold good in a well-ordered state.

In a well-ordered state where justice is administered every one is bound, if he would be accounted just, to demand penalties before the judge (see Lev. v. 1), not for the

sake of vengeance (Lev. xix. 17, 18), but in order to defend
justice and his country's laws, and to prevent the wicked
rejoicing in their wickedness.   All this is plainly in accordance with reason.   I might cite many other examples in
the same manner, but I think the foregoing are sufficient
to explain my meaning and the utility of this method, and
this is all my present purpose.   Hitherto we have only
shown how to investigate those passages of Scripture which
treat of practical conduct, and which, therefore, are more
easily examined, for on such subjects there was never really
any controversy among the writers of the Bible.

The purely speculative passages cannot be so easily
traced to their real meaning : the way becomes narrower,
for as the prophets differed in matters speculative among
themselves, and the narratives are in great measure adapted
to the prejudices of each age, we must not, on any account,
infer the intention of one prophet from clearer passages in
the writings of another ; nor must we so explain his meaning, unless it is perfectly plain that the two prophets were
at one in the matter.

How we are to arrive at the intention of the prophets in
such cases I will briefly explain.   Here, too, we must begin
from the most universal proposition, inquiring first from
the most clear Scriptural statements what is the nature of
prophecy or revelation, and wherein does it consist ; then
we must proceed to miracles, and so on to whatever is most
general till we come to the opinions of a particular prophet,
and, at last, to the meaning of a particular revelation,
prophecy, history, or miracle.   We have already pointed
out that great caution is necessary not to confound the
mind of a prophet or historian with the mind of the Holy
Spirit and the truth of the matter ; therefore I need not
dwell further on the subject.   I would, however, here remark concerning the meaning of revelation, that the present
method only teaches us what the prophets really saw or
heard, not what they desired to signify or represent by
symbols.   The latter may be guessed at but cannot be inferred with certainty from Scriptural premises.

We have thus shown the plan for interpreting Scripture,
and have, at the same time, demonstrated that it is the one
and surest way of investigating its true meaning.   I am

willing indeed to admit that those persons (if any such there be) would be more absolutely certainly right, who have received either a trustworthy tradition or an assurance from the prophets themselves, such as is claimed by the Pharisees; or who have a pontiff gifted with infallibility in the interpretation of Scripture, such as the Roman Catholics boast. But as we can never be perfectly sure, either of such a tradition or of the authority of the pontiff, we cannot found any certain conclusion on either: the one is denied by the oldest sect of Christians, the other by the oldest sect of Jews. Indeed, if we consider the series of years (to mention no other point) accepted by the Pharisees from their Rabbis, during which time they say they have handed down the tradition from Moses, we shall find that it is not correct, as I show elsewhere. Therefore such a tradition should be received with extreme suspicion; and although, according to our method, we are bound to consider as uncorrupted the tradition of the Jews, namely, the meaning of the Hebrew words which we received from them, we may accept the latter while retaining our doubts about the former.

No one has ever been able to change the meaning of a word in ordinary use, though many have changed the meaning of a particular sentence. Such a proceeding would be most difficult; for whoever attempted to change the meaning of a word, would be compelled, at the same time, to explain all the authors who employed it, each according to his temperament and intention, or else, with consummate cunning, to falsify them.

Further, the masses and the learned alike preserve language, but it is only the learned who preserve the meaning of particular sentences and books: thus, we may easily imagine that the learned having a very rare book in their power, might change or corrupt the meaning of a sentence in it, but they could not alter the signification of the words; moreover, if anyone wanted to change the meaning of a common word he would not be able to keep up the change among posterity, or in common parlance or writing.

For these and such-like reasons we may readily conclude that it would never enter into the mind of anyone to corrupt a language, though the intention of a writer may

often have been falsified by changing his phrases or interpreting them amiss. As then our method (based on the
principle that the knowledge of Scripture must be sought
from itself alone) is the sole true one, we must evidently
renounce any knowledge which it cannot furnish for the
complete understanding of Scripture. I will now point out
its difficulties and shortcomings, which prevent our gaining
a complete and assured knowlege of the Sacred Text.

Its first great difficulty consists in its requiring a
thorough knowledge of the Hebrew language.   Where is
such knowledge to be obtained?   The men of old who
employed the Hebrew tongue have left none of the principles and bases of their language to posterity; we have
from them absolutely nothing in the way of dictionary,
grammar, or rhetoric.

Now the Hebrew nation has lost all its grace and beauty
(as one would expect after the defeats and persecutions it
has gone through), and has only retained certain fragments
of its language and of a few books.   Nearly all the names
of fruits, birds, and fishes, and many other words have
perished in the wear and tear of time.   Further, the meaning of many nouns and verbs which occur in the Bible are
either utterly lost, or are subjects of dispute.   And not
only are these gone, but we are lacking in a knowledge of
Hebrew phraseology.   The devouring tooth of time has destroyed nearly all the phrases and turns of expression
peculiar to the Hebrews, so that we know them no more.
Therefore we cannot investigate as we would all the meanings of a sentence by the uses of the language; and there
are many phrases of which the meaning is most obscure or
altogether inexplicable, though the component words are
perfectly plain.

To this impossibility of tracing the history of the Hebrew
language must be added its particular nature and composition : these give rise to so many ambiguities that it is impossible to find a method which would enable us to gain a
certain knowledge of all the statements in Scripture.[1] In
addition to the sources of ambiguities common to all languages, there are many peculiar to Hebrew. These, I think,
it worth while to mention.

Firstly, an ambiguity often arises in the Bible from our

[1] See Note 7.

mistaking one letter for another similar one. ·The Hebrews divide the letters of the alphabet into five classes, according to the five organs of the mouth employed in pronouncing them, namely, the lips, the tongue, the teeth, the palate, and the throat, For instance, *Alpha, Ghet, Hgain, He,* are called gutturals, and are barely distinguishable, by any sign that we know, one from the other. *El,* which signifies *to,* is often taken for *hgal,* which signifies *above,* and *vice versâ.* Hence sentences are often rendered rather ambiguous or meaningless.

A second difficulty arises from the multiplied meaning of conjunctions and adverbs. For instance, *vau* serves promiscuously for a particle of union or of separation, meaning, *and, but, because, however, then: ki,* has seven or eight meanings, namely, *wherefore, although, if, when, inasmuch as, because, a burning,* &c., and so on with almost all particles.

The third very fertile source of doubt is the fact that Hebrew verbs in the indicative mood lack the present, the past imperfect, the pluperfect, the future perfect, and other tenses most frequently employed in other languages; in the imperative and infinitive moods they are wanting in all except the present, and a subjunctive mood does not exist. Now, although all these defects in moods and tenses may be supplied by certain fundamental rules of the language with ease and even elegance, the ancient writers evidently neglected such rules altogether, and employed indifferently future for present and past, and *vice versâ* past for future, and also indicative for imperative and subjunctive, with the result of considerable confusion.

Besides these sources of ambiguity there are two others, one very important. Firstly, there are in Hebrew no vowels; secondly, the sentences are not separated by any marks elucidating the meaning or separating the clauses. Though the want of these two has generally been supplied by points and accents, such substitutes cannot be accepted by us, inasmuch as they were invented and designed by men of an after age whose authority should carry no weight. The ancients wrote without points (that is, without vowels and accents), as is abundantly testified; their descendants added what was lacking, according to their own ideas of Scriptural interpretation; wherefore the existing accents and points are simply current interpretations, and are no more authoritative than any other commentaries.

Those who are ignorant of this fact cannot justify the author of the Epistle to the Hebrews for interpreting (chap. xi. 21) Genesis (xlvii. 31) very differently from the version given in our Hebrew text as at present pointed, as though the Apostle had been obliged to learn the meaning of Scripture from those who added the points. In my opinion the latter are clearly wrong. In order that everyone may judge for himself, and also see how the discrepancy arose simply from the want of vowels, I will give both interpretations. Those who pointed our version read, "And Israel bent himself over, or (changing *Hgain* into *Aleph*, a similar letter) towards, the head of the bed." The author of the Epistle reads, "And Israel bent himself over the head of his staff," substituting *mate* for *mita*, from which it only differs in respect of vowels. Now as in this narrative it is Jacob's age only that is in question, and not his illness, which is not touched on till the next chapter, it seems more likely that the historian intended to say that Jacob bent over the head of his staff (a thing commonly used by men of advanced age for their support) than that he bowed himself at the head of his bed, especially as for the former reading no substitution of letters is required. In this example I have desired not only to reconcile the passage in the Epistle with the passage in Genesis, but also and chiefly to illustrate how little trust should be placed in the points and accents which are found in our present Bible, and so to prove that he who would be without bias in interpreting Scripture should hesitate about accepting them, and inquire afresh for himself. Such being the nature and structure of the Hebrew language, one may easily understand that many difficulties are likely to arise, and that no possible method could solve all of them. It is useless to hope for a way out of our difficulties in the comparison of various parallel passages (we have shown that the only method of discovering the true sense of a passage out of many alternative ones is to see what are the usages of the language), for this comparison of parallel passages can only accidentally throw light on a difficult point, seeing that the prophets never wrote with the express object of explaining their own phrases or those of other people, and also because we cannot infer the meaning of one prophet or apostle by the meaning of another, unless on a purely practical question, not when the matter is speculative, or if a miracle, or history is being narrated. I might illustrate my point with instances, for there are many inexplicable phrases in Scripture, but I would rather pass on to consider the difficulties and imperfections of the method under discussion.

A further difficulty attends the method, from the fact that it requires the history of all that has happened to every book in the Bible; such a history we are often quite unable to furnish. Of the authors, or (if the expression be preferred), the writers of many of the books, we are either in complete ignorance, or at any rate in doubt, as I will point out at length. Further, we do not know either the occasions or the epochs when these books of unknown authorship were written; we cannot say into what hands they fell, nor how the numerous varying versions originated; nor, lastly, whether there were not other versions, now lost. I have briefly shown that such knowledge is necessary, but I passed over certain considerations which I will now draw attention to.

If we read a book which contains incredible or impossible narratives, or is written in a very obscure style, and if we know nothing of its author, nor of the time or occasion of its being written, we shall vainly endeavour to gain any certain knowledge of its true meaning. For being in ignorance on these points we cannot possibly know the aim or intended aim of the author; if we are fully informed, we so order our thoughts as not to be in any way prejudiced either in ascribing to the author or him for whom the author wrote either more or less than his meaning, and we only take into consideration what the author may have had in his mind, or what the time and occasion demanded. I think this must be tolerably evident to all.

It often happens that in different books we read histories in themselves similar, but which we judge very differently, according to the opinions we have formed of the authors. I remember once to have read in some book

that a man named Orlando Furioso used to drive a kind of
winged monster through the air, fly over any countries he
liked, kill unaided vast numbers of men and giants, and
such like fancies, which from the point of view of reason
are obviously absurd. A very similar story I read in Ovid
of Perseus, and also in the books of Judges and Kings of
Samson, who alone and unarmed killed thousands of men,
and of Elijah, who flew through the air, and at last went
up to heaven in a chariot of fire, with horses of fire. All
these stories are obviously alike, but we judge them very
differently. The first only sought to amuse, the second had
a political object, the third a religious object. We gather
this simply from the opinions we had previously formed of
the authors. Thus it is evidently necessary to know something of the authors of writings which are obscure or unintelligible, if we would interpret their meaning; and for
the same reason, in order to choose the proper reading from
among a great variety, we ought to have information as to
the versions in which the differences are found, and as to
the possibility of other readings having been discovered by
persons of greater authority.

A further difficulty attends this method in the case of
some of the books of Scripture, namely, that they are no
longer extant in their original language. The Gospel
according to Matthew, and certainly the Epistle to the
Hebrews, were written, it is thought, in Hebrew, though
they no longer exist in that form. Aben Ezra affirms in
his commentaries that the book of Job was translated into
Hebrew out of another language, and that its obscurity
arises from this fact. I say nothing of the apocryphal
books, for their authority stands on very inferior ground.

The foregoing difficulties in this method of interpreting
Scripture from its own history, I conceive to be so great
that I do not hesitate to say that the true meaning of
Scripture is in many places inexplicable, or at best mere
subject for guesswork; but I must again point out, on the
other hand, that such difficulties only arise when we endeavour to follow the meaning of a prophet in matters
which cannot be perceived, but only imagined, not in things,
whereof the understanding can give a clear and distinct idea,
and which are conceivable through themselves:[1] matters

[1] See Note 8.

which by their nature are easily perceived cannot be expressed so obscurely as to be unintelligible; as the proverb says, "a word is enough to the wise." Euclid, who only wrote of matters very simple and easily understood, can easily be comprehended by anyone in any language; we can follow his intention perfectly, and be certain of his true meaning, without having a thorough knowledge of the language in which he wrote; in fact, a quite rudimentary acquaintance is sufficient. We need make no researches concerning the life, the pursuits, or the habits of the author; nor need we inquire in what language, nor when he wrote, nor the vicissitudes of his book, nor its various readings, nor how, nor by whose advice it has been received.

What we here say of Euclid might equally be said of any book which treats of things by their nature perceptible: thus we conclude that we can easily follow the intention of Scripture in moral questions, from the history we possess of it, and we can be sure of its true meaning.

The precepts of true piety are expressed in very ordinary language, and are equally simple and easily understood. Further, as true salvation and blessedness consist in a true assent of the soul—and we truly assent only to what we clearly understand—it is most plain that we can follow with certainty the intention of Scripture in matters relating to salvation and necessary to blessedness; therefore, we need not be much troubled about what remains: such matters, inasmuch as we generally cannot grasp them with our reason and understanding, are more curious than profitable.

I think I have now set forth the true method of Scriptural interpretation, and have sufficiently explained my own opinion thereon. Besides, I do not doubt that everyone will see that such a method only requires the aid of natural reason. The nature and efficacy of the natural reason consists in deducing and proving the unknown from the known, or in carrying premises to their legitimate conclusions; and these are the very processes which our method desiderates. Though we must admit that it does not suffice to explain everything in the Bible, such imperfection does not spring from its own nature, but from the fact that the path which it teaches us, as the true one, has never been tended or trodden by men, and has thus, by the lapse of time, become very difficult, and almost impassable, as, indeed, I have shown in the difficulties I draw attention to.

There only remains to examine the opinions of those who differ from me.

The first which comes under our notice is, that the light of nature has no power to interpret Scripture, but that a supernatural faculty is required for the task. What is meant by this supernatural faculty I will leave to its propounders to explain. Personally, I can only suppose that they have adopted a very obscure way of stating their complete uncertainty about the true meaning of Scripture. If we look at their interpretations, they contain nothing supernatural, at least nothing but the merest conjectures.

Let them be placed side by side with the interpretations of those who frankly confess that they have no faculty beyond their natural ones; we shall see that the two are just alike—both human, both long pondered over, both laboriously invented. To say that the natural reason is insufficient for such results is plainly untrue, firstly, for the reasons above stated, namely, that the difficulty of interpreting Scripture arises from no defect in human reason, but simply from the carelessness (not to say malice) of men who neglected the history of the Bible while there were still materials for inquiry; secondly, from the fact (admitted, I think, by all) that the supernatural faculty is a Divine gift granted only to the faithful. But the prophets and apostles did not preach to the faithful only, but chiefly to the unfaithful and wicked. Such persons, therefore, were able to understand the intention of the prophets and apostles, otherwise the prophets and apostles would have seemed to be preaching to little boys and infants, not to men endowed with reason. Moses, too, would have given his laws in vain, if they could only be comprehended by the faithful, who need no law. Indeed, those who demand supernatural faculties for comprehending the meaning of the prophets and apostles seem truly lacking in natural faculties, so that we should hardly suppose such persons the possessors of a Divine supernatural gift.

The opinion of Maimonides was widely different. He

asserted that each passage in Scripture admits of various, nay, contrary, meanings; but that we could never be certain of any particular one till we knew that the passage, as we interpreted it, contained nothing contrary or repugnant to reason. If the literal meaning clashes with reason, though the passage seems in itself perfectly clear, it must be interpreted in some metaphorical sense. This doctrine he lays down very plainly in chap. xxv. part ii. of his book, "More Nebuchim," for he says: "Know that we shrink not from affirming that the world hath existed from eternity, because of what Scripture saith concerning the world's creation. For the texts which teach that the world was created are not more in number than those which teach that God hath a body; neither are the approaches in this matter of the world's creation closed, or even made hard to us: so that we should not be able to explain what is written, as we did when we showed that God hath no body, nay, peradventure, we could explain and make fast the doctrine of the world's eternity more easily than we did away with the doctrines that God hath a beatified body. Yet two things hinder me from doing as I have said, and believing that the world is eternal. As it hath been clearly shown that God hath not a body, we must perforce explain all those passages whereof the literal sense agreeth not with the demonstration, for sure it is that they can be so explained. But the eternity of the world hath not been so demonstrated, therefore it is not necessary to do violence to Scripture in support of some common opinion, whereof we might, at the bidding of reason, embrace the contrary."

Such are the words of Maimonides, and they are evidently sufficient to establish our point: for if he had been convinced by reason that the world is eternal, he would not have hesitated to twist and explain away the words of Scripture till he made them appear to teach this doctrine. He would have felt quite sure that Scripture, though everywhere plainly denying the eternity of the world, really intends to teach it. So that, however clear the meaning of Scripture may be, he would not feel certain of having grasped it, so long as he remained doubtful of the truth of what was written. For we are in doubt whether a thing is in conformity with reason, or contrary thereto, so long as we are uncertain of its truth, and, consequently, we cannot be sure whether the literal meaning of a passage be true or false.

If such a theory as this were sound, I would certainly grant that some faculty beyond the natural reason is required for interpreting Scripture. For nearly all things that we find in Scripture cannot be inferred from known principles of the natural reason, and, therefore, we should be unable to come to any conclusion about their truth, or about the real meaning and intention of Scripture, but should stand in need of some further assistance.

Further, the truth of this theory would involve that the masses, having generally no comprehension of, nor leisure for, detailed proofs, would be reduced to receiving all their knowledge of Scripture on the authority and testimony of philosophers, and, consequently, would be compelled to suppose that the interpretations given by philosophers were infallible.

Truly this would be a new form of ecclesiastical authority, and a new sort of priests or pontiffs, more likely to excite men's ridicule than their veneration. Certainly our method demands a knowledge of Hebrew for which the masses have no leisure; but no such objection as the foregoing can be brought against us. For the ordinary Jews or Gentiles, to whom the prophets and apostles preached and wrote, understood the language, and, consequently, the intention of the prophet or apostle addressing them; but they did not grasp the intrinsic reason of what was preached, which, according to Maimonides, would be necessary for an understanding of it.

There is nothing, then, in our method which renders it necessary that the masses should follow the testimony of commentators, for I point to a set of unlearned people who understood the language of the prophets and apostles; whereas Maimonides could not point to any such who could arrive at the prophetic or apostolic meaning through their knowledge of the causes of things.

As to the multitude of our own time, we have shown that whatsoever is necessary to salvation, though its reasons may be unknown, can easily be understood in any language, because it is thoroughly ordinary and usual; it is in such understanding as this that the masses acquiesce, not in the testimony of commentators; with regard to other questions, the ignorant and the learned fare alike.

But let us return to the opinion of Maimonides, and examine it more closely. In the first place, he supposes that the prophets were in entire agreement one with another, and that they were consummate philosophers and theologians; for he would have them to have based their conclusions on the absolute truth. Further, he supposes that the sense of Scripture cannot be made plain from Scripture itself, for the truth of things is not made plain therein (in that it does not prove any thing, nor teach the matters of which it speaks through their definitions and first causes), therefore, according to Maimonides, the true sense of Scripture cannot be made plain from itself, and must not be there sought.

The falsity of such a doctrine is shown in this very chapter, for we have shown both by reason and examples that the meaning of Scripture is only made plain through Scripture itself, and even in questions deducible from ordinary knowledge should be looked for from no other source.

Lastly, such a theory supposes that we may explain the words of Scripture according to our preconceived opinions, twisting them about, and reversing or completely changing the literal sense, however plain it may be. Such licence is utterly opposed to the teaching of this and the preceding chapters, and, moreover, will be evident to everyone as rash and excessive.

But if we grant all this licence, what can it effect after all? Absolutely nothing. Those things which cannot be demonstrated, and which make up the greater part of Scripture, cannot be examined by reason, and cannot therefore be explained or interpreted by this rule; whereas, on the contrary, by following our own method, we can explain many questions of this nature, and discuss them on a sure basis, as we have already shown, by reason and example. Those matters which are by their nature comprehensible we can easily explain, as has been pointed out, simply by means of the context.

Therefore, the method of Maimonides is clearly useless:

to which we may add, that it does away with all the certainty which the masses acquire by candid reading, or which is gained by any other persons in any other way. In conclusion, then, we dismiss Maimonides' theory as harmful, useless, and absurd.

As to the tradition of the Pharisees, we have already shown that it is not consistent, while the authority of the popes of Rome stands in need of more credible evidence; the latter, indeed, I reject simply on this ground, for if the popes could point out to us the meaning of Scripture as surely as did the high priests of the Jews, I should not be deterred by the fact that there have been heretic and impious Roman pontiffs; for among the Hebrew high-priests of old there were also heretics and impious men who gained the high-priesthood by improper means, but who, nevertheless, had Scriptural sanction for their supreme power of interpreting the law.   (See Deut. xvii. 11, 12, and xxxiii. 10, also Malachi ii. 8.)

However, as the popes can show no such sanction, their authority remains open to very grave doubt, nor should anyone be deceived by the example of the Jewish high-priests and think that the Catholic religion also stands in need of a pontiff; he should bear in mind that the laws of Moses being also the ordinary laws of the country, necessarily required some public authority to insure their observance; for, if everyone were free to interpret the laws of his country as he pleased, no state could stand, but would for that very reason be dissolved at once, and public rights would become private rights.

With religion the case is widely different. Inasmuch as it consists not so much in outward actions as in simplicity and truth of character, it stands outside the sphere of law and public authority. Simplicity and truth of character are not produced by the constraint of laws, nor by the authority of the state, no one the whole world over can be forced or legislated into a state of blessedness; the means required for such a consummation are faithful and brotherly admonition, sound education, and, above all, free use of the individual judgment.

Therefore, as the supreme right of free thinking, even on religion, is in every man's power, and as it is inconceivable that such power could be alienated, it is also in every man's power to wield the supreme right and authority of free judgment in this behalf, and to explain and interpret religion for himself. The only reason for vesting the supreme authority in the interpretation of law, and judgment on public affairs in the hands of the magistrates, is that it concerns questions of public right.   Similarly the supreme authority in explaining religion, and in passing judgment thereon, is lodged with the individual because it concerns questions of individual right. So far, then, from the authority of the Hebrew high-priests telling in confirmation of the authority of the Roman pontiffs to interpret religion, it would rather tend to establish individual freedom of judgment.   Thus in this way also, we have shown that our method of interpreting Scripture is the best.   For as the highest power of Scriptural interpretation belongs to every man, the rule for such interpretation should be nothing but the natural light of reason which is common to all—not any supernatural light nor any external authority; moreover, such a rule ought not to be so difficult that it can only be applied by very skilful philosophers, but should be adapted to the natural and ordinary faculties and capacity of mankind.   And such I have shown our method to be, for such difficulties as it has arise from men's carelessness, and are no part of its nature.

CHAPTER VIII.

OF THE AUTHORSHIP OF THE PENTATEUCH AND THE OTHER
HISTORICAL BOOKS OF THE OLD TESTAMENT.

IN the former chapter we treated of the foundations and
principles of Scriptural knowledge, and showed that
it consists solely in a trustworthy history of the sacred
writings; such a history, in spite of its indispensability,
the ancients neglected, or at any rate, whatever they may
have written or handed down has perished in the lapse of
time, consequently the groundwork for such an investigation is to a great extent, cut from under us.   This might
be put up with if succeeding generations had confined
themselves within the limits of truth, and had handed
down conscientiously what few particulars they had received or discovered without any additions from their own
brains: as it is, the history of the Bible is not so much
imperfect as untrustworthy: the foundations are not only
too scanty for building upon, but are also unsound.   It is
part of my purpose to remedy these defects, and to remove
common theological prejudices.   But I fear that I am
attempting my task too late, for men have arrived at the pitch
of not suffering contradiction, but defending obstinately
whatever they have adopted under the name of religion.
So widely have these prejudices taken possession of men's
minds, that very few, comparatively speaking, will listen to
reason.   However, I will make the attempt, and spare no
efforts, for there is no positive reason for despairing of
success.

In order to treat the subject methodically, I will begin
with the received opinions concerning the true authors of
the sacred books, and in the first place, speak of the author
of the Pentateuch, who is almost universally supposed to
have been Moses.   The Pharisees are so firmly convinced
of his identity, that they account as a heretic anyone who
differs from them on the subject.   Wherefore, Aben Ezra,

a man of enlightened intelligence, and no small learning, who was the first, so far as I know, to treat of this opinion, dared not express his meaning openly, but confined himself to dark hints which I shall not scruple to elucidate, thus throwing full light on the subject.

The words of Aben Ezra which occur in his commentary on Deuteronomy are as follows:—"Beyond Jordan, &c. . . . . If so be that thou understandest the mystery of the twelve . . . . moreover Moses wrote the law. . . . . The Canaanite was then in the land . . . . it shall be revealed on the mount of God . . . . then also behold his bed, his iron bed, then shalt thou know the truth." In these few words he hints, and also shows that it was not Moses who wrote the Pentateuch, but someone who lived long after him, and further, that the book which Moses wrote was something different from any now extant.

To prove this, I say, he draws attention to the facts—

I. That the preface to Deuteronomy could not have been written by Moses, inasmuch as he had never crossed the Jordan.

II. That the whole book of Moses was written at full length on the circumference of a single altar (Deut. xxvii. and Josh. viii. 37), which altar, according to the Rabbis, consisted of only twelve stones: therefore the book of Moses must have been of far less extent than the Pentateuch. This is what our author means, I think, by the mystery of the twelve, unless he is referring to the twelve curses contained in the chapter of Deuteronomy above cited, which he thought could not have been contained in the law, because Moses bade the Levites read them after the recital of the law, and so bind the people to its observance. Or again, he may have had in his mind the last chapter of Deuteronomy which treats of the death of Moses, and which contains twelve verses. But there is no need to dwell further on these and similar conjectures.

III. That in Deut. xxxi. 9, the expression occurs, "and Moses wrote the law:" words that cannot be ascribed to Moses, but must be those of some other writer narrating the deeds and writings of Moses.

IV. That in Genesis xii. 6, the historian, after narrating that Abraham journeyed through the land of Canaan, adds,

"and the Canaanite was then in the land," thus clearly excluding the time at which he wrote. So that this passage
must have been written after the death of Moses, when the
Canaanites had been driven out, and no longer possessed
the land.

Aben Ezra, in his commentary on the passage, alludes to
the difficulty as follows:—"And the Canaanite was then
in the land: it appears that Canaan, the grandson of Noah,
took from another the land which bears his name; if this be
not the true meaning, there lurks some mystery in the passage, and let him who understands it keep silence." That
is, if Canaan invaded those regions, the sense will be, the
Canaanite was then in the land, in contradistinction to the
time when it had been held by another: but if, as follows
from Gen. chap. x. Canaan was the first to inhabit the land,
the text must mean to exclude the time present, that is the
time at which it was written; therefore it cannot be the
work of Moses, in whose time the Canaanites still possessed
those territories: this is the mystery concerning which
silence is recommended.

V. That in Genesis xxii. 14 Mount Moriah is called
the mount of God,[1] a name which it did not acquire till after
the building of the Temple; the choice of the mountain
was not made in the time of Moses, for Moses does not
point out any spot as chosen by God; on the contrary, he
foretells that God will at some future time choose a spot
to which his name will be given.

VI. Lastly, that in Deut. chap. iii., in the passage relating to Og, king of Bashan, these words are inserted:
"For only Og king of Bashan remained of the remnant of
giants: behold, his bedstead was a bedstead of iron: is it
not in Rabbath of the children of Ammon? nine cubits
was the length thereof, and four cubits the breadth of it,
after the cubit of a man." This parenthesis most plainly
shows that its writer lived long after Moses; for this
mode of speaking is only employed by one treating of
things long past, and pointing to relics for the sake of
gaining credence: moreover, this bed was almost certainly
first discovered by David, who conquered the city of
Rabbath (2 Sam. xii. 30.) Again, the historian a little
further on inserts after the words of Moses, "Jair, the son

[1] See Note 9.

of Manasseh, took all the country of Argob unto the coasts
of Geshuri and Maachathi; and called them after his own
name, Bashan-havoth-jair, unto this day." This passage,
I say, is inserted to explain the words of Moses which pre-
cede it. "And the rest of Gilead, and all Bashan, being
the kingdom of Og, gave I unto the half tribe of Manasseh;
all the region of Argob, with all Bashan, which is called
the land of the giants." The Hebrews in the time of the
writer indisputably knew what territories belonged to the
tribe of Judah, but did not know them under the name of
the jurisdiction of Argob, or the land of the giants. Therefore the writer is compelled to explain what these places
were which were anciently so styled, and at the same time
to point out why they were at the time of his writing
known by the name of Jair, who was of the tribe of
Manasseh, not of Judah. We have thus made clear the
meaning of Aben Ezra and also the passages of the Pentateuch which he cites in proof of his contention. However,
Aben Ezra does not call attention to every instance, or
even the chief ones; there remain many of greater importance, which may be cited. Namely (I.), that the writer
of the books in question not only speaks of Moses in the
third person, but also bears witness to many details concerning him; for instance, "Moses talked with God;"
"The Lord spoke with Moses face to face;" "Moses was
the meekest of men" (Numb. xii. 3); "Moses was wrath
with the captains of the host;" Moses, the man of God;"
"Moses, the servant of the Lord, died;" "There was
never a prophet in Israel like unto Moses," &c. On the
other hand, in Deuteronomy, where the law which Moses
had expounded to the people and written is set forth,
Moses speaks and declares what he has done in the first
person: "God spake with me" (Deut. ii. 1, 17, &c.),
"I prayed to the Lord," &c. Except at the end of the
book, when the historian, after relating the words of
Moses, begins again to speak in the third person, and
to tell how Moses handed over the law which he had
expounded to the people in writing, again admonishing
them, and further, how Moses ended his life. All these
details, the manner of narration, the testimony, and the
context of the whole story lead to the plain conclusion

that these books were written by another, and not by Moses in person.

II. We must also remark that the history relates not only the manner of Moses' death and burial, and the thirty days' mourning of the Hebrews, but further compares him with all the prophets who came after him, and states that he surpassed them all. "There was never a prophet in Israel like unto Moses, whom the Lord knew face to face." Such testimony cannot have been given of Moses by himself, nor by any who immediately succeeded him, but it must come from someone who lived centuries afterwards, especially as the historian speaks of past times. "There was never a prophet," &c. And of the place of burial, "No one knows it to this day."

III. We must note that some places are not styled by the names they bore during Moses' lifetime, but by others which they obtained subsequently. For instance, Abraham is said to have pursued his enemies even unto Dan, a name not bestowed on the city till long after the death of Joshua (Gen. xiv. 14, Judges xviii. 29).

IV. The narrative is prolonged after the death of Moses, for in Exodus xvi. 34 we read that "the children of Israel did eat manna forty years until they came to a land inhabited, until they came unto the borders of the land of Canaan." In other words, until the time alluded to in Joshua vi. 12.

So, too, in Genesis xxxvi. 31 it is stated, "These are the kings that reigned in Edom before there reigned any king over the children of Israel." The historian, doubtless, here relates the kings of Idumæa before that territory was conquered by David[1] and garrisoned, as we read in 2 Sam. viii. 14.

From what has been said, it is thus clearer than the sun at noonday that the Pentateuch was not written by Moses, but by someone who lived long after Moses. Let us now turn our attention to the books which Moses actually did write, and which are cited in the Pentateuch; thus, also, shall we see that they were different from the Pentateuch. Firstly, it appears from Exodus xvii. 14 that Moses, by the command of God, wrote an account of the war against Amalek. The book in which he did so is not named in

---

[1] See Note 10.

the chapter just quoted, but in Numb. xxi. 12 a book is referred to under the title of the wars of God, and doubtless this war against Amalek and the castrametations said in Numb. xxxiii. 2 to have been written by Moses are therein described. We hear also in Exod. xxiv. 4 of another book called the Book of the Covenant, which Moses read before the Israelites when they first made a covenant with God. But this book or this writing contained very little, namely, the laws or commandments of God which we find in Exodus xx. 22 to the end of chap. xxiv., and this no one will deny who reads the aforesaid chapter rationally and impartially. It is there stated that as soon as Moses had learnt the feeling of the people on the subject of making a covenant with God, he immediately wrote down God's laws and utterances, and in the morning, after some ceremonies had been performed, read out the conditions of the covenant to an assembly of the whole people. When these had been gone through, and doubtless understood by all, the whole people gave their assent.

Now from the shortness of the time taken in its perusal and also from its nature as a compact, this document evidently contained nothing more than that which we have just described. Further, it is clear that Moses explained all the laws which he had received in the fortieth year after the exodus from Egypt; also that he bound over the people a second time to observe them, and that finally he committed them to writing (Deut. i. 5; xxix. 14; xxxi. 9), in a book which contained these laws explained, and the new covenant, and this book was therefore called the book of the law of God: the same which was afterwards added to by Joshua when he set forth the fresh covenant with which he bound over the people and which he entered into with God (Josh. xxiv. 25, 26).

Now, as we have extant no book containing this covenant of Moses and also the covenant of Joshua, we must perforce conclude that it has perished, unless, indeed, we adopt the wild conjecture of the Chaldean paraphrast Jonathan, and twist about the words of Scripture to our heart's content. This commentator, in the face of our present difficulty, preferred corrupting the sacred text to confessing his own ignorance. The passage in the book of Joshua which runs, "and Joshua wrote these words in the book of the law of God," he changes into "and Joshua wrote these words and kept them with the book of the law of God." What is to be done with persons who will only see what pleases them? What is such a proceeding if it is not denying Scripture, and inventing another Bible out of our own heads? We may therefore conclude that the book of the law of God which Moses wrote was not the Pentateuch, but something quite different, which the author of the Pentateuch duly inserted into his book. So much is abundantly plain both from what I have said and from what I am about to add. For in the passage of Deuteronomy above quoted, where it is related that Moses wrote the book of the law, the historian adds that he handed it over to the priests and bade them read it out at a stated time to the whole people. This shows that the work was of much less length than the Pentateuch, inasmuch as it could be read through at one sitting so as to be understood by all; further, we must not omit to notice that out of all the books which Moses wrote, this one book of the second covenant and the song (which latter he wrote afterwards so that all the people might learn it), was the only one which he caused to be religiously guarded and preserved. In the first covenant he had only bound over those who were present, but in the second covenant he bound over all their descendants also (Deut. xxix. 14), and therefore ordered this covenant with future ages to be religiously preserved, together with the Song, which was especially addressed to posterity: as, then, we have no proof that Moses wrote any book save this of the covenant, and as he committed no other to the care of posterity; and, lastly, as there are many passages in the Pentateuch which Moses could not have written, it follows that the belief that Moses was the author of the Pentateuch is ungrounded and even irrational.

Someone will perhaps ask whether Moses did not also write down other laws when they were first revealed to him —in other words, whether, during the course of forty years, he did not write down any of the laws which he promulgated, save only those few which I have stated to be contained in the book of the first covenant. To this I would answer, that although it seems reasonable to suppose that Moses wrote down the laws at the time when he wished to communicate them to the people, yet we are not warranted to take it as proved, for I have shown above that we must make no assertions in such matters which we do not gather from Scripture, or which do not flow as legitimate consequences from its fundamental principles. We must not accept whatever is reasonably probable. However, even reason in this case would not force such a conclusion upon us: for it may be that the assembly of elders wrote down the decrees of Moses and communicated them to the people, and the historian collected them, and duly set them forth in his narrative of the life of Moses. So much for the five books of Moses: it is now time for us to turn to the other sacred writings.

The book of Joshua may be proved not to be an autograph by reasons similar to those we have just employed: for it must be some other than Joshua who testifies that the fame of Joshua was spread over the whole world; that he omitted nothing of what Moses had taught (Josh. vi. 27; viii. last verse; xi. 15); that he grew old and summoned an assembly of the whole people, and finally that he departed this life. Furthermore, events are related which took place after Joshua's death. For instance, that the Israelites worshipped God, after his death, so long as there were any old men alive who remembered him; and in chap. xvi. 10, we read that "Ephraim and Manasseh did not drive out the Canaanites which dwelt in Gezer, but the Canaanite dwelt in the land of Ephraim unto this day, and was tributary to him." This is the same statement as that in Judges, chap. i., and the phrase "unto this day" shows that the writer was speaking of ancient times. With these texts we may compare the last verse of chap. xv., concerning the sons of Judah, and also the history of Caleb in the same chap. v. 14. Further, the building of an altar beyond Jordan by the two tribes and a half, chap. xxii. 10, *sqq.*, seems to have taken place after the death of Joshua, for in the whole narrative his name is never mentioned, but the people alone held council as to waging war, sent out legates, waited for their return, and finally approved of their answer.

Lastly, from chap. x. verse 14, it is clear that the book

was written many generations after the death of Joshua, for it bears witness "there was never any day like unto that day, either before or after, that the Lord hearkened to the voice of a man," &c. If, therefore, Joshua wrote any book at all, it was that which is quoted in the work now before us, chap. x. 13.

With regard to the book of Judges, I suppose no rational person persuades himself that it was written by the actual Judges. For the conclusion of the whole history contained in chap. ii. clearly shows that it is all the work of a single historian. Further, inasmuch as the writer frequently tells us that there was then no king in Israel, it is evident that the book was written after the establishment of the monarchy.

The books of Samuel need not detain us long, inasmuch as the narrative in them is continued long after Samuel's death; but I should like to draw attention to the fact that it was written many generations after Samuel's death. For in book i. chap. ix. verse 9, the historian remarks in a parenthesis, "Beforetime, in Israel, when a man went to inquire of God, thus he spake: Come, and let us go to the seer; for he that is now called a prophet was beforetime called a seer."

Lastly, the books of Kings, as we gather from internal evidence, were compiled from the books of King Solomon (1 Kings xi. 41), from the chronicles of the kings of Judah (1 Kings xiv. 19, 29), and the chronicles of the kings of Israel.

We may, therefore, conclude that all the books we have considered hitherto are compilations, and that the events therein are recorded as having happened in old time.

Now, if we turn our attention to the connection and argument of all these books, we shall easily see that they were all written by a single historian, who wished to relate the antiquities of the Jews from their first beginning down to the first destruction of the city. The way in which the several books are connected one with the other is alone enough to show us that they form the narrative of one and the same writer. For as soon as he has related the life of Moses, the historian thus passes on to the story of Joshua: "And it came to pass after that Moses the servant of the

Lord was dead, that God spake unto Joshua," &c., so in the same way, after the death of Joshua was concluded, he passes with identically the same transition and connection to the history of the Judges : "And it came to pass after that Joshua was dead, that the children of Israel sought from God," &c.   To the book of Judges he adds the story of Ruth, as a sort of appendix, in these words : "Now it came to pass in the days that the judges ruled, that there was a famine in the land."

The first book of Samuel is introduced with a similar phrase ; and so is the second book of Samuel.   Then, before the history of David is concluded, the historian passes in the same way to the first book of Kings, and, after David's death, to the second book of Kings.

The putting together, and the order of the narratives, show that they are all the work of one man, writing with a definite aim ; for the historian begins with relating the first origin of the Hebrew nation, and then sets forth in order the times and the occasions in which Moses put forth his laws, and made his predictions.   He then proceeds to relate how the Israelites invaded the promised land in accordance with Moses' prophecy (Deut. vii.) ; and how, when the land was subdued, they turned their backs on their laws, and thereby incurred many misfortunes (Deut. xxxi. 16, 17).   He tells how they wished to elect rulers, and how, according as these rulers observed the law, the people flourished or suffered (Deut. xxviii. 36) ; finally, how destruction came upon the nation, even as Moses had foretold.   In regard to other matters, which do not serve to confirm the law, the writer either passes over them in silence, or refers the reader to other books for information.   All that is set down in the books we have conduces to the sole object of setting forth the words and laws of Moses, and proving them by subsequent events.

When we put together these three considerations, namely, the unity of the subject of all the books, the connection between them, and the fact that they are compilations made many generations after the events they relate had taken place, we come to the conclusion, as I have just stated, that they are all the work of a single historian. Who this historian was, it is not so easy to show ; but I suspect that he was Ezra, and there are several strong reasons for adopting this hypothesis.

The historian whom we already know to be but one individual brings his history down to the liberation of Jehoiakim, and adds that he himself sat at the king's table all his life—that is, at the table either of Jehoiakim, or of the son of Nebuchadnezzar, for the sense of the passage is ambiguous: hence it follows that he did not live before the time of Ezra.   But Scripture does not testify of any except of Ezra (Ezra vii. 10), that he "prepared his heart to seek the law of the Lord, and to set it forth, and further that he was a ready scribe in the law of Moses."   Therefore, I cannot find anyone, save Ezra, to whom to attribute the sacred books.

Further, from this testimony concerning Ezra, we see that he prepared his heart, not only to seek the law of the Lord, but also to set it forth; and, in Nehemiah viii. 8, we read that "they read in the book of the law of God distinctly, and gave the sense, and caused them to understand the reading."

As, then, in Deuteronomy, we find not only the book of the law of Moses, or the greater part of it, but also many things inserted for its better explanation, I conjecture that this Deuteronomy is the book of the law of God, written, set forth, and explained by Ezra, which is referred to in the text above quoted.   Two examples of the way matters were inserted parenthetically in the text of Deuteronomy, with a view to its fuller explanation, we have already given, in speaking of Aben Ezra's opinion.   Many others are found in the course of the work: for instance, in chap. ii. verse 12: "The Horims dwelt also in Seir beforetime; but the children of Esau succeeded them, when they had destroyed them from before them, and dwelt in their stead; as Israel did unto the land of his possession, which the Lord gave unto them."   This explains verses 3 and 4 of the same chapter, where it is stated that Mount Seir, which had come to the children of Esau for a possession, did not fall into their hands uninhabited; but that they invaded it, and turned out and destroyed the Horims, who formerly dwelt therein, even as the children of Israel had done unto the Canaanites after the death of Moses.

So, also, verses 6, 7, 8, 9, of the tenth chapter are inserted parenthetically among the words of Moses. Everyone must see that verse 8, which begins, "At that time the Lord separated the tribe of Levi," necessarily refers to verse 5, and not to the death of Aaron, which is only mentioned here by Ezra because Moses, in telling of the golden calf worshipped by the people, stated that he had prayed for Aaron.

He then explains that at the time at which Moses spoke, God had chosen for Himself the tribe of Levi in order that He may point out the reason for their election, and for the fact of their not sharing in the inheritance; after this digression, he resumes the thread of Moses' speech. To these parentheses we must add the preface to the book, and all the passages in which Moses is spoken of in the third person, besides many which we cannot now distinguish, though, doubtless, they would have been plainly recognized by the writer's contemporaries.

If, I say, we were in possession of the book of the law as Moses wrote it, I do not doubt that we should find a great difference in the words of the precepts, the order in which they are given, and the reasons by which they are supported.

A comparison of the decalogue in Deuteronomy with the decalogue in Exodus, where its history is explicitly set forth, will be sufficient to show us a wide discrepancy in all these three particulars, for the fourth commandment is given not only in a different form, but at much greater length, while the reason for its observance differs wholly from that stated in Exodus. Again, the order in which the tenth commandment is explained differs in the two versions. I think that the differences here as elsewhere are the work of Ezra, who explained the law of God to his contemporaries, and who wrote this book of the law of God, before anything else; this I gather from the fact that it contains the laws of the country, of which the people stood in most need, and also because it is not joined to the book which precedes it by any connecting phrase, but begins with the independent statement, "these are the words of Moses." After this task was completed, I think Ezra set himself to give a complete account of the history of the Hebrew nation from the creation of the world to the entire destruction of the city, and in this account he inserted the book of Deuteronomy, and, possibly, he called the first five books by the name of Moses, because his life is chiefly contained therein, and forms their principal subject; for the same reason he called the sixth Joshua, the seventh Judges, the eighth Ruth, the ninth, and perhaps the tenth, Samuel, and, lastly, the eleventh and twelfth Kings. Whether Ezra put the finishing touches to this work and finished it as he intended, we will discuss in the next chapter.

CHAPTER IX.

OTHER QUESTIONS CONCERNING THE SAME BOOKS: NAMELY,
WHETHER THEY WERE COMPLETELY FINISHED BY EZRA,
AND, FURTHER, WHETHER THE MARGINAL NOTES WHICH
ARE FOUND IN THE HEBREW TEXTS WERE VARIOUS
READINGS.

HOW greatly the inquiry we have just made concerning
the real writer of the twelve books aids us in attaining a complete understanding of them, may be easily
gathered solely from the passages which we have adduced
in confirmation of our opinion, and which would be most
obscure without it.   But besides the question of the writer,
there are other points to notice which common superstition
forbids the multitude to apprehend.   Of these the chief is,
that Ezra (whom I will take to be the author of the aforesaid books until some more likely person be suggested) did
not put the finishing touches to the narratives contained
therein, but merely collected the histories from various
writers, and sometimes simply set them down, leaving
their examination and arrangement to posterity.

The cause (if it were not untimely death) which prevented him from completing his work in all its portions, I
cannot conjecture, but the fact remains most clear, although
we have lost the writings of the ancient Hebrew historians,
and can only judge from the few fragments which are still
extant.   For the history of Hezekiah (2 Kings xviii. 17), as
written in the vision of Isaiah, is related as it is found in
the chronicles of the kings of Judah.   We read the same
story, told with few exceptions [1] in the same words, in the
book of Isaiah which was contained in the chronicles of the
kings of Judah (2 Chron. xxxii. 32).   From this we must
conclude that there were various versions of this narrative
of Isaiah's, unless, indeed, anyone would dream that in this,
too, there lurks a mystery.   Further, the last chapter of

[1] See Note 11.

2 Kings 27-30 is repeated in the last chapter of Jeremiah, v. 31-34.

Again, we find 2 Sam. vii. repeated in 1 Chron. xvii., but the expressions in the two passages are so curiously varied,[1] that we can very easily see that these two chapters were taken from two different versions of the history of Nathan.

Lastly, the genealogy of the kings of Idumæa contained in Genesis xxxvi. 31, is repeated in the same words in 1 Chron. i., though we know that the author of the latter work took his materials from other historians, not from the twelve books we have ascribed to Ezra. We may therefore be sure that if we still possessed the writings of the historians, the matter would be made clear; however, as we have lost them, we can only examine the writings still extant, and from their order and connection, their various repetitions, and, lastly, the contradictions in dates which they contain, judge of the rest.

These, then, or the chief of them, we will now go through. First, in the story of Judah and Tamar (Gen. xxxviii.) the historian thus begins: "And it came to pass at that time that Judah went down from his brethren." This time cannot refer to what immediately precedes,[2] but must necessarily refer to something else, for from the time when Joseph was sold into Egypt to the time when the patriarch Jacob, with all his family, set out thither, cannot be reckoned as more than twenty-two years, for Joseph, when he was sold by his brethren, was seventeen years old, and when he was summoned by Pharaoh from prison was thirty; if to this we add the seven years of plenty and two of famine, the total amounts to twenty-two years. Now, in so short a period, no one can suppose that so many things happened as are described; that Judah had three children, one after the other, from one wife, whom he married at the beginning of the period; that the eldest of these, when he was old enough, married Tamar, and that after he died his next brother succeeded to her; that, after all this, Judah, without knowing it, had intercourse with his daughter-in-law, and that she bore him twins, and, finally, that the eldest of these twins became a father within the aforesaid period. As all these events

---

[1] See Note 12.   [2] See Note 13.

cannot have taken place within the period mentioned in Genesis, the reference must necessarily be to something treated of in another book: and Ezra in this instance simply related the story, and inserted it without examination among his other writings,

However, not only this chapter but the whole narrative of Joseph and Jacob is collected and set forth from various histories, inasmuch as it is quite inconsistent with itself. For in Gen. xlvii. we are told that Jacob, when he came at Joseph's bidding to salute Pharaoh, was 130 years old. If from this we deduct the twenty-two years which he passed sorrowing for the absence of Joseph and the seventeen years forming Joseph's age when he was sold, and, lastly, the seven years for which Jacob served for Rachel, we find that he was very advanced in life, namely, eighty-four, when he took Leah to wife, whereas Dinah was scarcely seven years old when she was violated by Shechem.[1] Simeon and Levi were aged respectively eleven and twelve when they spoiled the city and slew all the males therein with the sword.

There is no need that I should go through the whole Pentateuch. If anyone pays attention to the way in which all the histories and precepts in these five books are set down promiscuously and without order, with no regard for dates; and further, how the same story is often repeated, sometimes in a different version, he will easily, I say, discern that all the materials were promiscuously collected and heaped together, in order that they might at some subsequent time be more readily examined and reduced to order. Not only these five books, but also the narratives contained in the remaining seven, going down to the destruction of the city, are compiled in the same way. For who does not see that in Judges ii. 6 a new historian is being quoted, who had also written of the deeds of Joshua, and that his words are simply copied? For after our historian has stated in the last chapter of the book of Joshua that Joshua died and was buried, and has promised, in the first chapter of Judges, to relate what happened after his death, in what way, if he wished to continue the thread of his history, could he connect the statement here made about Joshua with what had gone before?

[1] See Note 14.

So, too, 1 Sam. 17, 18, are taken from another historian, who assigns a cause for David's first frequenting Saul's court very different from that given in chap. xvi. of the same book. For he did not think that David came to Saul in consequence of the advice of Saul's servants, as is narrated in chap. xvi., but that being sent by chance to the camp by his father on a message to his brothers, he was for the first time remarked by Saul on the occasion of his victory over Goliath the Philistine, and was retained at his court.

I suspect the same thing has taken place in chap. xxvi. of the same book, for the historian there seems to repeat the narrative given in chap. xxiv. according to another man's version. But I pass over this, and go on to the computation of dates.

In 1 Kings, chap. vi., it is said that Solomon built the Temple in the four hundred and eightieth year after the exodus from Egypt; but from the historians themselves we get a much longer period, for

	Years.
Moses governed the people in the desert	40
Joshua, who lived 110 years, did not, according to Josephus and others' opinion rule more than	26
Cushan Rishathaim held the people in subjection	8
Othniel, son of Kenag, was judge for	40[1]
Eglon, King of Moab, governed the people	18
Ehud and Shamgar were judges	80
Jachin, King of Canaan, held the people in subjection	20
The people was at peace subsequently for	40
It was under subjection to Midian	7
It obtained freedom under Gideon for	40
It fell under the rule of Abimelech	3
Tola, son of Puah, was judge	23
Jair was judge	22
The people was in subjection to the Philistines and Ammonites	18
Jephthah was judge	6
Ibzan, the Bethlehemite, was judge	7
Elon, the Zabulonite	10
Abdon, the Pirathonite	8

[1] See Note 15.

	Years.
The people was again subject to the Philistines .	40
Samson was judge	20[1]
Eli was judge	40
The people again fell into subjection to the Philistines, till they were delivered by Samuel. .	20
David reigned	40
Solomon reigned before he built the temple . .	4

All these periods added together make a total of 580 years. But to these must be added the years during which the Hebrew republic flourished after the death of Joshua, until it was conquered by Cushan Rishathaim, which I take to be very numerous, for I cannot bring myself to believe that immediately after the death of Joshua all those who had witnessed his miracles died simultaneously, nor that their successors at one stroke bid farewell to their laws, and plunged from the highest virtue into the depth of wickedness and obstinacy.

Nor, lastly, that Cushan Rishathaim subdued them on the instant; each one of these circumstances requires almost a generation, and there is no doubt that Judges ii. 7, 9, 10, comprehends a great many years which it passes over in silence. We must also add the years during which Samuel was judge, the number of which is not stated in Scripture, and also the years during which Saul reigned, which are not clearly shown from his history. It is, indeed, stated in 1 Sam. xiii. 1, that he reigned two years, but the text in that passage is mutilated, and the records of his reign lead us to suppose a longer period.   That the text is mutilated I suppose no one will doubt who has ever advanced so far as the threshold of the Hebrew language, for it runs as follows: " Saul was in his —— year, when he began to reign, and he reigned two years over Israel."   Who, I say, does not see that the number of the years of Saul's age when he began to reign has been omitted? That the record of the reign presupposes a greater number of years is equally beyond doubt, for in the same book, chap. xxvii. 7, it is stated that David sojourned among the Philistines, to whom he had fled on account of Saul, a year and four months ; thus the rest of the reign must have been

[1] See Note 16.

comprised in a space of eight months, which I think no one will credit. Josephus, at the end of the sixth book of his antiquities, thus corrects the text: Saul reigned eighteen years while Samuel was alive, and two years after his death. However, all the narrative in chap. xiii. is in complete disagreement with what goes before. At the end of chap. vii. it is narrated that the Philistines were so crushed by the Hebrews that they did not venture, during Samuel's life, to invade the borders of Israel; but in chap. xiii. we are told that the Hebrews were invaded during the life of Samuel by the Philistines, and reduced by them to such a state of wretchedness and poverty that they were deprived not only of weapons with which to defend themselves, but also of the means of making more. I should be at pains enough if I were to try and harmonize all the narratives contained in this first book of Samuel so that they should seem to be all written and arranged by a single historian. But I return to my object. The years, then, during which Saul reigned must be added to the above computation; and, lastly, I have not counted the years of the Hebrew anarchy, for I cannot from Scripture gather their number. I cannot, I say, be certain as to the period occupied by the events related in Judges chap. xvii. on till the end of the book.

It is thus abundantly evident that we cannot arrive at a true computation of years from the histories, and, further, that the histories are inconsistent themselves on the subject. We are compelled to confess that these histories were compiled from various writers without previous arrangement and examination. Not less discrepancy is found between the dates given in the Chronicles of the Kings of Judah, and those in the Chronicles of the Kings of Israel; in the latter, it is stated that Jehoram, the son of Ahab, began to reign in the second year of the reign of Jehoram, the son of Jehoshaphat (2 Kings i. 17), but in the former we read that Jehoram, the son of Jehoshaphat, began to reign in the fifth year of Jehoram, the son of Ahab (2 Kings viii. 16). Anyone who compares the narratives in Chronicles with the narratives in the books of Kings, will find many similar discrepancies. These there is no need for me to examine here, and still less am I called upon to treat of the commentaries of those who endeavour to harmonize them. The Rabbis evidently let their fancy run wild. Such commentators as I have read, dream, invent, and as a last resort, play fast and loose with the language. For instance, when it is said in 2 Chronicles, that Ahab was forty-two years old when he began to reign, they pretend that these years are computed from the reign of Omri, not from the birth of Ahab. If this can be shown to be the real meaning of the writer of the book of Chronicles, all I can say is, that he did not know how to state a fact. The commentators make many other assertions of this kind, which if true, would prove that the ancient Hebrews were ignorant both of their own language, and of the way to relate a plain narrative. I should in such case recognize no rule or reason in interpreting Scripture, but it would be permissible to hypothesize to one's heart's content,

If anyone thinks that I am speaking too generally, and without sufficient warrant, I would ask him to set himself to showing us some fixed plan in these histories which might be followed without blame by other writers of chronicles, and in his efforts at harmonizing and interpretation, so strictly to observe and explain the phrases and expressions, the order and the connections, that we may be able to imitate these also in our writings.[1] If he succeeds, I will at once give him my hand, and he shall be to me as great Apollo; for I confess that after long endeavours I have been unable to discover anything of the kind. I may add that I set down nothing here which I have not long reflected upon, and that, though I was imbued from my boyhood up with the ordinary opinions about the Scriptures, I have been unable to withstand the force of what I have urged.

However, there is no need to detain the reader with this question, and drive him to attempt an impossible task; I merely mentioned the fact in order to throw light on my intention.

I now pass on to other points concerning the treatment of these books. For we must remark, in addition to what has been shown, that these books were not guarded by posterity with such care that no faults crept in. The ancient scribes draw attention to many doubtful readings, and some mutilated passages, but not to all that exist: whether the

[1] See Note 17.

faults are of sufficient importance to greatly embarrass the reader I will not now discuss. I am inclined to think that they are of minor moment to those, at any rate, who read the Scriptures with enlightenment: and I can positively affirm that I have not noticed any fault or various reading in doctrinal passages sufficient to render them obscure or doubtful.

There are some people, however, who will not admit that there is any corruption, even in other passages, but maintain that by some unique exercise of providence God has preserved from corruption every word in the Bible: they say that the various readings are the symbols of profoundest mysteries, and that mighty secrets lie hid in the twenty-eight hiatus which occur, nay, even in the very form of the letters.

Whether they are actuated by folly and anile devotion, or whether by arrogance and malice so that they alone may be held to possess the secrets of God, I know not: this much I do know, that I find in their writings nothing which has the air of a Divine secret, but only childish lucubrations. I have read and known certain Kabbalistic triflers, whose insanity provokes my unceasing astonishment. That faults have crept in will, I think, be denied by no sensible person who reads the passage about Saul, above quoted (1 Sam. xiii. 1) and also 2 Sam. vi. 2: "And David arose and went with all the people that were with him from Judah, to bring up from thence the ark of God."

No one can fail to remark that the name of their destination, viz., Kirjath-jearim,[1] has been omitted: nor can we deny that 2 Sam. xiii. 37, has been tampered with and mutilated. "And Absalom fled, and went to Talmai, the son of Ammihud, king of Geshur. And he mourned for his son every day. So Absalom fled, and went to Geshur, and was there three years." I know that I have remarked other passages of the same kind, but I cannot recall them at the moment.

That the marginal notes which are found continually in the Hebrew Codices are doubtful readings will, I think, be evident to everyone who has noticed that they often arise from the great similarity of some of the Hebrew letters, such for instance, as the similarity between Kaph and

[1] See Note 18.

Beth, Jod and Vau, Daleth and Reth, &c. For example, the text in 2 Sam. v. 24, runs "in the time when thou hearest," and similarly in Judges xxi. 22, "And it shall be when their fathers or their brothers come unto us often," the marginal version is "come unto us to complain."

So also many various readings have arisen from the use of the letters named mutes, which are generally not sounded in pronunciation, and are taken promiscuously, one for the other. For example, in Levit. xxv. 29, it is written, "The house shall be established which is not in the walled city," but the margin has it, "which is in a walled city."

Though these matters are self-evident, it is necessary to answer the reasonings of certain Pharisees, by which they endeavour to convince us that the marginal notes serve to indicate some mystery and were added or pointed out by the writers of the sacred books. The first of these reasons, which, in my opinion, carries little weight, is taken from the practice of reading the Scriptures aloud.

If, it is urged, these notes were added to show various readings which could not be decided upon by posterity, why has custom prevailed that the marginal readings should always be retained? Why has the meaning which is preferred been set down in the margin when it ought to have been incorporated in the text, and not relegated to a side note?

The second reason is more specious, and is taken from the nature of the case. It is admitted that faults have crept into the sacred writings by chance and not by design; but they say that in the five books the word for a girl is, with one exception, written without the letter "he," contrary to all grammatical rules, whereas in the margin it is written correctly according to the universal rule of grammar. Can this have happened by mistake? Is it possible to imagine a clerical error to have been committed every time the word occurs? Moreover, it would have been easy to supply the emendation. Hence, when these readings are not accidental or corrections of manifest mistakes, it is supposed that they must have been set down on purpose by the original writers, and have a meaning. However, it is easy to answer such arguments; as to the question of custom having prevailed in the reading of the marginal versions,

I will not spare much time for its consideration: I know
not the promptings of superstition, and perhaps the practice may have arisen from the idea that both readings were
deemed equally good or tolerable, and therefore, lest either
should be neglected, one was appointed to be written, and
the other to be read. They feared to pronounce judgment in so
weighty a matter lest they should mistake the false for the
true, and therefore they would give preference to neither, as
they must necessarily have done if they had commanded one
only to be both read and written. This would be especially
the case where the marginal readings were not written down
in the sacred books: or the custom may have originated because some things though rightly written down were desired
to be read otherwise according to the marginal version, and
therefore the general rule was made that the marginal version should be followed in reading the Scriptures. The
cause which induced the scribes to expressly prescribe
certain passages to be read in the marginal version, I will
now touch on, for not all the marginal notes are various
readings, but some mark expressions which have passed
out of common use, obsolete words and terms which current
decency did not allow to be read in a public assembly.
The ancient writers, without any evil intention, employed
no courtly paraphrase, but called things by their plain
names. Afterwards, through the spread of evil thoughts
and luxury, words which could be used by the ancients
without offence, came to be considered obscene. There was
no need for this cause to change the text of Scripture.
Still, as a concession to the popular weakness, it became the
custom to substitute more decent terms for words denoting
sexual intercourse, excreta, &c., and to read them as they
were given in the margin.

At any rate, whatever may have been the origin of the
practice of reading Scripture according to the marginal
version, it was not that the true interpretation is contained
therein. For besides that, the Rabbins in the Talmud often
differ from the Massoretes, and give other readings which
they approve of, as I will shortly show, certain things are
found in the margin which appear less warranted by the
uses of the Hebrew language: For example, in 2 Samuel
xiv. 22, we read, "In that the king hath fulfilled the re-

quest of his servant," a construction plainly regular, and agreeing with that in chap. xvi. But the margin has it "of thy servant," which does not agree with the person of the verb. So, too, chap. xvi. 25 of the same book, we find, "As if one had inquired at the oracle of God," the margin adding "someone" to stand as a nominative to the verb. But the correction is not apparently warranted, for it is a common practice, well known to grammarians in the Hebrew language, to use the third person singular of the active verb impersonally.

The second argument advanced by the Pharisees is easily answered from what has just been said, namely, that the scribes besides the various readings called attention to obsolete words. For there is no doubt that in Hebrew as in other languages, changes of use made many words obsolete and antiquated, and such were found by the later scribes in the sacred books and noted by them with a view to the books being publicly read according to custom. For this reason the word *nahgar* is always found marked because its gender was originally common, and it had the same meaning as the Latin *juvenis* (a young person). So also the Hebrew capital was anciently called Jerusalem, not Jerusalaim. As to the pronouns himself and herself, I think that the later scribes changed *vau* into *jod* (a very frequent change in Hebrew) when they wished to express the feminine gender, but that the ancients only distinguished the two genders by a change of vowels. I may also remark that the irregular tenses of certain verbs differ in the ancient and modern forms, it being formerly considered a mark of elegance to employ certain letters agreeable to the ear.

In a word, I could easily multiply proofs of this kind if I were not afraid of abusing the patience of the reader. Perhaps I shall be asked how I became acquainted with the fact that all these expressions are obsolete. I reply that I have found them in the most ancient Hebrew writers in the Bible itself, and that they have not been imitated by subsequent authors, and thus they are recognized as antiquated, though the language in which they occur is dead. But perhaps someone may press the question why, if it be true, as I say, that the marginal notes of the Bible generally mark various readings, there are never more than two readings of a passage, that in the text and that in the margin, instead of three or more; and further, how the scribes can have hesitated between two readings, one of which is evidently contrary to grammar, and the other a plain correction.

The answer to these questions also is easy: I will premise that it is almost certain that there once were more various readings than those now recorded. For instance, one finds many in the Talmud which the Massoretes have neglected, and are so different one from the other that even the superstitious editor of the Bomberg Bible confesses that he cannot harmonize them. "We cannot say anything," he writes, "except what we have said above, namely, that the Talmud is generally in contradiction to the Massoretes." So that we are not bound to hold that there never were more than two readings of any passage, yet I am willing to admit, and indeed I believe that more than two readings are never found: and for the following reasons:—(I.) The cause of the differences of reading only admits of two, being generally the similarity of certain letters, so that the question resolved itself into which should be written Beth, or Kaf, Jod or Vau, Daleth or Reth: cases which are constantly occurring, and frequently yielding a fairly good meaning whichever alternative be adopted. Sometimes, too, it is a question whether a syllable be long or short, quantity being determined by the letters called mutes. Moreover, we never asserted that all the marginal versions, without exception, marked various readings; on the contrary, we have stated that many were due to motives of decency or a desire to explain obsolete words. (II.) I am inclined to attribute the fact that more than two readings are never found to the paucity of exemplars, perhaps not more than two or three, found by the scribes. In the treatise of the scribes, chap. vi., mention is made of three only, pretended to have been found in the time of Ezra, in order that the marginal versions might be attributed to him.

However that may be, if the scribes only had three codices we may easily imagine that in a given passage two of them would be in accord, for it would be extraordinary if each one of the three gave a different reading of the same text.

The dearth of copies after the time of Ezra will surprise no one who has read the 1st chapter of Maccabees, or Josephus's "Antiquities," Bk. 12, chap. 5. Nay, it appears wonderful considering the fierce and daily persecution, that even these few should have been preserved. This will, I think, be plain to even a cursory reader of the history of those times.

We have thus discovered the reasons why there are never more than two readings of a passage in the Bible, but this is a long way from supposing that we may therefore conclude that the Bible was purposely written incorrectly in such passages in order to signify some mystery. As to the second argument, that some passages are so faultily written that they are at plain variance with all grammar, and should have been corrected in the text and not in the margin, I attach little weight to it, for I am not concerned to say what religious motive the scribes may have had for acting as they did: possibly they did so from candour, wishing to transmit the few exemplars of the Bible which they had found exactly in their original state, marking the differences they discovered in the margin, not as doubtful readings, but as simple variants. I have myself called them doubtful readings, because it would be generally impossible to say which of the two versions is preferable.

Lastly, besides these doubtful readings the scribes have (by leaving a hiatus in the middle of a paragraph) marked several passages as mutilated. The Massoretes have counted up such instances, and they amount to eight-and-twenty. I do not know whether any mystery is thought to lurk in the number, at any rate the Pharisees religiously preserve a certain amount of empty space.

One of such hiatus occurs (to give an instance) in Gen. iv. 8, where it is written, "And Cain said to his brother . . . . and it came to pass while they were in the field, &c.," a space being left in which we should expect to hear what it was that Cain said.

Similarly there are (besides those points we have noticed) eight-and-twenty hiatus left by the scribes. Many of these would not be recognized as mutilated if it were not for the empty space left. But I have said enough on this subject.

CHAPTER X.

AN EXAMINATION OF THE REMAINING BOOKS OF THE OLD TESTAMENT ACCORDING TO THE PRECEDING METHOD.

I NOW pass on to the remaining books of the Old Testament.   Concerning the two books of Chronicles I have nothing particular or important to remark, except that they were certainly written after the time of Ezra, and possibly after the restoration of the Temple by Judas Maccabæus.[1] For in chap. ix. of the first book we find a reckoning of the families who were the first to live in Jerusalem, and in verse 17 the names of the porters, of which two recur in Nehemiah.   This shows that the books were certainly compiled after the rebuilding of the city.   As to their actual writer, their authority, utility, and doctrine, I come to no conclusion.   I have always been astonished that they have been included in the Bible by men who shut out from the canon the books of Wisdom, Tobit, and the others styled apocryphal.   I do not aim at disparaging their authority, but as they are universally received I will leave them as they are.

The Psalms were collected and divided into five books in the time of the second temple, for Ps. lxxxviii. was published, according to Philo-Judæus, while king Jehoiachin was still a prisoner in Babylon; and Ps. lxxxix. when the same king obtained his liberty : I do not think Philo would have made the statement unless either it had been the received opinion in his time, or else had been told him by trustworthy persons.

The Proverbs of Solomon were, I believe, collected at the same time, or at least in the time of King Josiah; for in chap. xxv. 1, it is written, " These are also proverbs of Solomon which the men of Hezekiah, king of Judah, copied out." I cannot here pass over in silence the audacity of the Rabbis who wished to exclude from the sacred canon both

[1] See Note 19.

the Proverbs and Ecclesiastes, and to put them both in the Apocrypha. In fact, they would actually have done so, if they had not lighted on certain passages in which the law of Moses is extolled. It is, indeed, grievous to think that the settling of the sacred canon lay in the hands of such men; however, I congratulate them, in this instance, on their suffering us to see these books in question, though I cannot refrain from doubting whether they have transmitted them in absolute good faith; but I will not now linger on this point.

I pass on, then, to the prophetic books. An examination of these assures me that the prophecies therein contained have been compiled from other books, and are not always set down in the exact order in which they were spoken or written by the prophets, but are only such as were collected here and there, so that they are but fragmentary.

Isaiah began to prophecy in the reign of Uzziah, as the writer himself testifies in the first verse. He not only prophesied at that time, but furthermore wrote the history of that king (see 2 Chron. xxvi. 22) in a volume now lost. That which we possess, we have shown to have been taken from the chronicles of the kings of Judah and Israel.

We may add that the Rabbis assert that this prophet prophesied in the reign of Manasseh, by whom he was eventually put to death, and, although this seems to be a myth, it yet shows that they did not think that all Isaiah's prophecies are extant.

The prophecies of Jeremiah, which are related historically are also taken from various chronicles; for not only are they heaped together confusedly, without any account being taken of dates, but also the same story is told in them differently in different passages. For instance, in chap. xxi. we are told that the cause of Jeremiah's arrest was that he had prophesied the destruction of the city to Zedekiah who consulted him. This narrative suddenly passes, in chap xxii., to the prophet's remonstrances to Jehoiakim (Zedekiah's predecessor), and the prediction he made of that king's captivity; then, in chap. xxv., come the revelations granted to the prophet previously, that is in the fourth year of Jehoiakim, and, further on still, the revelations received in the first year of the same reign. The continuator of Jeremiah goes on heaping prophecy upon prophecy without any regard to dates, until at last, in chap. xxxviii. (as if the intervening chapters had been a parenthesis), he takes up the thread dropped in chap. xxi.

In fact, the conjunction with which chap. xxxviii. begins, refers to the 8th, 9th, and 10th verses of chap. xxi. Jeremiah's last arrest is then very differently described, and a totally separate cause is given for his daily retention in the court of the prison.

We may thus clearly see that these portions of the book have been compiled from various sources, and are only from this point of view comprehensible. The prophecies contained in the remaining chapters, where Jeremiah speaks in the first person, seem to be taken from a book written by Baruch, at Jeremiah's dictation. These, however, only comprise (as appears from chap. xxxvi. 2) the prophecies revealed to the prophet from the time of Josiah to the fourth year of Jehoiakim, at which period the book begins. The contents of chap. xlv. 2, on to chap. li. 59, seem taken from the same volume.

That the book of Ezekiel is only a fragment, is clearly indicated by the first verse. For anyone may see that the conjunction with which it begins, refers to something already said, and connects what follows therewith. However, not only this conjunction, but the whole text of the discourse implies other writings. The fact of the present work beginning in the thirtieth year shows that the prophet is continuing, not commencing a discourse; and this is confirmed by the writer, who parenthetically states in verse 3, "The word of the Lord came often unto Ezekiel the priest, the son of Buzi, in the land of the Chaldeans," as if to say that the prophecies which he is about to relate are the sequel to revelations formerly received by Ezekiel from God. Furthermore, Josephus, "Antiq." x. 9, says that Ezekiel prophesied that Zedekiah should not see Babylon, whereas the book we now have not only contains no such statement, but contrariwise asserts in chap. xvii. that he should be taken to Babylon as a captive.[1]

Of Hosea I cannot positively state that he wrote more than is now extant in the book bearing his name, but I am

[1] See Note 20.

astonished at the smallness of the quantity we possess, for the sacred writer asserts that the prophet prophesied for more than eighty years.

We may assert, speaking generally, that the compiler of the prophetic books neither collected all the prophets, nor all the writings of those we have; for of the prophets who are said to have prophesied in the reign of Manasseh and of whom general mention is made in 2 Chron. xxxiii. 10, 18, we have, evidently, no prophecies extant; neither have we all the prophecies of the twelve who give their names to books. Of Jonah we have only the prophecy concerning the Ninevites, though he also prophesied to the children of Israel, as we learn in 2 Kings xiv. 25.

The book and the personality of Job have caused much controversy. Some think that the book is the work of Moses, and the whole narrative merely allegorical. Such is the opinion of the Rabbins recorded in the Talmud, and they are supported by Maimonides in his "More Nebuchim." Others believe it to be a true history, and some suppose that Job lived in the time of Jacob, and was married to his daughter Dinah. Aben Ezra, however, as I have already stated, affirms, in his commentaries, that the work is a translation into Hebrew from some other language: I could wish that he could advance more cogent arguments than he does, for we might then conclude that the Gentiles also had sacred books. I myself leave the matter undecided, but I conjecture Job to have been a Gentile, and a man of very stable character, who at first prospered, then was assailed with terrible calamities, and finally was restored to great happiness. (He is thus named, among others, by Ezekiel, xiv. 12.) I take it that the constancy of his mind amid the vicissitudes of his fortune occasioned many men to dispute about God's providence, or at least caused the writer of the book in question to compose his dialogues; for the contents, and also the style, seem to emanate far less from a man wretchedly ill and lying among ashes, than from one reflecting at ease in his study. I should also be inclined to agree with Aben Ezra that the book is a translation, for its poetry seems akin to that of the Gentiles; thus the Father of Gods summons a council, and Momus, here called Satan, criticizes the Divine decrees with the utmost freedom.

But these are mere conjectures without any solid foundation.

I pass on to the book of Daniel, which, from chap. viii. onwards, undoubtedly contains the writing of Daniel himself. Whence the first seven chapters are derived I cannot say; we may, however, conjecture that, as they were first written in Chaldean, they are taken from Chaldean chronicles. If this could be proved, it would form a very striking proof of the fact that the sacredness of Scripture depends on our understanding of the doctrines therein signified, and not on the words, the language, and the phrases in which these doctrines are conveyed to us; and it would further show us that books which teach and speak of whatever is highest and best are equally sacred, whatever be the tongue in which they are written, or the nation to which they belong.

We can, however, in this case only remark that the chapters in question were written in Chaldee, and yet are as sacred as the rest of the Bible.

The first book of Ezra is so intimately connected with the book of Daniel that both are plainly recognizable as the work of the same author, writing of Jewish history from the time of the first captivity onwards. I have no hesitation in joining to this the book of Esther, for the conjunction with which it begins can refer to nothing else. It cannot be the same work as that written by Mordecai, for, in chap. ix. 20-22, another person relates that Mordecai wrote letters, and tells us their contents; further, that Queen Esther confirmed the days of Purim in their times appointed, and that the decree was written in the book— that is (by a Hebraism), in a book known to all then living, which, as Aben Ezra and the rest confess, has now perished. Lastly, for the rest of the acts of Mordecai, the historian refers us to the chronicles of the kings of Persia. Thus there is no doubt that this book was written by the same person as he who recounted the history of Daniel and Ezra, and who wrote Nehemiah,[1] sometimes called the second book of Ezra. We may, then, affirm that all these books are from one hand; but we have no clue whatever to the personality of the author. However, in order to determine whence he, whoever he was, had gained a knowledge of

[1] See Note 21.

the histories which he had, perchance, in great measure himself written, we may remark that the governors or chiefs of the Jews, after the restoration of the Temple, kept scribes or historiographers, who wrote annals or chronicles of them. The chronicles of the kings are often quoted in the books of Kings, but the chronicles of the chiefs and priests are quoted for the first time in Nehemiah xii. 23, and again in 1 Macc. xvi. 24. This is undoubtedly the book referred to as containing the decree of Esther and the acts of Mordecai; and which, as we said with Aben Ezra, is now lost. From it were taken the whole contents of these four books, for no other authority is quoted by their writer, or is known to us.

That these books were not written by either Ezra or Nehemiah is plain from Nehemiah xii. 9, where the descendants of the high priest, Joshua are traced down to Jaddua, the sixth high priest, who went to meet Alexander the Great, when the Persian empire was almost subdued (Josephus, "Ant." ii. 108), or who, according to Philo-Judæus, was the sixth and last high priest under the Persians. In the same chapter of Nehemiah, verse 22, this point is clearly brought out: "The Levites in the days of Eliashib, Joiada, and Johanan, and Jaddua, were recorded chief of the fathers: also the priests, to the reign of Darius the Persian"—that is to say, in the chronicles; and, I suppose, no one thinks[1] that the lives of Nehemiah and Ezra were so prolonged that they outlived fourteen kings of Persia. Cyrus was the first who granted the Jews permission to rebuild their Temple: the period between his time and Darius, fourteenth and last king of Persia, extends over 230 years. I have, therefore, no doubt that these books were written after Judas Maccabæus had restored the worship in the Temple, for at that time false books of Daniel, Ezra, and Esther were published by evil-disposed persons, who were almost certainly Sadducees, for the writings were never recognized by the Pharisees, so far as I am aware; and, although certain myths in the fourth book of Ezra are repeated in the Talmud, they must not be set down to the Pharisees, for all but the most ignorant admit that they have been added by some trifler: in fact, I think, someone must have made such addi-

[1] See Note 22.

tions with a view to casting ridicule on all the traditions of the sect.

Perhaps these four books were written out and published at the time I have mentioned with a view to showing the people that the prophecies of Daniel had been fulfilled, and thus kindling their piety, and awakening a hope of future deliverance in the midst of their misfortunes. In spite of their recent origin, the books before us contain many errors, due, I suppose, to the haste with which they were written. Marginal readings, such as I have mentioned in the last chapter, are found here as elsewhere, and in even greater abundance; there are, moreover, certain passages which can only be accounted for by supposing some such cause as hurry.

However, before calling attention to the marginal readings, I will remark that, if the Pharisees are right in supposing them to have been ancient, and the work of the original scribes, we must perforce admit that these scribes (if there were more than one) set them down because they found that the text from which they were copying was inaccurate, and did yet not venture to alter what was written by their predecessors and superiors. I need not again go into the subject at length, and will, therefore, proceed to mention some discrepancies not noticed in the margin.

I. Some error has crept into the text of the second chapter of Ezra, for in verse 64 we are told that the total of all those mentioned in the rest of the chapter amounts to 42,360; but, when we come to add up the several items we get as result only 29,818. There must, therefore, be an error, either in the total, or in the details. The total is probably correct, for it would most likely be well known to all as a noteworthy thing; but with the details, the case would be different. If, then, any error had crept into the total, it would at once have been remarked, and easily corrected. This view is confirmed by Nehemiah vii., where this chapter of Ezra is mentioned, and a total is given in plain correspondence thereto; but the details are altogether different—some are larger, and some less, than those in Ezra, and altogether they amount to 31,089. We may, therefore, conclude that both in Ezra and in Nehemiah the details are erroneously given. The commentators who attempt to harmonize these evident contradictions draw on their imagination, each to the best of his ability ; and while professing adoration for each letter and word of Scripture, only succeed in holding up the sacred writers to ridicule, as though they knew not how to write or relate a plain narrative. Such persons effect nothing but to render the clearness of Scripture obscure. If the Bible could everywhere be interpreted after their fashion, there would be no such thing as a rational statement of which the meaning could be relied on. However, there is no need to dwell on the subject; only I am convinced that if any historian were to attempt to imitate the proceedings freely attributed to the writers of the Bible, the commentators would cover him with contempt. If it be blasphemy to assert that there are any errors in Scripture, what name shall we apply to those who foist into it their own fancies, who degrade the sacred writers till they seem to write confused nonsense, and who deny the plainest and most evident meanings? What in the whole Bible can be plainer than the fact that Ezra and his companions, in the second chapter of the book attributed to him, have given in detail the reckoning of all the Hebrews who set out with them for Jerusalem? This is proved by the reckoning being given, not only of those who told their lineage, but also of those who were unable to do so. Is it not equally clear from Nehemiah vii. 5, that the writer merely there copies the list given in Ezra? Those, therefore, who explain these passages otherwise, deny the plain meaning of Scripture—nay, they deny Scripture itself. They think it pious to reconcile one passage of Scripture with another—a pretty piety, forsooth, which accommodates the clear passages to the obscure, the correct to the faulty, the sound to the corrupt.

Far be it from me to call such commentators blasphemers, if their motives be pure: for to err is human. But I return to my subject.

Besides these errors in numerical details, there are others in the genealogies, in the history, and, I fear also in the prophecies. The prophecy of Jeremiah (chap. xxii.), concerning Jechoniah, evidently does not agree with his history as given in 1 Chronicles iii. 17-19, and especially with the last words of the chapter, nor do I see how the prophecy, "thou shalt die in peace," can be applied to Zedekiah, whose eyes were dug out after his sons had been slain before him. If prophecies are to be interpreted by their issue, we must make a change of name, and read Jechoniah for Zedekiah, and *vice versâ*. This, however, would be too paradoxical a proceeding; so I prefer to leave the matter unexplained, especially as the error, if error there be, must be set down to the historian, and not to any fault in the authorities.

Other difficulties I will not touch upon, as I should only weary the reader, and, moreover, be repeating the remarks of other writers. For R. Selomo, in face of the manifest contradiction in the above-mentioned genealogies, is compelled to break forth into these words (see his commentary on 1 Chron. viii.): "Ezra (whom he supposes to be the author of the book of Chronicles) gives different names and a different genealogy to the sons of Benjamin from those which we find in Genesis, and describes most of the Levites differently from Joshua, because he found original discrepancies." And, again, a little later: "The genealogy of Gibeon and others is described twice in different ways, from different tables of each genealogy, and in writing them down Ezra adopted the version given in the majority of the texts, and when the authority was equal he gave both." Thus granting that these books were compiled from sources originally incorrect and uncertain.

In fact the commentators, in seeking to harmonize difficulties, generally do no more than indicate their causes: for I suppose no sane person supposes that the sacred historians deliberately wrote with the object of appearing to contradict themselves freely.

Perhaps I shall be told that I am overthrowing the authority of Scripture, for that, according to me, anyone may suspect it of error in any passage; but, on the contrary, I have shown that my object has been to prevent the clear and uncorrupted passages being accommodated to and corrupted by the faulty ones; neither does the fact that some passages are corrupt warrant us in suspecting all. No book ever was completely free from faults, yet I would ask, who suspects all books to be everywhere faulty?

Surely no one, especially when the phraseology is clear and the intention of the author plain.

I have now finished the task I set myself with respect to the books of the Old Testament. We may easily conclude from what has been said, that before the time of the Maccabees there was no canon of sacred books,[1] but that those which we now possess were selected from a multitude of others at the period of the restoration of the Temple by the Pharisees (who also instituted the set form of prayers), who are alone responsible for their acceptance. Those, therefore, who would demonstrate the authority of Holy Scripture, are bound to show the authority of each separate book; it is not enough to prove the Divine origin of a single book in order to infer the Divine origin of the rest. In that case we should have to assume that the council of Pharisees was, in its choice of books, infallible, and this could never be proved. I am led to assert that the Pharisees alone selected the books of the Old Testament, and inserted them in the canon, from the fact that in Daniel ii. is proclaimed the doctrine of the Resurrection, which the Sadducees denied; and, furthermore, the Pharisees plainly assert in the Talmud that they so selected them. For in the treatise of Sabbathus, chapter ii., folio 30, page 2, it is written: "R. Jehuda, surnamed Rabbi, reports that the experts wished to conceal the book of Ecclesiastes because they found therein words opposed to the law (that is, to the book of the law of Moses). Why did they not hide it? Because it begins in accordance with the law, and ends according to the law;" and a little further on we read: "They sought also to conceal the book of Proverbs." And in the first chapter of the same treatise, fol. 13, page 2: "Verily, name one man for good, even he who was called Neghunja, the son of Hezekiah: for, save for him, the book of Ezekiel would been concealed, because it agreed not with the words of the law."

It is thus abundantly clear that men expert in the law summoned a council to decide which books should be received into the canon, and which excluded. If any man, therefore, wishes to be certified as to the authority of all the books, let him call a fresh council, and ask every member his reasons.

[1] See Note 23.

The time has now come for examining in the same manner the books in the New Testament; but as I learn that the task has been already performed by men highly skilled in science and languages, and as I do not myself possess a knowledge of Greek sufficiently exact for the task; lastly, as we have lost the originals of those books which were written in Hebrew, I prefer to decline the undertaking. However, I will touch on those points which have most bearing on my subject in the following chapter.

CHAPTER XI.

AN INQUIRY WHETHER THE APOSTLES WROTE THEIR EPIS-
TLES AS APOSTLES AND PROPHETS, OR MERELY AS
TEACHERS; AND AN EXPLANATION OF WHAT IS MEANT
BY AN APOSTLE.

NO reader of the New Testament can doubt that the
Apostles were prophets; but as a prophet does not
always speak by revelation, but only at rare intervals, as
we showed at the end of Chap. I., we may fairly inquire
whether the Apostles wrote their Epistles as prophets, by
revelation and express mandate, as Moses, Jeremiah, and
others did, or whether only as private individuals or
teachers, especially as Paul, in Corinthians xiv. 6, mentions
two sorts of preaching.

If we examine the style of the Epistles, we shall find it
totally different from that employed by the prophets.

The prophets are continually asserting that they speak
by the command of God: "Thus saith the Lord," "The
Lord of hosts saith," "The command of the Lord," &c.;
and this was their habit not only in assemblies of the prophets, but also in their epistles containing revelations, as
appears from the epistle of Elijah to Jehoram, 2 Chron. xxi.
12, which begins, "Thus saith the Lord."

In the Apostolic Epistles we find nothing of the sort.
Contrariwise, in 1 Cor. vii. 40 Paul speaks according to his
own opinion and in many passages we come across doubtful and perplexed phrases, such as, "We think, therefore,"
Rom. iii. 28; "Now I think,"[1] Rom. viii. 18, and so on.
Besides these, other expressions are met with very different
from those used by the prophets. For instance, 1 Cor.
vii. 6, "But I speak this by permission, not by commandment;" I give my judgment as one that hath obtained mercy
of the Lord to be faithful" (1 Cor. vii. 25), and so on in
many other passages. We must also remark that in the

[1] See Note 24.

aforesaid chapter the Apostle says that when he states that
he has or has not the precept or commandment of God, he
does not mean the precept or commandment of God revealed to himself, but only the words uttered by Christ in
His Sermon on the Mount.   Furthermore, if we examine
the manner in which the Apostles give out evangelical doctrine, we shall see that it differs materially from the
method adopted by the prophets. The Apostles everywhere
reason as if they were arguing rather than prophesying;
the prophecies, on the other hand, contain only dogmas and
commands.   God is therein introduced not as speaking to
reason, but as issuing decrees by His absolute fiat.   The
authority of the prophets does not submit to discussion,
for whosoever wishes to find rational ground for his arguments, by that very wish submits them to everyone's private
judgment. This Paul, inasmuch as he uses reason, appears
to have done, for he says in 1 Cor. x. 15, "I speak as to
wise men, judge ye what I say."   The prophets, as we
showed at the end of Chapter I., did not perceive what was
revealed by virtue of their natural reason, and though there
are certain passages in the Pentateuch which seem to be
appeals to induction, they turn out, on nearer examination,
to be nothing but peremptory commands.   For instance,
when Moses says, Deut. xxxi. 27, "Behold, while I am yet
alive with you, this day ye have been rebellious against the
Lord ; and how much more after my death," we must by
no means conclude that Moses wished to convince the
Israelites by reason that they would necessarily fall away
from the worship of the Lord after his death ; for the argument would have been false, as Scripture itself shows : the
Israelities continued faithful during the lives of Joshua and
the elders, and afterwards during the time of Samuel,
David, and Solomon.   Therefore the words of Moses are
merely a moral injunction, in which he predicts rhetorically
the future backsliding of the people so as to impress it
vividly on their imaginations.   I say that Moses spoke of
himself in order to lend likelihood to his prediction, and
not as a prophet by revelation, because in verse 21 of the
same chapter we are told that God revealed the same thing
to Moses in different words, and there was no need to make
Moses certain by argument of God's prediction and decree ;

it was only necessary that it should be vividly impressed on his imagination, and this could not be better accomplished than by imagining the existing contumacy of the people, of which he had had frequent experience, as likely to extend into the future.

All the arguments employed by Moses in the five books are to be understood in a similar manner; they are not drawn from the armoury of reason, but are merely modes of expression calculated to instil with efficacy, and present vividly to the imagination the commands of God.

However, I do not wish absolutely to deny that the prophets ever argued from revelation; I only maintain that the prophets made more legitimate use of argument in proportion as their knowledge approached more nearly to ordinary knowledge, and by this we know that they possessed a knowledge above the ordinary, inasmuch as they proclaimed absolute dogmas, decrees, or judgments. Thus Moses, the chief of the prophets, never used legitimate argument, and, on the other hand, the long deductions and arguments of Paul, such as we find in the Epistle to the Romans, are in nowise written from supernatural revelation.

The modes of expression and discourse adopted by the Apostles in the Epistles, show very clearly that the latter were not written by revelation and Divine command, but merely by the natural powers and judgment of the authors. They consist in brotherly admonitions and courteous expressions such as would never be employed in prophecy, as for instance, Paul's excuse in Romans xv. 15, "I have written the more boldly unto you in some sort, my brethren."

We may arrive at the same conclusion from observing that we never read that the Apostles were commanded to write, but only that they went everywhere preaching, and confirmed their words with signs. Their personal presence and signs were absolutely necessary for the conversion and establishment in religion of the Gentiles; as Paul himself expressly states in Rom. i. 11, "But I long to see you, that I may impart to you some spiritual gift, to the end that ye may be established."

It may be objected that we might prove in similar fashion that the Apostles did not preach as prophets, for they did not go to particular places, as the prophets did, by the

command of God. We read in the Old Testament that
Jonah went to Nineveh to preach, and at the same time that
he was expressly sent there, and told that he must preach.
So also it is related, at great length, of Moses that he went
to Egypt as the messenger of God, and was told at the
same time what he should say to the children of Israel and to
king Pharaoh, and what wonders he should work before them
to give credit to his words. Isaiah, Jeremiah, and Ezekiel
were expressly commanded to preach to the Israelites.

Lastly, the prophets only preached what we are assured
by Scripture they had received from God, whereas this is
hardly ever said of the Apostles in the New Testament,
when they went about to preach. On the contrary, we find
passages expressly implying that the Apostles chose the
places where they should preach on their own responsibility,
for there was a difference amounting to a quarrel between
Paul and Barnabas on the subject (Acts xv. 37, 38). Often
they wished to go to a place, but were prevented, as Paul
writes, Rom. i. 13, "Oftentimes I purposed to come to you,
but was let hitherto;" and in 1 Cor. xvi. 12, "As touching
our brother Apollos, I greatly desired him to come unto
you with the brethren, but his will was not at all to come
at this time: but he will come when he shall have convenient time."

From these expressions and differences of opinion among
the Apostles, and also from the fact that Scripture nowhere
testifies of them, as of the ancient prophets, that they went
by the command of God, one might conclude that they
preached as well as wrote in their capacity of teachers, and
not as prophets: but the question is easily solved if we
observe the difference between the mission of an Apostle
and that of an Old Testament prophet. The latter were not
called to preach and prophesy to all nations, but to certain
specified ones, and therefore an express and peculiar mandate was required for each of them; the Apostles, on the
other hand, were called to preach to all men absolutely,
and to turn all men to religion. Therefore, whithersoever
they went, they were fulfilling Christ's commandment;
there was no need to reveal to them beforehand what they
should preach, for they were the disciples of Christ to whom
their Master Himself said (Matt. x. 19, 20): "But, when

they deliver you up, take no thought how or what ye shall speak, for it shall be given you in that same hour what ye shall speak." We therefore conclude that the Apostles were only indebted to special revelation in what they orally preached and confirmed by signs (see the beginning of Chap. II.); that which they taught in speaking or writing without any confirmatory signs and wonders they taught from their natural knowledge. (See 1 Cor. xiv. 6.) We need not be deterred by the fact that all the Epistles begin by citing the imprimatur of the Apostleship, for the Apostles, as I will shortly show, were granted, not only the faculty of prophecy, but also the authority to teach. We may therefore admit that they wrote their Epistles as Apostles, and for this cause every one of them began by citing the Apostolic imprimatur, possibly with a view to gaining the attention of the reader by asserting that they were the persons who had made such mark among the faithful by their preaching, and had shown by many marvellous works that they were teaching true religion and the way of salvation. I observe that what is said in the Epistles with regard to the Apostolic vocation and the Holy Spirit of God which inspired them, has reference to their former preaching, except in those passages where the expressions of the Spirit of God and the Holy Spirit are used to signify a mind pure, upright, and devoted to God. For instance, in 1 Cor. vii. 40, Paul says: "But she is happier if she so abide, after my judgment, and I think also that I have the Spirit of God." By the Spirit of God the Apostle here refers to his mind, as we may see from the context: his meaning is as follows: "I account blessed a widow who does not wish to marry a second husband; such is my opinion, for I have settled to live unmarried, and I think that I am blessed." There are other similar passages which I need not now quote.

As we have seen that the Apostles wrote their Epistles solely by the light of natural reason, we must inquire how they were enabled to teach by natural knowledge matters outside its scope. However, if we bear in mind what we said in Chap. VII. of this treatise our difficulty will vanish: for although the contents of the Bible entirely surpass our understanding, we may safely discourse of them, provided

we assume nothing not told us in Scripture: by the same
method the Apostles, from what they saw and heard, and
from what was revealed to them, were enabled to form and
elicit many conclusions which they would have been able to
teach to men had it been permissible.

Further, although religion, as preached by the Apostles,
does not come within the sphere of reason, in so far as it
consists in the narration of the life of Christ, yet its essence,
which is chiefly moral, like the whole of Christ's doctrine, can readily be apprehended by the natural faculties
of all.

Lastly, the Apostles had no lack of supernatural illumi-
nation for the purpose of adapting the religion they had
attested by signs to the understanding of everyone so that
it might be readily received; nor for exhortations on the
subject: in fact, the object of the Epistles is to teach and
exhort men to lead that manner of life which each of the
Apostles judged best for confirming them in religion.
We may here repeat our former remark, that the Apostles
had received not only the faculty of preaching the history
of Christ as prophets, and confirming it with signs, but
also authority for teaching and exhorting according as each
thought best. Paul (2 Tim. i. 11), "Whereunto I am
appointed a preacher, and an apostle, and a teacher of
the Gentiles;" and again (1 Tim. ii. 7), "Whereunto I am
ordained a preacher and an apostle (I speak the truth in
Christ and lie not), a teacher of the Gentiles in faith and
verity." These passages, I say, show clearly the stamp
both of the apostleship and the teachership: the authority
for admonishing whomsoever and wheresoever he pleased
is asserted by Paul in the Epistle to Philemon, v. 8:
"Wherefore, though I might be much bold in Christ to
enjoin thee that which is convenient, yet," &c., where we
may remark that if Paul had received from God as a
prophet what he wished to enjoin Philemon, and had
been bound to speak in his prophetic capacity, he would
not have been able to change the command of God into
entreaties. We must therefore understand him to refer to
the permission to admonish which he had received as a
teacher, and not as a prophet. We have not yet made it
quite clear that the Apostles might each choose his own

way of teaching, but only that by virtue of their Apostleship they were teachers as well as prophets; however, if we
call reason to our aid we shall clearly see that an authority
to teach implies authority to choose the method.   It will
nevertheless be, perhaps, more satisfactory to draw all our
proofs from Scripture; we are there plainly told that each
Apostle chose his particular method (Rom. xv. 20): " Yea,
so have I strived to preach the gospel, not where Christ was
named, lest I should build upon another man's foundation."
If all the Apostles had adopted the same method of teaching,
and had all built up the Christian religion on the same foundation, Paul would have had no reason to call the work of a
fellow-Apostle "another man's foundation," inasmuch as
it would have been identical with his own: his calling it
another man's proved that each Apostle built up his religious instruction on different foundations, thus resem-
bling other teachers who have each their own method, and
prefer instructing quite ignorant people who have never
learnt under another master, whether the subject be science,
languages, or even the indisputable truths of mathematics.
Furthermore, if we go through the Epistles at all attentively, we shall see that the Apostles, while agreeing about
religion itself, are at variance as to the foundations it rests
on.   Paul, in order to strengthen men's religion, and show
them that salvation depends solely on the grace of God,
teaches that no one can boast of works, but only of faith,
and that no one can be justified by works (Rom. iii. 27, 28);
in fact, he preaches the complete doctrine of predestination.
James, on the other hand, states that man is justified by
works, and not by faith only (see his Epistle, ii. 24), and
omitting all the disputations of Paul, confines religion to a
very few elements.

Lastly, it is indisputable that from these different
grounds for religion selected by the Apostles, many quarrels
and schisms distracted the Church, even in the earliest
times, and doubtless they will continue so to distract it
for ever, or at least till religion is separated from philosophical speculations, and reduced to the few simple doctrines taught by Christ to His disciples; such a task was
impossible for the Apostles, because the Gospel was then
unknown to mankind, and lest its novelty should offend

men's ears it had to be adapted to the disposition of contemporaries (2 Cor. ix. 19, 20), and built up on the groundwork most familiar and accepted at the time.

Thus none of the Apostles philosophized more than did Paul, who was called to preach to the Gentiles; other Apostles preaching to the Jews, who despised philosophy, similarly adapted themselves to the temper of their hearers (see Gal. ii. 11), and preached a religion free from all philosophical speculations. How blest would our age be if it could witness a religion freed also from all the trammels of superstition!

CHAPTER XII.

OF THE TRUE ORIGINAL OF THE DIVINE LAW, AND WHERE-
FORE SCRIPTURE IS CALLED SACRED, AND THE WORD OF
GOD.   HOW THAT, IN SO FAR AS IT CONTAINS THE WORD
OF GOD, IT HAS COME DOWN TO US UNCORRUPTED.

THOSE who look upon the Bible as a message sent
down by God from Heaven to men, will doubtless cry
out that I have committed the sin against the Holy Ghost
because I have asserted that the Word of God is faulty,
mutilated, tampered with, and inconsistent; that we possess it only in fragments, and that the original of the
covenant which God made with the Jews has been lost.
However, I have no doubt that a little reflection will
cause them to desist from their uproar: for not only
reason but the expressed opinions of prophets and apostles
openly proclaim that God's eternal Word and covenant,
no less than true religion, is Divinely inscribed in human
hearts, that is, in the human mind, and that this is the
true original of God's covenant, stamped with His own
seal, namely, the idea of Himself, as it were, with the
image of His Godhood.

Religion was imparted to the early Hebrews as a law
written down, because they were at that time in the condition of children, but afterwards Moses (Deut. xxx. 6) and
Jeremiah (xxxi. 33) predicted a time coming when the
Lord should write His law in their hearts.   Thus only the
Jews, and amongst them chiefly the Sadducees, struggled
for the law written on tablets; least of all need those who
bear it inscribed on their hearts join in the contest. Those,
therefore, who reflect, will find nothing in what I have
written repugnant either to the Word of God or to true
religion and faith, or calculated to weaken either one or the
other: contrariwise, they will see that I have strengthened
religion, as I showed at the end of Chapter X.; indeed,

had it not been so, I should certainly have decided to hold
my peace, nay, I would even have asserted as a way out of
all difficulties that the Bible contains the most profound
hidden mysteries; however, as this doctrine has given rise
to gross superstition and other pernicious results spoken
of at the beginning of Chapter V., I have thought such a
course unnecessary, especially as religion stands in no
need of superstitious adornments, but is, on the contrary,
deprived by such trappings of some of her splendour.

Still, it will be said, though the law of God is written
in the heart, the Bible is none the less the Word of God,
and it is no more lawful to say of Scripture than of God's
Word that it is mutilated and corrupted. I fear that such
objectors are too anxious to be pious, and that they are
in danger of turning religion into superstition, and worshipping paper and ink in place of God's Word.

I am certified of thus much: I have said nothing unworthy of Scripture or God's Word, and I have made no
assertions which I could not prove by most plain argument to be true. I can, therefore, rest assured that I
have advanced nothing which is impious or even savours
of impiety.

I confess that some profane men, to whom religion is a
burden, may, from what I have said, assume a licence to
sin, and without any reason, at the simple dictates of their
lusts conclude that Scripture is everywhere faulty and
falsified, and that therefore its authority is null; but such
men are beyond the reach of help, for nothing, as the proverb has it, can be said so rightly that it cannot be twisted
into wrong. Those who wish to give rein to their lusts are
at no loss for an excuse, nor were those men of old who
possessed the original Scriptures, the ark of the covenant,
nay, the prophets and apostles in person among them, any
better than the people of to-day. Human nature, Jew as
well as Gentile, has always been the same, and in every
age virtue has been exceedingly rare.

Nevertheless, to remove every scruple, I will here show
in what sense the Bible or any inanimate thing should be
called sacred and Divine; also wherein the law of God consists, and how it cannot be contained in a certain number
of books; and, lastly, I will show that Scripture, in so far

as it teaches what is necessary for obedience and salvation, cannot have been corrupted. From these considerations everyone will be able to judge that I have neither said anything against the Word of God nor given any foothold to impiety.

A thing is called sacred and Divine when it is designed for promoting piety, and continues sacred so long as it is religiously used: if the users cease to be pious, the thing ceases to be sacred: if it be turned to base uses, that which was formerly sacred becomes unclean and profane. For instance, a certain spot was named by the patriarch Jacob the house of God, because he worshipped God there revealed to him: by the prophets the same spot was called the house of iniquity (see Amos v. 5, and Hosea x. 5), because the Israelites were wont, at the instigation of Jeroboam, to sacrifice there to idols. Another example puts the matter in the plainest light. Words gain their meaning solely from their usage, and if they are arranged according to their accepted signification so as to move those who read them to devotion, they will become sacred, and the book so written will be sacred also. But if their usage afterwards dies out so that the words have no meaning, or the book becomes utterly neglected, whether from unworthy motives, or because it is no longer needed, then the words and the book will lose both their use and their sanctity: lastly, if these same words be otherwise arranged, or if their customary meaning becomes perverted into its opposite, then both the words and the book containing them become, instead of sacred, impure and profane.

From this it follows that nothing is in itself absolutely sacred, or profane, and unclean, apart from the mind, but only relatively thereto. Thus much is clear from many passages in the Bible. Jeremiah (to select one case out of many) says (chap. vii. 4), that the Jews of his time were wrong in calling Solomon's Temple, the Temple of God, for, as he goes on to say in the same chapter, God's name would only be given to the Temple so long as it was frequented by men who worshipped Him, and defended justice, but that, if it became the resort of murderers, thieves, idolaters, and other wicked persons, it would be turned into a den of malefactors.

Scripture, curiously enough, nowhere tells us what became of the Ark of the Covenant, though there is no doubt that it was destroyed, or burnt together with the Temple; yet there was nothing which the Hebrews considered more sacred, or held in greater reverence.   Thus Scripture is sacred, and its words Divine so long as it stirs mankind to devotion towards God: but if it be utterly neglected, as it formerly was by the Jews, it becomes nothing but paper and ink, and is left to be desecrated or corrupted: still, though Scripture be thus corrupted or destroyed, we must not say that the Word of God has suffered in like manner, else we shall be like the Jews, who said that the Temple which would then be the Temple of God had perished in the flames.   Jeremiah tells us this in respect to the law, for he thus chides the ungodly of his time, "Wherefore say you we are masters, and the law of the Lord is with us? Surely it has been given in vain, it is in vain that the pen of the scribes" (has been made)—that is, you say falsely that the Scripture is in your power, and that you possess the law of God; for ye have made it of none effect.

So also, when Moses broke the first tables of the law, he did not by any means cast the Word of God from his hands in anger and shatter it—such an action would be inconceivable, either of Moses or of God's Word—he only broke the tables of stone, which, though they had before been holy from containing the covenant wherewith the Jews had bound themselves in obedience to God, had entirely lost their sanctity when the covenant had been violated by the worship of the calf, and were, therefore, as liable to perish as the ark of the covenant.   It is thus scarcely to be wondered at, that the original documents of Moses are no longer extant, nor that the books we possess met with the fate we have described, when we consider that the true original of the Divine covenant, the most sacred object of all, has totally perished.

Let them cease, therefore, who accuse us of impiety, inasmuch as we have said nothing against the Word of God, neither have we corrupted it, but let them keep their anger, if they would wreak it justly, for the ancients whose malice desecrated the Ark, the Temple, and the Law of God, and all that was held sacred, subjecting them to corruption.   Fur-

thermore, if, according to the saying of the Apostle in
2 Cor. iii. 3, they possessed "the Epistle of Christ, written
not with ink, but with the Spirit of the living God, not in
tables of stone, but in the fleshy tables of the heart," let
them cease to worship the letter, and be so anxious concerning it.

I think I have now sufficiently shown in what respect
Scripture should be accounted sacred and Divine; we may
now see what should rightly be understood by the expression, the Word of the Lord; *debar* (the Hebrew original)
signifies word, speech, command, and thing. The causes
for which a thing is in Hebrew said to be of God, or is
referred to Him, have been already detailed in Chap. I.,
and we can therefrom easily gather what meaning Scripture
attaches to the phrases, the word, the speech, the command,
or the thing of God. I need not, therefore, repeat what I
there said, nor what was shown under the third head in
the chapter on miracles. It is enough to mention the
repetition for the better understanding of what I am about
to say—viz., that the Word of the Lord when it has reference
to anyone but God Himself, signifies that Divine law
treated of in Chap. IV.; in other words, religion, universal
and catholic to the whole human race, as Isaiah describes
it (chap. i. 10), teaching that the true way of life consists,
not in ceremonies, but in charity, and a true heart, and
calling it indifferently God's Law and God's Word.

The expression is also used metaphorically for the order
of nature and destiny (which, indeed, actually depend and
follow from the eternal mandate of the Divine nature), and
especially for such parts of such order as were foreseen by
the prophets, for the prophets did not perceive future events
as the result of natural causes, but as the fiats and decrees
of God. Lastly, it is employed for the command of any
prophet, in so far as he had perceived it by his peculiar
faculty or prophetic gift, and not by the natural light of
reason; this use springs chiefly from the usual prophetic
conception of God as a legislator, which we remarked in
Chap. IV. There are, then, three causes for the Bible's
being called the Word of God: because it teaches true religion, of which God is the eternal Founder; because it narrates predictions of future events as though they were

decrees of God; because its actual authors generally perceived things not by their ordinary natural faculties, but by a power peculiar to themselves, and introduced these things perceived, as told them by God.

Although Scripture contains much that is merely historical and can be perceived by natural reason, yet its name is acquired from its chief subject matter.

We can thus easily see how God can be said to be the Author of the Bible : it is because of the true religion therein contained, and not because He wished to communicate to men a certain number of books. We can also learn from hence the reason for the division into Old and New Testament. It was made because the prophets who preached religion before Christ, preached it as a national law in virtue of the covenant entered into under Moses; while the Apostles who came after Christ, preached it to all men as a universal religion solely in virtue of Christ's Passion : the cause for the division is not that the two parts are different in doctrine, nor that they were written as originals of the covenant, nor, lastly, that the catholic religion (which is in entire harmony with our nature) was new except in relation to those who had not known it : "it was in the world," as John the Evangelist says, "and the world knew it not."

Thus, even if we had fewer books of the Old and New Testament than we have, we should still not be deprived of the Word of God (which, as we have said, is identical with true religion), even as we do not now hold ourselves to be deprived of it, though we lack many cardinal writings such as the Book of the Law, which was religiously guarded in the Temple as the original of the Covenant, also the Book of Wars, the Book of Chronicles, and many others, from whence the extant Old Testament was taken and compiled. The above conclusion may be supported by many reasons.

I. Because the books of both Testaments were not written by express command at one place for all ages, but are a fortuitous collection of the works of men, writing each as his period and disposition dictated. So much is clearly shown by the call of the prophets who were bade to admonish the ungodly of their time, and also by the Apostolic Epistles.

II. Because it is one thing to understand the meaning of

Scripture and the prophets, and quite another thing to understand the meaning of God, or the actual truth. This follows from what we said in Chap. II. We showed, in Chap. VI., that it applied to historic narratives, and to miracles: but it by no means applies to questions concerning true religion and virtue.

III. Because the books of the Old Testament were selected from many, and were collected and sanctioned by a council of the Pharisees, as we showed in Chap. X. The books of the New Testament were also chosen from many by councils which rejected as spurious other books held sacred by many. But these councils, both Pharisee and Christian, were not composed of prophets, but only of learned men and teachers. Still, we must grant that they were guided in their choice by a regard for the Word of God; and they must, therefore, have known what the law of God was.

IV. Because the Apostles wrote not as prophets, but as teachers (see last Chapter), and chose whatever method they thought best adapted for those whom they addressed: and consequently, there are many things in the Epistles (as we showed at the end of the last Chapter) which are not necessary to salvation.

V. Lastly, because there are four Evangelists in the New Testament, and it is scarcely credible that God can have designed to narrate the life of Christ four times over, and to communicate it thus to mankind. For though there are some details related in one Gospel which are not in another, and one often helps us to understand another, we cannot thence conclude that all that is set down is of vital importance to us, and that God chose the four Evangelists in order that the life of Christ might be better understood; for each one preached his Gospel in a separate locality, each wrote it down as he preached it, in simple language, in order that the history of Christ might be clearly told, not with any view of explaining his fellow-Evangelists.

If there are some passages which can be better, and more easily understood by comparing the various versions, they are the result of chance, and are not numerous: their continuance in obscurity would have impaired neither the clearness of the narrative nor the blessedness of mankind.

We have now shown that Scripture can only be called

the Word of God in so far as it affects religion, or the Divine
law ; we must now point out that, in respect to these questions, it is neither faulty, tampered with, nor corrupt.   By
faulty, tampered with, and corrupt, I here mean written so
incorrectly that the meaning cannot be arrived at by a study
of the language, nor from the authority of Scripture.   I
will not go to such lengths as to say that the Bible, in so far
as it contains the Divine law, has always preserved the
same vowel-points, the same letters, or the same words (I
leave this to be proved by the Massoretes and other wor-
shippers of the letter), I only maintain that the meaning
by which alone an utterance is entitled to be called Divine,
has come down to us uncorrupted, even though the original
wording may have been more often changed than we suppose.   Such alterations, as I have said above, detract
nothing from the Divinity of the Bible, for the Bible would
have been no less Divine had it been written in different
words or a different language.   That the Divine law has
in this sense come down to us uncorrupted, is an assertion
which admits of no dispute.   For from the Bible itself we
learn, without the smallest difficulty or ambiguity, that
its cardinal precept is : To love God above all things, and
one's neighbour as one's self.   This cannot be a spurious
passage, nor due to a hasty and mistaken scribe, for if
the Bible had ever put forth a different doctrine it would
have had to change the whole of its teaching, for this is
the corner-stone of religion, without which the whole fabric
would fall headlong to the ground.   The Bible would not
be the work we have been examining, but something quite
different.

We remain, then, unshaken in our belief that this has
always been the doctrine of Scripture, and, consequently,
that no error sufficient to vitiate it can have crept in without being instantly observed by all ; nor can anyone have
succeeded in tampering with it and escaped the discovery
of his malice.

As this corner-stone is intact, we must perforce admit the
same of whatever other passages are indisputably dependent on it, and are also fundamental, as, for instance, that
a God exists, that He foresees all things, that He is Almighty, that by His decree the good prosper and the wicked

come to naught, and, finally, that our salvation depends
solely on His grace.

These are doctrines which Scripture plainly teaches
throughout, and which it is bound to teach, else all the
rest would be empty and baseless; nor can we be less positive about other moral doctrines, which plainly are built
upon this universal foundation—for instance, to uphold
justice, to aid the weak, to do no murder, to covet no man's
goods, &c. Precepts, I repeat, such as these, human
malice and the lapse of ages are alike powerless to destroy,
for if any part of them perished, its loss would immediately be supplied from the fundamental principle, especially the doctrine of charity, which is everywhere in both
Testaments extolled above all others. Moreover, though it
be true that there is no conceivable crime so heinous that
it has never been committed, still there is no one who
would attempt in excuse for his crimes to destroy the law,
or introduce an impious doctrine in the place of what is
eternal and salutary; men's nature is so constituted that
everyone (be he king or subject) who has committed a base
action, tries to deck out his conduct with spurious excuses,
till he seems to have done nothing but what is just and
right.

We may conclude, therefore, that the whole Divine law,
as taught by Scripture, has come down to us uncorrupted.
Besides this there are certain facts which we may be sure
have been transmitted in good faith. For instance, the
main facts of Hebrew history, which were perfectly well
known to everyone. The Jewish people were accustomed
in former times to chant the ancient history of their nation
in psalms. The main facts, also, of Christ's life and passion were immediately spread abroad through the whole
Roman empire. It is therefore scarcely credible, unless
nearly everybody consented thereto, which we cannot suppose, that successive generations have handed down the
broad outline of the Gospel narrative otherwise than as
they received it.

Whatsoever, therefore, is spurious or faulty can only
have reference to details—some circumstances in one or
the other history or prophecy designed to stir the people
to greater devotion; or in some miracle, with a view of

confounding philosophers; or, lastly, in speculative matters after they had become mixed up with religion, so that some individual might prop up his own inventions with a pretext of Divine authority.   But such matters have little to do with salvation, whether they be corrupted little or much, as I will show in detail in the next chapter, though I think the question sufficiently plain from what I have said already, especially in Chapter II.

CHAPTER XIII.

IT IS SHOWN THAT SCRIPTURE TEACHES ONLY VERY SIMPLE DOCTRINES, SUCH AS SUFFICE FOR RIGHT CONDUCT.

IN the second chapter of this treatise we pointed out that the prophets were gifted with extraordinary powers of imagination, but not of understanding; also that God only revealed to them such things as are very simple—not philosophic mysteries,—and that He adapted His communications to their previous opinions. We further showed in Chap. V. that Scripture only transmits and teaches truths which can readily be comprehended by all; not deducing and concatenating its conclusions from definitions and axioms, but narrating quite simply, and confirming its statements, with a view to inspiring belief, by an appeal to experience as exemplified in miracles and history, and setting forth its truths in the style and phraseology which would most appeal to the popular mind (cf. Chap. VI., third division).

Lastly, we demonstrated in Chap. VII. that the difficulty of understanding Scripture lies in the language only, and not in the abstruseness of the argument.

To these considerations we may add that the Prophets did not preach only to the learned, but to all Jews, without exception, while the Apostles were wont to teach the gospel doctrine in churches where there were public meetings; whence it follows that Scriptural doctrine contains no lofty speculations nor philosophic reasoning, but only very simple matters, such as could be understood by the slowest intelligence.

I am consequently lost in wonder at the ingenuity of those whom I have already mentioned, who detect in the Bible mysteries so profound that they cannot be explained in human language, and who have introduced so many philosophic speculations into religion that the Church seems like an academy, and religion like a science, or rather a dispute.

It is not to be wondered at that men, who boast of possessing supernatural intelligence, should be unwilling to yield the palm of knowledge to philosophers who have only their ordinary faculties; still I should be surprised if I found them teaching any new speculative doctrine, which was not a commonplace to those Gentile philosophers whom, in spite of all, they stigmatize as blind; for, if one inquires what these mysteries lurking in Scripture may be, one is confronted with nothing but the reflections of Plato or Aristotle, or the like, which it would often be easier for an ignorant man to dream than for the most accomplished scholar to wrest out of the Bible.

However, I do not wish to affirm absolutely that Scripture contains no doctrines in the sphere of philosophy, for in the last chapter I pointed out some of the kind, as fundamental principles; but I go so far as to say that such doctrines are very few and very simple. Their precise nature and definition I will now set forth. The task will be easy, for we know that Scripture does not aim at imparting scientific knowledge, and, therefore, it demands from men nothing but obedience, and censures obstinacy, but not ignorance.

Furthermore, as obedience to God consists solely in love to our neighbour—for whosoever loveth his neighbour, as a means of obeying God, hath, as St. Paul says (Rom. xiii. 8), fulfilled the law,—it follows that no knowledge is commended in the Bible save that which is necessary for enabling all men to obey God in the manner stated, and without which they would become rebellious, or without the discipline of obedience.

Other speculative questions, which have no direct bearing on this object, or are concerned with the knowledge of natural events, do not affect Scripture, and should be entirely separated from religion.

Now, though everyone, as we have said, is now quite able to see this truth for himself, I should nevertheless wish, considering that the whole of Religion depends thereon, to explain the entire question more accurately and clearly. To this end I must first prove that the intellectual or accurate knowledge of God is not a gift, bestowed upon all good men like obedience; and, further, that the knowledge of God, required by Him through His prophets from everyone without exception, as needful to be known, is simply a knowledge of His Divine justice and charity. Both these points are easily proved from Scripture. The first plainly follows from Exodus vi. 2, where God, in order to show the singular grace bestowed upon Moses, says to him: "And I appeared unto Abraham, unto Isaac, and unto Jacob by the name of El Sadai (A. V. God Almighty); but by my name Jehovah was I not known to them"—for the better understanding of which passage I may remark that *El Sadai*, in Hebrew, signifies the God who suffices, in that He gives to every man that which suffices for him; and, although *Sadai* is often used by itself, to signify God, we cannot doubt that the word *El* (God) is everywhere understood. Furthermore, we must note that Jehovah is the only word found in Scripture with the meaning of the absolute essence of God, without reference to created things. The Jews maintain, for this reason, that this is, strictly speaking, the only name of God; that the rest of the words used are merely titles; and, in truth, the other names of God, whether they be substantives or adjectives, are merely attributive, and belong to Him, in so far as He is conceived of in relation to created things, or manifested through them. Thus *El*, or *Eloah*, signifies powerful, as is well known, and only applies to God in respect to His supremacy, as when we call Paul an apostle; the faculties of his power are set forth in an accompanying adjective, as *El*, great, awful, just, merciful, &c., or else all are understood at once by the use of *El* in the plural number, with a singular signification, an expression frequently adopted in Scripture.

Now, as God tells Moses that He was not known to the patriarchs by the name of Jehovah, it follows that they were not cognizant of any attribute of God which expresses His absolute essence, but only of His deeds and promises—that is, of His power, as manifested in visible things. God does not thus speak to Moses in order to accuse the patriarchs of infidelity, but, on the contrary, as a means of extolling their belief and faith, inasmuch as, though they possessed no extraordinary knowledge of God (such as Moses had), they yet accepted His promises as fixed and certain; whereas Moses, though his thoughts about God were more exalted, nevertheless doubted about the Divine promises, and complained to God that, instead of the promised deliverance, the prospects of the Israelites had darkened.

As the patriarchs did not know the distinctive name of God, and as God mentions the fact to Moses, in praise of their faith and single-heartedness, and in contrast to the extraordinary grace granted to Moses, it follows, as we stated at first, that men are not bound by decree to have knowledge of the attributes of God, such knowledge being only granted to a few of the faithful: it is hardly worth while to quote further examples from Scripture, for everyone must recognize that knowledge of God is not equal among all good men.   Moreover, a man cannot be ordered to be wise any more than he can be ordered to live and exist.   Men, women, and children are all alike able to obey by commandment, but not to be wise.   If any tell us that it is not necessary to understand the Divine attributes, but that we must believe them simply without proof, he is plainly trifling.   For what is invisible and can only be perceived by the mind, cannot be apprehended by any other means than proofs; if these are absent the object remains ungrasped; the repetition of what has been heard on such subjects no more indicates or attains to their meaning than the words of a parrot or a puppet speaking without sense or signification.

Before I proceed I ought to explain how it comes that we are often told in Genesis that the patriarchs preached in the name of Jehovah, this being in plain contradiction to the text above quoted.   A reference to what was said in Chap. VIII. will readily explain the difficulty.   It was there shown that the writer of the Pentateuch did not always speak of things and places by the names they bore in the times of which he was writing, but by the names best known to his contemporaries.   God is thus said in the Pentateuch to have been preached by the patriarchs under the name of Jehovah, not because such was the name by which the patriarchs knew Him, but because this name was the one most reverenced by the Jews.   This point, I say, must necessarily be noticed, for in Exodus it is expressly stated that God was not known to the patriarchs by this name; and in chap. iii. 13, it is said that Moses desired to know the name of God.   Now, if this name had been already known it would have been known to Moses.   We must therefore draw the conclusion indicated, namely, that the faithful patriarchs did not know this name of God, and that the knowledge of God is bestowed and not commanded by the Deity.

It is now time to pass on to our second point, and show that God through His prophets required from men no other knowledge of Himself than is contained in a knowledge of His justice and charity—that is, of attributes which a certain manner of life will enable men to imitate.   Jeremiah states this in so many words (xxii. 15, 16): "Did not thy father eat, and drink, and do judgment and justice? and then it was well with him.   He judged the cause of the poor and needy; then it was well with him: was not this to know Me? saith the Lord."   The words in chap. ix. 24 of the same book are equally clear.   "But let him that glorieth glory in this, that he understandeth and knoweth Me, that I am the Lord which exercise loving-kindness, judgment, and righteousness in the earth; for in these things I delight, saith the Lord."   The same doctrine may be gathered from Exod. xxxiv. 6, where God revealed to Moses only those of His attributes which display the Divine justice and charity.   Lastly, we may call attention to a passage in John which we shall discuss at more length hereafter; the Apostle explains the nature of God (inasmuch as no one has beheld Him) through charity only, and concludes that he who possesses charity possesses, and in very truth knows God.

We have thus seen that Moses, Jeremiah, and John sum up in a very short compass the knowledge of God needful for all, and that they state it to consist in exactly what we said, namely, that God is supremely just, and supremely merciful—in other words, the one perfect pattern of the true life.   We may add that Scripture nowhere gives an express definition of God, and does not point out any other of His attributes which should be apprehended save these, nor does it in set terms praise any others.   Wherefore we may draw the general conclusion that an intellectual knowledge of God, which takes cognizance of His nature in so far as it actually is, and which cannot by any manner of living be imitated by mankind or followed as an example, has no bearing whatever on true rules of conduct, on faith, or on revealed religion; consequently that men may be in complete error on the subject without incurring the charge of sinfulness.   We need now no longer wonder that God adapted Himself to the existing opinions and imaginations of the prophets, or that the faithful held different ideas of God, as we showed in Chap. II.; or, again, that the sacred books speak very inaccurately of God, attributing to Him hands, feet, eyes, ears, a mind, and motion from one place to another; or that they ascribe to Him emotions, such as jealousy, mercy, &c., or, lastly, that they describe Him as a Judge in heaven sitting on a royal throne with Christ on His right hand.   Such expressions are adapted to the understanding of the multitude, it being the object of the Bible to make men not learned but obedient.

In spite of this the general run of theologians, when they come upon any of these phrases which they cannot rationally harmonize with the Divine nature, maintain that they should be interpreted metaphorically, passages they cannot understand they say should be interpreted literally. But if every expression of this kind in the Bible is necessarily to be interpreted and understood metaphorically, Scripture must have been written, not for the people and the unlearned masses, but chiefly for accomplished experts and philosophers.

If it were indeed a sin to hold piously and simply the ideas about God we have just quoted, the prophets ought to have been strictly on their guard against the use of such expressions, seeing the weak-mindedness of the people, and ought, on the other hand, to have set forth first of all, duly and clearly, those attributes of God which are needful to be understood.

This they have nowhere done; we cannot, therefore, think that opinions taken in themselves without respect to actions are either pious or impious, but must maintain that a man is pious or impious in his beliefs only in so far as he is thereby incited to obedience, or derives from them license to sin and rebel. If a man, by believing what is true, becomes rebellious, his creed is impious; if by believing what is false he becomes obedient, his creed is pious; for the true knowledge of God comes not by commandment, but by Divine gift. God has required nothing from man but a knowledge of His Divine justice and charity, and that not as necessary to scientific accuracy, but to obedience.

CHAPTER XIV.

DEFINITIONS OF FAITH, THE FAITH, AND THE FOUNDATIONS
OF FAITH, WHICH IS ONCE FOR ALL SEPARATED FROM
PHILOSOPHY.

FOR a true knowledge of faith it is above all things
necessary to understand that the Bible was adapted
to the intelligence, not only of the prophets, but also of
the diverse and fickle Jewish multitude.   This will be
recognized by all who give any thought to the subject, for
they will see that a person who accepted promiscuously
everything in Scripture as being the universal and absolute teaching of God, without accurately defining what
was adapted to the popular intelligence, would find it
impossible to escape confounding the opinions of the masses
with the Divine doctrines, praising the judgments and
comments of man as the teaching of God, and making a
wrong use of Scriptural authority.   Who, I say, does not
perceive that this is the chief reason why so many sectaries
teach contradictory opinions as Divine documents, and
support their contentions with numerous Scriptural texts,
till it has passed in Belgium into a proverb, *geen ketter
sonder letter*—no heretic without a text? The sacred books
were not written by one man, nor for the people of a single
period, but by many authors of different temperaments, at
times extending from first to last over nearly two thousand
years, and perhaps much longer. We will not, however,
accuse the sectaries of impiety because they have adapted
the words of Scripture to their own opinions; it is thus
that these words were adapted to the understanding of
the masses originally, and everyone is at liberty so to
treat them if he sees that he can thus obey God in matters
relating to justice and charity with a more full consent:
but we do accuse those who will not grant this freedom
to their fellows, but who persecute all who differ from

them, as God's enemies, however honourable and virtuous be their lives; while, on the other hand, they cherish those who agree with them, however foolish they may be, as God's elect.   Such conduct is as wicked and dangerous to the state as any that can be conceived.

In order, therefore, to establish the limits to which individual freedom should extend, and to decide what persons, in spite of the diversity of their opinions, are to be looked upon as the faithful, we must define faith and its essentials. This task I hope to accomplish in the present chapter, and also to separate faith from philosophy, which is the chief aim of the whole treatise.

In order to proceed duly to the demonstration let us recapitulate the chief aim and object of Scripture; this will indicate a standard by which we may define faith.

We have said in a former chapter that the aim and object of Scripture is only to teach obedience.   Thus much, I think, no one can question.   Who does not see that both Testaments are nothing else but schools for this object, and have neither of them any aim beyond inspiring mankind with a voluntary obedience?   For (not to repeat what I said in the last chapter) I will remark that Moses did not seek to convince the Jews by reason, but bound them by a covenant, by oaths, and by conferring benefits; further, he threatened the people with punishment if they should infringe the law, and promised rewards if they should obey it.   All these are not means for teaching knowledge, but for inspiring obedience.   The doctrine of the Gospels enjoins nothing but simple faith, namely, to believe in God and to honour Him, which is the same thing as to obey Him.   There is no occasion for me to throw further light on a question so plain by citing Scriptural texts commending obedience, such as may be found in great numbers in both Testaments.   Moreover, the Bible teaches very clearly in a great many passages what everyone ought to do in order to obey God; the whole duty is summed up in love to one's neighbour.   It cannot, therefore, be denied that he who by God's command loves his neighbour as himself is truly obedient and blessed according to the law, whereas he who hates his neighbour or neglects him is rebellious and obstinate.

Lastly, it is plain to everyone that the Bible was not written and disseminated only for the learned, but for men of every age and race; wherefore we may rest assured that we are not bound by Scriptural command to believe anything beyond what is absolutely necessary for fulfilling its main precept.

This precept, then, is the only standard of the whole Catholic faith, and by it alone all the dogmas needful to be believed should be determined. So much being abundantly manifest, as is also the fact that all other doctrines of the faith can be legitimately deduced therefrom by reason alone, I leave it to every man to decide for himself how it comes to pass that so many divisions have arisen in the Church: can it be from any other cause than those suggested at the beginning of Chap. VII.? It is these same causes which compel me to explain the method of determining the dogmas of the faith from the foundation we have discovered, for if I neglected to do so, and put the question on a regular basis, I might justly be said to have promised too lavishly, for that anyone might, by my showing, introduce any doctrine he liked into religion, under the pretext that it was a necessary means to obedience: especially would this be the case in questions respecting the Divine attributes.

In order, therefore, to set forth the whole matter methodically, I will begin with a definition of faith, which on the principle above given, should be as follows:—

Faith consists in a knowledge of God, without which obedience to Him would be impossible, and which the mere fact of obedience to Him implies. This definition is so clear, and follows so plainly from what we have already proved, that it needs no explanation. The consequences involved therein I will now briefly show. (I.) Faith is not salutary in itself, but only in respect to the obedience it implies, or as James puts it in his Epistle, ii. 17, "Faith without works is dead" (see the whole of the chapter quoted). (II.) He who is truly obedient necessarily possesses true and saving faith; for if obedience be granted, faith must be granted also, as the same Apostle expressly says in these words (ii. 18), "Show me thy faith without thy works, and I will show thee my faith by my works." So also John, 1 Ep. iv. 7: "Everyone that loveth is born of God, and

knoweth God: he that loveth not, knoweth not God; for
God is love." From these texts, I repeat, it follows that we
can only judge a man faithful or unfaithful by his works.
If his works be good, he is faithful, however much his doctrines may differ from those of the rest of the faithful: if
his works be evil, though he may verbally conform, he is
unfaithful. For obedience implies faith, and faith without
works is dead.

John, in the 13th verse of the chapter above quoted, expressly teaches the same doctrine: "Hereby," he says,
"know we that we dwell in Him and He in us, because He
hath given us of His Spirit," *i.e.* love. He had said before
that God is love, and therefore he concludes (on his own
received principles), that whoso possesses love possesses
truly the Spirit of God. As no one has beheld God he
infers that no one has knowledge or consciousness of God,
except from love towards his neighbour, and also that no
one can have knowledge of any of God's attributes, except
this of love, in so far as we participate therein.

If these arguments are not conclusive, they, at any rate,
show the Apostle's meaning, but the words in chap. ii. v.
3, 4, of the same Epistle are much clearer, for they state in
so many words our precise contention: "And hereby we
do know that we know Him, if we keep His commandments.
He that saith, I know Him, and keepeth not His commandments, is a liar, and the truth is not in him."

From all this, I repeat, it follows that they are the true
enemies of Christ who persecute honourable and justice-
loving men because they differ from them, and do not
uphold the same religious dogmas as themselves: for whosoever loves justice and charity we know, by that very fact,
to be faithful: whosoever persecutes the faithful, is an
enemy to Christ.

Lastly, it follows that faith does not demand that
dogmas should be true as that they should be pious—that
is, such as will stir up the heart to obey; though there be
many such which contain not a shadow of truth, so long as
they be held in good faith, otherwise their adherents are
disobedient, for how can anyone, desirous of loving justice
and obeying God, adore as Divine what he knows to be
alien from the Divine nature? However, men may err from

simplicity of mind, and Scripture, as we have seen, does not condemn ignorance, but obstinacy. This is the necessary result of our definition of faith, and all its branches should spring from the universal rule above given, and from the evident aim and object of the Bible, unless we choose to mix our own inventions therewith. Thus it is not true doctrines which are expressly required by the Bible, so much as doctrines necessary for obedience, and to confirm in our hearts the love of our neighbour, wherein (to adopt the words of John) we are in God, and God in us.

As, then, each man's faith must be judged pious or impious only in respect of its producing obedience or obstinacy, and not in respect of its truth; and as no one will dispute that men's dispositions are exceedingly varied, that all do not acquiesce in the same things, but are ruled some by one opinion some by another, so that what moves one to devotion moves another to laughter and contempt, it follows that there can be no doctrines in the Catholic, or universal, religion, which can give rise to controversy among good men. Such doctrines might be pious to some and impious to others, whereas they should be judged solely by their fruits.

To the universal religion, then, belong only such dogmas as are absolutely required in order to attain obedience to God, and without which such obedience would be impossible; as for the rest, each man—seeing that he is the best judge of his own character—should adopt whatever he thinks best adapted to strengthen his love of justice. If this were so, I think there would be no further occasion for controversies in the Church.

I have now no further fear in enumerating the dogmas of universal faith or the fundamental dogmas of the whole of Scripture, inasmuch as they all tend (as may be seen from what has been said) to this one doctrine, namely, that there exists a God, that is, a Supreme Being, Who loves justice and charity, and Who must be obeyed by whosoever would be saved; that the worship of this Being consists in the practice of justice and love towards one's neighbour, and that they contain nothing beyond the following doctrines :—

I. That God or a Supreme Being exists, sovereignly just and merciful, the Exemplar of the true life; that whosoever is ignorant of or disbelieves in His existence cannot obey Him or know Him as a Judge.

II. That He is One. Nobody will dispute that this doctrine is absolutely necessary for entire devotion, admiration, and love towards God. For devotion, admiration, and love spring from the superiority of one over all else.

III. That He is omnipresent, or that all things are open to Him, for if anything could be supposed to be concealed from Him, or to be unnoticed by Him, we might doubt or be ignorant of the equity of His judgment as directing all things.

IV. That He has supreme right and dominion over all things, and that He does nothing under compulsion, but by His absolute fiat and grace. All things are bound to obey Him, He is not bound to obey any.

V. That the worship of God consists only in justice and charity, or love towards one's neighbour.

VI. That all those, and those only, who obey God by their manner of life are saved; the rest of mankind, who live under the sway of their pleasures, are lost. If we did not believe this, there would be no reason for obeying God rather than pleasure.

VII. Lastly, that God forgives the sins of those who repent. No one is free from sin, so that without this belief all would despair of salvation, and there would be no reason for believing in the mercy of God. He who firmly believes that God, out of the mercy and grace with which He directs all things, forgives the sins of men, and who feels his love of God kindled thereby, he, I say, does really know Christ according to the Spirit, and Christ is in him.

No one can deny that all these doctrines are before all things necessary to be believed, in order that every man, without exception, may be able to obey God according to the bidding of the Law above explained, for if one of these precepts be disregarded obedience is destroyed. But as to what God, or the Exemplar of the true life, may be, whether fire, or spirit, or light, or thought, or what not, this, I say, has nothing to do with faith any more than has the question how He comes to be the Exemplar of the true life, whether it be because He has a just and merciful mind, or because all things exist and act through Him, and consequently that we understand through Him, and through Him see what is truly just and good. Everyone may think on such questions as he likes,

Furthermore, faith is not affected, whether we hold that God is omnipresent essentially or potentially; that He directs all things by absolute fiat, or by the necessity of His nature; that He dictates laws like a prince, or that He sets them forth as eternal truths; that man obeys Him by virtue of free will, or by virtue of the necessity of the Divine decree; lastly, that the reward of the good and the punishment of the wicked is natural or supernatural: these and such like questions have no bearing on faith, except in so far as they are used as means to give us license to sin more, or to obey God less. I will go further, and maintain that every man is bound to adapt these dogmas to his own way of thinking, and to interpret them according as he feels that he can give them his fullest and most unhesitating assent, so that he may the more easily obey God with his whole heart.

Such was the manner, as we have already pointed out, in which the faith was in old time revealed and written, in accordance with the understanding and opinions of the prophets and people of the period; so, in like fashion, every man is bound to adapt it to his own opinions, so that he may accept it without any hesitation or mental repugnance. We have shown that faith does not so much require truth as piety, and that it is only quickening and pious through obedience, consequently no one is faithful save by obedience alone. The best faith is not necessarily possessed by him who displays the best reasons, but by him who displays the best fruits of justice and charity. How salutary and necessary this doctrine is for a state, in order that men may dwell together in peace and concord; and how many and how great causes of disturbance and crime are thereby cut off, I leave everyone to judge for himself!

Before we go further, I may remark that we can, by means of what we have just proved, easily answer the objections raised in Chap. I., when we were discussing God's speaking with the Israelites on Mount Sinai. For, though the voice heard by the Israelites could not give those men any philosophical or mathematical certitude of God's existence, it was yet sufficient to thrill them with admiration for God, as they already knew Him, and to stir them up to obedience: and such was the object of the display. God did not wish to teach the Israelites the absolute attributes of His essence (none of which He then revealed), but to break down their hardness of heart, and to draw them to obedience: therefore He did not appeal to them with reasons, but with the sound of trumpets, thunder, and lightnings.

It remains for me to show that between faith or theology, and philosophy, there is no connection, nor affinity. I think no one will dispute the fact who has knowledge of the aim and foundations of the two subjects, for they are as wide apart as the poles.

Philosophy has no end in view save truth: faith, as we have abundantly proved, looks for nothing but obedience and piety. Again, philosophy is based on axioms which must be sought from nature alone: faith is based on history and language, and must be sought for only in Scripture and revelation, as we showed in Chap. VII. Faith, therefore, allows the greatest latitude in philosophic speculation, allowing us without blame to think what we like about anything, and only condemning, as heretics and schismatics, those who teach opinions which tend to produce obstinacy, hatred, strife, and anger; while, on the other hand, only considering as faithful those who persuade us, as far as their reason and faculties will permit, to follow justice and charity.

Lastly, as what we are now setting forth are the most important subjects of my treatise, I would most urgently beg the reader, before I proceed, to read these two chapters with especial attention, and to take the trouble to weigh them well in his mind: let him take for granted that I have not written with a view to introducing novelties, but in order to do away with abuses, such as I hope I may, at some future time, at last see reformed.

CHAPTER XV.

THEOLOGY IS SHOWN NOT TO BE SUBSERVIENT TO REASON,
NOR REASON TO THEOLOGY: A DEFINITION OF THE REASON
WHICH ENABLES US TO ACCEPT THE AUTHORITY OF THE
BIBLE.

THOSE who know not that philosophy and reason are distinct, dispute whether Scripture should be made subservient to reason, or reason to Scripture: that is, whether
the meaning of Scripture should be made to agreed with
reason; or whether reason should be made to agree with
Scripture: the latter position is assumed by the sceptics
who deny the certitude of reason, the former by the dog-
matists.   Both parties are, as I have shown, utterly in the
wrong, for either doctrine would require us to tamper with
reason or with Scripture.

We have shown that Scripture does not teach philosophy,
but merely obedience, and that all it contains has been
adapted to the understanding and established opinions of
the multitude.   Those, therefore, who wish to adapt it to
philosophy, must needs ascribe to the prophets many ideas
which they never even dreamed of, and give an extremely
forced interpretation to their words: those on the other
hand, who would make reason and philosophy subservient
to theology, will be forced to accept as Divine utterances
the prejudices of the ancient Jews, and to fill and confuse
their mind therewith.   In short, one party will run wild
with the aid of reason, and the other will run wild without
the aid of reason.

The first among the Pharisees who openly maintained
that Scripture should be made to agree with reason, was
Maimonides, whose opinion we reviewed, and abundantly
refuted in Chap. VII.: now, although this writer had much
authority among his contemporaries, he was deserted on
this question by almost all, and the majority went straight

over to the opinion of a certain R. Jehuda Alpakhar, who, in his anxiety to avoid the error of Maimonides, fell into another, which was its exact contrary. He held that reason should be made subservient, and entirely give way to Scripture. He thought that a passage should not be interpreted metaphorically, simply because it was repugnant to reason, but only in the cases when it is inconsistent with Scripture itself—that is, with its clear doctrines. Therefore he laid down the universal rule, that whatsoever Scripture teaches dogmatically, and affirms expressly, must on its own sole authority be admitted as absolutely true: that there is no doctrine in the Bible which directly contradicts the general tenour of the whole: but only some which appear to involve a difference, for the phrases of Scripture often seem to imply something contrary to what has been expressly taught. Such phrases, and such phrases only, we may interpret metaphorically.

For instance, Scripture clearly teaches the unity of God (see Deut. vi. 4), nor is there any text distinctly asserting a plurality of gods; but in several passages God speaks of Himself, and the prophets speak of Him, in the plural number; such phrases are simply a manner of speaking, and do not mean that there actually are several gods: they are to be explained metaphorically, not because a plurality of gods is repugnant to reason, but because Scripture distinctly asserts that there is only one.

So, again, as Scripture asserts (as Alpakhar thinks) in Deut. iv. 15, that God is incorporeal, we are bound, solely by the authority of this text, and not by reason, to believe that God has no body: consequently we must explain metaphorically, on the sole authority of Scripture, all those passages which attribute to God hands, feet, &c., and take them merely as figures of speech. Such is the opinion of Alpakhar. In so far as he seeks to explain Scripture by Scripture, I praise him, but I marvel that a man gifted with reason should wish to debase that faculty. It is true that Scripture should be explained by Scripture, so long as we are in difficulties about the meaning and intention of the prophets, but when we have elicited the true meaning, we must of necessity make use of our judgment and reason in order to assent thereto. If reason, however, much as she rebels, is to be entirely subjected to Scripture, I ask, are we to effect her submission by her own aid, or without her, and blindly? If the latter, we shall surely act foolishly and injudiciously; if the former, we assent to Scripture under the dominion of reason, and should not assent to it without her. Moreover, I may ask now, is a man to assent to anything against his reason? What is denial if it be not reason's refusal to assent? In short, I am astonished that anyone should wish to subject reason, the greatest of gifts and a light from on high, to the dead letter which may have been corrupted by human malice; that it should be thought no crime to speak with contempt of mind, the true handwriting of God's Word, calling it corrupt, blind, and lost, while it is considered the greatest of crimes to say the same of the letter, which is merely the reflection and image of God's Word. Men think it pious to trust nothing to reason and their own judgment, and impious to doubt the faith of those who have transmitted to us the sacred books. Such conduct is not piety, but mere folly. And, after all, why are they so anxious? What are they afraid of? Do they think that faith and religion cannot be upheld unless men purposely keep themselves in ignorance, and turn their backs on reason? If this be so, they have but a timid trust in Scripture.

However, be it far from me to say that religion should seek to enslave reason, or reason religion, or that both should not be able to keep their sovereignity in perfect harmony. I will revert to this question presently, for I wish now to discuss Alpakhar's rule.

He requires, as we have stated, that we should accept as true, or reject as false, everything asserted or denied by Scripture, and he further states that Scripture never expressly asserts or denies anything which contradicts its assertions or negations elsewhere. The rashness of such a requirement and statement can escape no one. For (passing over the fact that he does not notice that Scripture consists of different books, written at different times, for different people, by different authors: and also that his requirement is made on his own authority without any corroboration from reason or Scripture) he would be bound to show that all passages which are indirectly contradictory of the rest, can be satisfactorily explained metaphorically through the nature of the language and the context: further, that Scripture has come down to us untampered with. However, we will go into the matter at length.

Firstly, I ask what shall we do if reason prove recalcitrant? Shall we still be bound to affirm whatever Scripture affirms, and to deny whatever Scripture denies? Perhaps it will be answered that Scripture contains nothing repugnant to reason. But I insist that it expressly affirms and teaches that God is jealous (namely, in the decalogue itself, and in Exod. xxxiv. 14, and in Deut. iv. 24, and in many other places), and I assert that such a doctrine is repugnant to reason. It must, I suppose, in spite of all, be accepted as true. If there are any passages in Scripture which imply that God is not jealous, they must be taken metaphorically as meaning nothing of the kind. So, also, Scripture expressly states (Exod. xix. 20, &c.) that God came down to Mount Sinai, and it attributes to Him other movements from place to place, nowhere directly stating that God does not so move. Wherefore, we must take the passage literally, and Solomon's words (1 Kings viii. 27), "But will God dwell on the earth? Behold the heavens and earth cannot contain thee," inasmuch as they do not expressly state that God does not move from place to place, but only imply it, must be explained away till they have no further semblance of denying locomotion to the Deity. So also we must believe that the sky is the habitation and throne of God, for Scripture expressly says so; and similarly many passages expressing the opinions of the prophets or the multitude, which reason and philosophy, but not Scripture, tell us to be false, must be taken as true if we are to follow the guidance of our author, for according to him, reason has nothing to do with the matter. Further, it is untrue that Scripture never contradicts itself directly, but only by implication. For Moses says, in so many words (Deut. iv. 24), "The Lord thy God is a consuming fire," and elsewhere expressly denies that God has any likeness to visible things. (Deut. iv. 12.) If it be decided that the latter passage only contradicts the former by implication, and must be adapted thereto, lest it seem to negative it, let us grant that God is a fire; or rather, lest

we should seem to have taken leave of our senses, let us
pass the matter over and take another example.

Samuel expressly denies that God ever repents, "for he
is not a man that he should repent" (1 Sam. xv. 29).
Jeremiah, on the other hand, asserts that God does repent,
both of the evil and of the good which He had intended to
do (Jer. xviii. 8-10). What? Are not these two texts
directly contradictory? Which of the two, then, would
our author want to explain metaphorically? Both statements are general, and each is the opposite of the other—
what one flatly affirms, the other flatly denies. So, by his
own rule, he would be obliged at once to reject them as
false, and to accept them as true.

Again, what is the point of one passage, not being contradicted by another directly, but only by implication, if the
implication is clear, and the nature and context of the passage preclude metaphorical interpretation? There are many
such instances in the Bible, as we saw in Chap. II. (where
we pointed out that the prophets held different and contradictory opinions), and also in Chaps. IX. and X., where we
drew attention to the contradictions in the historical narratives. There is no need for me to go through them all
again, for what I have said sufficiently exposes the absurdities which would follow from an opinion and rule such as
we are discussing, and shows the hastiness of its pro-
pounder.

We may, therefore, put this theory, as well as that of
Maimonides, entirely out of court; and we may take it
for indisputable that theology is not bound to serve reason, nor reason theology, but that each has her own
domain.

The sphere of reason is, as we have said, truth and
wisdom; the sphere of theology is piety and obedience.
The power of reason does not extend so far as to determine
for us that men may be blessed through simple obedience,
without understanding. Theology tells us nothing else,
enjoins on us no command save obedience, and has neither
the will nor the power to oppose reason: she defines the
dogmas of faith (as we pointed out in the last chapter) only
in so far as they may be necessary for obedience, and leaves
reason to determine their precise truth: for reason is the

light of the mind, and without her all things are dreams and phantoms.

By theology, I here mean, strictly speaking, revelation, in so far as it indicates the object aimed at by Scripture—namely, the scheme and manner of obedience, or the true dogmas of piety and faith. This may truly be called the Word of God, which does not consist in a certain number of books (see Chap. XII.). Theology thus understood, if we regard its precepts or rules of life, will be found in accordance with reason; and, if we look to its aim and object, will be seen to be in nowise repugnant thereto, wherefore it is universal to all men.

As for its bearing on Scripture, we have shown in Chap. VII. that the meaning of Scripture should be gathered from its own history, and not from the history of nature in general, which is the basis of philosophy.

We ought not to be hindered if we find that our investigation of the meaning of Scripture thus conducted shows us that it is here and there repugnant to reason; for whatever we may find of this sort in the Bible, which men may be in ignorance of, without injury to their charity, has, we may be sure, no bearing on theology or the Word of God, and may, therefore, without blame, be viewed by every one as he pleases.

To sum up, we may draw the absolute conclusion that the Bible must not be accommodated to reason, nor reason to the Bible.

Now, inasmuch as the basis of theology—the doctrine that man may be saved by obedience alone—cannot be proved by reason whether it be true or false, we may be asked, Why, then, should we believe it? If we do so without the aid of reason, we accept it blindly, and act foolishly and injudiciously; if, on the other hand, we settle that it can be proved by reason, theology becomes a part of philosophy, and inseparable therefrom. But I make answer that I have absolutely established that this basis of theology cannot be investigated by the natural light of reason, or, at any rate, that no one ever has proved it by such means, and, therefore, revelation was necessary. We should, however, make use of our reason, in order to grasp with moral certainty what is revealed—I say, with moral certainty, for we cannot hope to attain greater certainty than the prophets: yet their certainty was only moral, as I showed in Chap. II.

Those, therefore, who attempt to set forth the authority of Scripture with mathematical demonstrations are wholly in error: for the authority of the Bible is dependent on the authority of the prophets, and can be supported by no stronger arguments than those employed in old time by the prophets for convincing the people of their own authority. Our certainty on the same subject can be founded on no other basis than that which served as foundation for the certainty of the prophets.

Now the certainty of the prophets consisted (as we pointed out) in these three elements :—(I.) A distinct and vivid imagination. (II.) A sign. (III.) Lastly, and chiefly, a mind turned to what is just and good. It was based on no other reasons than these, and consequently they cannot prove their authority by any other reasons, either to the multitude whom they addressed orally, nor to us whom they address in writing.

The first of these reasons, namely, the vivid imagination, could be valid only for the prophets; therefore, our certainty concerning revelation must, and ought to be, based on the remaining two—namely, the sign and the teaching. Such is the express doctrine of Moses, for (in Deut. xviii.) he bids the people obey the prophet who should give a true sign in the name of the Lord, but if he should predict falsely, even though it were in the name of the Lord, he should be put to death, as should also he who strives to lead away the people from the true religion, though he confirm his authority with signs and portents. We may compare with the above Deut. xiii. Whence it follows that a true prophet could be distinguished from a false one, both by his doctrine and by the miracles he wrought, for Moses declares such an one to be a true prophet, and bids the people trust him without fear of deceit. He condemns as false, and worthy of death, those who predict anything falsely even in the name of the Lord, or who preach false gods, even though their miracles be real.

The only reason, then, which we have for belief in Scripture or the writings of the prophets, is the doctrine we find therein, and the signs by which it is confirmed. For as we see that the prophets extol charity and justice above all things, and have no other object, we conclude that they did not write from unworthy motives, but because they really thought that men might become blessed through obedience and faith : further, as we see that they confirmed their teaching with signs and wonders, we become persuaded that they did not speak at random, nor run riot in their prophecies. We are further strengthened in our conclusion by the fact that the morality they teach is in evident agreement with reason, for it is no accidental coincidence that the Word of God which we find in the prophets coincides with the Word of God written in our hearts. We may, I say, conclude this from the sacred books as certainly as did the Jews of old from the living voice of the prophets : for we showed in Chap. XII. that Scripture has come down to us intact in respect to its doctrine and main narratives.

Therefore this whole basis of theology and Scripture, though it does not admit of mathematical proof, may yet be accepted with the approval of our judgment. It would be folly to refuse to accept what is confirmed by such ample prophetic testimony, and what has proved such a comfort to those whose reason is comparatively weak, and such a benefit to the state; a doctrine, moreover, which we may believe in without the slightest peril or hurt, and should reject simply because it cannot be mathematically proved : it is as though we should admit nothing as true, or as a wise rule of life, which could ever, in any possible way, be called in question; or as though most of our actions were not full of uncertainty and hazard.

I admit that those who believe that theology and philosophy are mutually contradictory, and that therefore either one or the other must be thrust from its throne—I admit, I say, that such persons are not unreasonable in attempting to put theology on a firm basis, and to demonstrate its truth mathematically. Who, unless he were desperate or mad, would wish to bid an incontinent farewell to reason, or to despise the arts and sciences, or to deny reason's certitude? But, in the meanwhile, we cannot wholly absolve them from blame, inasmuch as they invoke the aid of reason for her own defeat, and attempt infallibly to prove her fallible.

While they are trying to prove mathematically the authority and truth of theology, and to take away the authority of natural reason, they are in reality only bringing theology under reason's dominion, and proving that her authority has no weight unless natural reason be at the back of it.

If they boast that they themselves assent because of the inward testimony of the Holy Spirit, and that they only invoke the aid of reason because of unbelievers, in order to convince them, not even so can this meet with our approval, for we can easily show that they have spoken either from emotion or vain-glory. It most clearly follows from the last chapter that the Holy Spirit only gives its testimony in favour of works, called by Paul (in Gal. v. 22) the fruits of the Spirit, and is in itself really nothing but the mental acquiescence which follows a good action in our souls. No spirit gives testimony concerning the certitude of matters within the sphere of speculation, save only reason, who is mistress, as we have shown, of the whole realm of truth. If then they assert that they possess this Spirit which makes them certain of truth, they speak falsely, and according to the prejudices of the emotions, or else they are in great dread lest they should be vanquished by philosophers and exposed to public ridicule, and therefore they flee, as it were, to the altar; but their refuge is vain, for what altar will shelter a man who has outraged reason? However, I pass such persons over, for I think I have fulfilled my purpose, and shown how philosophy should be separated from theology, and wherein each consists; that neither should be subservient to the other, but that each should keep her unopposed dominion. Lastly, as occasion offered, I have pointed out the absurdities, the inconveniences, and the evils following from the extraordinary confusion which has hitherto prevailed between the two subjects, owing to their not being properly distinguished and separated. Before I go further I would expressly state (though I have said it before) that I consider the utility and the need for Holy Scripture or Revelation to be very great. For as we cannot perceive by the natural light of reason that simple obedience is the path of salvation,[1] and are taught by revelation only that it is so by the special grace of God, which our reason cannot attain, it follows that the Bible has

[1] See Note 25.

brought a very great consolation to mankind. All are able to obey, whereas there are but very few, compared with the aggregate of humanity, who can acquire the habit of virtue under the unaided guidance of reason. Thus if we had not the testimony of Scripture, we should doubt of the salvation of nearly all men.

CHAPTER XVI.

OF THE FOUNDATIONS OF A STATE; OF THE NATURAL AND
CIVIL RIGHTS OF INDIVIDUALS; AND OF THE RIGHTS OF
THE SOVEREIGN POWER.

HITHERTO our care has been to separate philosophy
from theology, and to show the freedom of thought
which such separation insures to both. It is now time to
determine the limits to which such freedom of thought and
discussion may extend itself in the ideal state. For the
due consideration of this question we must examine the
foundations of a state, first turning our attention to the
natural rights of individuals, and afterwards to religion
and the state as a whole.

By the right and ordinance of nature, I merely mean
those natural laws wherewith we conceive every individual
to be conditioned by nature, so as to live and act in a given
way. For instance, fishes are naturally conditioned for
swimming, and the greater for devouring the less; therefore fishes enjoy the water, and the greater devour the less
by sovereign natural right. For it is certain that nature,
taken in the abstract, has sovereign right to do anything
she can; in other words, her right is co-extensive with her
power. The power of nature is the power of God, which
has sovereign right over all things; and, inasmuch as the
power of nature is simply the aggregate of the powers of
all her individual components, it follows that every individual has sovereign right to do all that he can; in other
words, the rights of an individual extend to the utmost
limits of his power as it has been conditioned. Now it is
the sovereign law and right of nature that each individual
should endeavour to preserve itself as it is, without regard
to anything but itself; therefore this sovereign law and

right belongs to every individual, namely, to exist and act according to its natural conditions. We do not here acknowledge any difference between mankind and other individual natural entities, nor between men endowed with reason and those to whom reason is unknown; nor between fools, madmen, and sane men. Whatsoever an individual does by the laws of its nature it has a sovereign right to do, inasmuch as it acts as it was conditioned by nature, and cannot act otherwise. Wherefore among men, so long as they are considered as living under the sway of nature, he who does not yet know reason, or who has not yet acquired the habit of virtue, acts solely according to the laws of his desire with as sovereign a right as he who orders his life entirely by the laws of reason.

That is, as the wise man has sovereign right to do all that reason dictates, or to live according to the laws of reason, so also the ignorant and foolish man has sovereign right to do all that desire dictates, or to live according to the laws of desire. This is identical with the teaching of Paul, who acknowledges that previous to the law—that is, so long as men are considered of as living under the sway of nature, there is no sin.

The natural right of the individual man is thus determined, not by sound reason, but by desire and power. All are not naturally conditioned so as to act according to the laws and rules of reason; nay, on the contrary, all men are born ignorant, and before they can learn the right way of life and acquire the habit of virtue, the greater part of their life, even if they have been well brought up, has passed away. Nevertheless, they are in the meanwhile bound to live and preserve themselves as far as they can by the unaided impulses of desire. Nature has given them no other guide, and has denied them the present power of living according to sound reason; so that they are no more bound to live by the dictates of an enlightened mind, than a cat is bound to live by the laws of the nature of a lion.

Whatsoever, therefore, an individual (considered as under the sway of nature) thinks useful for himself, whether led by sound reason or impelled by the passions, that he has a sovereign right to seek and to take for himself as he best can, whether by force, cunning, entreaty, or any other means; consequently he may regard as an enemy anyone who hinders the accomplishment of his purpose.

It follows from what we have said that the right and ordinance of nature, under which all men are born, and under which they mostly live, only prohibits such things as no one desires, and no one can attain: it does not forbid strife, nor hatred, nor anger, nor deceit, nor, indeed, any of the means suggested by desire.

This we need not wonder at, for nature is not bounded by the laws of human reason, which aims only at man's true benefit and preservation; her limits are infinitely wider, and have reference to the eternal order of nature, wherein man is but a speck; it is by the necessity of this alone that all individuals are conditioned for living and acting in a particular way. If anything, therefore, in nature seems to us ridiculous, absurd, or evil, it is because we only know in part, and are almost entirely ignorant of the order and interdependence of nature as a whole, and also because we want everything to be arranged according to the dictates of our human reason; in reality that which reason considers evil, is not evil in respect to the order and laws of nature as a whole, but only in respect to the laws of our reason.

Nevertheless, no one can doubt that it is much better for us to live according to the laws and assured dictates of reason, for, as we said, they have men's true good for their object. Moreover, everyone wishes to live as far as possible securely beyond the reach of fear, and this would be quite impossible so long as everyone did everything he liked, and reason's claim was lowered to a par with those of hatred and anger; there is no one who is not ill at ease in the midst of enmity, hatred, anger, and deceit, and who does not seek to avoid them as much as he can. When we reflect that men without mutual help, or the aid of reason, must needs live most miserably, as we clearly proved in Chap. V., we shall plainly see that men must necessarily come to an agreement to live together as securely and well as possible if they are to enjoy as a whole the rights which naturally belong to them as individuals, and their life should be no more conditioned by the force and desire of individuals, but by the power and will of the whole body. This end they will be unable to attain if desire be their only guide (for by the laws of desire each man is drawn in a different direction) ; they must, therefore, most firmly decree and establish that they will be guided in everything by reason (which nobody will dare openly to repudiate lest he should be taken for a madman), and will restrain any desire which is injurious to a man's fellows, that they will do to all as they would be done by, and that they will defend their neighbour's rights as their own.

How such a compact as this should be entered into, how ratified and established, we will now inquire.

Now it is a universal law of human nature that no one ever neglects anything which he judges to be good, except with the hope of gaining a greater good, or from the fear of a greater evil; nor does anyone endure an evil except for the sake of avoiding a greater evil, or gaining a greater good. That is, everyone will, of two goods, choose that which he thinks the greatest; and, of two evils, that which he thinks the least. I say advisedly that which he thinks the greatest or the least, for it does not necessarily follow that he judges right. This law is so deeply implanted in the human mind that it ought to be counted among eternal truths and axioms.

As a necessary consequence of the principle just enunciated, no one can honestly promise to forego the right which he has over all things,[1] and in general no one will abide by his promises, unless under the fear of a greater evil, or the hope of a greater good. An example will make the matter clearer. Suppose that a robber forces me to promise that I will give him my goods at his will and pleasure. It is plain (inasmuch as my natural right is, as I have shown, co-extensive with my power) that if I can free myself from this robber by stratagem, by assenting to his demands, I have the natural right to do so, and to pretend to accept his conditions. Or again, suppose I have genuinely promised someone that for the space of twenty days I will not taste food or any nourishment; and suppose I afterwards find that my promise was foolish, and cannot be kept without very great injury to myself; as I am bound by natural law and right to choose the least of two evils, I

[1] See Note 26.

have complete right to break my compact, and act as if my promise had never been uttered. I say that I should have perfect natural right to do so, whether I was actuated by true and evident reason, or whether I was actuated by mere opinion in thinking I had promised rashly; whether my reasons were true or false, I should be in fear of a greater evil, which, by the ordinance of nature, I should strive to avoid by every means in my power.

We may, therefore, conclude that a compact is only made valid by its utility, without which it becomes null and void. It is, therefore, foolish to ask a man to keep his faith with us for ever, unless we also endeavour that the violation of the compact we enter into shall involve for the violator more harm than good. This consideration should have very great weight in forming a state. However, if all men could be easily led by reason alone, and could recognize what is best and most useful for a state, there would be no one who would not forswear deceit, for everyone would keep most religiously to their compact in their desire for the chief good, namely, the preservation of the state, and would cherish good faith above all things as the shield and buckler of the commonwealth. However, it is far from being the case that all men can always be easily led by reason alone; everyone is drawn away by his pleasure, while avarice, ambition, envy, hatred, and the like so engross the mind that reason has no place therein. Hence, though men make promises with all the appearances of good faith, and agree that they will keep to their engagement, no one can absolutely rely on another man's promise unless there is something behind it. Everyone has by nature a right to act deceitfully, and to break his compacts, unless he be restrained by the hope of some greater good, or the fear of some greater evil.

However, as we have shown that the natural right of the individual is only limited by his power, it is clear that by transferring, either willingly or under compulsion, this power into the hands of another, he in so doing necessarily cedes also a part of his right; and further, that the sovereign right over all men belongs to him who has sovereign power, wherewith he can compel men by force, or restrain them by threats of the universally feared punishment of death; such sovereign right he will retain only so long as he can maintain his power of enforcing his will; otherwise he will totter on his throne, and no one who is stronger than he will be bound unwillingly to obey him.

In this manner a society can be formed without any violation of natural right, and the covenant can always be strictly kept—that is, if each individual hands over the whole of his power to the body politic, the latter will then possess sovereign natural right over all things; that is, it will have sole and unquestioned dominion, and everyone will be bound to obey, under pain of the severest punishment. A body politic of this kind is called a Democracy, which may be defined as a society which wields all its power as a whole. The sovereign power is not restrained by any laws, but everyone is bound to obey it in all things; such is the state of things implied when men either tacitly or expressly handed over to it all their power of self-defence, or in other words, all their right. For if they had wished to retain any right for themselves, they ought to have taken precautions for its defence and preservation; as they have not done so, and indeed could not have done so without dividing and consequently ruining the state, they placed themselves absolutely at the mercy of the sovereign power; and, therefore, having acted (as we have shown) as reason and necessity demanded, they are obliged to fulfil the commands of the sovereign power, however absurd these may be, else they will be public enemies, and will act against reason, which urges the preservation of the state as a primary duty. For reason bids us choose the least of two evils.

Furthermore, this danger of submitting absolutely to the dominion and will of another, is one which may be incurred with a light heart: for we have shown that sovereigns only possess this right of imposing their will, so long as they have the full power to enforce it: if such power be lost their right to command is lost also, or lapses to those who have assumed it and can keep it. Thus it is very rare for sovereigns to impose thoroughly irrational commands, for they are bound to consult their own interests, and retain their power by consulting the public good and acting according to the dictates of reason, as Seneca says, " vio-

lenta imperia nemo continuit diu." No one can long
retain a tyrant's sway.

In a democracy, irrational commands are still less to be
feared: for it is almost impossible that the majority of a
people, especially if it be a large one, should agree in an
irrational design: and, moreover, the basis and aim of a
democracy is to avoid the desires as irrational, and to bring
men as far as possible under the control of reason, so that
they may live in peace and harmony: if this basis be
removed the whole fabric falls to ruin.

Such being the ends in view for the sovereign power, the
duty of subjects is, as I have said, to obey its commands,
and to recognize no right save that which it sanctions.

It will, perhaps, be thought that we are turning subjects
into slaves: for slaves obey commands and free men live
as they like; but this idea is based on a misconception, for
the true slave is he who is led away by his pleasures and
can neither see what is good for him nor act accordingly:
he alone is free who lives with free consent under the entire
guidance of reason.

Action in obedience to orders does take away freedom in
a certain sense, but it does not, therefore, make a man a
slave, all depends on the object of the action. If the
object of the action be the good of the state, and not the
good of the agent, the latter is a slave and does himself no
good: but in a state or kingdom where the weal of the
whole people, and not that of the ruler, is the supreme law,
obedience to the sovereign power does not make a man a
slave, of no use to himself, but a subject. Therefore,
that state is the freest whose laws are founded on sound
reason, so that every member of it may, if he will, be free;[1]
that is, live with full consent under the entire guidance of
reason.

Children, though they are bound to obey all the commands of their parents, are yet not slaves: for the commands of parents look generally to the children's benefit.

We must, therefore, acknowledge a great difference between a slave, a son, and a subject; their positions may be
thus defined. A slave is one who is bound to obey his
master's orders, though they are given solely in the master's
interest: a son is one who obeys his father's orders, given

1 See Note 27.

in his own interest; a subject obeys the orders of the sovereign power, given for the common interest, wherein he is included.

I think I have now shown sufficiently clearly the basis of a democracy: I have especially desired to do so, for I believe it to be of all forms of government the most natural, and the most consonant with individual liberty. In it no one transfers his natural right so absolutely that he has no further voice in affairs, he only hands it over to the majority of a society, whereof he is a unit. Thus all men remain, as they were in the state of nature, equals.

This is the only form of government which I have treated of at length, for it is the one most akin to my purpose of showing the benefits of freedom in a state.

I may pass over the fundamental principles of other forms of government, for we may gather from what has been said whence their right arises without going into its origin. The possessor of sovereign power, whether he be one, or many, or the whole body politic, has the sovereign right of imposing any commands he pleases: and he who has either voluntarily, or under compulsion, transferred the right to defend him to another, has, in so doing, renounced his natural right and is therefore bound to obey, in all things, the commands of the sovereign power; and will be bound so to do so long as the king, or nobles, or the people preserve the sovereign power which formed the basis of the original transfer. I need add no more.

The bases and rights of dominion being thus displayed, we shall readily be able to define private civil right, wrong, justice, and injustice, with their relations to the state; and also to determine what constitutes an ally, or an enemy, or the crime of treason.

By private civil right we can only mean the liberty every man possesses to preserve his existence, a liberty limited by the edicts of the sovereign power, and preserved only by its authority: for when a man has transferred to another his right of living as he likes, which was only limited by his power, that is, has transferred his liberty and power of self-defence, he is bound to live as that other dictates, and to trust to him entirely for his defence. Wrong takes place when a citizen, or subject, is forced by another to undergo some loss or pain in contradiction to the authority of the law, or the edict of the sovereign power.

Wrong is conceivable only in an organized community: nor can it ever accrue to subjects from any act of the sovereign, who has the right to do what he likes. It can only arise, therefore, between private persons, who are bound by law and right not to injure one another. Justice consists in the habitual rendering to every man his lawful due: injustice consists in depriving a man, under the pretence of legality, of what the laws, rightly interpreted, would allow him. These last are also called equity and iniquity, because those who administer the laws are bound to show no respect of persons, but to account all men equal, and to defend every man's right equally, neither envying the rich nor despising the poor.

The men of two states become allies, when for the sake of avoiding war, or for some other advantage, they covenant to do each other no hurt, but on the contrary, to assist each other if necessity arises, each retaining his independence. Such a covenant is valid so long as its basis of danger or advantage is in force: no one enters into an engagement, or is bound to stand by his compacts unless there be a hope of some accruing good, or the fear of some evil: if this basis be removed the compact thereby becomes void: this has been abundantly shown by experience. For although different states make treaties not to harm one another, they always take every possible precaution against such treaties being broken by the stronger party, and do not rely on the compact, unless there is a sufficiently obvious object and advantage to both parties in observing it. Otherwise they would fear a breach of faith, nor would there be any wrong done thereby: for who in his proper senses, and aware of the right of the sovereign power, would trust in the promises of one who has the will and the power to do what he likes, and who aims solely at the safety and advantage of his dominion? Moreover, if we consult loyalty and religion, we shall see that no one in possession of power ought to abide by his promises to the injury of his dominion; for he cannot keep such promises without breaking the engagement he made with his subjects, by which both he and they are most solemnly bound.

An enemy is one who lives apart from the state, and does not recognize its authority either as a subject or as an ally. It is not hatred which makes a man an enemy, but the rights of the state. The rights of the state are the same in regard to him who does not recognize by any compact the state authority, as they are against him who has done the state an injury: it has the right to force him as best it can, either to submit, or to contract an alliance.

Lastly, treason can only be committed by subjects, who by compact, either tacit or expressed, have transferred all their rights to the state: a subject is said to have committed this crime when he has attempted, for whatever reason, to seize the sovereign power, or to place it in different hands. I say, *has attempted,* for if punishment were not to overtake him till he had succeeded, it would often come too late, the sovereign rights would have been acquired or transferred already.

I also say, *has attempted, for whatever reason, to seize the sovereign power,* and I recognize no difference whether such an attempt should be followed by public loss or public gain. Whatever be his reason for acting, the crime is treason, and he is rightly condemned: in war, everyone would admit the justice of his sentence. If a man does not keep to his post, but approaches the enemy without the knowledge of his commander, whatever may be his motive, so long as he acts on his own motion, even if he advances with the design of defeating the enemy, he is rightly put to death, because he has violated his oath, and infringed the rights of his commander. That all citizens are equally bound by these rights in time of peace, is not so generally recognized, but the reasons for obedience are in both cases, identical. The state must be preserved and directed by the sole authority of the sovereign, and such authority and right have been accorded by universal consent to him alone: if, therefore, anyone else attempts, without his consent, to execute any public enterprise, even though the state might (as we said) reap benefit therefrom, such person has none the less infringed the sovereign's right, and would be rightly punished for treason.

In order that every scruple may be removed, we may now answer the inquiry, whether our former assertion that everyone who has not the practice of reason, may, in the state of nature, live by sovereign natural right, according to the laws of his desires, is not in direct opposition to the law and right of God as revealed. For as all men absolutely (whether they be less endowed with reason or more) are equally bound by the Divine command to love their neighbour as themselves, it may be said that they cannot, without wrong, do injury to anyone, or live according to their desires.

This objection, so far as the state of nature is concerned, can be easily answered, for the state of nature is, both in nature and in time, prior to religion. No one knows by nature that he owes any obedience to God,[1] nor can he attain thereto by any exercise of his reason, but solely by revelation confirmed by signs. Therefore, previous to revelation, no one is bound by a Divine law and right of which he is necessarily in ignorance. The state of nature must by no means be confounded with a state of religion, but must be conceived as without either religion or law, and consequently without sin or wrong: this is how we have described it, and we are confirmed by the authority of Paul. It is not only in respect of ignorance that we conceive the state of nature as prior to, and lacking the Divine revealed law and right; but in respect of freedom also, wherewith all men are born endowed.

If men were naturally bound by the Divine law and right, or if the Divine law and right were a natural necessity, there would have been no need for God to make a covenant with mankind, and to bind them thereto with an oath and agreement.

We must, then, fully grant that the Divine law and right originated at the time when men by express covenant agreed to obey God in all things, and ceded, as it were, their natural freedom, transferring their rights to God in the manner described in speaking of the formation of a state.

However, I will treat of these matters more at length presently.

It may be insisted that sovereigns are as much bound by the Divine law as subjects: whereas we have asserted that they retain their natural rights, and may do whatever they like.

1 See Note 28.

In order to clear up the whole difficulty, which arises rather concerning the natural right than the natural state, I maintain that everyone is bound, in the state of nature, to live according to Divine law, in the same way as he is bound to live according to the dictates of sound reason; namely, inasmuch as it is to his advantage, and necessary for his salvation; but, if he will not so live, he may do otherwise at his own risk. He is thus bound to live according to his own laws, not according to anyone else's, and to recognize no man as a judge, or as a superior in religion. Such, in my opinion, is the position of a sovereign, for he may take advice from his fellow-men, but he is not bound to recognize any as a judge, nor anyone besides himself as an arbitrator on any question of right, unless it be a prophet sent expressly by God. and attesting his mission by indisputable signs. Even then he does not recognize a man, but God Himself as His judge.

If a sovereign refuses to obey God as revealed in His law, he does so at his own risk and loss, but without violating any civil or natural right. For the civil right is dependent on his own decree; and natural right is dependent on the laws of nature, which latter are not adapted to religion, whose sole aim is the good of humanity, but to the order of nature—that is, to God's eternal decree unknown to us.

This truth seems to be adumbrated in a somewhat obscurer form by those who maintain that men can sin against God's revelation, but not against the eternal decree by which He has ordained all things.

We may be asked, what should we do if the sovereign commands anything contrary to religion, and the obedience which we have expressly vowed to God? should we obey the Divine law or the human law? I shall treat of this question at length hereafter, and will therefore merely say now, that God should be obeyed before all else, when we have a certain and indisputable revelation of His will: but men are very prone to error on religious subjects, and, according to the diversity of their dispositions, are wont with considerable stir to put forward their own inventions, as experience more than sufficiently attests, so that if no one were bound to obey the state in matters which, in his own opinion concern religion, the rights of the state would be dependent on every man's judgment and passions. No one would consider himself bound to obey laws framed against his faith or superstition; and on this pretext he might assume unbounded license. In this way, the rights of the civil authorities would be utterly set at nought, so that we must conclude that the sovereign power, which alone is bound both by Divine and natural right to preserve and guard the laws of the state, should have supreme authority for making any laws about religion which it thinks fit; all are bound to obey its behests on the subject in accordance with their promise which God bids them to keep.

However, if the sovereign power be heathen, we should either enter into no engagements therewith, and yield up our lives sooner than transfer to it any of our rights; or, if the engagement be made, and our rights transferred, we should (inasmuch as we should have ourselves transferred the right of defending ourselves and our religion) be bound to obey them, and to keep our word: we might even rightly be bound so to do, except in those cases where God, by indisputable revelation, has promised His special aid against tyranny, or given us special exemption from obedience. Thus we see that, of all the Jews in Babylon, there were only three youths who were certain of the help of God, and, therefore, refused to obey Nebuchadnezzar. All the rest, with the sole exception of Daniel, who was beloved by the king, were doubtless compelled by right to obey, perhaps thinking that they had been delivered up by God into the hands of the king, and that the king had obtained and preserved his dominion by God's design. On the other hand, Eleazar, before his country had utterly fallen, wished to give a proof of his constancy to his compatriots, in order that they might follow in his footsteps, and go to any lengths, rather than allow their right and power to be transferred to the Greeks, or brave any torture rather than swear allegiance to the heathen. Instances are occurring every day in confirmation of what I here advance. The rulers of Christian kingdoms do not hesitate, with a view to strengthening their dominion, to make treaties with Turks and heathen, and to give orders to their subjects who settle among such peoples not to assume more freedom, either in things secular or religious, than is set down in the treaty, or allowed by the foreign government. We may see this exemplified in the Dutch treaty with the Japanese, which I have already mentioned.

CHAPTER XVII.

IT IS SHOWN THAT NO ONE CAN, OR NEED, TRANSFER ALL
HIS RIGHTS TO THE SOVEREIGN POWER.   OF THE HEBREW
REPUBLIC, AS IT WAS DURING THE LIFETIME OF MOSES,
AND AFTER HIS DEATH, TILL THE FOUNDATION OF THE
MONARCHY; AND OF ITS EXCELLENCE.   LASTLY, OF THE
CAUSES WHY THE THEOCRATIC REPUBLIC FELL, AND
WHY IT COULD HARDLY HAVE CONTINUED WITHOUT
DISSENSION.

THE theory put forward in the last chapter, of the universal rights of the sovereign power, and of the natural
rights of the individual transferred thereto, though it corre-
sponds in many respects with actual practice, and though
practice may be so arranged as to conform to it more and
more, must nevertheless always remain in many respects
purely ideal.   No one can ever so utterly transfer to
another his power and, consequently, his rights, as to cease
to be a man; nor can there ever be a power so sovereign
that it can carry out every possible wish.   It will always
be vain to order a subject to hate what he believes brings
him advantage, or to love what brings him loss, or not to
be offended at insults, or not to wish to be free from fear,
or a hundred other things of the sort, which necessarily
follow from the laws of human nature.   So much, I think,
is abundantly shown by experience: for men have never so
far ceded their power as to cease to be an object of fear to
the rulers who received such power and right; and dominions have always been in as much danger from their own
subjects as from external enemies.   If it were really the
case that men could be deprived of their natural rights so
utterly as never to have any further influence on affairs,[1]
except with the permission of the holders of sovereign
right, it would then be possible to maintain with impunity

[1] See Note 29.

the most violent tyranny, which, I suppose, no one would for an instant admit.

We must, therefore, grant that every man retains some part of his right, in dependence on his own decision, and no one else's.

However, in order correctly to understand the extent of the sovereign's right and power, we must take notice that it does not cover only those actions to which it can compel men by fear, but absolutely every action which it can induce men to perform: for it is the fact of obedience, not the motive for obedience, which makes a man a subject.

Whatever be the cause which leads a man to obey the commands of the sovereign, whether it be fear or hope, or love of his country, or any other emotion—the fact remains that the man takes counsel with himself, and nevertheless acts as his sovereign orders. We must not, therefore, assert that all actions resulting from a man's deliberation with himself are done in obedience to the rights of the individual rather than the sovereign: as a matter of fact, all actions spring from a man's deliberation with himself, whether the determining motive be love or fear of punishment; therefore, either dominion does not exist, and has no rights over its subjects, or else it extends over every instance in which it can prevail on men to decide to obey it. Consequently, every action which a subject performs in accordance with the commands of the sovereign, whether such action springs from love, or fear, or (as is more frequently the case) from hope and fear together, or from reverence compounded of fear and admiration, or, indeed, any motive whatever, is performed in virtue of his submission to the sovereign, and not in virtue of his own authority.

This point is made still more clear by the fact that obedience does not consist so much in the outward act as in the mental state of the person obeying; so that he is most under the dominion of another who with his whole heart determines to obey another's commands; and consequently the firmest dominion belongs to the sovereign who has most influence over the minds of his subjects; if those who are most feared possessed the firmest dominion, the firmest dominion would belong to the subjects of a tyrant, for they are always greatly feared by their ruler. Furthermore, though it is impossible to govern the mind as completely as the tongue, nevertheless minds are, to a certain extent, under the control of the sovereign, for he can in many ways bring about that the greatest part of his subjects should follow his wishes in their beliefs, their loves, and their hates.   Though such emotions do not arise at the express command of the sovereign they often result (as experience shows) from the authority of his power, and from his direction ; in other words, in virtue of his right ; we may, therefore, without doing violence to our understanding, conceive men who follow the instigation of their sovereign in their beliefs, their loves, their hates, their contempt, and all other emotions whatsoever.

Though the powers of government, as thus conceived, are sufficiently ample, they can never become large enough to execute every possible wish of their possessors.   This, I think, I have already shown clearly enough.   The method of forming a dominion which should prove lasting I do not, as I have said, intend to discuss, but in order to arrive at the object I have in view, I will touch on the teaching of Divine revelation to Moses in this respect, and we will consider the history and the success of the Jews, gathering therefrom what should be the chief concessions made by sovereigns to their subjects with a view to the security and increase of their dominion.

That the preservation of a state chiefly depends on the subjects' fidelity and constancy in carrying out the orders they receive, is most clearly taught both by reason and experience ; how subjects ought to be guided so as best to preserve their fidelity and virtue is not so obvious.   All, both rulers and ruled, are men, and prone to follow after their lusts.   The fickle disposition of the multitude almost reduces those who have experience of it to despair, for it is governed solely by emotions, not by reason : it rushes headlong into every enterprise, and is easily corrupted either by avarice or luxury : everyone thinks himself omniscient and wishes to fashion all things to his liking, judging a thing to be just or unjust, lawful or unlawful, according as he thinks it will bring him profit or loss : vanity leads him to despise his equals, and refuse their guidance : envy of superior fame or fortune (for such gifts are never equally distributed) leads him to desire and rejoice in his neigh-bour's downfall. I need not go through the whole list, everyone knows already how much crime results from dis-gust at the present—desire for change, headlong anger, and contempt for poverty—and how men's minds are engrossed and kept in turmoil thereby.

To guard against all these evils, and form a dominion where no room is left for deceit; to frame our institutions so that every man, whatever his disposition, may prefer public right to private advantage, this is the task and this the toil. Necessity is often the mother of invention, but she has never yet succeeded in framing a dominion that was in less danger from its own citizens than from open enemies, or whose rulers did not fear the latter less than the former. Witness the state of Rome, invincible by her enemies, but many times conquered and sorely oppressed by her own citizens, especially in the war between Ves-pasian and Vitellius. (See Tacitus, Hist. bk. iv. for a de-scription of the pitiable state of the city.)

Alexander thought prestige abroad more easy to acquire than prestige at home, and believed that his greatness could be destroyed by his own followers. Fearing such a disaster, he thus addressed his friends: "Keep me safe from internal treachery and domestic plots, and I will front without fear the dangers of battle and of war. Philip was more secure in the battle array than in the theatre: he often escaped from the hands of the enemy, he could not escape from his own subjects. If you think over the deaths of kings, you will count up more who have died by the assassin than by the open foe." (Q. Curtius, chap. vi.)

For the sake of making themselves secure, kings who seized the throne in ancient times used to try to spread the idea that they were descended from the immortal gods, thinking that if their subjects and the rest of mankind did not look on them as equals, but believed them to be gods, they would willingly submit to their rule, and obey their commands. Thus Augustus persuaded the Romans that he was descended from Æneas, who was the son of Venus, and numbered among the gods. "He wished himself to be worshipped in temples, like the gods, with flamens and priests." (Tacitus, Ann. i. 10.)

Alexander wished to be saluted as the son of Jupiter, not from motives of pride but of policy, as he showed by his answer to the invective of Hermolaus: "It is almost laughable," said he, "that Hermolaus asked me to contradict Jupiter, by whose oracle I am recognized. Am I responsible for the answers of the gods? It offered me the name of son; acquiescence was by no means foreign to my present designs. Would that the Indians also would believe me to be a god! Wars are carried through by prestige, falsehoods that are believed often gain the force of truth." (Curtius, viii. § 8.) In these few words he cleverly contrives to palm off a fiction on the ignorant, and at the same time hints at the motive for the deception.

Cleon, in his speech persuading the Macedonians to obey their king, adopted a similar device: for after going through the praises of Alexander with admiration, and recalling his merits, he proceeds, "the Persians are not only pious, but prudent in worshipping their kings as gods: for kingship is the shield of public safety," and he ends thus, "I, myself, when the king enters a banquet hall, should prostrate my body on the ground; other men should do the like, especially those who are wise" (Curtius, viii. § 65). However, the Macedonians were more prudent—indeed, it is only complete barbarians who can be so openly cajoled, and can suffer themselves to be turned from subjects into slaves without interests of their own. Others, notwithstanding, have been able more easily to spread the belief that kingship is sacred, and plays the part of God on the earth, that it has been instituted by God, not by the suffrage and consent of men; and that it is preserved and guarded by Divine special providence and aid. Similar fictions have been promulgated by monarchs, with the object of strengthening their dominion, but these I will pass over, and in order to arrive at my main purpose, will merely recall and discuss the teaching on the subject of Divine revelation to Moses in ancient times.

We have said in Chap. V. that after the Hebrews came up out of Egypt they were not bound by the law and right of any other nation, but were at liberty to institute any new rites at their pleasure, and to occupy whatever territory they chose. After their liberation from the intolerable bondage of the Egyptians, they were bound by no covenant to any man; and, therefore, every man entered into his natural right, and was free to retain it or to give it up, and transfer it to another. Being, then, in the state of nature, they followed the advice of Moses, in whom they chiefly trusted, and decided to transfer their right to no human being, but only to God; without further delay they all, with one voice, promised to obey all the commands of the Deity, and to acknowledge no right that He did not proclaim as such by prophetic revelation. This promise, or transference of right to God, was effected in the same manner as we have conceived it to have been in ordinary societies, when men agree to divest themselves of their natural rights. It is, in fact, in virtue of a set covenant, and an oath (see Exod. xxxiv. 7), that the Jews freely, and not under compulsion or threats, surrendered their rights and transferred them to God. Moreover, in order that this covenant might be ratified and settled, and might be free from all suspicion of deceit, God did not enter into it till the Jews had had experience of His wonderful power by which alone they had been, or could be, preserved in a state of prosperity (Exod. xix. 4, 5). It is because they believed that nothing but God's power could preserve them that they surrendered to God the natural power of self-preservation, which they formerly, perhaps, thought they possessed, and consequently they surrendered at the same time all their natural right.

God alone, therefore, held dominion over the Hebrews, whose state was in virtue of the covenant called God's kingdom, and God was said to be their king; consequently the enemies of the Jews were said to be the enemies of God, and the citizens who tried to seize the dominion were guilty of treason against God; and, lastly, the laws of the state were called the laws and commandments of God. Thus in the Hebrew state the civil and religious authority, each consisting solely of obedience to God, were one and the same. The dogmas of religion were not precepts, but laws and ordinances; piety was regarded as the same as loyalty, impiety as the same as disaffection. Everyone who fell away from religion ceased to be a citizen, and was, on that ground alone, accounted an

enemy: those who died for the sake of religion, were held
to have died for their country; in fact, between civil and
religious law and right there was no distinction whatever.
For this reason the government could be called a Theocracy,
inasmuch as the citizens were not bound by anything save
the revelations of God.

However, this state of things existed rather in theory
than in practice, for it will appear from what we are about
to say, that the Hebrews, as a matter of fact, retained
absolutely in their own hands the right of sovereignty:
this is shown by the method and plan by which the government was carried on, as I will now explain.

Inasmuch as the Hebrews did not transfer their rights
to any other person but, as in a democracy, all surrendered
their rights equally, and cried out with one voice, "Whatsoever God shall speak (no mediator or mouthpiece being
named) that will we do," it follows that all were equally
bound by the covenant, and that all had an equal right to
consult the Deity, to accept and to interpret His laws, so
that all had an exactly equal share in the government. Thus
at first they all approached God together, so that they
might learn His commands, but in this first salutation,
they were so thoroughly terrified and so astounded to hear
God speaking, that they thought their last hour was at
hand: full of fear, therefore, they went afresh to Moses,
and said, "Lo, we have heard God speaking in the fire,
and there is no cause why we should wish to die: surely
this great fire will consume us: if we hear again the voice
of God, we shall surely die.   Thou, therefore, go near, and
hear all the words of our God, and thou (not God) shalt
speak with us: all that God shall tell us, that will we
hearken to and perform."

They thus clearly abrogated their former covenant, and
absolutely transferred to Moses their right to consult God
and interpret His commands: for they do not here promise
obedience to all that God shall tell them, but to all that
God shall tell Moses (see Deut. v. after the Decalogue, and
chap. xviii. v. 15, 16).   Moses, therefore, remained the sole
promulgator and interpreter of the Divine laws, and consequently also the sovereign judge, who could not be arraigned himself, and who acted among the Hebrews the

part of God; in other words, held the sovereign kingship: he alone had the right to consult God, to give the Divine answers to the people, and to see that they were carried out. I say he alone, for if anyone during the life of Moses was desirous of preaching anything in the name of the Lord, he was, even if a true prophet, considered guilty and a usurper of the sovereign right (Numb. xi. 28).[1] We may here notice, that though the people had elected Moses, they could not rightfully elect Moses's successor; for having transferred to Moses their right of consulting God, and absolutely promised to regard him as a Divine oracle, they had plainly forfeited the whole of their right, and were bound to accept as chosen by God anyone proclaimed by Moses as his successor. If Moses had so chosen his successor, who like him should wield the sole right of government, possessing the sole right of consulting God, and consequently of making and abrogating laws, of deciding on peace or war, of sending ambassadors, appointing judges—in fact, discharging all the functions of a sovereign, the state would have become simply a monarchy, only differing from other monarchies in the fact, that the latter are, or should be, carried on in accordance with God's decree, unknown even to the monarch, whereas the Hebrew monarch would have been the only person to whom the decree was revealed. A difference which increases, rather than diminishes the monarch's authority. As far as the people in both cases are concerned, each would be equally subject, and equally ignorant of the Divine decree, for each would be dependent on the monarch's words, and would learn from him alone, what was lawful or unlawful: nor would the fact that the people believed that the monarch was only issuing commands in accordance with God's decree revealed to him, make it less in subjection, but rather more. However, Moses elected no such successor, but left the dominion to those who came after him in a condition which could not be called a popular government, nor an aristocracy, nor a monarchy, but a Theocracy. For the right of interpreting laws was vested in one man, while the right and power of administering the state according to the

---

[1] See Note 30.

laws thus interpreted, was vested in another man (see Numb. xxvii. 21).[1]

In order that the question may be thoroughly understood, I will duly set forth the administration of the whole state.

First, the people were commanded to build a tabernacle, which should be, as it were, the dwelling of God—that is, of the sovereign authority of the state. This tabernacle was to be erected at the cost of the whole people, not of one man, in order that the place where God was consulted might be public property. The Levites were chosen as courtiers and administrators of this royal abode; while Aaron, the brother of Moses, was chosen to be their chief and second, as it were, to God their King, being succeeded in the office by his legitimate sons.

He, as the nearest to God, was the sovereign interpreter of the Divine laws; he communicated the answers of the Divine oracle to the people, and entreated God's favour for them. If, in addition to these privileges, he had possessed the right of ruling, he would have been neither more nor less than an absolute monarch; but, in respect to government, he was only a private citizen: the whole tribe of Levi was so completely divested of governing rights that it did not even take its share with the others in the partition of territory. Moses provided for its support by inspiring the common people with great reverence for it, as the only tribe dedicated to God.

Further, the army, formed from the remaining twelve tribes, was commanded to invade the land of Canaan, to divide it into twelve portions, and to distribute it among the tribes by lot. For this task twelve captains were chosen, one from every tribe, and were, together with Joshua and Eleazar, the high priest, empowered to divide the land into twelve equal parts, and distribute it by lot. Joshua was chosen for the chief command of the army, inasmuch as none but he had the right to consult God in emergencies, not like Moses, alone in his tent, or in the tabernacle, but through the high priest, to whom only the answers of God were revealed. Furthermore, he was empowered to execute, and cause the people to obey God's commands, transmitted through the high priests; to find,

[1] See Note 31.

and to make use of, means for carrying them out; to choose
as many army captains as he liked; to make whatever
choice he thought best; to send ambassadors in his own
name; and, in short, to have the entire control of the war.
To his office there was no rightful successor—indeed, the
post was only filled by the direct order of the Deity, on occasions of public emergency. In ordinary times, all the
management of peace and war was vested in the captains
of the tribes, as I will shortly point out. Lastly, all men
between the ages of twenty and sixty were ordered to bear
arms, and form a citizen army, owing allegiance, not to its
general-in-chief, nor to the high priest, but to Religion and
to God. The army, or the hosts, were called the army of
God, or the hosts of God. For this reason God was called
by the Hebrews the God of Armies; and the ark of the
covenant was borne in the midst of the army in important
battles, when the safety or destruction of the whole people
hung upon the issue, so that the people might, as it were,
see their King among them, and put forth all their strength.

From these directions, left by Moses to his successors,
we plainly see that he chose administrators, rather than
despots, to come after him; for he invested no one with the
power of consulting God, where he liked and alone, consequently, no one had the power possessed by himself of ordaining and abrogating laws, of deciding on war or peace,
of choosing men to fill offices both religious and secular:
all these are the prerogatives of a sovereign. The high
priest, indeed, had the right of interpreting laws, and communicating the answers of God, but he could not do so
when he liked, as Moses could, but only when he was asked
by the general-in-chief of the army, the council, or some
similar authority. The general-in-chief and the council
could consult God when they liked, but could only receive
His answers through the high priest; so that the utterances
of God, as reported by the high priest, were not decrees, as
they were when reported by Moses, but only answers; they
were accepted by Joshua and the council, and only then had
the force of commands and decrees.

The high priest, both in the case of Aaron and of his son
Eleazar, was chosen by Moses; nor had anyone, after
Moses' death, a right to elect to the office, which became

hereditary. The general-in-chief of the army was also
chosen by Moses, and assumed his functions in virtue of
the commands, not of the high priest, but of Moses: indeed, after the death of Joshua, the high priest did not
appoint anyone in his place, and the captains did not consult God afresh about a general-in-chief, but each retained
Joshua's power in respect to the contingent of his own
tribe, and all retained it collectively, in respect to the whole
army. There seems to have been no need of a general-in-
chief, except when they were obliged to unite their forces
against a common enemy. This occurred most frequently
during the time of Joshua, when they had no fixed dwelling-
place, and possessed all things in common. After all the
tribes had gained their territories by right of conquest, and
had divided their allotted gains, they became separated,
having no longer their possessions in common, so that the
need for a single commander ceased, for the different tribes
should be considered rather in the light of confederated
states than of bodies of fellow-citizens. In respect to their
God and their religion, they were fellow-citizens; but, in
respect to the rights which one possessed with regard to
another, they were only confederated: they were, in fact,
in much the same position (if one excepts the Temple
common to all) as the United States of the Netherlands.
The division of property held in common is only another
phrase for the possession of his share by each of the owners
singly, and the surrender by the others of their rights over
such share. This is why Moses elected captains of the
tribes—namely, that when the dominion was divided, each
might take care of his own part; consulting God through
the high priest on the affairs of his tribe, ruling over his
army, building and fortifying cities, appointing judges,
attacking the enemies of his own dominion, and having
complete control over all civil and military affairs. He was
not bound to acknowledge any superior judge save God,[1] or
a prophet whom God should expressly send. If he departed
from the worship of God, the rest of the tribes did not
arraign him as a subject, but attacked him as an enemy.
Of this we have examples in Scripture. When Joshua was

[1] See Note 32.

dead, the children of Israel (not a fresh general-in-chief) consulted God; it being decided that the tribe of Judah should be the first to attack its enemies, the tribe in question contracted a single alliance with the tribe of Simeon, for uniting their forces, and attacking their common enemy, the rest of the tribes not being included in the alliance (Judges i. 1, 2, 3). Each tribe separately made war against its own enemies, and, according to its pleasure, received them as subjects or allies, though it had been commanded not to spare them on any conditions, but to destroy them utterly. Such disobedience met with reproof from the rest of the tribes, but did not cause the offending tribe to be arraigned: it was not considered a sufficient reason for proclaiming a civil war, or interfering in one another's affairs. But when the tribe of Benjamin offended against the others, and so loosened the bonds of peace that none of the confederated tribes could find refuge within its borders, they attacked it as an enemy, and gaining the victory over it after three battles, put to death both guilty and innocent, according to the laws of war: an act which they subsequently bewailed with tardy repentance.

These examples plainly confirm what we have said concerning the rights of each tribe. Perhaps we shall be asked who elected the successors to the captains of each tribe; on this point I can gather no positive information in Scripture, but I conjecture that as the tribes were divided into families, each headed by its senior member, the senior of all these heads of families succeeded by right to the office of captain, for Moses chose from among these seniors his seventy coadjutors, who formed with himself the supreme council. Those who administered the government after the death of Joshua were called elders, and elder is a very common Hebrew expression in the sense of judge, as I suppose everyone knows; however, it is not very important for us to make up our minds on this point. It is enough to have shown that after the death of Moses no one man wielded all the power of a sovereign; as affairs were not all managed by one man, nor by a single council, nor by the popular vote, but partly by one tribe, partly by the rest in equal shares, it is most evident that the government, after the death of Moses, was neither monarchic, nor aristocratic, nor popular, but, as we have said, Theocratic. The reasons for applying this name are:

I. Because the royal seat of government was the Temple, and in respect to it alone, as we have shown, all the tribes were fellow-citizens,

II. Because all the people owed allegiance to God, their supreme Judge, to whom only they had promised implicit obedience in all things.

III. Because the general-in-chief or dictator, when there was need of such, was elected by none save God alone. This was expressly commanded by Moses in the name of God (Deut. xix. 15), and witnessed by the actual choice of Gideon, of Samson, and of Samuel; wherefrom we may conclude that the other faithful leaders were chosen in the same manner, though it is not expressly told us.

These preliminaries being stated, it is now time to inquire the effects of forming a dominion on this plan, and to see whether it so effectually kept within bounds both rulers and ruled, that the former were never tyrannical and the latter never rebellious.

Those who administer or possess governing power, always try to surround their high-handed actions with a cloak of legality, and to persuade the people that they act from good motives; this they are easily able to effect when they are the sole interpreters of the law; for it is evident that they are thus able to assume a far greater freedom to carry out their wishes and desires than if the interpretation of the law is vested in someone else, or if the laws were so self-evident that no one could be in doubt as to their meaning. We thus see that the power of evil-doing was greatly curtailed for the Hebrew captains by the fact that the whole interpretation of the law was vested in the Levites (Deut. xxi. 5), who, on their part, had no share in the government, and depended for all their support and consideration on a correct interpretation of the laws entrusted to them. Moreover, the whole people was commanded to come together at a certain place every seven years and be instructed in the law by the high-priest; further, each individual was bidden to read the book of the law through and through continually with scrupulous care. (Deut. xxxi. 9, and vi. 7.)

The captains were thus for their own sakes bound to take great care to administer everything according to the laws laid down, and well known to all, if they wished to be held in high honour by the people, who would regard them as the administrators of God's dominion, and as God's vicegerents; otherwise they could not have escaped all the virulence of theological hatred. There was another very important check on the unbridled license of the captains, in the fact, that the army was formed from the whole body of the citizens, between the ages of twenty and sixty, without exception, and that the captains were not able to hire any foreign soldiery. This I say was very important, for it is well known that princes can oppress their peoples with the single aid of the soldiery in their pay; while there is nothing more formidable to them than the freedom of citizen soldiers, who have established the freedom and glory of their country by their valour, their toil, and their blood. Thus Alexander, when he was about to make war on Darius, a second time, after hearing the advice of Parmenio, did not chide him who gave the advice, but Polysperchon, who was standing by. For, as Curtius says (iv. § 13), he did not venture to reproach Parmenio again after having shortly before reproved him too sharply. This freedom of the Macedonians, which he so dreaded, he was not able to subdue till after the number of captives enlisted in the army surpassed that of his own people: then, but not till then, he gave rein to his anger so long checked by the independence of his chief fellow-countrymen.

If this independence of citizen soldiers can restrain the princes of ordinary states who are wont to usurp the whole glory of victories, it must have been still more effectual against the Hebrew captains, whose soldiers were fighting, not for the glory of a prince, but for the glory of God, and who did not go forth to battle till the Divine assent had been given.

We must also remember that the Hebrew captains were associated only by the bonds of religion: therefore, if any one of them had transgressed, and begun to violate the Divine right, he might have been treated by the rest as an enemy and lawfully subdued.

An additional check may be found in the fear of a new

prophet arising, for if a man of unblemished life could show by certain signs that he was really a prophet, he *ipso facto* obtained the sovereign right to rule, which was given to him, as to Moses formerly, in the name of God, as revealed to himself alone; not merely through the high priest, as in the case of the captains.   There is no doubt that such an one would easily be able to enlist an oppressed people in his cause, and by trifling signs persuade them of anything he wished: on the other hand, if affairs were well ordered, the captain would be able to make provision in time; that the prophet should be submitted to his approval, and be examined whether he were really of unblemished life, and possessed indisputable signs of his mission: also, whether the teaching he proposed to set forth in the name of the Lord agreed with received doctrines, and the general laws of the country; if his credentials were insufficient, or his doctrines new, he could lawfully be put to death, or else received on the captain's sole responsibility and authority.

Again, the captains were not superior to the others in nobility or birth, but only administered the government in virtue of their age and personal qualities.   Lastly, neither captains nor army had any reason for preferring war to peace.   The army, as we have stated, consisted entirely of citizens, so that affairs were managed by the same persons both in peace and war.   The man who was a soldier in the camp was a citizen in the market-place, he who was a leader in the camp was a judge in the law courts, he who was a general in the camp was a ruler in the state.   Thus no one could desire war for its own sake, but only for the sake of preserving peace and liberty; possibly the captains avoided change as far as possible, so as not to be obliged to consult the high priest and submit to the indignity of standing in his presence.

So much for the precautions for keeping the captains within bounds.   We must now look for the restraints upon the people: these, however, are very clearly indicated in the very groundwork of the social fabric.

Anyone who gives the subject the slightest attention, will see that the state was so ordered as to inspire the most ardent patriotism in the hearts of the citizens, so that the latter would be very hard to persuade to betray their country, and be ready to endure anything rather than submit to a foreign yoke. After they had transferred their right to God, they thought that their kingdom belonged to God, and that they themselves were God's children. Other nations they looked upon as God's enemies, and regarded with intense hatred (which they took to be piety, see Psalm cxxxix. 21, 22): nothing would have been more abhorrent to them than swearing allegiance to a foreigner, and promising him obedience: nor could they conceive any greater or more execrable crime than the betrayal of their country, the kingdom of the God whom they adored.

It was considered wicked for anyone to settle outside of the country, inasmuch as the worship of God by which they were bound could not be carried on elsewhere: their own land alone was considered holy, the rest of the earth unclean and profane.

David, who was forced to live in exile, complained before Saul as follows: "But if they be the children of men who have stirred thee up against me, cursed be they before the Lord; for they have driven me out this day from abiding in the inheritance of the Lord, saying, Go, serve other gods." (1 Sam. xxvi. 19.) For the same reason no citizen, as we should especially remark, was ever sent into exile: he who sinned was liable to punishment, but not to disgrace.

Thus the love of the Hebrews for their country was not only patriotism, but also piety, and was cherished and nurtured by daily rites till, like their hatred of other nations, it must have passed into their nature. Their daily worship was not only different from that of other nations (as it might well be, considering that they were a peculiar people and entirely apart from the rest), it was absolutely contrary. Such daily reprobation naturally gave rise to a lasting hatred, deeply implanted in the heart: for of all hatreds none is more deep and tenacious than that which springs from extreme devoutness or piety, and is itself cherished as pious. Nor was a general cause lacking for inflaming such hatred more and more, inasmuch as it was reciprocated; the surrounding nations regarding the Jews with a hatred just as intense.

How great was the effect of all these causes, namely, freedom from man's dominion; devotion to their country;

absolute rights over all other men; a hatred not only permitted but pious; a contempt for their fellow-men; the
singularity of their customs and religious rites; the effect,
I repeat, of all these causes in strengthening the hearts of
the Jews to bear all things for their country, with extraordinary constancy and valour, will at once be discerned
by reason and attested by experience. Never, so long as
the city was standing, could they endure to remain under
foreign dominion; and therefore they called Jerusalem "a
rebellious city" (Ezra iv. 12). Their state after its re-
establishment (which was a mere shadow of the first, for
the high priests had usurped the rights of the tribal
captains) was, with great difficulty, destroyed by the
Romans, as Tacitus bears witness (Hist. ii. 4):—"Ves-
pasian had closed the war against the Jews, abandoning
the siege of Jerusalem as an enterprise difficult and
arduous, rather from the character of the people and the
obstinacy of their superstition, than from the strength left
to the besieged for meeting their necessities." But besides
these characteristics, which are merely ascribed by an individual opinion, there was one feature peculiar to this state
and of great importance in retaining the affections of the
citizens, and checking all thoughts of desertion, or aban-
donment of the country: namely, self-interest, the strength
and life of all human action. This was peculiarly engaged
in the Hebrew state, for nowhere else did citizens possess
their goods so securely as did the subjects of this community, for the latter possessed as large a share in the land
and the fields as did their chiefs, and were owners of their
plots of ground in perpetuity; for if any man was compelled
by poverty to sell his farm or his pasture, he received it
back again intact at the year of jubilee: there were other
similar enactments against the possibility of alienating real
property.

Again, poverty was nowhere more endurable than in a
country where duty towards one's neighbour, that is, one's
fellow-citizen, was practised with the utmost piety, as a
means of gaining the favour of God the King. Thus the
Hebrew citizens would nowhere be so well off as in their
own country; outside its limits they met with nothing but
loss and disgrace.

The following considerations were of weight, not only in keeping them at home, but also in preventing civil war and removing causes of strife: no one was bound to serve his equal, but only to serve God, while charity and love towards fellow-citizens was accounted the highest piety; this last feeling was not a little fostered by the general hatred with which they regarded foreign nations and were regarded by them. Furthermore, the strict discipline of obedience in which they were brought up, was a very important factor; for they were bound to carry on all their actions according to the set rules of the law: a man might not plough when he liked, but only at certain times, in certain years, and with one sort of beast at a time; so, too, he might only sow and reap in a certain method and season—in fact, his whole life was one long school of obedience (see Chap. V. on the use of ceremonies); such a habit was thus engendered, that conformity seemed freedom instead of servitude, and men desired what was commanded rather than what was forbidden. This result was not a little aided by the fact that the people were bound, at certain seasons of the year, to give themselves up to rest and rejoicing, not for their own pleasure, but in order that they might worship God cheerfully.

Three times in the year they feasted before the Lord; on the seventh day of every week they were bidden to abstain from all work and to rest; besides these, there were other occasions when innocent rejoicing and feasting were not only allowed but enjoined. I do not think any better means of influencing men's minds could be devised; for there is no more powerful attraction than joy springing from devotion, a mixture of admiration and love. It was not easy to be wearied by constant repetition, for the rites on the various festivals were varied and recurred seldom. We may add the deep reverence for the Temple which all most religiously fostered, on account of the peculiar rites and duties that they were obliged to perform before approaching thither. Even now, Jews cannot read without horror of the crime of Manasseh, who dared to place an idol in the Temple. The laws, scrupulously preserved in the inmost sanctuary, were objects of equal reverence to the people. Popular reports and misconceptions were, therefore, very little to be feared in this quarter, for no one dared decide on sacred matters, but all felt bound to obey, without consulting their reason, all the commands given by the answers of God received in the Temple, and all the laws which God had ordained.

I think I have now explained clearly, though briefly, the main features of the Hebrew commonwealth. I must now inquire into the causes which led the people so often to fall away from the law, which brought about their frequent subjection, and, finally, the complete destruction of their dominion. Perhaps I shall be told that it sprang from their hardness of heart; but this is childish, for why should this people be more hard of heart than others; was it by nature?

But nature forms individuals, not peoples; the latter are only distinguishable by the difference of their language, their customs, and their laws; while from the two last— *i.e.*, customs and laws,—it may arise that they have a peculiar disposition, a peculiar manner of life, and peculiar prejudices. If, then, the Hebrews were harder of heart than other nations, the fault lay with their laws or customs.

This is certainly true, in the sense that, if God had wished their dominion to be more lasting, He would have given them other rites and laws, and would have instituted a different form of government. We can, therefore, only say that their God was angry with them, not only, as Jeremiah says, from the building of the city, but even from the founding of their laws.

This is borne witness to by Ezekiel xx. 25: "Wherefore I gave them also statutes that were not good, and judgments whereby they should not live; and I polluted them in their own gifts, in that they caused to pass through the fire all that openeth the womb; that I might make them desolate, to the end that they might know that I am the Lord."

In order that we may understand these words, and the destruction of the Hebrew commonwealth, we must bear in mind that it had at first been intended to entrust the whole duties of the priesthood to the firstborn, and not to the Levites (see Numb. viii. 17). It was only when all the tribes, except the Levites, worshipped the golden calf, that the firstborn were rejected and defiled, and the Levites chosen in their stead (Deut. x. 8). When I reflect on this change, I feel disposed to break forth with the words of Tacitus. God's object at that time was not the safety of the Jews, but vengeance. I am greatly astonished that the celestial mind was so inflamed with anger that it ordained laws, which always are supposed to promote the honour, well-being, and security of a people, with the purpose of vengeance, for the sake of punishment; so that the laws do not seem so much laws—that is, the safeguard of the people—as pains and penalties.

The gifts which the people were obliged to bestow on the Levites and priests—the redemption of the firstborn, the poll-tax due to the Levites, the privilege possessed by the latter of the sole performance of sacred rites—all these, I say, were a continual reproach to the people, a continual reminder of their defilement and rejection. Moreover, we may be sure that the Levites were for ever heaping reproaches upon them: for among so many thousands there must have been many importunate dabblers in theology. Hence the people got into the way of watching the acts of the Levites, who were but human; of accusing the whole body of the faults of one member, and continually murmuring.

Besides this, there was the obligation to keep in idleness men hateful to them, and connected by no ties of blood. Especially would this seem grievous when provisions were dear. What wonder, then, if in times of peace, when striking miracles had ceased, and no men of paramount authority were forthcoming, the irritable and greedy temper of the people began to wax cold, and at length to fall away from a worship, which, though Divine, was also humiliating, and even hostile, and to seek after something fresh; or can we be surprised that the captains, who always adopt the popular course, in order to gain the sovereign power for themselves by enlisting the sympathies of the people, and alienating the high priest, should have yielded to their demands, and introduced a new worship? If the state had been formed according to the original intention, the rights and honour of all the tribes would have been equal, and everything would have rested on a firm basis. Who is there who would willingly violate the religious rights of his kindred? What could a man desire more than to support his own brothers and parents, thus fulfilling the duties of religion? Who would not rejoice in being taught by them the interpretation of the laws, and receiving through them the answers of God?

The tribes would thus have been united by a far closer bond, if all alike had possessed the right to the priesthood. All danger would have been obviated, if the choice of the Levites had not been dictated by anger and revenge. But, as we have said, the Hebrews had offended their God, Who, as Ezekiel says, polluted them in their own gifts by rejecting all that openeth the womb, so that He might destroy them.

This passage is also confirmed by their history. As soon as the people in the wilderness began to live in ease and plenty, certain men of no mean birth began to rebel against the choice of the Levites, and to make it a cause for believing that Moses had not acted by the commands of God, but for his own good pleasure, inasmuch as he had chosen his own tribe before all the rest, and had bestowed the high priesthood in perpetuity on his own brother. They, therefore, stirred up a tumult, and came to him, crying out that all men were equally sacred, and that he had exalted himself above his fellows wrongfully. Moses was not able to pacify them with reasons; but by the intervention of a miracle, in proof of the faith, they all perished. A fresh sedition then arose among the whole people, who believed that their champions had not been put to death by the judgment of God, but by the device of Moses. After a great slaughter, or pestilence, the rising subsided from inanition, but in such a manner that all preferred death to life under such conditions.

We should rather say that sedition ceased than that harmony was re-established. This is witnessed by Scripture (Deut. xxxi. 21), where God, after predicting to Moses that the people after his death will fall away from the Divine worship, speaks thus: "For I know their imagination which they go about, even now before I have brought them into the land which I sware;" and, a little while after (xxxi. 27), Moses says: "For I know thy rebellion and thy stiff neck: behold, while I am yet alive with you this day, ye have been rebellious against the Lord; and how much more after my death!"

Indeed, it happened according to his words, as we all know. Great changes, extreme license, luxury, and hardness of heart grew up; things went from bad to worse, till at last the people, after being frequently conquered, came to an open rupture with the Divine right, and wished for a mortal king, so that the seat of government might be the Court, instead of the Temple, and that the tribes might remain fellow-citizens in respect to their king, instead of in respect to Divine right and the high priesthood.

A vast material for new seditions was thus produced, eventually resulting in the ruin of the entire state. Kings are above all things jealous of a precarious rule, and can in nowise brook a dominion within their own. The first monarchs, being chosen from the ranks of private citizens, were content with the amount of dignity to which they had risen; but their sons, who obtained the throne by right of inheritance, began gradually to introduce changes, so as to get all the sovereign rights into their own hands. This they were generally unable to accomplish, so long as the right of legislation did not rest with them, but with the high priest, who kept the laws in the sanctuary, and interpreted them to the people. The kings were thus bound to obey the laws as much as were the subjects, and were unable to abrogate them, or to ordain new laws of equal authority; moreover, they were prevented by the Levites from administering the affairs of religion, king and subject being alike unclean. Lastly, the whole safety of their dominion depended on the will of one man, if that man appeared to be a prophet; and of this they had seen an example, namely, how completely Samuel had been able to command Saul, and how easily, because of a single disobedience, he had been able to transfer the right of sovereignty to David. Thus the kings found a dominion within their own, and wielded a precarious sovereignty.

In order to surmount these difficulties, they allowed other temples to be dedicated to the gods, so that there might be no further need of consulting the Levites; they also sought out many who prophesied in the name of God, so that they might have creatures of their own to oppose to the true prophets. However, in spite of all their attempts, they never attained their end. For the prophets, prepared against every emergency, waited for a favourable opportunity, such as the beginning of a new reign, which is always precarious, while the memory of the previous reign remains green. At these times they could easily pronounce by Divine authority that the king was tyrannical, and could produce a champion of distinguished virtue to vindicate the Divine right, and lawfully to claim dominion, or a share in it. Still, not even so could the prophets effect much. They could, indeed, remove a tyrant; but there were reasons which prevented them from doing more than setting up, at great cost of civil bloodshed, another tyrant in his stead. Of discords and civil wars there was no end, for the causes for the violation of Divine right remained always the same, and could only be removed by a complete re-modelling of the state.

We have now seen how religion was introduced into the Hebrew commonwealth, and how the dominion might have lasted for ever, if the just wrath of the Lawgiver had allowed it. As this was impossible, it was bound in time to perish. I am now speaking only of the first common-wealth, for the second was a mere shadow of the first, inasmuch as the people were bound by the rights of the Persians to whom they were subject. After the restoration of free-dom, the high priests usurped the rights of the secular chiefs, and thus obtained absolute dominion. The priests were inflamed with an intense desire to wield the powers of the sovereignty and the high priesthood at the same time. I have, therefore, no need to speak further of the second commonwealth. Whether the first, in so far as we deem it to have been durable, is capable of imitation, and whether it would be pious to copy it as far as possible, will appear from what follows. I wish only to draw attention, as a crown-ing conclusion, to the principle indicated already—namely, that it is evident, from what we have stated in this chapter, that the Divine right, or the right of religion, originates in a compact: without such compact, none but natural rights exist. The Hebrews were not bound by their religion to evince any pious care for other nations not included in the compact, but only for their own fellow-citizens.

CHAPTER XVIII.

FROM THE COMMONWEALTH OF THE HEBREWS, AND THEIR HISTORY, CERTAIN POLITICAL DOCTRINES ARE DEDUCED.

ALTHOUGH the commonwealth of the Hebrews, as we have conceived it, might have lasted for ever, it would be impossible to imitate it at the present day, nor would it be advisable so to do. If a people wished to transfer their rights to God it would be necessary to make an express covenant with Him, and for this would be needed not only the consent of those transferring their rights, but also the consent of God. God, however, has revealed through his Apostles that the covenant of God is no longer written in ink, or on tables of stone, but with the Spirit of God in the fleshy tables of the heart.

Furthermore, such a form of government would only be available for those who desire to have no foreign relations, but to shut themselves up within their own frontiers, and to live apart from the rest of the world; it would be useless to men who must have dealings with other nations; so that the cases where it could be adopted are very few indeed.

Nevertheless, though it could not be copied in its entirety, it possessed many excellent features which might be brought to our notice, and perhaps imitated with advantage. My intention, however, is not to write a treatise on forms of government, so I will pass over most of such points in silence, and will only touch on those which bear upon my purpose.

God's kingdom is not infringed upon by the choice of an earthly ruler endowed with sovereign rights; for after the Hebrews had transferred their rights to God, they conferred the sovereign right of ruling on Moses, investing him with the sole power of instituting and abrogating laws in the name of God, of choosing priests, of judging, of teaching, of punishing—in fact, all the prerogatives of an absolute monarch.

Again, though the priests were the interpreters of the laws, they had no power to judge the citizens, or to excommunicate anyone: this could only be done by the judges and chiefs chosen from among the people. A consideration of the successes and the histories of the Hebrews will bring to light other considerations worthy of note. To wit:

I. That there were no religious sects, till after the high priests, in the second commonwealth, possessed the authority to make decrees, and transact the business of government. In order that such authority might last for ever, the high priests usurped the rights of secular rulers, and at last wished to be styled kings. The reason for this is ready to hand; in the first commonwealth no decrees could bear the name of the high priest, for he had no right to ordain laws, but only to give the answers of God to questions asked by the captains or the councils: he had, therefore, no motive for making changes in the law, but took care, on the contrary, to administer and guard what had already been received and accepted. His only means of preserving his freedom in safety against the will of the captains lay in cherishing the law intact. After the high priests had assumed the power of carrying on the government, and added the rights of secular rulers to those they already possessed, each one began both in things religious and in things secular, to seek for the glorification of his own name, settling everything by sacerdotal authority, and issuing every day, concerning ceremonies, faith, and all else, new decrees which he sought to make as sacred and authoritative as the laws of Moses. Religion thus sank into a degrading superstition, while the true meaning and interpretation of the laws became corrupted. Furthermore, while the high priests were paving their way to the secular rule just after the restoration, they attempted to gain popular favour by assenting to every demand; approving whatever the people did, however impious, and accommodating Scripture to the very depraved current morals. Malachi bears witness to this in no measured terms: he chides the priests of his time as despisers of the name of God, and then goes on with his invective as follows (Mal.

ii. 7, 8): "For the priest's lips should keep knowledge, and they should seek the law at his mouth: for he is the messenger of the Lord of hosts. But ye are departed out of the way; ye have caused many to stumble at the law, ye have corrupted the covenant of Levi, saith the Lord of hosts." He further accuses them of interpreting the laws according to their own pleasure, and paying no respect to God but only to persons. It is certain that the high priests were never so cautious in their conduct as to escape the remark of the more shrewd among the people, for the latter were at length emboldened to assert that no laws ought to be kept save those that were written, and that the decrees which the Pharisees (consisting, as Josephus says in his "Antiquities," chiefly of the common people), were deceived into calling the traditions of the fathers, should not be observed at all. However this may be, we can in nowise doubt that flattery of the high priest, the corruption of religion and the laws, and the enormous increase of the extent of the last-named, gave very great and frequent occasion for disputes and altercations impossible to allay. When men begin to quarrel with all the ardour of superstition, and the magistracy to back up one side or the other, they can never come to a compromise, but are bound to split into sects.

II. It is worthy of remark that the prophets, who were in a private station of life, rather irritated than reformed mankind by their freedom of warning, rebuke, and censure; whereas the kings, by their reproofs and punishments, could always produce an effect. The prophets were often intolerable even to pious kings, on account of the authority they assumed for judging whether an action was right or wrong, or for reproving the kings themselves if they dared to transact any business, whether public or private, without prophetic sanction. King Asa who, according to the testimony of Scripture, reigned piously, put the prophet Hanani into a prison-house because he had ventured freely to chide and reprove him for entering into a covenant with the king of Armenia.

Other examples might be cited, tending to prove that religion gained more harm than good by such freedom, not to speak of the further consequence, that if the prophets had retained their rights, great civil wars would have resulted.

III. It is remarkable that during all the period, during which the people held the reins of power, there was only one civil war, and that one was completely extinguished, the conquerors taking such pity on the conquered, that they endeavoured in every way to reinstate them in their former dignity and power. But after that the people, little accus-omed to kings, changed its first form of government into ι monarchy, civil war raged almost continuously; and ɔattles were so fierce as to exceed all others recorded; in ɔne engagement (taxing our faith to the utmost) five hun-lred thousand Israelites were slaughtered by the men of Judah, and in another the Israelites slew great numbers of the men of Judah (the figures are not given in Scripture), almost razed to the ground the walls of Jerusalem, and sacked the Temple in their unbridled fury. At length, laden with the spoils of their brethren, satiated with blood, they took hostages, and leaving the king in his well-nigh devastated kingdom, laid down their arms, relying on the weakness rather than the good faith of their foes. A few years after, the men of Judah, with recruited strength, again took the field, but were a second time beaten by the Israelites, and slain to the number of a hundred and twenty thousand, two hundred thousand of their wives and children were led into captivity, and a great booty again seized. Worn out with these and similar battles set forth at length in their histories, the Jews at length fell a prey to their enemies.

Furthermore, if we reckon up the times during which peace prevailed under each form of government, we shall find a great discrepancy. Before the monarchy forty years and more often passed, and once eighty years (an almost unparalleled period), without any war, foreign or civil. After the kings acquired sovereign power, the fighting was no longer for peace and liberty, but for glory; accordingly we find that they all, with the exception of Solomon (whose virtue and wisdom would be better displayed in peace than in war) waged war, and finally a fatal desire for power gained ground, which, in many cases, made the path to the throne a bloody one.

Lastly, the laws, during the rule of the people, remained

uncorrupted and were studiously observed. Before the monarchy there were very few prophets to admonish the people, but after the establishment of kings there were a great number at the same time. Obadiah saved a hundred from death and hid them away, lest they should be slain with the rest. The people, so far as we can see, were never deceived by false prophets till after the power had been vested in kings, whose creatures many of the prophets were. Again, the people, whose heart was generally proud or humble according to its circumstances, easily corrected itself under misfortune, turned again to God, restored His laws, and so freed itself from all peril; but the kings, whose hearts were always equally puffed up, and who could not be corrected without humiliation, clung pertinaciously to their vices, even till the last overthrow of the city.

We may now clearly see from what I have said :—

I. How hurtful to religion and the state is the concession to ministers of religion of any power of issuing decrees or transacting the business of government: how, on the contrary, far greater stability is afforded, if the said ministers are only allowed to give answers to questions duly put to them, and are, as a rule, obliged to preach and practise the received and accepted doctrines.

II. How dangerous it is to refer to Divine right matters merely speculative and subject or liable to dispute. The most tyrannical governments are those which make crimes of opinions, for everyone has an inalienable right over his thoughts—nay, such a state of things leads to the rule of popular passion.

Pontius Pilate made concession to the passion of the Pharisees in consenting to the crucifixion of Christ, whom he knew to be innocent. Again, the Pharisees, in order to shake the position of men richer than themselves, began to set on foot questions of religion, and accused the Sadducees of impiety, and, following their example, the vilest hypocrites, stirred, as they pretended, by the same holy wrath which they called zeal for the Lord, persecuted men whose unblemished character and distinguished virtue had excited the popular hatred, publicly denounced their opinions, and inflamed the fierce passions of the people against them.

This wanton licence being cloaked with the specious garb

of religion could not easily be repressed, especially when the sovereign authorities introduced a sect of which they were not the head; they were then regarded not as interpreters of Divine right, but as sectarians—that is, as persons recognizing the right of Divine interpretation assumed by the leaders of the sect. The authority of the magistrates thus became of little account in such matters in comparison with the authority of sectarian leaders before whose interpretations kings were obliged to bow.

To avoid such evils in a state, there is no safer way than to make piety and religion to consist in acts only—that is, in the practice of justice and charity, leaving everyone's judgment in other respects free. But I will speak of this more at length presently.

III. We see how necessary it is, both in the interests of the state and in the interests of religion, to confer on the sovereign power the right of deciding what is lawful or the reverse. If this right of judging actions could not be given to the very prophets of God without great injury to the state and religion, how much less should it be entrusted to those who can neither foretell the future nor work miracles! But this again I will treat of more fully hereafter.

IV. Lastly, we see how disastrous it is for a people unaccustomed to kings, and possessing a complete code of laws, to set up a monarchy. Neither can the subjects brook such a sway, nor the royal authority submit to laws and popular rights set up by anyone inferior to itself. Still less can a king be expected to defend such laws, for they were not framed to support his dominion, but the dominion of the people, or some council which formerly ruled, so that in guarding the popular rights the king would seem to be a slave rather than a master. The representative of a new monarchy will employ all his zeal in attempting to frame new laws, so as to wrest the rights of dominion to his own use, and to reduce the people till they find it easier to increase than to curtail the royal prerogative. I must not, however, omit to state that it is no less dangerous to remove a monarch, though he is on all hands admitted to be a tyrant. For his people are accustomed to royal authority and will obey no other, despising and mocking at any less august control.

It is therefore necessary, as the prophets discovered of old, if one king be removed, that he should be replaced by another, who will be a tyrant from necessity rather than choice. For how will he be able to endure the sight of the hands of the citizens reeking with royal blood, and to rejoice in their regicide as a glorious exploit? Was not the deed perpetrated as an example and warning for himself?

If he really wishes to be king, and not to acknowledge the people as the judge of kings and the master of himself, or to wield a precarious sway, he must avenge the death of his predecessor, making an example for his own sake, lest the people should venture to repeat a similar crime. He will not, however, be able easily to avenge the death of the tyrant by the slaughter of citizens unless he defends the cause of tyranny and approves the deeds of his predecessor, thus following in his footsteps.

Hence it comes to pass that peoples have often changed their tyrants, but never removed them or changed the monarchical form of government into any other.

The English people furnish us with a terrible example of this fact. They sought how to depose their monarch under the forms of law, but when he had been removed, they were utterly unable to change the form of government, and after much bloodshed only brought it about, that a new monarch should be hailed under a different name (as though it had been a mere question of names); this new monarch could only consolidate his power by completely destroying the royal stock, putting to death the king's friends, real or supposed, and disturbing with war the peace which might encourage discontent, in order that the populace might be engrossed with novelties and divert its mind from brooding over the slaughter of the king. At last, however, the people reflected that it had accomplished nothing for the good of the country beyond violating the rights of the lawful king and changing everything for the worse. It therefore decided to retrace its steps as soon as possible, and never rested till it had seen a complete restoration of the original state of affairs.

It may perhaps be objected that the Roman people was easily able to remove its tyrants, but I gather from its history a strong confirmation of my contention. Though the

Roman people was much more than ordinarily capable of removing their tyrants and changing their form of government, inasmuch as it held in its own hands the power of
electing its king and his successor, and being composed of
rebels and criminals had not long been used to the royal
yoke (out of its six kings it had put to death three), nevertheless it could accomplish nothing beyond electing several
tyrants in place of one, who kept it groaning under a continual state of war, both foreign and civil, till at last it
changed its government again to a form differing from
monarchy, as in England, only in name.

As for the United States of the Netherlands, they have
never, as we know, had a king, but only counts, who never
attained the full rights of dominion. The States of the
Netherlands evidently acted as principals in the settlement
made by them at the time of the Earl of Leicester's
mission: they always reserved for themselves the authority
to keep the counts up to their duties, and the power to
preserve this authority and the liberty of the citizens.
They had ample means of vindicating their rights if their
rulers should prove tyrannical, and could impose such restraints that nothing could be done without their consent
and approval.

Thus the rights of sovereign power have always been
vested in the States, though the last count endeavoured to
usurp them. It is therefore little likely that the States
should give them up, especially as they have just restored
their original dominion, lately almost lost.

These examples, then, confirm us in our belief, that
every dominion should retain its original form, and, indeed,
cannot change it without danger of the utter ruin of the
whole state. Such are the points I have here thought
worthy of remark.

CHAPTER XIX.

IT IS SHOWN THAT THE RIGHT OVER MATTERS SPIRITUAL
LIES WHOLLY WITH THE SOVEREIGN, AND THAT THE OUT-
WARD FORMS OF RELIGION SHOULD BE IN ACCORDANCE
WITH PUBLIC PEACE, IF WE WOULD OBEY GOD ARIGHT.

WHEN I said that the possessors of sovereign power
have rights over everything, and that all rights are
dependent on their decree, I did not merely mean temporal
rights, but also spiritual rights; of the latter, no less than the
former, they ought to be the interpreters and the champions.
I wish to draw special attention to this point, and to discuss
it fully in this chapter, because many persons deny that
the right of deciding religious questions belongs to the
sovereign power, and refuse to acknowledge it as the interpreter of Divine right. They accordingly assume full
licence to accuse and arraign it, nay, even to excommunicate it from the Church, as Ambrosius treated the Emperor
Theodosius in old time. However, I will show later on in
this chapter that they take this means of dividing the government, and paving the way to their own ascendency. I
wish, however, first to point out that religion acquires its
force as law solely from the decrees of the sovereign. God
has no special kingdom among men except in so far as He
reigns through temporal rulers. Moreover, the rites of religion and the outward observances of piety should be in
accordance with the public peace and well-being, and should
therefore be determined by the sovereign power alone. I
speak here only of the outward observances of piety and
the external rites of religion, not of piety itself, nor of the
inward worship of God, nor the means by which the mind
is inwardly led to do homage to God in singleness of heart.
Inward worship of God and piety in itself are within the
sphere of everyone's private rights, and cannot be alienated
(as I showed at the end of Chapter VII.). What I here

mean by the kingdom of God is, I think, sufficiently clear
from what has been said in Chapter XIV. I there showed
that a man best fulfils God's law who worships Him, according to His command, through acts of justice and
charity; it follows, therefore, that wherever justice and
charity have the force of law and ordinance, there is God's
kingdom.

I recognize no difference between the cases where God
teaches and commands the practice of justice and charity
through our natural faculties, and those where He makes
special revelations; nor is the form of the revelation of importance so long as such practice is revealed and becomes
a sovereign and supreme law to men. If, therefore, I show
that justice and charity can only acquire the force of right
and law through the rights of rulers, I shall be able readily
to arrive at the conclusion (seeing that the rights of rulers
are in the possession of the sovereign), that religion can
only acquire the force of right by means of those who have
the right to command, and that God only rules among men
through the instrumentality of earthly potentates. It
follows from what has been said, that the practice of justice
and charity only acquires the force of law through the
rights of the sovereign authority; for we showed in
Chapter XVI. that in the state of nature reason has no
more rights than desire, but that men living either by the
laws of the former or the laws of the latter, possess rights
co-extensive with their powers.

For this reason we could not conceive sin to exist in the
state of nature, nor imagine God as a judge punishing
man's transgressions; but we supposed all things to happen according to the general laws of universal nature, there
being no difference between pious and impious, between
him that was pure (as Solomon says) and him that was
impure, because there was no possibility either of justice or
charity.

In order that the true doctrines of reason, that is (as we
showed in Chapter IV.), the true Divine doctrines might
obtain absolutely the force of law and right, it was necessary
that each individual should cede his natural right, and
transfer it either to society as a whole, or to a certain body
of men, or to one man. Then, and not till then, does it first

dawn upon us what is justice and what is injustice, what is equity and what is iniquity.

Justice, therefore, and absolutely all the precepts of reason, including love towards one's neighbour, receive the force of laws and ordinances solely through the rights of dominion, that is (as we showed in the same chapter) solely on the decree of those who possess the right to rule. Inasmuch as the kingdom of God consists entirely in rights applied to justice and charity or to true religion, it follows that (as we asserted) the kingdom of God can only exist among men through the means of the sovereign powers; nor does it make any difference whether religion be apprehended by our natural faculties or by revelation : the argument is sound in both cases, inasmuch as religion is one and the same, and is equally revealed by God, whatever be the manner in which it becomes known to men.

Thus, in order that the religion revealed by the prophets might have the force of law among the Jews, it was necessary that every man of them should yield up his natural right, and that all should, with one accord, agree that they would only obey such commands as God should reveal to them through the prophets. Just as we have shown to take place in a democracy, where men with one consent agree to live according to the dictates of reason. Although the Hebrews furthermore transferred their right to God, they were able to do so rather in theory than in practice, for, as a matter of fact (as we pointed out above) they absolutely retained the right of dominion till they transferred it to Moses, who in his turn became absolute king, so that it was only through him that God reigned over the Hebrews. For this reason (namely, that religion only acquires the force of law by means of the sovereign power) Moses was not able to punish those who, before the covenant, and consequently while still in possession of their rights, violated the Sabbath (Exod. xvi. 27), but was able to do so after the covenant (Numb. xv. 36), because everyone had then yielded up his natural rights, and the ordinance of the Sabbath had received the force of law.

Lastly, for the same reason, after the destruction of the Hebrew dominion, revealed religion ceased to have the force of law; for we cannot doubt that as soon as the Jews

transferred their right to the king of Babylon, the kingdom of God and the Divine right forthwith ceased. For
the covenant wherewith they promised to obey all the
utterances of God was abrogated; God's kingdom, which
was based thereupon, also ceased. The Hebrews could no
longer abide thereby, inasmuch as their rights no longer
belonged to them but to the king of Babylon, whom (as we
showed in Chapter XVI.) they were bound to obey in all
things. Jeremiah (chap. xxix. verse 7) expressly admo-
nishes them of this fact: "And seek the peace of the city,
whither I have caused you to be carried away captives, and
pray unto the Lord for it; for in the peace thereof shall
ye have peace." Now, they could not seek the peace of the
city as having a share in its government, but only as slaves,
being, as they were, captives; by obedience in all things,
with a view to avoiding seditions, and by observing all the
laws of the country, however different from their own. It
is thus abundantly evident that religion among the
Hebrews only acquired the form of law through the right
of the sovereign rule; when that rule was destroyed, it could
no longer be received as the law of a particular kingdom,
but only as the universal precept of reason. I say of
reason, for the universal religion had not yet become known
by revelation. We may therefore draw the general conclusion that religion, whether revealed through our natural
faculties or through prophets, receives the force of a command solely through the decrees of the holders of sovereign
power; and, further, that God has no special kingdom
among men, except in so far as He reigns through earthly
potentates.

We may now see in a clearer light what was stated in
Chapter IV., namely, that all the decrees of God involve
eternal truth and necessity, so that we cannot conceive
God as a prince or legislator giving laws to mankind. For
this reason the Divine precepts, whether revealed through
our natural faculties, or through prophets, do not receive
immediately from God the force of a command, but only
from those, or through the mediation of those, who possess
the right of ruling and legislating. It is only through
these latter means that God rules among men, and directs
human affairs with justice and equity.

This conclusion is supported by experience, for we find traces of Divine justice only in places where just men bear sway; elsewhere the same lot (to repeat again Solomon's words) befalls the just and the unjust, the pure and the impure: a state of things which causes Divine Providence to be doubted by many who think that God immediately reigns among men, and directs all nature for their benefit.

As, then, both reason and experience tell us that the Divine right is entirely dependent on the decrees of secular rulers, it follows that secular rulers are its proper interpreters. How this is so we shall now see, for it is time to show that the outward observances of religion, and all the external practices of piety should be brought into accordance with the public peace and well-being if we would obey God rightly. When this has been shown we shall easily understand how the sovereign rulers are the proper interpreters of religion and piety.

It is certain that duties towards one's country are the highest that man can fulfil; for, if government be taken away, no good thing can last, all falls into dispute, anger and anarchy reign unchecked amid universal fear. Consequently there can be no duty towards our neighbour which would not become an offence if it involved injury to the whole state, nor can there be any offence against our duty towards our neighbour, or anything but loyalty in what we do for the sake of preserving the state. For instance: it is in the abstract my duty when my neighbour quarrels with me and wishes to take my cloak, to give him my coat also; but if it be thought that such conduct is hurtful to the maintenance of the state, I ought to bring him to trial, even at the risk of his being condemned to death.

For this reason Manlius Torquatus is held up to honour, inasmuch as the public welfare outweighed with him his duty towards his children. This being so, it follows that the public welfare is the sovereign law to which all others, Divine and human, should be made to conform.

Now, it is the function of the sovereign only to decide what is necesssary for the public welfare and the safety of the state, and to give orders accordingly; therefore it is also the function of the sovereign only to decide the limits of

our duty towards our neighbour—in other words, to determine how we should obey God. We can now clearly understand how the sovereign is the interpreter of religion, and
further, that no one can obey God rightly, if the practices
of his piety do not conform to the public welfare; or, consequently, if he does not implicitly obey all the commands
of the sovereign. For as by God's command we are bound
to do our duty to all men without exception, and to do no
man an injury, we are also bound not to help one man at
another's loss, still less at a loss to the whole state. Now,
no private citizen can know what is good for the state, except he learn it through the sovereign power, who alone
has the right to transact public business: therefore no one
can rightly practise piety or obedience to God, unless he
obey the sovereign power's commands in all things. This
proposition is confirmed by the facts of experience. For if
the sovereign adjudge a man to be worthy of death or an
enemy, whether he be a citizen or a foreigner, a private
individual or a separate ruler, no subject is allowed to give
him assistance. So also though the Jews were bidden to
love their fellow-citizens as themselves (Levit. xix. 17, 18),
they were nevertheless bound, if a man offended against
the law, to point him out to the judge (Levit. v. 1, and
Deut. xiii. 8, 9), and, if he should be condemned to death,
to slay him (Deut. xvii. 7).

Further, in order that the Hebrews might preserve the
liberty they had gained, and might retain absolute sway
over the territory they had conquered, it was necessary, as
we showed in Chapter XVII., that their religion should be
adapted to their particular government, and that they
should separate themselves from the rest of the nations:
wherefore it was commanded to them, "Love thy neighbour and hate thine enemy" (Matt. v. 43), but after they
had lost their dominion and had gone into captivity in
Babylon, Jeremiah bid them take thought for the safety of
the state into which they had been led captive; and Christ
when He saw that they would be spread over the whole
world, told them to do their duty by all men without exception; all of which instances show that religion has always
been made to conform to the public welfare. Perhaps
someone will ask: By what right, then, did the disciples

of Christ, being private citizens, preach a new religion? I answer that they did so by the right of the power which they had received from Christ against unclean spirits (see Matt. x. 1). I have already stated in Chapter XVI. that all are bound to obey a tyrant, unless they have received from God through undoubted revelation a promise of aid against him; so let no one take example from the Apostles unless he too has the power of working miracles. The point is brought out more clearly by Christ's command to His disciples, "Fear not those who kill the body" (Matt. x. 28). If this command were imposed on everyone, governments would be founded in vain, and Solomon's words (Prov. xxiv. 21), "My son, fear God and the king," would be impious, which they certainly are not; we must therefore admit that the authority which Christ gave to His disciples was given to them only, and must not be taken as an example for others.

I do not pause to consider the arguments of those who wish to separate secular rights from spiritual rights, placing the former under the control of the sovereign, and the latter under the control of the universal Church; such pretensions are too frivolous to merit refutation. I cannot, however, pass over in silence the fact that such persons are woefully deceived when they seek to support their seditious opinions (I ask pardon for the somewhat harsh epithet) by the example of the Jewish high priest, who, in ancient times, had the right of administering the sacred offices. Did not the high priests receive their right by the decree of Moses (who, as I have shown, retained the sole right to rule), and could they not by the same means be deprived of it? Moses himself chose not only Aaron, but also his son Eleazar, and his grandson Phineas, and bestowed on them the right of administering the office of high priest. This right was retained by the high priests afterwards, but none the less were they delegates of Moses—that is, of the sovereign power. Moses, as we have shown, left no successor to his dominion, but so distributed his prerogatives, that those who came after him seemed, as it were, regents who administer the government when a king is absent but not dead.

In the second commonwealth the high priests held their

right absolutely, after they had obtained the rights of principality in addition. Wherefore the rights of the high priesthood always depended on the edict of the sovereign, and the high priests did not possess them till they became sovereigns also. Rights in matters spiritual always remained under the control of the kings absolutely (as I will show at the end of this chapter), except in the single particular that they were not allowed to administer in person the sacred duties in the Temple, inasmuch as they were not of the family of Aaron, and were therefore considered unclean, a reservation which would have no force in a Christian community.

We cannot, therefore, doubt that the daily sacred rites (whose performance does not require a particular genealogy but only a special mode of life, and from which the holders of sovereign power are not excluded as unclean) are under the sole control of the sovereign power; no one, save by the authority or concession of such sovereign, has the right or power of administering them, of choosing others to administer them, of defining or strengthening the foundations of the Church and her doctrines; of judging on questions of morality or acts of piety; of receiving anyone into the Church or excommunicating him therefrom, or, lastly, of providing for the poor.

These doctrines are proved to be not only true (as we have already pointed out), but also of primary necessity for the preservation of religion and the state. We all know what weight spiritual right and authority carries in the popular mind: how everyone hangs on the lips, as it were, of those who possess it. We may even say that those who wield such authority have the most complete sway over the popular mind.

Whosoever, therefore, wishes to take this right away from the sovereign power, is desirous of dividing the dominion; from such division, contentions, and strife will necessarily spring up, as they did of old between the Jewish kings and high priests, and will defy all attempts to allay them. Nay, further, he who strives to deprive the sovereign power of such authority, is aiming (as we have said), at gaining dominion for himself. What is left for the sovereign power to decide on, if this right be denied him?

Certainly nothing concerning either war or peace, if he has to ask another man's opinion as to whether what he believes to be beneficial would be pious or impious. Everything would depend on the verdict of him who had the right of deciding and judging what was pious or impious, right or wrong.

When such a right was bestowed on the Pope of Rome absolutely, he gradually acquired complete control over the kings, till at last he himself mounted to the summits of dominion; however much monarchs, and especially the German emperors, strove to curtail his authority, were it only by a hair's-breadth, they effected nothing, but on the contrary by their very endeavours largely increased it. That which no monarch could accomplish with fire and sword, ecclesiastics could bring about with a stroke of the pen; whereby we may easily see the force and power at the command of the Church, and also how necessary it is for sovereigns to reserve such prerogatives for themselves.

If we reflect on what was said in the last chapter we shall see that such reservation conduced not a little to the increase of religion and piety; for we observed that the prophets themselves, though gifted with Divine efficacy, being merely private citizens, rather irritated than reformed the people by their freedom of warning, reproof, and denunciation, whereas the kings by warnings and punishments easily bent men to their will. Furthermore, the kings themselves, not possessing the right in question absolutely, very often fell away from religion and took with them nearly the whole people. The same thing has often happened from the same cause in Christian states.

Perhaps I shall be asked, "But if the holders of sovereign power choose to be wicked, who will be the rightful champion of piety? Should the sovereigns still be its interpreters?" I meet them with the counter-question, "But if ecclesiastics (who are also human, and private citizens, and who ought to mind only their own affairs), or if others whom it is proposed to entrust with spiritual authority, choose to be wicked, should they still be considered as piety's rightful interpreters?" It is quite certain that when sovereigns wish to follow their own pleasure, whether they have control over spiritual matters or not, the whole state, spiritual and secular, will go to ruin, and it will go much faster if private citizens seditiously assume the championship of the Divine rights.

Thus we see that not only is nothing gained by denying such rights to sovereigns, but on the contrary, great evil ensues. For (as happened with the Jewish kings who did not possess such rights absolutely) rulers are thus driven into wickedness, and the injury and loss to the state become certain and inevitable, instead of uncertain and possible. Whether we look to the abstract truth, or the security of states, or the increase of piety, we are compelled to maintain that the Divine right, or the right of control over spiritual matters, depends absolutely on the decree of the sovereign, who is its legitimate interpreter and champion. Therefore the true ministers of God's word are those who teach piety to the people in obedience to the authority of the sovereign rulers by whose decree it has been brought into conformity with the public welfare.

There remains for me to point out the cause for the frequent disputes on the subject of these spiritual rights in Christian states; whereas the Hebrews, so far as I know, never had any doubts about the matter. It seems monstrous that a question so plain and so vitally important should thus have remained undecided, and that the secular rulers could never obtain the prerogative without controversy, nay, nor without great danger of sedition and injury to religion. If no cause for this state of things were forthcoming, I could easily persuade myself that all I have said in this chapter is mere theorizing, or a kind of speculative reasoning which can never be of any practical use. However, when we reflect on the beginnings of Christianity the cause at once becomes manifest. The Christian religion was not taught at first by kings, but by private persons, who, against the wishes of those in power, whose subjects they were, were for a long time accustomed to hold meetings in secret churches, to institute and perform sacred rites, and on their own authority to settle and decide on their affairs without regard to the state, When, after the lapse of many years, the religion was taken up by the authorities, the ecclesiastics were obliged to teach it to the emperors themselves as they had defined it : wherefore

they easily gained recognition as its teachers and interpreters, and the church pastors were looked upon as vicars
of God. The ecclesiastics took good care that the Christian
kings should not assume their authority, by prohibiting
marriage to the chief ministers of religion and to its
highest interpreter. They furthermore effected their purpose by multiplying the dogmas of religion to such an
extent and so blending them with philosophy that their
chief interpreter was bound to be a skilled philosopher and
theologian, and to have leisure for a host of idle speculations : conditions which could only be fulfilled by a private
individual with much time on his hands.

Among the Hebrews things were very differently arranged : for their Church began at the same time as their
dominion, and Moses, their absolute ruler, taught religion
to the people, arranged their sacred rites, and chose their
spiritual ministers. Thus the royal authority carried very
great weight with the people, and the kings kept a firm
hold on their spiritual prerogatives.

Although, after the death of Moses, no one held absolute
sway, yet the power of deciding both in matters spiritual and
matters temporal was in the hands of the secular chief, as I
have already pointed out. Further, in order that it might
be taught religion and piety, the people was bound to consult the supreme judge no less than the high priest (Deut.
xvii. 9, 11). Lastly, though the kings had not as much
power as Moses, nearly the whole arrangement and choice
of the sacred ministry depended on their decision. Thus
David arranged the whole service of the Temple (see
1 Chron. xxviii. 11, 12, &c.) ; from all the Levites he chose
twenty-four thousand for the sacred psalms ; six thousand of these formed the body from which were chosen the
judges and prætors, four thousand were porters, and four
thousand to play on instruments (see 1 Chron. xxiii. 4, 5).
He further divided them into companies (of whom he chose
the chiefs), so that each in rotation, at the allotted time,
might perform the sacred rites. The priests he also divided
into as many companies ; I will not go through the whole
catalogue, but refer the reader to 2 Chron. viii. 13, where
it is stated, "Then Solomon offered burnt offerings to the
Lord . . . . after a certain rate every day, offering accord-

ing to the commandments of Moses;" and in verse 14, "And he appointed, according to the order of David his father, the courses of the priests to their service . . . . for so had David the man of God commanded." Lastly, the historian bears witness in verse 15 : "And they departed not from the commandment of the king unto the priests and Levites concerning any matter, or concerning the treasuries."

From these and other histories of the kings it is abundantly evident, that the whole practice of religion and the sacred ministry depended entirely on the commands of the king.

When I said above that the kings had not the same right as Moses to elect the high priest, to consult God without intermediaries, and to condemn the prophets who prophesied during their reign; I said so simply because the prophets could, in virtue of their mission, choose a new king and give absolution for regicide, not because they could call a king who offended against the law to judgment, or could rightly act against him.[1]

Wherefore if there had been no prophets who, in virtue of a special revelation, could give absolution for regicide, the kings would have possessed absolute rights over all matters both spiritual and temporal. Consequently the rulers of modern times, who have no prophets and would not rightly be bound in any case to receive them (for they are not subject to Jewish law), have absolute possession of the spiritual prerogative, although they are not celibates, and they will always retain it, if they will refuse to allow religious dogmas to be unduly multiplied or confounded with philosophy.

[1] See Note 33.

CHAPTER XX.

THAT IN A FREE STATE EVERY MAN MAY THINK WHAT HE LIKES, AND SAY WHAT HE THINKS.

IF men's minds were as easily controlled as their tongues, every king would sit safely on his throne, and government by compulsion would cease; for every subject would shape his life according to the intentions of his rulers, and would esteem a thing true or false, good or evil, just or unjust, in obedience to their dictates. However, we have shown already (Chapter XVII.) that no man's mind can possibly lie wholly at the disposition of another, for no one can willingly transfer his natural right of free reason and judgment, or be compelled so to do. For this reason government which attempts to control minds is accounted tyrannical, and it is considered an abuse of sovereignty and a usurpation of the rights of subjects, to seek to prescribe what shall be accepted as true, or rejected as false, or what opinions should actuate men in their worship of God. All these questions fall within a man's natural right, which he cannot abdicate even with his own consent.

I admit that the judgment can be biassed in many ways, and to an almost incredible degree, so that while exempt from direct external control it may be so dependent on another man's words, that it may fitly be said to be ruled by him; but although this influence is carried to great lengths, it has never gone so far as to invalidate the statement, that every man's understanding is his own, and that brains are as diverse as palates.

Moses, not by fraud, but by Divine virtue, gained such a hold over the popular judgment that he was accounted superhuman, and believed to speak and act through the inspiration of the Deity; nevertheless, even he could not escape murmurs and evil interpretations. How much less then can other monarchs avoid them! Yet such unlimited power, if it exists at all, must belong to a monarch, and least of all to a democracy, where the whole or a great part of the people wield authority collectively. This is a fact which I think everyone can explain for himself.

However unlimited, therefore, the power of a sovereign may be, however implicitly it is trusted as the exponent of law and religion, it can never prevent men from forming judgments according to their intellect, or being influenced by any given emotion. It is true that it has the right to treat as enemies all men whose opinions do not, on all subjects, entirely coincide with its own; but we are not discussing its strict rights, but its proper course of action. I grant that it has the right to rule in the most violent manner, and to put citizens to death for very trivial causes, but no one supposes it can do this with the approval of sound judgment. Nay, inasmuch as such things cannot be done without extreme peril to itself, we may even deny that it has the absolute power to do them, or, consequently, the absolute right; for the rights of the sovereign are limited by his power.

Since, therefore, no one can abdicate his freedom of judgment and feeling; since every man is by indefeasible natural right the master of his own thoughts, it follows that men thinking in diverse and contradictory fashions, cannot, without disastrous results, be compelled to speak only according to the dictates of the supreme power. Not even the most experienced, to say nothing of the multitude, know how to keep silence. Men's common failing is to confide their plans to others, though there be need for secrecy, so that a government would be most harsh which deprived the individual of his freedom of saying and teaching what he thought; and would be moderate if such freedom were granted. Still we cannot deny that authority may be as much injured by words as by actions; hence, although the freedom we are discussing cannot be entirely denied to subjects, its unlimited concession would be most baneful; we must, therefore, now inquire, how far such freedom can and ought to be conceded without danger to the peace of the state, or the power of the rulers; and this, as I said at the beginning of Chapter XVI., is my principal object.

It follows, plainly, from the explanation given above, of the foundations of a state, that the ultimate aim of government is not to rule, or restrain, by fear, nor to exact obedience, but contrariwise, to free every man from fear, that he may live in all possible security; in other words, to strengthen his natural right to exist and work without injury to himself or others.

No, the object of government is not to change men from rational beings into beasts or puppets, but to enable them to develope their minds and bodies in security, and to employ their reason unshackled; neither showing hatred, anger, or deceit, nor watched with the eyes of jealousy and injustice. In fact, the true aim of government is liberty.

Now we have seen that in forming a state the power of making laws must either be vested in the body of the citizens, or in a portion of them, or in one man. For, although men's free judgments are very diverse, each one thinking that he alone knows everything, and although complete unanimity of feeling and speech is out of the question, it is impossible to preserve peace, unless individuals abdicate their right of acting entirely on their own judgment. Therefore, the individual justly cedes the right of free action, though not of free reason and judgment; no one can act against the authorities without danger to the state, though his feelings and judgment may be at variance therewith; he may even speak against them, provided that he does so from rational conviction, not from fraud, anger, or hatred, and provided that he does not attempt to introduce any change on his private authority.

For instance, supposing a man shows that a law is repugnant to sound reason, and should therefore be repealed; if he submits his opinion to the judgment of the authorities (who, alone, have the right of making and repealing laws), and meanwhile acts in nowise contrary to that law, he has deserved well of the state, and has behaved as a good citizen should; but if he accuses the authorities of injustice, and stirs up the people against them, or if he seditiously strives to abrogate the law without their consent, he is a mere agitator and rebel.

Thus we see how an individual may declare and teach what he believes, without injury to the authority of his rulers, or to the public peace; namely, by leaving in their hands the entire power of legislation as it affects action,

and by doing nothing against their laws, though he be compelled often to act in contradiction to what he believes, and
openly feels, to be best.

Such a course can be taken without detriment to justice
and dutifulness, nay, it is the one which a just and dutiful
man would adopt. We have shown that justice is dependent on the laws of the authorities, so that no one who
contravenes their accepted decrees can be just, while the
highest regard for duty, as we have pointed out in the preceding chapter, is exercised in maintaining public peace
and tranquillity; these could not be preserved if every man
were to live as he pleased; therefore it is no less than undu-
tiful for a man to act contrary to his country's laws, for if
the practice became universal the ruin of states would
necessarily follow.

Hence, so long as a man acts in obedience to the laws of
his rulers, he in nowise contravenes his reason, for in obedience to reason he transferred the right of controlling his
actions from his own hands to theirs. This doctrine we
can confirm from actual custom, for in a conference of great
and small powers, schemes are seldom carried unanimously,
yet all unite in carrying out what is decided on, whether they
voted for or against. But I return to my proposition.

From the fundamental notions of a state, we have discovered how a man may exercise free judgment without
detriment to the supreme power: from the same premises
we can no less easily determine what opinions would be
seditious. Evidently those which by their very nature
nullify the compact by which the right of free action was
ceded. For instance, a man who holds that the supreme
power has no rights over him, or that promises ought not to
be kept, or that everyone should live as he pleases, or
other doctrines of this nature in direct opposition to the
above-mentioned contract, is seditious, not so much from
his actual opinions and judgment, as from the deeds which
they involve; for he who maintains such theories abrogates
the contract which tacitly, or openly, he made with his
rulers. Other opinions which do not involve acts violating
the contract, such as revenge, anger, and the like, are not
seditious, unless it be in some corrupt state, where superstitious and ambitious persons, unable to endure men of

learning, are so popular with the multitude that their word is more valued than the law.

However, I do not deny that there are some doctrines which, while they are apparently only concerned with abstract truths and falsehoods, are yet propounded and published with unworthy motives. This question we have discussed in Chapter XV., and shown that reason should nevertheless remain unshackled. If we hold to the principle that a man's loyalty to the state should be judged, like his loyalty to God, from his actions only—namely, from his charity towards his neighbours; we cannot doubt that the best government will allow freedom of philosophical speculation no less than of religious belief. I confess that from such freedom inconveniences may sometimes arise, but what question was ever settled so wisely that no abuses could possibly spring therefrom? He who seeks to regulate everything by law, is more likely to arouse vices than to reform them. It is best to grant what cannot be abolished, even though it be in itself harmful. How many evils spring from luxury, envy, avarice, drunkenness, and the like, yet these are tolerated—vices as they are—because they cannot be prevented by legal enactments. How much more then should free thought be granted, seeing that it is in itself a virtue and that it cannot be crushed! Besides, the evil results can easily be checked, as I will show, by the secular authorities, not to mention that such freedom is absolutely necessary for progress in science and the liberal arts: for no man follows such pursuits to advantage unless his judgment be entirely free and unhampered.

But let it be granted that freedom may be crushed, and men be so bound down, that they do not dare to utter a whisper, save at the bidding of their rulers; nevertheless this can never be carried to the pitch of making them think according to authority, so that the necessary consequences would be that men would daily be thinking one thing and saying another, to the corruption of good faith, that mainstay of government, and to the fostering of hateful flattery and perfidy, whence spring stratagems, and the corruption of every good art.

It is far from possible to impose uniformity of speech, for the more rulers strive to curtail freedom of speech, the

more obstinately are they resisted; not indeed by the
avaricious, the flatterers, and other numskulls, who think
supreme salvation consists in filling their stomachs and gloat-
ing over their money-bags, but by those whom good education, sound morality, and virtue have rendered more free.
Men, as generally constituted, are most prone to resent the
branding as criminal of opinions which they believe to be
true, and the proscription as wicked of that which inspires
them with piety towards God and man; hence they are
ready to forswear the laws and conspire against the authorities, thinking it not shameful but honourable to stir up
seditions and perpetuate any sort of crime with this end in
view. Such being the constitution of human nature, we see
that laws directed against opinions affect the generous-
minded rather than the wicked, and are adapted less for
coercing criminals than for irritating the upright; so that
they cannot be maintained without great peril to the state.

Moreover, such laws are almost always useless, for those
who hold that the opinions proscribed are sound, cannot
possibly obey the law; whereas those who already reject
them as false, accept the law as a kind of privilege, and
make such boast of it, that authority is powerless to repeal
it, even if such a course be subsequently desired.

To these considerations may be added what we said in
Chapter XVIII. in treating of the history of the Hebrews.
And, lastly, how many schisms have arisen in the Church
from the attempt of the authorities to decide by law the
intricacies of theological controversy! If men were not
allured by the hope of getting the law and the authorities on
their side, of triumphing over their adversaries in the sight
of an applauding multitude, and of acquiring honourable
distinctions, they would not strive so maliciously, nor would
such fury sway their minds. This is taught not only by
reason but by daily examples, for laws of this kind pre-
scribing what every man shall believe and forbidding anyone to speak or write to the contrary, have often been
passed, as sops or concessions to the anger of those who
cannot tolerate men of enlightenment, and who, by such
harsh and crooked enactments, can easily turn the devotion
of the masses into fury and direct it against whom they
will.

How much better would it be to restrain popular anger and fury, instead of passing useless laws, which can only be broken by those who love virtue and the·liberal arts, thus paring down the state till it is too small to harbour men of talent. What greater misfortune for a state can be conceived than that honourable men should be sent like criminals into exile, because they hold diverse opinions which they cannot disguise? What, I say, can be more hurtful than that men who have committed no crime or wickedness should, simply because they are enlightened, be treated as enemies and put to death, and that the scaffold, the terror of evil-doers, should become the arena where the highest examples of tolerance and virtue are displayed to the people with all the marks of ignominy that authority can devise?

He that knows himself to be upright does not fear the death of a criminal, and shrinks from no punishment; his mind is not wrung with remorse for any disgraceful deed: he holds that death in a good cause is no punishment, but an honour, and that death for freedom is glory.

What purpose then is served by the death of such men, what example is proclaimed? the cause for which they die is unknown to the idle and the foolish, hateful to the turbulent, loved by the upright. The only lesson we can draw from such scenes is to flatter the persecutor, or else to imitate the victim.

If formal assent is not to be esteemed above conviction, and if governments are to retain a firm hold of authority and not be compelled to yield to agitators, it is imperative that freedom of judgment should be granted, so that men may live together in harmony, however diverse, or even openly contradictory their opinions may be. We cannot doubt that such is the best system of government and open to the fewest objections, since it is the one most in harmony with human nature. In a democracy (the most natural form of government, as we have shown in Chapter XVI.) everyone submits to the control of authority over his actions, but not over his judgment and reason; that is, seeing that all cannot think alike, the voice of the majority has the force of law, subject to repeal if circumstances bring about a change of opinion. In proportion as the power of free judgment is withheld we depart from the natural condition of mankind, and consequently the government becomes more tyrannical.

In order to prove that from such freedom no inconvenience arises, which cannot easily be checked by the exercise of the sovereign power, and that men's actions can easily be kept in bounds, though their opinions be at open variance, it will be well to cite an example. Such an one is not very far to seek. The city of Amsterdam reaps the fruit of this freedom in its own great prosperity and in the admiration of all other people. For in this most flourishing state, and most splendid city, men of every nation and religion live together in the greatest harmony, and ask no questions before trusting their goods to a fellow-citizen, save whether he be rich or poor, and whether he generally acts honestly, or the reverse. His religion and sect is considered of no importance: for it has no effect before the judges in gaining or losing a cause, and there is no sect so despised that its followers, provided that they harm no one, pay every man his due, and live uprightly, are deprived of the protection of the magisterial authority.

On the other hand, when the religious controversy between Remonstrants and Counter-Remonstrants began to be taken up by politicians and the States, it grew into a schism, and abundantly showed that laws dealing with religion and seeking to settle its controversies are much more calculated to irritate than to reform, and that they give rise to extreme licence: further, it was seen that schisms do not originate in a love of truth, which is a source of courtesy and gentleness, but rather in an inordinate desire for supremacv, From all these considerations it is clearer than the sun at noonday, that the true schismatics are those who condemn other men's writings, and seditiously stir up the quarrelsome masses against their authors, rather than those authors themselves, who generally write only for the learned, and appeal solely to reason. In fact, the real disturbers of the peace are those who, in a free state, seek to curtail the liberty of judgment which they are unable to tyrannize over.

I have thus shown:—I. That it is impossible to deprive men of the liberty of saying what they think. II. That such liberty can be conceded to every man without injury to the rights and authority of the sovereign power, and that every man may retain it without injury to such rights, provided that he does not presume upon it to the extent of introducing any new rights into the state, or acting in any way contrary to the existing laws. III. That every man may enjoy this liberty without detriment to the public peace, and that no inconveniences arise therefrom which cannot easily be checked. IV. That every man may enjoy it without injury to his allegiance. V. That laws dealing with speculative problems are entirely useless. VI. Lastly, that not only may such liberty be granted without prejudice to the public peace, to loyalty, and to the rights of rulers, but that it is even necessary for their preservation. For when people try to take it away, and bring to trial, not only the acts which alone are capable of offending, but also the opinions of mankind, they only succeed in surrounding their victims with an appearance of martyrdom, and raise feelings of pity and revenge rather than of terror. Uprightness and good faith are thus corrupted, flatterers and traitors are encouraged, and sectarians triumph, inasmuch as concessions have been made to their animosity, and they have gained the state sanction for the doctrines of which they are the interpreters. Hence they arrogate to themselves the state authority and rights, and do not scruple to assert that they have been directly chosen by God, and that their laws are Divine, whereas the laws of the state are human, and should therefore yield obedience to the laws of God—in other words, to their own laws. Everyone must see that this is not a state of affairs conducive to public welfare. Wherefore, as we have shown in Chapter XVIII., the safest way for a state is to lay down the rule that religion is comprised solely in the exercise of charity and justice, and that the rights of rulers in sacred, no less than in secular matters, should merely have to do with actions, but that every man should think what he likes and say what he thinks.

I have thus fulfilled the task I set myself in this treatise. It remains only to call attention to the fact that I have written nothing which I do not most willingly submit to the examination and approval of my country's rulers; and

that I am willing to retract anything which they shall decide to be repugnant to the laws, or prejudicial to the public
good.   I know that I am a man, and as a man liable to
error, but against error I have taken scrupulous care, and
have striven to keep in entire accordance with the laws of
my country, with loyalty, and with morality.

AUTHOR'S NOTES TO THE THEOLOGICO-POLITICAL TREATISE.

AUTHOR'S NOTES TO THE THEOLOGICO-POLITICAL TREATISE.

Chapter I.

Note 1 (*p.* 13). The word *nabi* is rightly interpreted by Rabbi Salomon Jarchi, but the sense is hardly caught by Aben Ezra, who was not so good a Hebraist. We must also remark that this Hebrew word for prophecy has a universal meaning and embraces all kinds of prophecy. Other terms are more special, and denote this or that sort of prophecy, as I believe is well known to the learned.

Note 2 (*p.* 14). "*Although ordinary knowledge is Divine, its professors cannot be called prophets.*" That is, interpreters of God. For he alone is an interpreter of God, who interprets the decrees which God has revealed to him, to others who have not received such revelation, and whose belief, therefore, rests merely on the prophet's authority and the confidence reposed in him. If it were otherwise, and all who listen to prophets became prophets themselves, as all who listen to philosophers become philosophers, a prophet would no longer be the interpreter of Divine decrees, inasmuch as his hearers would know the truth, not on the authority of the prophet, but by means of actual Divine revelation and inward testimony. Thus the sovereign powers are the interpreters of their own rights of sway, because these are defended only by their authority and supported by their testimony.

Note 3 (*p.* 24). "*Prophets were endowed with a peculiar and extraordinary power.*" Though some men enjoy gifts which nature has not bestowed on their fellows, they are not said to surpass the bounds of human nature, unless their special qualities are such as cannot be said to be deducible from the definition of human nature. For instance, a giant is a rarity, but still human. The gift of composing poetry *extempore* is given to very few, yet it is human. The same may, therefore, be said of the faculty possessed by some of imagining things as vividly as though they saw them before them, and this not while asleep, but while

awake. But if anyone could be found who possessed òther
means and other foundations for knowledge, he might be said
to transcend the limits of human nature.

CHAPTER III.

Note 4 (*p.* 47). In Gen. xv. it is written that God promised Abraham to protect him, and to grant him ample rewards. Abraham
answered that he could expect nothing which could be of any
value to him, as he was childless and well stricken in years.

Note 5 (*p.* 47). That a keeping of the commandments of the
Old Testament is not sufficient for eternal life, appears from
Mark x. 21.

CHAPTER VI.

Note 6 (*p.* 84). We doubt of the existence of God, and consequently of all else, so long as we have no clear and distinct idea of
God, but only a confused one. For as he who knows not rightly
the nature of a triangle, knows not that its three angles are equal
to two right angles, so he who conceives the Divine nature confusedly, does not see that it pertains to the nature of God to
exist. Now, to conceive the nature of God clearly and distinctly,
it is necessary to pay attention to a certain number of very simple
notions, called general notions, and by their help to associate the
conceptions which we form of the attributes of the Divine nature.
It then, for the first time, becomes clear to us, that God exists
necessarily, that He is omnipresent, and that all our conceptions
involve in themselves the nature of God and are conceived
through it. Lastly, we see that all our adequate ideas are true.
Compare on this point the prologomena to my book, "*Principles of Descartes's philosophy set forth geometrically.*"

CHAPTER VII.

Note 7 (*p.* 108). "*It is impossible to find a method which would
enable us to gain a certain knowledge of all the statements in Scripture.*" I mean impossible for us who have not the habitual use of
the language, and have lost the precise meaning of its phraseology.

Note 8 (*p.* 112). "*Not in things whereof the understanding can gain
a clear and distinct idea, and which are conceivable through themselves.*" By things conceivable I mean not only those which are
rigidly proved, but also those whereof we are morally certain,
and are wont to hear without wonder, though they are incapable
of proof. Everyone can see the truth of Euclid's propositions
before they are proved. So also the histories of things both
future and past which do not surpass human credence, laws,

institutions, manners, I call conceivable and clear, though they cannot be proved mathematically. But hieroglyphics and histories which seem to pass the bounds of belief I call inconceivable; yet even among these last there are many which our method enables us to investigate, and to discover the meaning of their narrator.

Chapter VIII.

Note 9 (*p.* 122). " *Mount Moriah is called the mount of God.*" That is by the historian, not by Abraham, for he says that the place now called "In the mount of the Lord it shall be revealed," was called by Abraham, "the Lord shall provide."

Note 10 (*p.* 124). " *Before that territory* [*Idumœa*] *was conquered by David.*" From this time to the reign of Jehoram when they again separated from the Jewish kingdom (2 Kings viii. 20), the Idumæans had no king, princes appointed by the Jews supplied the place of kings (1 Kings xxii. 48), in fact the prince of Idumæa is called a king (2 Kings iii. 9).

It may be doubted whether the last of the Idumæan kings had begun to reign before the accession of Saul, or whether Scripture in this chapter of Genesis wished to enumerate only such kings as were independent. It is evidently mere trifling to wish to enrol among Hebrew kings the name of Moses, who set up a dominion entirely different from a monarchy.

Chapter IX.

Note 11 (*p.* 133). " *With few exceptions.*" One of these exceptions is found in 2 Kings xviii. 20, where we read, " Thou sayest (but they are but vain words)," the second person being used. In Isaiah xxxvi. 5, we read " I say (but they are but vain words) I have counsel and strength for war," and in the twenty-second verse of the chapter in Kings it is written, " But if ye say," the plural number being used, whereas Isaiah gives the singular. The text in Isaiah does not contain the words found in 2 Kings xxxii. 32. Thus there are several cases of various readings where it is impossible to distinguish the best.

Note 12 (*p.* 134). " *The expressions in the two passages are so varied.*" For instance we read in 2 Sam. vii. 6, "But I have walked in a tent and in a tabernacle." Whereas in 1 Chron. xvii. 5, "but have gone from tent to tent and from one tabernacle to another." In 2 Sam. vii. 10, we read, "to afflict them," whereas in 1 Chron. vii. 9, we find a different expression. I could point out other differences still greater, but a single reading of the chapters in question will suffice to make them manifest to all who are neither blind nor devoid of sense.

Note 13 (*p.* 134). "*This time cannot refer to what immediately precedes.*" It is plain from the context that this passage must allude to the time when Joseph was sold by his brethren. But this is not all. We may draw the same conclusion from the age of Judah, who was then twenty-two years old at most, taking as basis of calculation his own history just narrated. It follows, indeed, from the last verse of Gen. xxx., that Judah was born in the tenth of the years of Jacob's servitude to Laban, and Joseph in the fourteenth. Now, as we know that Joseph was seventeen years old when sold by his brethren, Judah was then not more than twenty-one. Hence, those writers who assert that Judah's long absence from his father's house took place before Joseph was sold, only seek to delude themselves and to call in question the Scriptural authority which they are anxious to protect.

Note 14 (*p.* 135). "*Dinah was scarcely seven years old when she was violated by Schechem.*" The opinion held by some that Jacob wandered about for eight or ten years between Mesopotamia and Bethel, savours of the ridiculous; if respect for Aben Ezra allows me to say so. For it is clear that Jacob had two reasons for haste: first, the desire to see his old parents; secondly, and chiefly to perform, the vow made when he fled from his brother (Gen. xxviii. 10 and xxxi. 13, and xxxv. 1). We read (Gen. xxxi. 3), that God had commanded him to fulfil his vow, and promised him help for returning to his country. If these considerations seem conjectures rather than reasons, I will waive the point and admit that Jacob, more unfortunate than Ulysses,· spent eight or ten years or even longer, in this short journey. At any rate it cannot be denied that Benjamin was born in the last year of this wandering, that is by the reckoning of the objectors, when Joseph was sixteen or seventeen years old, for Jacob left Laban seven years after Joseph's birth. Now from the seventeenth year of Joseph's age till the patriarch went into Egypt, not more than twenty-two years elapsed, as we have shown in this chapter. Consequently Benjamin, at the time of the journey to Egypt, was twenty-three or twenty-four at the most. He would therefore have been a grandfather in the flower of his age (Gen. xlvi. 21, cf. Numb. xxvi. 38, 40, and 1 Chron. viii. 1), for it is certain that Bela, Benjamin's eldest son, had at that time, two sons, Addai and Naaman. This is just as absurd as the statement that Dinah was violated at the age of seven, not to mention other impossibilities which would result from the truth of the narrative. Thus we see that unskilful endeavours to solve difficulties, only raise fresh ones, and make confusion worse confounded.

Note 15 (*p.* 136). "*Othniel, son of Kenag, was judge for forty years.*" Rabbi Levi Ben Gerson and others believe that these forty years which the Bible says were passed in freedom, should be counted

from the death of Joshua, and consequently include the eight
years during which the people were subject to Kushan Rishathaim, while the following eighteen years must be added on to
the eighty years of Ehud's and Shamgar's judgeships. In this
case it would be necessary to reckon the other years of subjection
among those said by the Bible to have been passed in freedom.
But the Bible expressly notes the number of years of subjection,
and the number of years of freedom, and further declares
(Judges ii. 18) that the Hebrew state was prosperous during the
whole time of the judges. Therefore it is evident that Levi Ben
Gerson (certainly a very learned man), and those who follow
him, correct rather than interpret the Scriptures.

The same fault is committed by those who assert, that Scripture, by this general calculation of years, only intended to mark
the period of the regular administration of the Hebrew state,
leaving out the years of anarchy and subjection as periods of
misfortune and interregnum. Scripture certainly passes over in
silence periods of anarchy, but does not, as they dream, refuse
to reckon them or wipe them out of the country's annals. It is
clear that Ezra, in 1 Kings vi., wished to reckon absolutely all
the years since the flight from Egypt. This is so plain, that no
one versed in the Scriptures can doubt it. For, without going
back to the precise words of the text, we may see that the
genealogy of David given at the end of the book of Ruth, and
1 Chron. ii., scarcely accounts for so great a number of years.
For Nahshon, who was prince of the tribe of Judah (Numb. vii.
11), two years after the Exodus, died in the desert, and his son
Salmon passed the Jordan with Joshua. Now this Salmon, according to the genealogy, was David's great-grandfather. De-
ducting, then, from the total of 480 years, four years for Solomon's
reign, seventy for David's life, and forty for the time passed in
the desert, we find that David was born 366 years after the passage of the Jordan. Hence we must believe that David's father,
grandfather, great-grandfather, and great-great-grandfather be-
gat children when they were ninety years old.

Note 16 (*p.* 137). " *Samson was judge for twenty years.*'
Samson was born after the Hebrews had fallen under the
dominion of the Philistines.

Note 17 (*p.* 139). Otherwise, they rather correct than explain
Scripture.

Note 18 (*p.* 140). "*Kirjath-jearim.*" Kirjath-jearim is also called
Baale of Judah. Hence Kimchi and others think that the words
Baale Judah, which I have translated " the people of Judah,"
are the name of a town. But this is not so, for the word Baale
is in the plural. Moreover, comparing this text in Samuel with
1 Chron. xiii. 5, we find that David did not rise up and go forth
out of Baale, but that he went thither. If the author of the book

of Samuel had meant to name the place whence David took the
ark, he would, if he spoke Hebrew correctly, have said, "David
rose up, and set forth from Baale Judah, and took the ark from
thence."

CHAPTER X.

Note 19 (*p.* 146). "*After the restoration of the Temple by Judas
Maccabæus.*" This conjecture, if such it be, is founded on
the genealogy of King Jeconiah, given in 1 Chron. iii., which
finishes at the sons of Elioenai, the thirteenth in direct descent
from him: whereon we must observe that Jeconiah, before his
captivity, had no children; but it is probable that he had two
while he was in prison, if we may draw any inference from
the names he gave them. As to his grandchildren, it is evident
that they were born after his deliverance, if the names be any
guide, for his grandson, Pedaiah (a name meaning *God hath
delivered me*), who, according to this chapter, was the father of
Zerubbabel, was born in the thirty-seventh or thirty-eighth year
of Jeconiah's life, that is thirty-three years before the restoration
of liberty to the Jews by Cyrus. Therefore Zerubbabel, to whom
Cyrus gave the principality of Judæa, was thirteen or fourteen
years old. But we need not carry the inquiry so far: we need
only read attentively the chapter of 1 Chron., already quoted,
where (*v.* 17, *sqq.*) mention is made of all the posterity of Jeconiah, and compare it with the Septuagint version to see clearly
that these books were not published, till after Maccabæus had
restored the Temple, the sceptre no longer belonging to the house
of Jeconiah.

Note 20 (*p.* 148). "*Zedekiah should be taken to Babylon.*"
No one could then have suspected that the prophecy of Ezekiel
contradicted that of Jeremiah, but the suspicion occurs to everyone who reads the narrative of Josephus. The event proved
that both prophets were in the right.

Note 21 (*p.* 150). "*And who wrote Nehemiah.*" That the
greater part of the book of Nehemiah was taken from the work
composed by the prophet Nehemiah himself, follows from the
testimony of its author. (See chap. i.). But it is obvious that
the whole of the passage contained between chap. viii. and
chap. xii. verse 26, together with the two last verses of chap.
xii., which form a sort of parenthesis to Nehemiah's words,
were added by the historian himself, who outlived Nehemiah.

Note 22 (*p.* 151). "*I suppose no one thinks*" that Ezra was the
uncle of the first high priest, named Joshua (see Ezra vii., and
1 Chron. vi. 14), and went to Jerusalem from Babylon with
Zerubbabel (see Nehemiah xii. 1). But it appears that when
he saw, that the Jews were in a state of anarchy, he returned
to Babylon, as also did others (Nehem. i. 2), and remained

there till the reign of Artaxerxes, when his requests were granted and he went a second time to Jerusalem. Nehemiah also went to Jerusalem with Zerubbabel in the time of Cyrus (Ezra ii. 2 and 63, cf. x. 9, and Nehemiah x. 1). The version given of the Hebrew word, translated "ambassador," is not supported by any authority, while it is certain that fresh names were given to those Jews who frequented the court. Thus Daniel was named Balteshazzar, and Zerubbabel Sheshbazzar (Dan. i. 7). Nehemiah was called Atirsata, while in virtue of his office he was styled governor, or president. (Nehem. v. 24, xii. 26.)

Note 23 (*p.* 155). "*Before the time of the Maccabees there was no canon of sacred books.*" The synagogue styled "the great" did not begin before the subjugation of Asia by the Macedonians. The contention of Maimonides, Rabbi Abraham, Ben-David, and others, that the presidents of this synagogue were Ezra, Daniel, Nehemiah, Haggai, Zechariah, &c., is a pure fiction, resting only on rabbinical tradition. Indeed they assert that the dominion of the Persians only lasted thirty-four years, and this is their chief reason for maintaining that the decrees of the "great synagogue," or synod (rejected by the Sadducees, but accepted by the Pharisees) were ratified by the prophets, who received them from former prophets, and so in direct succession from Moses, who received them from God Himself. Such is the doctrine which the Pharisees maintain with their wonted obstinacy. Enlightened persons, however, who know the reasons for the convoking of councils, or synods, and are no strangers to the differences between Pharisees and Sadducees, can easily divine the causes which led to the assembling of this great synagogue. It is very certain that no prophet was there present, and that the decrees of the Pharisees, which they style their traditions, derive all their authority from it.

Chapter XI.

Note 24 (*p.* 157). "*Now I think.*" The translators render the word λογίζομαι here by *I infer*, and assert that Paul uses it as synonymous with συλλογίζομαι. But the former word has, in Greek, the same meaning as the Hebrew word rendered to think, to esteem, to judge. And this signification would be in entire agreement with the Syriac translation. This Syriac translation (if it be a translation, which is very doubtful, for we know neither the time of its appearance, nor the translator, and Syriac was the vernacular of the Apostles) renders the text before us in a way well explained by Tremellius as "we think, therefore."

CHAPTER XV.

Note 25 (*p.* 198). "*That simple obedience is the path of salvation.*" In other words, it is enough for salvation or blessedness, that we should embrace the Divine decrees as laws or commands; there is no need to conceive them as eternal truths. This can be taught us by Revelation, not Reason, as appears from the demonstrations given in Chapter IV.

CHAPTER XVI.

Note 26 (*p.* 203). "*No one can honestly promise to forego the right which he has over all things.*" In the state of social life, where general right determines what is good or evil, stratagem is rightly distinguished as of two kinds, good and evil. But in the state of Nature, where every man is his own judge, possessing the absolute right to lay down laws for himself, to interpret them as he pleases, or to abrogate them if he thinks it convenient, it is not conceivable that stratagem should be evil.

Note 27 (*p.* 206). "*Every member of it may, if he will, be free.*" Whatever be the social state a man finds himself in, he may be free. For certainly a man is free, in so far as he is led by reason. Now reason (though Hobbes thinks otherwise) is always on the side of peace, which cannot be attained unless the general laws of the state be respected. Therefore the more a man is led by reason—in other words, the more he is free, the more constantly will he respect the laws of his country, and obey the commands of the sovereign power to which he is subject.

Note 28 (*p.* 210). "*No one knows by nature that he owes any obedience to God.*" When Paul says that men have in themselves no refuge, he speaks as a man : for in the ninth chapter of the same epistle he expressly teaches that God has mercy on whom He will, and that men are without excuse, only because they are in God's power like clay in the hands of a potter, who out of the same lump makes vessels, some for honour and some for dishonour, not because they have been forewarned. As regards the Divine natural law whereof the chief commandment is, as we have said, to love God, I have called it a law in the same sense, as philosophers style laws those general rules of nature, according to which everything happens. For the love of God is not a state of obedience : it is a virtue which necesarily exists in a man who knows God rightly. Obedience has regard to the will of a ruler, not to necessity and truth. Now as we are ignorant of the nature of God's will, and on the other hand know that everything happens solely by God's power, we cannot, except through revelation, know whether God wishes in any way to be honoured as a sovereign.

Again; we have shown that the Divine rights appear to us in the light of rights or commands, only so long as we are ignorant of their cause: as soon as their cause is known, they cease to be rights, and we embrace them no longer as rights but as eternal truths; in other words, obedience passes into love of God, which emanates from true knowledge as necessarily as light emanates from the sun. Reason then leads us to love God, but cannot lead us to obey Him ; for we cannot embrace the commands of God as Divine, while we are in ignorance of their cause, neither can we rationally conceive God as a sovereign laying down laws as a sovereign.

CHAPTER XVII.

Note 29 (*p*. 214). "*If men could lose their natural rights so as to be absolutely unable for the future to oppose the will of the sovereign.*"
Two common soldiers undertook to change the Roman dominion, and did change it. (Tacitus, Hist. i. 7.)
Note 30 (*p.* 221). See *Numbers* xi. 28. In this passage it is written that two men prophesied in the camp, and that Joshua wished to punish them. This he would not have done, if it had been lawful for anyone to deliver the Divine oracles to the people without the consent of Moses. But Moses thought good to pardon the two men, and rebuked Joshua for exhorting him to use his royal prerogative, at a time when he was so weary of reigning, that he preferred death to holding undivided sway (Numb. xi. 14). For he made answer to Joshua, "Enviest thou for my sake? Would God that all the Lord's people were prophets, and that the Lord would put His spirit upon them." That is to say, would God that the right of taking counsel of God were general, and the power were in the hands of the people. Thus Joshua was not mistaken as to the right, but only as to the time for using it, for which he was rebuked by Moses, in the same way as Abishai was rebuked by David for counselling that Shimei, who had undoubtedly been guilty of treason, should be put to death. See 2 Sam. xix. 22, 23.
Note 31 (*p.* 222). See *Numbers* xxvii. 21. The translators of the Bible have rendered incorrectly verses 19 and 23 of this chapter. The passage does not mean that Moses gave precepts or advice to Joshua, but that he made or established him chief of the Hebrews. The phrase is very frequent in Scripture (see Exodus, xviii. 23; 1 Sam. xiii. 15; Joshua i. 9; 1 Sam. xxv. 30).
Note 32 (*p.* 224). "*There was no judge over each of the captains save God.*" The Rabbis and some Christians equally foolish pretend that the Sanhedrin, called "the great" was instituted by Moses. As a matter of fact, Moses chose seventy colleagues to assist him in governing, because he was not able to bear alone the

burden of the whole people; but he never passed any law for forming a college of seventy members; on the contrary he ordered every tribe to appoint for itself, in the cities which God had given it, judges to settle disputes according to the laws which he himself had laid down. In cases where the opinions of the judges differed as to the interpretation of these laws, Moses bade them take counsel of the High Priest (who was the chief interpreter of the law), or of the chief judge, to whom they were then subordinate (who had the right of consulting the High Priest), and to decide the dispute in accordance with the answer obtained. If any subordinate judge should assert, that he was not bound by the decision of the High Priest, received either directly or through the chief of his state, such an one was to be put to death (Deut. xvii. 9) by the chief judge, whoever he might be, to whom he was a subordinate. This chief judge would either be Joshua, the supreme captain of the whole people, or one of the tribal chiefs who had been entrusted, after the division of the tribes, with the right of consulting the high priest concerning the affairs of his tribe, of deciding on peace or war, of fortifying towns, of appointing inferior judges, &c. Or, again, it might be the king, in whom all or some of the tribes had vested their rights.

I could cite many instances in confirmation of what I here advance. I will confine myself to one, which appears to me the most important of all. When the Shilomitish prophet anointed Jeroboam king, he, in so doing, gave him the right of consulting the high priest, of appointing judges, &c. In fact he endowed him with all the rights over the ten tribes, which Rehoboam retained over the two tribes. Consequently Jeroboam could set up a supreme council in his court with as much right as Jehoshaphat could at Jerusalem (2 Chron. xix. 8). For it is plain that neither Jeroboam, who was king by God's command, nor Jeroboam's subjects, were bound by the Law of Moses to accept the judgments of Rehoboam, who was not their king. Still less were they under the jurisdiction of the judge, whom Rehoboam had set up in Jerusalem as subordinate to himself. According, therefore, as the Hebrew dominion was divided, so was a supreme council set up in each division. Those who neglect the variations in the constitution of the Hebrew States, and confuse them all together in one, fall into numerous difficulties.

CHAPTER XIX.

Note 33 (*p.* 256). I must here bespeak special attention for what was said in Chap. XVI. concerning rights.

BENEDICT DE SPINOZA'S POLITICAL TREATISE,

WHEREIN IS DEMONSTRATED, HOW THE SOCIETY IN

WHICH MONARCHICAL DOMINION FINDS PLACE,

AS ALSO THAT IN WHICH THE DOMINION

IS ARISTOCRATIC, SHOULD BE ORDERED,

SO AS NOT TO LAPSE INTO A

TYRANNY, BUT TO PRESERVE

INVIOLATE THE PEACE

AND FREEDOM OF

THE CITIZENS.

[*TRACTATUS POLITICUS.*]

FROM THE EDITOR'S PREFACE TO THE POSTHUMOUS WORKS OF BENEDICT DE SPINOZA.

OUR author composed the Political Treatise shortly before his death. Its reasonings are exact, its style clear. Abandoning the opinions of many political writers, he most firmly propounds therein his own judgment; and throughout draws his conclusions from his premisses. In the first five chapters, he treats of political science in general—in the sixth and seventh, of monarchy; in the eighth, ninth, and tenth, of aristocracy; lastly, the eleventh begins the subject of democratic government. But his untimely death was the reason that he did not finish this treatise, and that he did not deal with the subject of laws, nor with the various questions about politics, as may be seen from the following "Letter of the Author to a Friend, which may properly be prefixed to this Political Treatise, and serve it for a Preface:"—

"Dear Friend,—Your welcome letter was delivered to me yesterday. I heartily thank you for the kind interest you take in me. I would not miss this opportunity, were I not engaged in something, which I think more useful, and which, I believe, will please you more—that is, in preparing a Political Treatise, which I began some time since, upon your advice. Of this treatise, six chapters are already finished. The first contains a kind of introduction to the actual work; the second treats of natural right; the third, of the right of supreme authorities. In the fourth, I inquire, what political matters are subject to the direction of supreme authorities; in the fifth, what is the ultimate and highest end which a society can contemplate; and, in the sixth, how a monarchy should be ordered, so as not to lapse into a tyranny. I am at present writing the seventh chapter, wherein I make a regular demonstration of all the heads of my preceding sixth chapter, concerning the ordering of a well-regulated monarchy. I shall afterwards pass to the subjects of aristocratic and popular dominion, and, lastly, to that of laws and other particular questions about politics. And so, farewell."

The author's aim appears clearly from this letter; but being hindered by illness, and snatched away by death, he was unable, as the reader will find for himself, to continue this work further than to the end of the subject of aristocracy.

CONTENTS.

CHAPTER I. INTRODUCTION.

PAGE

1-3. Of the theory and practice of political science . . . 287
4. Of the author's design 288
5. Of the force of the passions in men 289
6, 7. That we must not look to proofs of reason for the causes
and foundations of dominion, but deduce them from the
general nature or condition of mankind . . . 289

CHAPTER II. OF NATURAL RIGHT.

1. Right, natural and civil 291
2. Essence, ideal and real 291
3-5. What natural right is 291
6. The vulgar opinion about liberty. Of the first man's fall . 292
7-10. Of liberty and necessity 294
11. He is free, who is led by reason 295
12. Of giving and breaking one's word by natural right . 296
13. Of alliances formed between men 296
14. Men naturally enemies 296
15. The more there are that come together, the more right all
collectively have 296
16. Every one has so much the less right, the more the rest
collectively exceed him in power 297
17. Of dominion and its three kinds 297
18. That in the state of nature one can do no wrong . 297
19-21. What wrong-doing and obedience are . . . 298
22. The free man 299
23. The just and unjust man 299
24. Praise and blame 300

CHAPTER III. OF THE RIGHT OF SUPREME AUTHORITIES.

1. A commonwealth, affairs of state, citizens, subjects . . 301
2. Right of a dominion same as natural right . . 301
3-4. By the ordinance of the commonwealth a citizen may not
live after his own mind 301
5-9. Every citizen is dependent not on himself, but on the commonwealth 302
10. A question about religion 305

PAGE

11, 12. Of the right of supreme authorities against the world at
large 306
13. Two commonwealths naturally hostile 306
14-18. Of the state of treaty, war, and peace 307

CHAPTER IV. OF THE FUNCTIONS OF SUPREME AUTHORITIES.

1-3. What matters are affairs of state 309
4-6. In what sense it can, in what it cannot be said, that a commonwealth does wrong 310

CHAPTER V. OF THE BEST STATE OF A DOMINION.

1. That is best which is ordered according to the dictate of
reason 313
2-6. The end of the civil state. The best dominion . . 313
7. Machiavelli and his design 315

CHAPTER VI. OF MONARCHY.

1-3. Of the causes of establishing a dominion . . . 316
4. Of conferring the authority on one man . . . 317
5-8. Of the nature of a monarchy. Of the foundations of a
monarchical dominion 317
9. Of cities 319
10. Of the militia and its commanders 319
11. Of dividing the citizens into clans 319
12. Of lands and houses 319
13, 14. Of the election of the king and of the nobles . . 320
15, 16. Of the king's counsellors 320
17-25. Of the supreme council's functions 321
26-29. Of another council for administering justice . . 323
30. Of other subordinate councils 324
31. Of the payment of the militia 324
32. Of the rights of foreigners 325
33. Of ambassadors 325
34. Of the king's servants and body-guard . . . 325
35. Of waging war 325
36. Of the king's marriage 326
37, 38. Of the heir to the dominion 326
39. Of the obedience of the citizens 326
40. Of religion 326

CHAPTER VII. OF MONARCHY. PROOF OF THE FOUNDATIONS OF
A MONARCHICAL DOMINION.

1. The monarch is not chosen unconditionally. The Persian
kings. Ulysses 327
2. Nature of our monarchy the best and true one . . 328
3. It is necessary that the monarch have counsellors . 328

PAGE

    4. The counsellors must necessarily be representative . . 329
    5. The king's right is to select one of the opinions offered by
        the council 329
 6-11. The great advantages of this council 330
   12. The militia to be composed of citizens only . . . 332
   13. How the counsellors are to be chosen 333
14, 15. King's safety. Evidence of history 333
   16. Cities to be fortified 334
   17. Of mercenaries and military commanders 335
   18. Citizens to be divided into clans 336
   19. The soil to be the common property of the commonwealth 336
   20. None to be noble but the issue of kings 336
   21. Judges to be appointed for a term of years . . . 337
   22. The militia to be given no pay 337
   23. Of foreigners and the king's kinsmen 338
   24. Of the dangers from the king's marriage. Evidence of
       history 338
   25. Of the right of succession to the kingdom 339
   26. Of the right of worshipping God 340
   27. All men's nature is one and the same 340
   28. Of the most durable dominion of all 341
   29. Of hardly concealing the plans of the dominion . . . 342
   30. The example of the dominion of the Arragonese . . 342
   31. That the multitude may preserve under a king an ample
       enough liberty 344

CHAPTER VIII. OF ARISTOCRACY.

    1. What aristocracy is. Patricians 345
    2. An aristocracy should consist of a large number of patri-
       cians 345
    3. Difference between monarchy and aristocracy . . . 346
 4-6. Aristocracy approaches nearer to absolutism than monarchy 347-8
    7. Is also fitter to maintain liberty. Foundations of an aris-
       tocracy where one city is head of a whole dominion . 348
    8. Of fortifying towns 348
    9. Of the military and its leaders 349
   10. Of the sale of lands and farms 350
   11. Of the supreme council of patricians 350
   12. Of the causes of the destruction of an aristocracy . . 351
   13. The primary law of this dominion, to prevent its lapsing
       into oligarchy 351
14, 15. Patricians to be chosen out of certain families . . . 352
   16. Of the place and time of assembling 352
   17. Of the supreme council's functions 353
   18. Of the ruler or chief of the council 353
   19. Equality to be observed among patricians 353
20-25. Of the syndics and their functions 354
26, 27. Of the ministers of the dominion 356
   28. Voting to be by ballot 357

PAGE

29-33. Of the senate or second council 358
34-36. Of the presidents of the senate and their deputies. Consuls 361
37-41. Of the bench or college of judges 363
   42. Governors of cities and provinces. Right of the neigh-
        bouring cities 366
   43. Judges to be appointed in every city 367
   44. Ministers of dominion to be chosen from the commons . 367
   45. Of the tribunes of the treasury 368
   46. Of freedom of worship and speech 368
   47. Of the bearing and state of the patricians . . . 368
   48. Of the oath 369
   49. Of academies and liberty of teaching 369

CHAPTER IX. OF ARISTOCRACY.

   1. Of the aristocratic dominion held by more than one city . 370
   2. Confederate cities 370
   3. Of points common to both kinds of aristocracy . . 370
   4. Of the common bond of the cities by a senate and tribunal 371
   5. Supreme council and senate 371
   6. Of assembling this council, of choosing generals and am-
        bassadors, of the presidents of the orders, judges, &c. . 372
   7. Of commanders of battalions and military tribunes . 373
   8. Of tributes 373
   9. Of the senators' emoluments and place of meeting . 374
  10. Of the councils and syndics of the separate cities . 374
  11. Consuls of cities 374
  12. Judges of cities 375
  13. Of dependent cities 375
14, 15. This kind of aristocracy to be preferred to the other. 375

CHAPTER X. OF ARISTOCRACY.

   1. Primary cause, why aristocracies are dissolved. Of a
        dictator 378
   2. Of the supreme council 379
   3. Of the tribunes of the commons among the Romans . 380
   4. Of the authority of the syndics 380
   5. Sumptuary laws 381
6, 7. Vices not to be forbidden directly, but indirectly . 381
   8. Honours and rewards rejected 382
9, 10. An aristocracy may be stable 383

CHAPTER XI. OF DEMOCRACY.

1, 2. Difference between democracy and aristocracy . . 385
   3. Of the nature of democracy 386
   4. Women to be excluded from government . . . 387

A

POLITICAL TREATISE.

CHAPTER I.

INTRODUCTION.

PHILOSOPHERS conceive of the passions which harass us as vices into which men fall by their own fault, and, therefore, generally deride, bewail, or blame them, or execrate them, if they wish to seem unusually pious. And so they think they are doing something wonderful, and reaching the pinnacle of learning, when they are clever enough to bestow manifold praise on such human nature, as is nowhere to be found, and to make verbal attacks on that which, in fact, exists. For they conceive of men, not as they are, but as they themselves would like them to be. Whence it has come to pass that, instead of ethics, they have generally written satire, and that they have never conceived a theory of politics, which could be turned to use, but such as might be taken for a chimera, or might have been formed in Utopia, or in that golden age of the poets when, to be sure, there was least need of it. Accordingly, as in all sciences, which have a useful application, so especially in that of politics, theory is supposed to be at variance with practice; and no men are esteemed less fit to direct public affairs than theorists or philosophers.

2. But statesmen, on the other hand, are suspected of plotting against mankind, rather than consulting their

interests, and are esteemed more crafty than learned. No
doubt nature has taught them, that vices will exist, while
men do. And so, while they study to anticipate human
wickedness, and that by arts, which experience and long
practice have taught, and which men generally use under
the guidance more of fear than of reason, they are thought
to be enemies of religion, especially by divines, who believe
that supreme authorities should handle public affairs in
accordance with the same rules of piety, as bind a private
individual. Yet there can be no doubt, that statesmen
have written about politics far more happily than philosophers. For, as they had experience for their mistress,
they taught nothing that was inconsistent with practice.

3. And, certainly, I am fully persuaded that experience
has revealed all conceivable sorts of commonwealth, which
are consistent with men's living in unity, and likewise the
means by which the multitude may be guided or kept
within fixed bounds. So that I do not believe that we can
by meditation discover in this matter anything not yet tried
and ascertained, which shall be consistent with experience
or practice. For men are so situated, that they cannot live
without some general law. But general laws and public
affairs are ordained and managed by men of the utmost
acuteness, or, if you like, of great cunning or craft. And
so it is hardly credible, that we should be able to conceive
of anything serviceable to a general society, that occasion or
chance has not offered, or that men, intent upon their
common affairs, and seeking their own safety, have not seen
for themselves.

4. Therefore, on applying my mind to politics, I have resolved to demonstrate by a certain and undoubted course
of argument, or to deduce from the very condition of
human nature, not what is new and unheard of, but only
such things as agree best with practice. And that I might
investigate the subject-matter of this science with the same
freedom of spirit as we generally use in mathematics, I
have laboured carefully, not to mock, lament, or execrate,
but to understand human actions; and to this end I have
looked upon passions, such as love, hatred, anger, envy,
ambition, pity, and the other perturbations of the mind,
not in the light of vices of human nature, but as properties,

just as pertinent to it, as are heat, cold, storm, thunder, and the like to the nature of the atmosphere, which phenomena, though inconvenient, are yet necessary, and have fixed causes, by means of which we endeavour to understand their nature, and the mind has just as much pleasure in viewing them aright, as in knowing such things as flatter the senses.

5. For this is certain, and we have proved its truth in our Ethics,[1] that men are of necessity liable to passions, and so constituted as to pity those who are ill, and envy those who are well off; and to be prone to vengeance more than to mercy: and moreover, that every individual wishes the rest to live after his own mind, and to approve what he approves, and reject what he rejects. And so it comes to pass, that, as all are equally eager to be first, they fall to strife, and do their utmost mutually to oppress one another; and he who comes out conqueror is more proud of the harm he has done to the other, than of the good he has done to himself. And although all are persuaded, that religion, on the contrary, teaches every man to love his neighbour as himself, that is to defend another's right just as much as his own, yet we showed that this persuasion has too little power over the passions. It avails, indeed, in the hour of death, when disease has subdued the very passions, and man lies inert, or in temples, where men hold no traffic, but least of all, where it is most needed, in the law-court or the palace. We showed too, that reason can, indeed, do much to restrain and moderate the passions, but we saw at the same time, that the road, which reason herself points out, is very steep;[2] so that such as persuade themselves, that the multitude or men distracted by politics can ever be induced to live according to the bare dictate of reason, must be dreaming of the poetic golden age, or of a stage-play.

6. A dominion then, whose well-being depends on any man's good faith, and whose affairs cannot be properly administered, unless those who are engaged in them will act honestly, will be very unstable. On the contrary, to insure its permanence, its public affairs should be so

[1] Ethics, iv. 4, Coroll. iii. 31, note; 32, note.
[2] Ibid., v. 42, note.

290 A POLITICAL TREATISE. [SECS. 6-7.

ordered, that those who administer them, whether guided
by reason or passion, cannot be led to act treacherously or
basely.   Nor does it matter to the security of a dominion,
in what spirit men are led to rightly administer its affairs.
For liberality of spirit, or courage, is a private virtue ; but
the virtue of a state is its security.

7. Lastly, inasmuch as all men, whether barbarous or
civilized, everywhere frame customs, and form some kind
of civil state, we must not, therefore, look to proofs of
reason for the causes and natural bases of dominion, but
derive them from the general nature or position of mankind, as I mean to do in the next chapter.

CHAPTER II.

OF NATURAL RIGHT.

IN our Theologico-Political Treatise we have treated of natural and civil right,[1] and in our Ethics have explained the nature of wrong-doing, merit, justice, injustice,[2] and lastly, of human liberty.[3] Yet, lest the readers of the present treatise should have to seek elsewhere those points, which especially concern it, I have determined to explain them here again, and give a deductive proof of them.

2. Any natural thing whatever can be just as well conceived, whether it exists or does not exist. As then the beginning of the existence of natural things cannot be inferred from their definition, so neither can their continuing to exist. For their ideal essence is the same, after they have begun to exist, as it was before they existed. As then their beginning to exist cannot be inferred from their essence, so neither can their continuing to exist; but they need the same power to enable them to go on existing, as to enable them to begin to exist. From which it follows, that the power, by which natural things exist, and therefore that by which they operate, can be no other than the eternal power of God itself. For were it another and a created power, it could not preserve itself, much less natural things, but it would itself, in order to continue to exist, have need of the same power which it needed to be created.

3. From this fact therefore, that is, that the power whereby natural things exist and operate is the very power of God itself, we easily understand what natural right is. For as God has a right to everything, and God's right is nothing else, but his very power, as far as the latter is con-

---

[1] Theologico-Political Treatise, Chap. xvi.
[2] Ethics, iv. 37, note 2.   [3] Ibid., ii. 48, 49, note.

sidered to be absolutely free; it follows from this, that every natural thing has by nature as much right, as it has power to exist and operate; since the natural power of every natural thing, whereby it exists and operates, is nothing else but the power of God, which is absolutely free.

4. And so by natural right I understand the very laws or rules of nature, in accordance with which everything takes place, in other words, the power of nature itself. And so the natural right of universal nature, and consequently of every individual thing, extends as far as its power: and accordingly, whatever any man does after the laws of his nature, he does by the highest natural right, and he has as much right over nature as he has power.

5. If then human nature had been so constituted, that men should live according to the mere dictate of reason, and attempt nothing inconsistent therewith, in that case natural right, considered as special to mankind, would be determined by the power of reason only. But men are more led by blind desire, than by reason: and therefore the natural power or right of human beings should be limited, not by reason, but by every appetite, whereby they are determined to action, or seek their own preservation. I, for my part, admit, that those desires, which arise not from reason, are not so much actions as passive affections of man. But as we are treating here of the universal power or right of nature, we cannot here recognize any distinction between desires, which are engendered in us by reason, and those which are engendered by other causes; since the latter, as much as the former, are effects of nature, and display the natural impulse, by which man strives to continue in existence. For man, be he learned or ignorant, is part of nature, and everything, by which any man is determined to action, ought to be referred to the power of nature, that is, to that power, as it is limited by the nature of this or that man. For man, whether guided by reason or mere desire, does nothing save in accordance with the laws and rules of nature, that is, by natural right. (Section 4.)

6. But most people believe, that the ignorant rather disturb than follow the course of nature, and conceive of

mankind in nature as of one dominion within another. For they maintain, that the human mind is produced by no natural causes, but created directly by God, and is so independent of other things, that it has an absolute power to determine itself, and make a right use of reason. Experience, however, teaches us but too well, that it is no more in our power to have a sound mind, than a sound body. Next, inasmuch as everything whatever, as far as in it lies, strives to preserve its own existence, we cannot at all doubt, that, were it as much in our power to live after the dictate of reason, as to be led by blind desire, all would be led by reason, and order their lives wisely; which is very far from being the case. For

"Each is attracted by his own delight."[1]

Nor do divines remove this difficulty, at least not by deciding, that the cause of this want of power is a vice or sin in human nature, deriving its origin from our first parents' fall. For if it was even in the first man's power as much to stand as to fall, and he was in possession of his senses, and had his nature unimpaired, how could it be, that he fell in spite of his knowledge and foresight? But they say, that he was deceived by the devil. Who then was it, that deceived the devil himself? Who, I say, so maddened the very being that excelled all other created intelligences, that he wished to be greater than God? For was not *his* effort too, supposing him of sound mind, to preserve himself and his existence, as far as in him lay? Besides, how could it happen, that the first man himself, being in his senses, and master of his own will, should be led astray, and suffer himself to be taken mentally captive? For if he had the power to make a right use of reason, it was not possible for him to be deceived, for as far as in him lay, he of necessity strove to preserve his existence and his soundness of mind. But the hypothesis is, that he had this in his power; therefore he of necessity maintained his soundness of mind, and could not be deceived. But this from his history, is known to be false. And, accordingly, it must be admitted, that it was not in the first man's

---

[1] Virgil, Ecl. ii. 65.

power to make a right use of reason, but that, like us, he was subject to passions.

7. But that man, like other beings, as far as in him lies, strives to preserve his existence, no one can deny. For if any distinction could be conceived on this point, it must arise from man's having a free will. But the freer we conceived man to be, the more we should be forced to maintain, that he must of necessity preserve his existence and be in possession of his senses; as anyone will easily grant me, that does not confound liberty with contingency. For liberty is a virtue, or excellence. Whatever, therefore, convicts a man of weakness cannot be ascribed to his liberty. And so man can by no means be called free, because he is able not to exist or not to use his reason, but only in so far as he preserves the power of existing and operating according to the laws of human nature. The more, therefore, we consider man to be free, the less we can say, that he can neglect to use reason, or choose evil in preference to good; and, therefore, God, who exists in absolute liberty, also understands and operates of necessity, that is, exists, understands, and operates according to the necessity of his own nature. For there is no doubt, that God operates by the same liberty whereby he exists. As then he exists by the necessity of his own nature, by the necessity of his own nature also he acts, that is, he acts with absolute liberty.

8. So we conclude, that it is not in the power of any man always to use his reason, and be at the highest pitch of human liberty, and yet that everyone always, as far as in him lies, strives to preserve his own existence; and that (since each has as much right as he has power) whatever anyone, be he learned or ignorant, attempts and does, he attempts and does by supreme natural right. From which it follows that the law and ordinance of nature, under which all men are born, and for the most part live, forbids nothing but what no one wishes or is able to do, and is not opposed to strifes, hatred, anger, treachery, or, in general, anything that appetite suggests. For the bounds of nature are not the laws of human reason, which do but pursue the true interest and preservation of mankind, but other infinite laws, which regard the eternal order of universal nature,

whereof man is an atom ; and according to the necessity of this order only are all individual beings determined in a fixed manner to exist and operate. Whenever, then, anything in nature seems to us ridiculous, absurd, or evil, it is because we have but a partial knowledge of things, and are in the main ignorant of the order and coherence of nature as a whole, and because we want everything to be arranged according to the dictate of our own reason; although, in fact, what our reason pronounces bad, is not bad as regards the order and laws of universal nature, but only as regards the laws of our own nature taken separately.

9. Besides, it follows that everyone is so far rightfully dependent on another, as he is under that other's authority, and so far independent, as he is able to repel all violence, and avenge to his heart's content all damage done to him, and in general to live after his own mind.

10. He has another under his authority, who holds him bound, or has taken from him arms and means of defence or escape, or inspired him with fear, or so attached him to himself by past favour, that the man obliged would rather please his benefactor than himself, and live after his mind than after his own. He that has another under authority in the first or second of these ways, holds but his body, not his mind. But in the third or fourth way he has made dependent on himself as well the mind as the body of the other ; yet only as long as the fear or hope lasts, for upon the removal of the feeling the other is left independent.

11. The judgment can be dependent on another, only as far as that other can deceive the mind ; whence it follows that the mind is so far independent, as it uses reason aright. Nay, inasmuch as human power is to be reckoned less by physical vigour than by mental strength, it follows that those men are most independent whose reason is strongest, and who are most guided thereby. And so I am altogether for calling a man so far free, as he is led by reason ; because so far he is determined to action by such causes, as can be adequately understood by his unassisted nature, although by these causes he be necessarily determined to action. For liberty, as we showed above

(Sec. 7), does not take away the necessity of acting, but supposes it.

12. The pledging of faith to any man, where one has but verbally promised to do this or that, which one might rightfully leave undone, or *vice versâ*, remains so long valid as the will of him that gave his word remains unchanged. For he that has authority to break faith has, in fact, bated nothing of his own right, but only made a present of words. If, then, he, being by natural right judge in his own case, comes to the conclusion, rightly or wrongly (for "to err is human"), that more harm than profit will come of his promise, by the judgment of his own mind he decides that the promise should be broken, and by natural right (Sec. 9) he will break the same.

13. If two come together and unite their strength, they have jointly more power, and consequently more right over nature than both of them separately, and the more there are that have so joined in alliance, the more right they all collectively will possess.

14. In so far as men are tormented by anger, envy, or any passion implying hatred, they are drawn asunder and made contrary one to another, and therefore are so much the more to be feared, as they are more powerful, crafty, and cunning than the other animals. And because men are in the highest degree liable to these passions (Chap. I, Sec. 5), therefore men are naturally enemies. For he is my greatest enemy, whom I must most fear and be on my guard against.

15. But inasmuch as (Sec. 6) in the state of nature each is so long independent, as he can guard against oppression by another, and it is in vain for one man alone to try and guard against all, it follows hence that so long as the natural right of man is determined by the power of every individual, and belongs to everyone, so long it is a nonentity, existing in opinion rather than fact, as there is no assurance of making it good. And it is certain that the greater cause of fear every individual has, the less power, and consequently the less right, he possesses. To this must be added, that without mutual help men can hardly support life and cultivate the mind. And so our conclusion is, that that natural right, which is special to the human race,

can hardly be conceived, except where men have general rights, and combine to defend the possession of the lands they inhabit and cultivate, to protect themselves, to repel all violence, and to live according to the general judgment of all. For (Sec. 13) the more there are that combine together, the more right they collectively possess. And if this is why the schoolmen want to call man a sociable animal—I mean because men in the state of nature can hardly be independent—I have nothing to say against them.

16. Where men have general rights, and are all guided, as it were, by one mind, it is certain (Sec. 13), that every individual has the less right the more the rest collectively exceed him in power; that is, he has, in fact, no right over nature but that which the common law allows him. But whatever he is ordered by the general consent, he is bound to execute, or may rightfully be compelled thereto (Sec. 4).

17. This right, which is determined by the power of a multitude, is generally called Dominion. And, speaking generally, he holds dominion, to whom are entrusted by common consent affairs of state—such as the laying down, interpretation, and abrogation of laws, the fortification of cities, deciding on war and peace, &c. But if this charge belong to a council, composed of the general multitude, then the dominion is called a democracy; if the council be composed of certain chosen persons, then it is an aristocracy; and if, lastly, the care of affairs of state and, consequently, the dominion rest with one man, then it has the name of monarchy.

18. From what we have proved in this chapter, it becomes clear to us that, in the state of nature, wrong-doing is impossible; or, if anyone does wrong, it is to himself, not to another. For no one by the law of nature is bound to please another, unless he chooses, nor to hold anything to be good or evil, but what he himself, according to his own temperament, pronounces to be so; and, to speak generally, nothing is forbidden by the law of nature, except what is beyond everyone's power (Secs. 5 and 8). But wrong-doing is action, which cannot lawfully be committed. But if men by the ordinance of nature were bound to be led by

reason, then all of necessity would be so led. For the
ordinances of nature are the ordinances of God (Secs. 2, 3),
which God has instituted by the liberty, whereby he exists,
and they follow, therefore, from the necessity of the divine
nature (Sec. 7), and, consequently, are eternal, and cannot
be broken.   But men are chiefly guided by appetite, without reason; yet for all this they do not disturb the course
of nature, but follow it of necessity. And, therefore, a man
ignorant and weak of mind, is no more bound by natural
law to order his life wisely, than a sick man is bound to be
sound of body.

19. Therefore wrong-doing cannot be conceived of, but
under dominion—that is, where, by the general right of
the whole dominion, it is decided what is good and what
evil, and where no one does anything rightfully, save what
he does in accordance with the general decree or consent
(Sec. 16). For that, as we said in the last section, is
wrong-doing, which cannot lawfully be committed, or is by
law forbidden.   But obedience is the constant will to
execute that, which by law is good, and by the general
decree ought to be done.

20. Yet we are accustomed to call that also wrong,
which is done against the sentence of sound reason, and
to give the name of obedience to the constant will to
moderate the appetite according to the dictate of reason :
a manner of speech which I should quite approve, did
human liberty consist in the licence of appetite, and
slavery in the dominion of reason.   But as human liberty
is the greater, the more man can be guided by reason,
and moderate his appetite, we cannot without great im-
propriety call a rational life obedience, and give the name
of wrong-doing to that which is, in fact, a weakness of
the mind, not a licence of the mind directed against itself,
and for which a man may be called a slave, rather than
free (Secs. 7 and 11).

21. However, as reason teaches one to practise piety, and
be of a calm and gentle spirit, which cannot be done save
under dominion; and, further, as it is impossible for a
multitude to be guided, as it were, by one mind, as under
dominion is required, unless it has laws ordained according
to the dictate of reason; men who are accustomed to live

under dominion are not, therefore, using words so improperly, when they call that wrong-doing which is done against the sentence of reason, because the laws of the best dominion ought to be framed according to that dictate (Sec. 18). But, as for my saying (Sec. 18) that man in a state of nature, if he does wrong at all, does it against himself, see, on this point, Chap. IV., Secs. 4, 5, where is shown, in what sense we can say, that he who holds dominion and possesses natural right, is bound by laws and can do wrong.

22. As far as religion is concerned, it is further clear, that a man is most free and most obedient to himself when he most loves God, and worships him in sincerity. But so far as we regard, not the course of nature, which we do not understand, but the dictates of reason only, which respect religion, and likewise reflect that these dictates are revealed to us by God, speaking, as it were, within ourselves, or else were revealed to prophets as laws; so far, speaking in human fashion, we say that man obeys God when he worships him in sincerity, and, on the contrary, does wrong when he is led by blind desire. But, at the same time, we should remember that we are subject to God's authority, as clay to that of the potter, who of the same lump makes some vessels unto honour, and others unto dishonour.[1] And thus man can, indeed, act contrarily to the decrees of God, as far as they have been written like laws in the minds of ourselves or the prophets, but against that eternal decree of God, which is written in universal nature, and has regard to the course of nature as a whole, he can do nothing.

23. As, then, wrong-doing and obedience, in their strict sense, so also justice and injustice cannot be conceived of, except under dominion. For nature offers nothing that can be called this man's rather than another's; but under nature everything belongs to all—that is, they have authority to claim it for themselves. But under dominion, where it is by common law determined what belongs to this man, and what to that, he is called just who has a constant will to render to every man his own, but he unjust who strives,

---

[1] Romans ix. 21.

on the contrary; to make his own that which belongs to another.

24. But that praise and blame are emotions of joy and sadness, accompanied by an idea of human excellence or weakness as their cause, we have explained in our Ethics.

CHAPTER III.

OF THE RIGHT OF SUPREME AUTHORITIES.

UNDER every dominion the state is said to be Civil; but the entire body subject to a dominion is called a Commonwealth, and the general business of the dominion, subject to the direction of him that holds it, has the name of Affairs of State. Next we call men Citizens, as far as they enjoy by the civil law all the advantages of the commonwealth, and Subjects, as far as they are bound to obey its ordinances or laws. Lastly, we have already said that, of the civil state, there are three kinds—democracy, aristocracy, and monarchy (Chap. II. Sec. 17). Now, before I begin to treat of each kind separately, I will first deduce all the properties of the civil state in general. And of these, first of all comes to be considered the supreme right of the commonwealth, or the right of the supreme authorities.

2. From Chap. II. Sec. 15, it is clear that the right of the supreme authorities is nothing else than simple natural right, limited, indeed, by the power, not of every individual, but of the multitude, which is guided, as it were, by one mind—that is, as each individual in the state of nature, so the body and mind of a dominion have as much right as they have power. And thus each single citizen or subject has the less right, the more the commonwealth exceeds him in power (Chap. II. Sec. 16), and each citizen consequently does and has nothing, but what he may by the general decree of the commonwealth defend.

3. If the commonwealth grant to any man the right, and therewith the authority (for else it is but a gift of words, Chap. II. Sec. 12), to live after his own mind, by that very act it abandons its own right, and transfers the same

to him, to whom it has given such authority. But if it
has given this authority to two or more, I mean authority
to live each after his own mind, by that very act it has
divided the dominion, and if, lastly, it has given this same
authority to every citizen, it has thereby destroyed itself,
and there remains no more a commonwealth, but everything returns to the state of nature; all of which is very
manifest from what goes before. And thus it follows,
that it can by no means be conceived, that every citizen
should by the ordinance of the commonwealth live after
his own mind, and accordingly this natural right of being
one's own judge ceases in the civil state. I say expressly
" by the ordinance of the commonwealth," for, if we weigh
the matter aright, the natural right of every man does not
cease in the civil state. For man, alike in the natural and
in the civil state, acts according to the laws of his own
nature, and consults his own interest. Man, I say, in each
state is led by fear or hope to do or leave undone this or
that; but the main difference between the two states is
this, that in the civil state all fear the same things, and all
have the same ground of security, and manner of life ; and
this certainly does not do away with the individual's faculty
of judgment. For he that is minded to obey all the
commonwealth's orders, whether through fear of its power
or through love of quiet, certainly consults after his own
heart his own safety and interest.

4. Moreover, we cannot even conceive, that every citizen
should be allowed to interpret the commonwealth's decrees
or laws. For were every citizen allowed this, he would
thereby be his own judge, because each would easily be
able to give a colour of right to his own deeds, which by
the last section is absurd.

5. We see then, that every citizen depends not on himself, but on the commonwealth, all whose commands he is
bound to execute, and has no right to decide, what is
equitable or iniquitous, just or unjust. But, on the contrary, as the body of the dominion should, so to speak, be
guided by one mind, and consequently the will of the
commonwealth must be taken to be the will of all; what
the state decides to be just and good must be held to be
so decided by every individual. And so, however iniquitous

the subject may think the commonwealth's decisions, he is none the less bound to execute them.

6. But (it may be objected) is it not contrary to the dictate of reason to subject one's self wholly to the judgment of another, and consequently, is not the civil state repugnant to reason? Whence it would follow, that the civil state is irrational, and could only be created by men destitute of reason, not at all by such as are led by it. But since reason teaches nothing contrary to nature, sound reason cannot therefore dictate, that every one should remain independent, so long as men are liable to passions (Chap. II. Sec. 15), that is, reason pronounces against such independence (Chap. I. Sec. 5). Besides, reason altogether teaches to seek peace, and peace cannot be maintained, unless the commonwealth's general laws be kept unbroken. And so, the more a man is guided by reason, that is (Chap. II. Sec. 11), the more he is free, the more constantly he will keep the laws of the commonwealth, and execute the commands of the supreme authority, whose subject he is. Furthermore, the civil state is naturally ordained to remove general fear, and prevent general sufferings, and therefore pursues above everything the very end, after which everyone, who is led by reason, strives, but in the natural state strives vainly (Chap. II. Sec. 15). Wherefore, if a man, who is led by reason, has sometimes to do by the commonwealth's order what he knows to be repugnant to reason, that harm is far compensated by the good, which he derives from the existence of a civil state. For it is reason's own law, to choose the less of two evils; and accordingly we may conclude, that no one is acting against the dictate of his own reason, so far as he does what by the law of the commonwealth is to be done. And this anyone will more easily grant us, after we have explained, how far the power and consequently the right of the commonwealth extends.

7. For, first of all, it must be considered, that, as in the state of nature the man who is led by reason is most powerful and most independent, so too that commonwealth will be most powerful and most independent, which is founded and guided by reason. For the right of the commonwealth is determined by the power of the multitude, which is led, as it were, by one mind. But this

unity of mind can in no wise be conceived, unless the commonwealth pursues chiefly the very end, which sound reason teaches is to the interest of all men.

8. In the second place it comes to be considered, that subjects are so far dependent not on themselves, but on the commonwealth, as they fear its power or threats, or as they love the civil state (Chap. II. Sect. 10). Whence it follows, that such things, as no one can be induced to do by rewards or threats, do not fall within the rights of the commonwealth. For instance, by reason of his faculty of judgment, it is in no man's power to believe. For by what rewards or threats can a man be brought to believe, that the whole is not greater than its part, or that God does not exist, or that that is an infinite being, which he sees to be finite, or generally anything contrary to his sense or thought? So, too, by what rewards or threats can a man be brought to love one, whom he hates, or to hate one, whom he loves? And to this head must likewise be referred such things as are so abhorrent to human nature, that it regards them as actually worse than any evil, as that a man should be witness against himself, or torture himself, or kill his parents, or not strive to avoid death, and the like, to which no one can be induced by rewards or threats. But if we still choose to say, that the commonwealth has the right or authority to order such things, we can conceive of it in no other sense, than that in which one might say, that a man has the right to be mad or delirious. For what but a delirious fancy would such a right be, as could bind no one? And here I am speaking expressly of such things as cannot be subject to the right of a commonwealth and are abhorrent to human nature in general. For the fact, that a fool or madman can by no rewards or threats be induced to execute orders, or that this or that person, because he is attached to this or that religion, judges the laws of a dominion worse than any possible evil, in no wise makes void the laws of the commonwealth, since by them most of the citizens are restrained. And so, as those who are without fear or hope are so far independent (Chap. II. Sec. 10), they are, therefore, enemies of the dominion (Chap. II. Sec. 14), and may lawfully be coerced by force.

9. Thirdly and lastly, it comes to be considered, that those things are not so much within the commonwealth's right, which cause indignation in the majority. For it is certain, that by the guidance of nature men conspire together, either through common fear, or with the desire to avenge some common hurt; and as the right of the commonwealth is determined by the common power of the multitude, it is certain that the power and right of the commonwealth are so far diminished, as it gives occasion for many to conspire together. There are certainly some subjects of fear for a commonwealth, and as every separate citizen or in the state of nature every man, so a commonwealth is the less independent, the greater reason it has to fear. So much for the right of supreme authorities over subjects. Now before I treat of the right of the said authorities as against others, we had better resolve a question commonly mooted about religion.

10. For it may be objected to us, Do not the civil state, and the obedience of subjects, such as we have shown is required in the civil state, do away with religion, whereby we are bound to worship God? But if we consider the matter, as it really is, we shall find nothing that can suggest a scruple. For the mind, so far as it makes use of reason, is dependent, not on the supreme authorities, but on itself (Chap. II. Sec. 11). And so the true knowledge and the love of God cannot be subject to the dominion of any, nor yet can charity towards one's neighbour (Sec. 8). And if we further reflect, that the highest exercise of charity is that which aims at keeping peace and joining in unity, we shall not doubt that he does his duty, who helps everyone, so far as the commonwealth's laws, that is so far as unity and quiet allow. As for external rites, it is certain, that they can do no good or harm at all in respect of the true knowledge of God, and the love which necessarily results from it; and so they ought not to be held of such importance, that it should be thought worth while on their account to disturb public peace and quiet. Moreover it is certain, that I am not a champion of religion by the law of nature, that is (Chap. II. Sec. 3), by the divine decree. For I have no authority, as once the disciples of Christ had, to cast out unclean spirits and work miracles; which

authority is yet so necessary to the propagating of religion in places where it is forbidden, that without it one not only, as they say, wastes one's time [1] and trouble, but causes besides very many inconveniences, whereof all ages have seen most mournful examples.   Everyone therefore, wherever he may be, can worship God with true religion, and mind his own business, which is the duty of a private man. But the care of propagating religion should be left to God, or the supreme authorities, upon whom alone falls the charge of affairs of state.   But I return to my subject.

11. After explaining the right of supreme authorities over citizens and the duty of subjects, it remains to consider the right of such authorities against the world at large, which is now easily intelligible from what has been said.   For since (Sec. 2) the right of the supreme authorities is nothing else but simple natural right, it follows that two dominions stand towards each other in the same relation as do two men in the state of nature, with this exception, that a commonwealth can provide against being oppressed by another ; which a man in the state of nature cannot do, seeing that he is overcome daily by sleep, often by disease or mental infirmity, and in the end by old age, and is besides liable to other inconveniences, from which a commonwealth can secure itself.

12. A commonwealth then is so far independent, as it can plan and provide against oppression by another (Chap. II. Secs. 9, 15), and so far dependent on another commonwealth, as it fears that other's power, or is hindered by it from executing its own wishes, or lastly, as it needs its help for its own preservation or increase (Chap. II. Secs. 10, 15).   For we cannot at all doubt, that if two commonwealths are willing to offer each other mutual help, both together are more powerful, and therefore have more right, than either alone (Chap. II. Sec. 13).

13. But this will be more clearly intelligible, if we reflect, that two commonwealths are naturally enemies. For men in the state of nature are enemies (Chap. II. Sec. 14). Those, then, who stand outside a commonwealth, and retain their natural rights, continue enemies.   Accord-

---

[1] Literally, "oil and trouble"—a common proverbial expression in Latin.

ingly, if one commonwealth wishes to make war on another and employ extreme measures to make that other dependent on itself, it may lawfully make the attempt, since it needs but the bare will of the commonwealth for war to be waged.   But concerning peace it can decide nothing, save with the concurrence of another commonwealth's will. Whence it follows, that laws of war regard every commonwealth by itself, but laws of peace regard not one, but at the least two commonwealths, which are therefore called " contracting powers."

14. This "contract" remains so long unmoved as the motive for entering into it, that is, fear of hurt or hope of gain, subsists.   But take away from either commonwealth this hope or fear, and it is left independent (Chap. II. Sec. 10), and the link, whereby the commonwealths were mutually bound, breaks of itself.   And therefore every commonwealth has the right to break its contract, whenever it chooses, and cannot be said to act treacherously or perfidiously in breaking its word, as soon as the motive of hope or fear is removed.   For every contracting party was on equal terms in this respect, that whichever could first free itself of fear should be independent, and make use of its independence after its own mind; and, besides, no one makes a contract respecting the future, but on the hypothesis of certain precedent circumstances.   But when these circumstances change, the reason of policy applicable to the whole position changes with them; and therefore every one of the contracting commonwealths retains the right of consulting its own interest, and consequently endeavours, as far as possible, to be free from fear and thereby independent, and to prevent another from coming out of the contract with greater power. If then a commonwealth complains that it has been deceived, it cannot properly blame the bad faith of another contracting commonwealth, but only its own folly in having entrusted its own welfare to another party, that was independent, and had for its highest law the welfare of its own dominion.

15. To commonwealths, which have contracted a treaty of peace, it belongs to decide the questions, which may be mooted about the terms or rules of peace, whereby they have mutually bound themselves, inasmuch as laws of

peace regard not one commonwealth, but the commonwealths which contract taken together (Sec. 13). But if
they cannot agree together about the conditions, they by
that very fact return to a state of war.

16. The more commonwealths there are, that have contracted a joint treaty of peace, the less each of them by
itself is an object of fear to the remainder, or the less it
has the authority to make war. But it is so much the
more bound to observe the conditions of peace; that is
(Sec. 13), the less independent, and the more bound to ac-
commodate itself to the general will of the contracting
parties.

17. But the good faith, inculcated by sound reason and
religion, is not hereby made void; for neither reason nor
Scripture teaches one to keep one's word in every case.
For if I have promised a man, for instance, to keep safe a
sum of money he has secretly deposited with me, I am not
bound to keep my word, from the time that I know or
believe the deposit to have been stolen, but I shall act
more rightly in endeavouring to restore it to its owners.
So likewise, if the supreme authority has promised another
to do something, which subsequently occasion or reason
shows or seems to show is contrary to the welfare of its
subjects, it is surely bound to break its word. As then
Scripture only teaches us to keep our word in general, and
leaves to every individual's judgment the special cases of
exception, it teaches nothing repugnant to what we have
just proved.

18. But that I may not have so often to break the
thread of my discourse, and to resolve hereafter similar objections, I would have it known that all this demonstration
of mine proceeds from the necessity of human nature, considered in what light you will—I mean, from the universal
effort of all men after self-preservation, an effort inherent
in all men, whether learned or unlearned. And therefore,
however one considers men are led, whether by passion or
by reason, it will be the same thing; for the demonstration,
as we have said, is of universal application.

CHAPTER IV.

OF THE FUNCTIONS OF SUPREME AUTHORITIES.

THAT the right of the supreme authorities is limited by their power, we showed in the last chapter, and saw that the most important part of that right is, that they are, as it were, the mind of the dominion, whereby all ought to be guided; and accordingly, that such authorities alone have the right of deciding what is good, evil, equitable, or iniquitous, that ·is, what must be done or left undone by the subjects severally or collectively. And, accordingly, we saw that they have the sole right of laying down laws, and of interpreting the same, whenever their meaning is disputed, and of deciding whether a given case is in conformity with or violation of the law (Chap. III. Secs. 3-5); and, lastly, of waging war, and of drawing up and offering propositions for peace, or of accepting such when offered (Chap. III. Secs. 12, 13).

2. As all these functions, and also the means required to execute them, are matters which regard the whole body of the dominion, that is, are affairs of state, it follows, that affairs of state depend on the direction of him only, who holds supreme dominion.   And hence it follows, that it is the right of the supreme authority alone to judge the deeds of every individual, and demand of him an account of the same; to punish criminals, and decide questions of law between citizens, or appoint jurists acquainted with the existing laws, to administer these matters on its behalf; and, further, to use and order all means to war and peace, as to found and fortify cities, levy soldiers, assign military posts, and order what it would have done, and, with a view to peace, to send and give audience to ambassadors; and, finally, to levy the costs of all this.

3. Since, then, it is the right of the supreme authority

alone to handle public matters, or choose officials to do so,
it follows, that that subject is a pretender to the dominion,
who, without the supreme council's knowledge, enters upon
any public matter, although he believe that his design will
be to the best interest of the commonwealth.

4. But it is often asked, whether the supreme authority
is bound by laws, and, consequently, whether it can do
wrong. Now as the words "law" and "wrong-doing"
often refer not merely to the laws of a commonwealth, but
also to the general rules which concern all natural things,
and especially to the general rules of reason, we cannot,
without qualification, say that the commonwealth is bound
by no laws, or can do no wrong. For were the commonwealth bound by no laws or rules, which removed, the
commonwealth were no commonwealth, we should have to
regard it not as a natural thing, but as a chimera. A
commonwealth then does wrong, when it does, or suffers to
be done, things which may be the cause of its own ruin;
and we can say that it then does wrong, in the sense in
which philosophers or doctors say that nature does wrong;
and in this sense we can say, that a commonwealth does
wrong, when it acts against the dictate of reason. For a
commonwealth is most independent when it acts according
to the dictate of reason (Chap. III. Sec. 7); so far, then,
as it acts against reason, it fails itself, or does wrong. And
we shall be able more easily to understand this if we reflect, that when we say, that a man can do what he will
with his own, this authority must be limited not only by
the power of the agent, but by the capacity of the object.
If, for instance, I say that I can rightfully do what I will
with this table, I do not certainly mean, that I have the
right to make it eat grass. So, too, though we say, that
men depend not on themselves, but on the commonwealth,
we do not mean, that men lose their human nature and put
on another; nor yet that the commonwealth has the right
to make men wish for this or that, or (what is just as impossible) regard with honour things which excite ridicule
or disgust. But it is implied, that there are certain intervening circumstances, which supposed, one likewise supposes the reverence and fear of the subjects towards the
commonwealth, and which abstracted, one makes abstrac-

tion likewise of that fear and reverence, and therewith of the commonwealth itself. The commonwealth, then, to maintain its independence, is bound to preserve the causes of fear and reverence, otherwise it ceases to be a commonwealth. For the person or persons that hold dominion, can no more combine with the keeping up of majesty the running with harlots drunk or naked about the streets, or the performances of a stage-player, or the open violation or contempt of laws passed by themselves, than they can combine existence with non-existence. But to proceed to slay and rob subjects, ravish maidens, and the like, turns fear into indignation and the civil state into a state of enmity.

5. We see, then, in what sense we may say, that a commonwealth is bound by laws and can do wrong. But if by "law" we understand civil law, and by "wrong" that which, by civil law, is forbidden to be done, that is, if these words be taken in their proper sense, we cannot at all say, that a commonwealth is bound by laws, or can do wrong. For the maxims and motives of fear and reverence, which a commonwealth is bound to observe in its own interest, pertain not to civil jurisprudence, but to the law of nature, since (Sec. 4) they cannot be vindicated by the civil law, but by the law of war. And a commonwealth is bound by them in no other sense than that in which in the state of nature a man is bound to take heed, that he preserve his independence and be not his own enemy, lest he should destroy himself; and in this taking heed lies not the subjection, but the liberty of human nature. But civil jurisprudence depends on the mere decree of the commonwealth, which is not bound to please any but itself, nor to hold anything to be good or bad, but what it judges to be such for itself. And, accordingly, it has not merely the right to avenge itself, or to lay down and interpret laws, but also to abolish the same, and to pardon any guilty person out of the fulness of its power.

6. Contracts or laws, whereby the multitude transfers its right to one council or man, should without doubt be broken, when it is expedient for the general welfare to do so. But to decide this point, whether, that is, it be expedient for the general welfare to break them or not, is

within the right of no private person, but of him only who holds dominion (Sec. 3) ; therefore of these laws he who holds dominion remains sole interpreter. Moreover, no private person can by right vindicate these laws, and so they do not really bind him who holds dominion. Notwithstanding, if they are of such a nature that they cannot be broken, without at the same time weakening the commonwealth's strength, that is, without at the same time changing to indignation the common fear of most of the citizens, by this very fact the commonwealth is dissolved, and the contract comes to an end ; and therefore such contract is vindicated not by the civil law, but by the law of war. And so he who holds dominion is not bound to observe the terms of the contract by any other cause than that, which bids a man in the state of nature to beware of being his own enemy, lest he should destroy himself, as we said in the last section.

CHAPTER V.

OF THE BEST STATE OF A DOMINION.

IN Chap. II. Sec. 2, we showed, that man is then most independent, when he is most led by reason, and, in consequence (Chap. III. Sec. 7), that that commonwealth is most powerful and most independent, which is founded and guided by reason. But, as the best plan of living, so as to assure to the utmost self-preservation, is that which is framed according to the dictate of reason, therefore it follows, that that in every kind is best done, which a man or commonwealth does, so far as he or it is in the highest degree independent. For it is one thing to till a field by right, and another to till it in the best way. One thing, I say, to defend or preserve one's self, and to pass judgment by right, and another to defend or preserve one's self in the best way, and to pass the best judgment; and, consequently, it is one thing to have dominion and care of affairs of state by right, and another to exercise dominion and direct affairs of state in the best way. And so, as we have treated of the right of every commonwealth in general, it is time to treat of the best state of every dominion.

2. Now the quality of the state of any dominion is easily perceived from the end of the civil state, which end is nothing else but peace and security of life. And therefore that dominion is the best, where men pass their lives in unity, and the laws are kept unbroken. For it is certain, that seditions, wars, and contempt or breach of the laws are not so much to be imputed to the wickedness of the subjects, as to the bad state of a dominion. For men are not born fit for citizenship, but must be made so. Besides, men's natural passions are everywhere the same; and if wickedness more prevails, and more offences are committed in one commonwealth than in another, it is certain that the

former has not enough pursued the end of unity, nor framed its laws with sufficient forethought; and that, therefore, it has failed in making quite good its right as a commonwealth. For a civil state, which has not done away with the causes of seditions, where war is a perpetual object of fear, and where, lastly, the laws are often broken, differs but little from the mere state of nature, in which everyone lives after his own mind at the great risk of his life.

3. But as the vices and inordinate licence and contumacy of subjects must be imputed to the commonwealth, so, on the other hand, their virtue and constant obedience to the laws are to be ascribed in the main to the virtue and perfect right of the commonwealth, as is clear from Chap. II. Sec. 15. And so it is deservedly reckoned to Hannibal as an extraordinary virtue, that in his army there never arose a sedition.[1]

4. Of a commonwealth, whose subjects are but hindered by terror from taking arms, it should rather be said, that it is free from war, than that it has peace. For peace is not mere absence of war, but is a virtue that springs from force of character: for obedience (Chap. II. Sec. 19) is the constant will to execute what, by the general decree of the commonwealth, ought to be done. Besides that commonwealth, whose peace depends on the sluggishness of its subjects, that are led about like sheep, to learn but slavery, may more properly be called a desert than a commonwealth.

5. When, then, we call that dominion best, where men pass their lives in unity, I understand a human life, defined not by mere circulation of the blood, and other qualities common to all animals, but above all by reason, the true excellence and life of the mind.

6. But be it remarked that, by the dominion which I have said is established for this end, I intend that which has been established by a free multitude, not that which is acquired over a multitude by right of war. For a free multitude is guided more by hope than fear; a conquered one, more by fear than hope: inasmuch as the former aims

---

[1] Justin, Histories, xxxii. iv. 12.

at making use of life, the latter but at escaping death.
The former, I say, aims at living for its own ends, the
latter is forced to belong to the conqueror; and so we say
that this is enslaved, but that free. And, therefore, the
end of a dominion, which one gets by right of war, is to be
master, and have rather slaves than subjects. And although
between the dominion created by a free multitude, and that
gained by right of war, if we regard generally the right of
each, we can make no essential distinction; yet their ends,
as we have already shown, and further the means to the
preservation of each are very different.

7. But what means a prince, whose sole motive is lust of
mastery, should use to establish and maintain his dominion,
the most ingenious Machiavelli has set forth at large,[1] but
with what design one can hardly be sure. If, however, he
had some good design, as one should believe of a learned
man, it seems to have been to show, with how little foresight many attempt to remove a tyrant, though thereby the
causes which make the prince a tyrant can in no wise be
removed, but, on the contrary, are so much the more
established, as the prince is given more cause to fear, which
happens when the multitude has made an example of its
prince, and glories in the parricide as in a thing well done.
Moreover, he perhaps wished to show how cautious a free
multitude should be of entrusting its welfare absolutely to
one man, who, unless in his vanity he thinks he can please
everybody, must be in daily fear of plots, and so is forced
to look chiefly after his own interest, and, as for the multitude, rather to plot against it than consult its good. And
I am the more led to this opinion concerning that most far-
seeing man, because it is known that he was favourable to
liberty, for the maintenance of which he has besides given
the most wholesome advice.

[1] In his book called " Il Principe," or " The Prince."

CHAPTER VI.

OF MONARCHY.

INASMUCH as men are led, as we have said, more by
passion than reason, it follows, that a multitude comes
together, and wishes to be guided, as it were, by one mind,
not at the suggestion of reason, but of some common passion—that is (Chap. III. Sec. 9), common hope, or fear, or
the desire of avenging some common hurt. But since fear
of solitude exists in all men, because no one in solitude is
strong enough to defend himself, and procure the necessaries of life, it follows that men naturally aspire to the civil
state; nor can it happen that men should ever utterly
dissolve it.

2. Accordingly, from the quarrels and seditions which
are often stirred up in a commonwealth, it never results
that the citizens dissolve it, as often happens in the case of
other associations; but only that they change its form into
some other—that is, of course, if the disputes cannot be
settled, and the features of the commonwealth at the same
time preserved. Wherefore, by means necessary to preserve
a dominion, I intend such things as are necessary to preserve
the existing form of the dominion, without any notable
change.

3. But if human nature were so constituted, that men
most desired what is most useful, no art would be needed
to produce unity and confidence. But, as it is admittedly
far otherwise with human nature, a dominion must of
necessity be so ordered, that all, governing and governed
alike, whether they will or no, shall do what makes for the
general welfare; that is, that all, whether of their own
impulse, or by force or necessity, shall be compelled to
live according to the dictate of reason. And this is the

case, if the affairs of the dominion be so managed, that
nothing which affects the general welfare is entirely entrusted to the good faith of any one. For no man is so
watchful, that he never falls asleep; and no man ever had
a character so vigorous and honest, but he sometimes, and
that just when strength of character was most wanted, was
diverted from his purpose and let himself be overcome.
And it is surely folly to require of another what one can
never obtain from one's self; I mean, that he should be more
watchful for another's interest than his own, that he should
be free from avarice, envy, and ambition, and so on;
especially when he is one, who is subject daily to the
strongest temptations of every passion.

4. But, on the other hand, experience is thought to
teach, that it makes for peace and concord, to confer the
whole authority upon one man. For no dominion has
stood so long without any notable change, as that of the
Turks, and on the other hand there were none so little
lasting, as those, which were popular or democratic, nor
any in which so many seditions arose. Yet if slavery,
barbarism, and desolation are to be called peace, men can
have no worse misfortune. No doubt there are usually
more and sharper quarrels between parents and children,
than between masters and slaves; yet it advances not the
art of housekeeping, to change a father's right into a right
of property, and count children but as slaves. Slavery
then, not peace, is furthered by handing over to one man
the whole authority. For peace, as we said before, consists not in mere absence of war, but in a union or agreement of minds,

5. And in fact they are much mistaken, who suppose
that one man *can* by himself hold the supreme right of a
commonwealth. For the only limit of right, as we showed
(Chap. II.), is power. But the power of one man is very
inadequate to support so great a load. And hence it
arises, that the man, whom the multitude has chosen
king, looks out for himself generals, or counsellors, or
friends, to whom he entrusts his own and the common
welfare; so that the dominion, which is thought to be a
perfect monarchy, is in actual working an aristocracy, not,
indeed, an open but a hidden one, and therefore the worst

of all.   Besides which, a king, who is a boy, or ill, or overcome by age, is but king on sufferance; and those in this
case have the supreme authority, who administer the
highest business of the dominion, or are near the king's
person; not to mention, that a lascivious king often
manages everything at the caprice of this or that mistress
or minion.   "I had heard," says Orsines, "that women
once reigned in Asia, but for a eunuch to reign is something new." [1]

6. It is also certain, that a commonwealth is always in
greater danger from its citizens than from its enemies;
for the good are few.   Whence it follows, that he, upon
whom the whole right of the dominion has been conferred,
will always be more afraid of citizens than of enemies, and
therefore will look to his own safety, and not try to consult
his subjects' interests, but to plot against them, especially
against those who are renowned for learning, or have influence through wealth.

7. It must besides be added, that kings fear their sons
also more than they love them, and so much the more as
the latter are skilled in the arts of war and peace, and
endeared to the subjects by their virtues.   Whence it
comes, that kings try so to educate their sons, that they
may have no reason to fear them.   Wherein ministers very
readily obey the king, and will be at the utmost pains, that
the successor may be an inexperienced king, whom they
can hold tightly in hand.

8. From all which it follows, that the more absolutely
the commonwealth's right is transferred to the king, the
less independent he is, and the more unhappy is the condition of his subjects.   And so, that a monarchical dominion may be duly established, it is necessary to lay
solid foundations, to build it on; from which may result
to the monarch safety, and to the multitude peace; and,
therefore, to lay them in such a way, that the monarch
may then be most independent, when he most consults the
multitude's welfare.   But I will first briefly state, what
these foundations of a monarchical dominion are, and afterwards prove them in order.

---

[1] Curtius, x. 1.

9. One or more cities must be founded and fortified, whose citizens, whether they live within the walls, or outside for purposes of agriculture, are all to enjoy the same right in the commonwealth; yet on this condition, that every city provide an ascertained number of citizens for its own and the general defence. But a city, which cannot supply this, must be held in subjection on other terms.

10. The militia must be formed out of citizens alone, none being exempt, and of no others. And, therefore, all are to be bound to have arms, and no one to be admitted into the number of the citizens, till he has learnt his drill, and promised to practise it at stated times in the year. Next, the militia of each clan is to be divided into battalions and regiments, and no captain of a battalion chosen, that is not acquainted with military engineering. Moreover, though the commanders of battalions and regiments are to be chosen for life, yet the commander of the militia of a whole clan is to be chosen only in time of war, to hold command for a year at most, without power of being continued or afterwards re-appointed. And these last are to be selected out of the king's counsellors, of whom we shall speak in the fifteenth and following sections, or out of those who have filled the post of counsellor.

11. The townsmen and countrymen of every city, that is, the whole of the citizens, are to be divided into clans, distinguished by some name and badge, and all persons born of any of these clans are to be received into the number of citizens, and their names inscribed on the roll of their clan, as soon as they have reached the age, when they can carry arms and know their duty; with the exception of those, who are infamous from some crime, or dumb, or mad, or menials supporting life by some servile office.

12. The fields, and the whole soil, and, if it can be managed, the houses should be public property, that is, the property of him, who holds the right of the commonwealth: and let him let them at a yearly rent to the citizens, whether townsmen or countrymen, and with this exception let them all be free or exempt from every kind of taxation in time of peace. And of this rent a part is to be applied to the defences of the state, a part to the king's private use. For

it is necessary in time of peace to fortify cities against war, and also to have ready ships and other munitions of war.

13. After the selection of the king from one of the clans, none are to be held noble, but his descendants, who are therefore to be distinguished by royal insignia from their own and the other clans.

14. Those male nobles, who are the reigning king's collaterals, and stand to him in the third or fourth degree of consanguinity, must not marry, and any children they may have had, are to be accounted bastards, and unworthy of any dignity, nor may they be recognized as heirs to their parents, whose goods must revert to the king.

15. Moreover the king's counsellors, who are next to him in dignity, must be numerous, and chosen out of the citizens only; that is (supposing there to be no more than six hundred clans) from every clan three or four or five, who will form together one section of this council; and not for life, but for three, four, or five years, so that every year a third, fourth, or fifth part may be replaced by selection, in which selection it must be observed as a first condition, that out of every clan at least one counsellor chosen be a jurist.

16. The selection must be made by the king himself, who should fix a time of year for the choice of fresh counsellors. Each clan must then submit to the king the names of all its citizens, who have reached their fiftieth year, and have been duly put forward as candidates for this office, and out of these the king will choose whom he pleases. But in that year, when the jurist of any clan is to be replaced, only the names of jurists are to be submitted to the king. Those who have filled this office of counsellor for the appointed time, are not to be continued therein, nor to be replaced on the list of candidates for five years or more. But the reason why one is to be chosen every year out of every clan is, that the council may not be composed alternately of untried novices, and of veterans versed in affairs, which must necessarily be the case, were all to retire at once, and new men to succeed them. But if every year one be chosen out of every family, then only a fifth, fourth, or at most a third part of the council will con-

sist of novices.   Further, if the king be prevented by other
business, or for any other reason, from being able to spare
time for this choice, then let the counsellors themselves
choose others for a time, until the king either chooses
different ones, or confirms the choice of the council.

17. Let the primary function of this council be to defend
the fundamental laws of the dominion, and to give advice
about administration, that the king may know, what for
the public good ought to be decreed : and that on the
understanding, that the king may not decide in any matter,
without first hearing the opinion of this council. But if, as
will generally happen, the council is not of one mind, but
is divided in opinion, even after discussing the same subject two or three times, there must be no further delay, but
the different opinions are to be submitted to the king, as
in the twenty-fifth section of this chapter we shall show.

18. Let it be also the duty of this council to publish the
king's orders or decrees, and to see to the execution of any
decree concerning affairs of state, and to supervise the administration of the whole dominion, as the king's deputies.

19. The citizens should have no access to the king, save
through this council, to which are to be handed all demands or petitions, that they may be presented to the
king.   Nor should the envoys of other commonwealths be
allowed to obtain permission to address the king, but
through the council.   Letters, too, sent from elsewhere to
the king, must be handed to him by the council.   And in
general the king is to be accounted as the mind of the
commonwealth, but the council as the senses outside the
mind, or the commonwealth's body, through whose intervention the mind understands the state of the commonwealth, and acts as it judges best for itself.

20. The care of the education of the king's sons should
also fall on this council, and the guardianship, where a
king has died, leaving as his successor an infant or boy.
Yet lest meanwhile the council should be left without a
king, one of the elder nobles of the commonwealth should
be chosen to fill the king's place, till the legitimate heir has
reached the age at which he can support the weight of
government.

21. Let the candidates for election to this council be such

as know the system of government, and the foundations,
and state or condition of the commonwealth, whose subjects
they are.   But he that would fill the place of a jurist must,
besides the government and condition of the commonwealth, whose subject he is, be likewise acquainted with
those of the other commonwealths, with which it has any
intercourse.   But none are to be placed upon the list of
candidates, unless they have reached their fiftieth year
without being convicted of crime.

22. In this council no decision is to be taken about the
affairs of the dominion, but in the presence of all the
members.   But if anyone be unable through illness or
other cause to attend, he must send in his stead one of the
same clan, who has filled the office of counsellor or been put
on the list of candidates.   Which if he neglect to do, and
the council through his absence be forced to adjourn any
matter, let him be fined a considerable sum.   But this
must be understood to mean, when the question is of a
matter affecting the whole dominion, as of peace or war, of
abrogating or establishing a law, of trade, &c.   But if the
question be one that affects only a particular city or two,
as about petitions, &c., it will suffice that a majority of the
council attend.

23. To maintain a perfect equality between the clans,
and a regular order in sitting, making proposals, and
speaking, every clan is to take in turn the presidency at
the sittings, a different clan at every sitting, and that
which was first at one sitting is to be last at the next. But
among members of the same clan, let precedence go by
priority of election.

24. This council should be summoned at least four times
a year, to demand of the ministers account of their administration of the dominion, to ascertain the state of
affairs, and see if anything else needs deciding.   For it
seems impossible for so large a number of citizens to have
constant leisure for public business.   But as in the mean-
time public business must none the less be carried on,
therefore fifty or more are to be chosen out of this council
to supply its place after its dismissal; and these should
meet daily in a chamber next the king's, and so have daily
care of the treasury, the cities, the fortifications, the edu-

cation of the king's son, and in general of all those duties
of the great council, which we have just enumerated, except that they cannot take counsel about new matters, concerning which no decision has been taken.

25. On the meeting of the council, before anything is
proposed in it, let five, six, or more jurists of the clans,
which stand first in order of place at that session, attend on
the king, to deliver to him petitions or letters, if they have
any, to declare to him the state of affairs, and, lastly, to
understand from him what he bids them propose in his
council; and when they have heard this, let them return
to the council, and let the first in precedence open the
matter of debate. But, in matters which seem to any of
them to be of some moment, let not the votes be taken at
once, but let the voting be adjourned to such a date as the
urgency of the matter allows. When, then, the council
stands adjourned till the appointed time, the counsellors of
every clan will meanwhile be able to debate the matter
separately, and, if they think it of great moment, to consult
others that have been counsellors, or are candidates for the
council. And if within the appointed time the counsellors
of any clan cannot agree among themselves, that clan shall
lose its vote, for every clan can give but one vote. But,
otherwise, let the jurist of the clan lay before the council
the opinion they have decided to be best; and so with
the rest. And if the majority of the council think fit, after
hearing the grounds of every opinion, to consider the
matter again, let the council be again adjourned to a date,
at which every clan shall pronounce its final opinion; and
then, at last, before the entire council, let the votes be
taken, and that opinion be invalidated which has not at
least a hundred votes. But let the other opinions be submitted to the king by all the jurists present at the council,
that, after hearing every party's arguments, he may select
which opinion he pleases. And then let the jurists leave
him, and return to the council; and there let all await the
king at the time fixed by himself, that all may hear which
opinion of those proposed he thinks fit to adopt, and what
he decides should be done.

26. For the administration of justice, another council is
to be formed of jurists, whose business should be to decide

suits, and punish criminals, but so that all the judgments they deliver be tested by those who are for the time members of the great council—that is, as to their having been delivered according to the due process of justice, and without partiality. But if the losing party can prove, that any judge has been bribed by the adversary, or that there is some mutual cause of friendship between the judge and the adversary, or of hatred between the judge and himself, or, lastly, that the usual process of justice has not been observed, let such party be restored to his original position. But this would, perhaps, not be observed by such as love to convict the accused in a criminal case, rather by torture than proofs. But, for all that, I can conceive on this point of no other process of justice than the above, that befits the best system of governing a commonwealth.

27. Of these judges, there should be a large and odd number—for instance, sixty-one, or at least forty-one,—and not more than one is to be chosen of one clan, and that not for life, but every year a certain proportion are to retire, and be replaced by as many others out of different clans, that have reached their fortieth year.

28. In this council, let no judgment be pronounced save in the presence of all the judges. But if any judge, from disease or other cause, shall for a long time be unable to attend the council, let another be chosen for that time to fill his place. But in giving their votes, they are all not to utter their opinions aloud, but to signify them by ballot.

29. Let those who supply others' places in this and the first-mentioned council first be paid out of the goods of those whom they have condemned to death, and also out of the fines of which any are mulcted. Next, after every judgment they pronounce in a civil suit, let them receive a certain proportion of the whole sum at stake for the benefit of both councils.

30. Let there be in every city other subordinate councils, whose members likewise must not be chosen for life, but must be partially renewed every year, out of the clans who live there only. But there is no need to pursue this further.

31. No military pay is to be granted in time of peace; but, in time of war, military pay is to be allowed to those

only, who support their lives by daily labour. But the commanders and other officers of the battalions are to expect no other advantage from war but the spoil of the enemy.

32. If a foreigner takes to wife the daughter of a citizen, his children are to be counted citizens, and put on the roll of their mother's clan. But those who are born and bred within the dominion of foreign parents should be allowed to purchase at a fixed price the right of citizenship from the captains of thousands of any clan, and to be enrolled in that clan. For no harm can arise thence to the dominion, even though the captains of thousands, for a bribe, admit a foreigner into the number of their citizens for less than the fixed price; but, on the contrary, means should be devised for more easily increasing the number of citizens, and producing a large confluence of men. As for those who are not enrolled as citizens, it is but fair that, at least in war-time, they should pay for their exemption from service by some forced labour or tax.

33. The envoys to be sent in time of peace to other commonwealths must be chosen out of the nobles only, and their expenses met by the state treasury, and not the king's privy purse.

34. Those that attend the court, and are the king's servants, and are paid out of his privy purse, must be excluded from every appointment and office in the commonwealth. I say expressly, "and are paid out of the king's privy purse," to except the body-guard. For there should be no other body-guard, but the citizens of the king's city, who should take turns to keep guard at court before the king's door.

35. War is only to be made for the sake of peace, so that, at its end, one may be rid of arms. And so, when cities have been taken by right of war, and terms of peace are to be made after the enemies are subdued, the captured cities must not be garrisoned and kept; but either the enemy, on accepting the terms of peace, should be allowed to redeem them at a price, or, if by following that policy, there would, by reason of the danger of the position, remain a constant lurking anxiety, they must be utterly destroyed, and the inhabitants removed elsewhere.

36. The king must not be allowed to contract a foreign marriage, but only to take to wife one of his kindred, or of the citizens; yet, on condition that, if he marries a citizen, her near relations become incapable of holding office in the commonweath.

37. The dominion must be indivisible. And so, if the king leaves more than one child, let the eldest one succeed; but by no means be it allowed to divide the dominion between them, or to give it undivided to all or several of them, much less to give a part of it as a daughter's dowry. For that daughters should be admitted to the inheritance of a dominion is in no wise to be allowed.

38. If the king die leaving no male issue, let the next to him in blood be held the heir to the dominion, unless he chance to have married a foreign wife, whom he will not put away.

39. As for the citizens, it is manifest (Chap. III. Sec. 5) that every one of them ought to obey all the commands of the king, and the decrees published by the great council, although he believe them to be most absurd, and otherwise he may rightfully be forced to obey. And these are the foundations of a monarchical dominion, on which it must be built, if it is to be stable, as we shall show in the next chapter.

40. As for religion, no temples whatever ought to be built at the public expense; nor ought laws to be established about opinions, unless they be seditious and overthrow the foundations of the commonwealth. And so let such as are allowed the public exercise of their religion build a temple at their own expense. But the king may have in his palace a chapel of his own, that he may practise the religion to which he belongs.

CHAPTER VII.

OF MONARCHY (CONTINUATION).

AFTER explaining the foundations of a monarchical dominion, I have taken in hand to prove here in order the fitness of such foundations. And to this end the first point to be noted is, that it is in no way repugnant to experience, for laws to be so firmly fixed, that not the king himself can abolish them. For though the Persians worshipped their kings as gods, yet had not the kings themselves authority to revoke laws once established, as appears from Daniel,[1] and nowhere, as far as I know, is a monarch chosen absolutely without any conditions expressed. Nor yet is it repugnant to reason or the absolute obedience due to a king. For the foundations of the dominion are to be considered as eternal decrees of the king, so that his ministers entirely obey him in refusing to execute his orders, when he commands anything contrary to the same. Which we can make plain by the example of Ulysses.[2] For his comrades were executing his own order, when they would not untie him, when he was bound to the mast and captivated by the Sirens' song, although he gave them manifold orders to do so, and that with threats. And it is ascribed to his forethought, that he afterwards thanked his comrades for obeying him according to his first intention. And, after this example of Ulysses, kings often instruct judges, to administer justice without respect of persons, not even of the king himself, if by some singular accident he order anything contrary to established law. For kings are not gods, but men, who are often led captive by the Sirens' song. If then everything depended on the inconstant will of one man, nothing would be fixed. And so, that a monarchical dominion may be stable, it must be

---

[1] Daniel vi. 15. [2] Hom. "Odys.," xii. 156-200.

ordered, so that everything be done by the king's decree only, that is, so that every law be an explicit will of the king, but not every will of the king a law; as to which see Chap. VI. Sects. 3, 5, 6.

2. It must next be observed, that in laying foundations it is very necessary to study the human passions: and it is not enough to have shown, what ought to be done, but it ought, above all, to be shown how it can be effected, that men, whether led by passion or reason, should yet keep the laws firm and unbroken. For if the constitution of the dominion, or the public liberty depends only on the weak assistance of the laws, not only will the citizens have no security for its maintenance (as we showed in the third section of the last chapter), but it will even turn to their ruin. For this is certain, that no condition of a commonwealth is more wretched than that of the best, when it begins to totter, unless at one blow it falls with a rush into slavery, which seems to be quite impossible. And, therefore, it would be far better for the subjects to transfer their rights absolutely to one man, than to bargain for unascertained and empty, that is unmeaning, terms of liberty, and so prepare for their posterity a way to the most cruel servitude. But if I succeed in showing that the foundation of monarchical dominion, which I stated in the last chapter, are firm and cannot be plucked up, without the indignation of the larger part of an armed multitude, and that from them follow peace and security for king and multitude, and if I deduce this from general human nature, no one will be able to doubt, that these foundations are the best and the true ones (Chap. III. Sec. 9, and Chap. VI. Sects. 3, 8). But that such is their nature, I will show as briefly as possible.

3. That the duty of him, who holds the dominion, is always to know its state and condition, to watch over the common welfare of all, and to execute whatever is to the interest of the majority of the subjects, is admitted by all. But as one person alone is unable to examine into everything, and cannot always have his mind ready and turn it to meditation, and is often hindered by disease, or old age, or other causes, from having leisure for public business; therefore it is necessary that the monarch have counsellors

to know the state of affairs, and help the king with their
advice, and frequently supply his place; and that so it
come to pass, that the dominion or commonwealth may
continue always in one and the same mind.

4. But as human nature is so constituted, that everyone
seeks with the utmost passion his own advantage, and
judges those laws to be most equitable, which he thinks
necessary to preserve and increase his substance, and
defends another's cause so far only as he thinks he is
thereby establishing his own; it follows hence, that the
counsellors chosen must be such, that their private affairs
and their own interests depend on the general welfare and
peace of all.   And so it is evident, that if from every sort
or class of citizens a certain number be chosen, what has
most votes in such a council will be to the interest of
the greater part of the subjects.   And though this council,
because it is composed of so large a number of citizens,
must of necessity be attended by many of very simple
intellect, yet this is certain, that everyone is pretty clever
and sagacious in business which he has long and eagerly
practised.   And, therefore, if none be chosen but such as
have till their fiftieth year practised their own business
without disgrace, they will be fit enough to give their
advice about their own affairs, especially if, in matters of
considerable importance, a time be allowed for consideration.   Besides, it is far from being the fact, that a council
composed of a few is not frequented by this kind of men.
For, on the contrary, its greatest part must consist of such,
since everyone, in that case, tries hard to have dullards for
colleagues, that they may hang on his words, for which
there is no opportunity in large councils.

5. Furthermore, it is certain, that everyone would rather
rule than be ruled.   "For no one of his own will yields
up dominion to another," as Sallust has it in his first
speech to Cæsar.[1]   And, therefore, it is clear, that a whole
multitude will never transfer its right to a few or to one,
if it can come to an agreement with itself, without proceeding from the controversies, which generally arise in large
councils, to seditions.   And so the multitude does not, if

---

[1] Chap. I. Sec. 4 of the speech, or rather letter, which is not now
admitted to be a genuine work of Sallust.

it is free, transfer to the king anything but that, which it
cannot itself have absolutely within its authority, namely,
the ending of controversies and the using despatch in
decisions. For as to the case which often arises, where a
king is chosen on account of war, that is, because war is
much more happily conducted by kings, it is manifest
folly, I say, that men should choose slavery in time of
peace for the sake of better fortune in war; if, indeed,
peace can be conceived of in a dominion, where merely for
the sake of war the highest authority is transferred to one
man, who is, therefore, best able to show his worth and the
importance to everyone of his single self in time of war;
whereas, on the contrary, democracy has this advantage,
that its excellence is greater in peace than in war. However, for whatever reason a king is chosen, he cannot by
himself, as we said just now, know what will be to the
interest of the dominion: but for this purpose, as we
showed in the last section, will need many citizens for his
counsellors. And as we cannot at all suppose, that any
opinion can be conceived about a matter proposed for discussion, which can have escaped the notice of so large a
number of men, it follows, that no opinion can be conceived
tending to the people's welfare, besides all the opinions of
this council, which are submitted to the king. And so,
since the people's welfare is the highest law, or the king's
utmost right, it follows, that the king's utmost right is but
to choose one of the opinions offered by the council, not to
decree anything, or offer any opinion contrary to the mind
of all the council at once (Chap. VI. Sec. 25). But if all
the opinions offered in the council were to be submitted to
the king, then it might happen that the king would always
favour the small cities, which have the fewest votes. For
though by the constitution of the council it be ordained,
that the opinions should be submitted to the king without
mention of their supporters, yet they will never be able to
take such good care, but that some opinion will get
divulged. And, therefore, it must of necessity be provided,
that that opinion, which has not gained at least a hundred
votes, shall be held void; and this law the larger cities
will be sure to defend with all their might.

6. And here, did I not study brevity, I would show

other advantages of this council; yet one, which seems of the greatest importance, I will allege. I mean, that there can be given no greater inducement to virtue, than this general hope of the highest honour. For by ambition are we all most led, as in our Ethics we showed to be the case.[1]

7. But it cannot be doubted that the majority of this council will never be minded to wage war, but rather always pursue and love peace. For besides that war will always cause them fear of losing their property and liberty, it is to be added, that war requires fresh expenditure, which they must meet, and also that their own children and relatives, though intent on their domestic cares, will be forced to turn their attention to war and go a-soldiering, whence they will never bring back anything but unpaid-for scars. For, as we said (Chap. VI. Sec. 31), no pay is to be given to the militia, and (Chap. VI. Sec. 10) it is to be formed out of citizens only and no others.

8. There is another accession to the cause of peace and concord, which is also of great weight: I mean, that no citizen can have immovable property (Chap. VI. Sec. 12). Hence all will have nearly an equal risk in war. For all will be obliged, for the sake of gain, to practise trade, or lend money to one another, if, as formerly by the Athenians, a law be passed, forbidding to lend money at interest to any but inhabitants; and thus they will be engaged in business, which either is mutually involved, one man's with another's, or needs the same means for its furtherance. And thus the greatest part of this council will generally have one and the same mind about their common affairs and the arts of peace. For, as we said (Sec. 4), every man defends another's cause, so far as he thinks thereby to establish his own.

9. It cannot be doubted, that it will never occur to anyone to corrupt this council with bribes. For were any man to draw over to his side some one or two out of so great a number of men, he would gain nothing. For, as we said, the opinion, which does not gain at least a hundred votes, is void.

10. We shall also easily see, that, once this council is established its members cannot be reduced to a less num-

---

[1] Ethics, iii. 29, &c.

ber, if we consider the common passions of mankind. For all are guided mostly by ambition, and there is no man who lives in health but hopes to attain extreme old age. If then we calculate the number of those who actually reach their fiftieth or sixtieth year, and further take into account the number that are every year chosen of this great council, we shall see, that there can hardly be a man of those who bear arms, but is under the influence of a great hope of attaining this dignity. And so they will all, to the best of their power, defend this law of the council. For be it noted, that corruption, unless it creep in gradually, is easily prevented. But as it can be more easily supposed, and would be less invidious, that a less number should be chosen out of every clan, than that a less number should be chosen out of a few clans, or that one or two clans should be altogether excluded ; therefore (Chap. VI. Sec. 15) the number of counsellors cannot be reduced, unless a third, fourth, or fifth part be removed simultaneously, which change is a very great one, and therefore quite repugnant to common practice. Nor need one be afraid of delay or negligence in choosing, because this is remedied by the council itself. See Chap. VI. Sec. 16.

11. The king, then, whether he is induced by fear of the multitude, or aims at binding to himself the majority of an armed multitude, or is guided by a generous spirit, a wish that is, to consult the public interest, will always confirm that opinion, which has gained most votes, that is (Sec. 5),[1] which is to the interest of the greater part of the dominion ; and will study to reconcile the divergent opinions referred to him, if it can be done, that he may attach all to himself (in which he will exert all his powers), and that alike in peace and war they may find out, what an advantage his single self is to them. And thus he will then be most in-dependent, and most in possession of dominion, when he most consults the general welfare of the multitude.

12. For the king by himself cannot restrain all by fear. But his power, as we have said, rests upon the number of

---

[1] This seems to be a mistake for Sec. 4, " Id majori subditorum parti utile erit, quod in hoc concilio plurima habuerit suffragia." " What has most votes in such a council, will be to the interest of the greater part of the subjects."

his soldiers, and especially on their valour and faith, which will always remain so long enduring between men, as with them is joined need, be that need honourable or disgraceful. And this is why kings usually are fonder of exciting than restraining their soldiery, and shut their eyes more to their vices than to their virtues, and generally, to hold under the best of them, seek out, distinguish, and assist with money or favour the idle, and those who have ruined themselves by debauchery, and shake hands with them, and throw them kisses, and for the sake of mastery stoop to every servile action. In order therefore that the citizens may be distinguished by the king before all others, and, as far as the civil state and equity permit, may remain independent, it is necessary that the militia should consist of citizens only, and that citizens should be his counsellors; and on the contrary citizens are altogether subdued, and are laying the foundations of eternal war, from the moment that they suffer mercenaries to be levied, whose trade is war, and who have most power in strifes and seditions.

13. That the king's counsellors ought not to be elected for life, but for three, four, or five years, is clear as well from the tenth, as from what we said in the ninth section of this chapter. For if they were chosen for life, not only could the greatest part of the citizens conceive hardly any hope of obtaining this honour, and thus there would arise a great inequality, and thence envy, and constant murmurs, and at last seditions, which, no doubt, would be welcome to kings greedy of mastery: but also the counsellors, being rid of the fear of their successors, would assume a great licence in all respects, which the king would be far from opposing. For the more the citizens hate them, the more they will cling to the king, and be ready to flatter him. Nay, the interval of five years seems even too much, for in such a space of time it does not seem so impossible to corrupt by bribes or favour a very large part of the council, however large it be. And therefore it will be far safer, if every year two out of every clan retire, and be replaced by as many more (supposing that there are to be five counsellors of each clan), except in the year in which the jurist of any clan retires, and a fresh one is chosen in his place.

14. Moreover, no king can promise himself more safety,

than he who reigns in a commonwealth of this sort.   For
besides that a king soon perishes, when his soldiers cease
to desire his safety, it is certain that kings are always in the
greatest danger from those who are nearest their persons.
The fewer counsellors, then, there are, and the more powerful
they consequently are, the more the king is in danger of
their transferring the dominion to another.   Nothing in
fact more alarmed David, than that his own counsellor
Ahitophel sided with Absalom.[1]   Still more is this the case,
if the whole authority has been transferred absolutely to
one man, because it can then be more easily transferred
from one to another.   For two private soldiers once took
in hand to transfer the Roman empire, and did transfer it.[2]
I omit the arts and cunning wiles, whereby counsellors have
to assure themselves against falling victims to their unpopularity; for they are but too well known, and no one,
who has read history, can be ignorant, that the good faith
of counsellors has generally turned to their ruin.   And so,
for their own safety, it behoves them to be cunning, not
faithful.   But if the counsellors are too numerous to unite
in the same crime, and are all equal, and do not hold their
office beyond a period of four years, they cannot be at all objects of fear to the king, except he attempt to take away
their liberty, wherein he will offend all the citizens equally.
For, as Antonio Perez[3] excellently observes, an absolute
dominion is to the prince very dangerous, to the subjects
very hateful, and to the institutes of God and man alike
opposed, as innumerable instances show.

15. Besides these we have, in the last chapter, laid other
foundations, by which the king is greatly secured in his
dominion, and the citizens in their hold of peace and liberty,
which foundations we will reason out in their proper places.
For I was anxious above everything to reason out all those,
which refer to the great council and are of the greatest importance.   Now I will continue with the others, in the
same order in which I stated them.

16. It is undoubted, that citizens are more powerful,

---

[1] 2 Sam. xv. 31.

[2] Tacitus, Histories, i., 7.

[3] Antonio Perez, a publicist, and professor of law in the University
of Louvain in the first part of the seventeenth century.

and, therefore, more independent, the larger and better fortified their towns are. For the safer the place is, in which they are, the better they can defend their liberty, and the less they need fear an enemy, whether without or within; and it is certain that the more powerful men are by their riches, the more they by nature study their own safety. But cities which need the help of another for their preservation are not on terms of equal right with that other, but are so far dependent on his right as they need his help. For we showed in the second chapter, that right is determined by power alone.

17. For the same reason, also, I mean that the citizens may continue independent, and defend their liberty, the militia ought to be composed of the citizens only, and none of them to be exempted. For an armed man is more independent than an unarmed (Sec. 12); and those citizens transfer absolutely their own right to another, and entrust it entirely to his good faith, who have given him their arms and the defences of their cities. Human avarice, by which most men are very much led, adds its weight to this view. For it cannot be, that a mercenary force be hired without great expense; and citizens can hardly endure the exactions required to maintain an idle soldiery. But that no man, who commands the whole or a large part of the militia, should, except under pressure of necessity, be chosen for the extreme term of a year, all are aware, who have read history, alike sacred and profane. For there is nothing that reason more clearly teaches. For surely the might of dominion is altogether entrusted to him, who is allowed enough time to gain military glory, and raise his fame above the king's, or to make the army faithful to himself by flattery, largesses, and the other arts, whereby generals are accustomed to procure the enslavement of others, and the mastery for themselves. Lastly, I have added this point for the greater safety of the whole dominion, that these commanders of the militia are to be selected from the king's counsellors or ex-counsellors—that is, from men who have reached the age at which mankind generally prefer what is old and safe to what is new and dangerous.[1]

[1] Chap. VI. Sec. 10.

18. I said that the citizens were to be divided into clans,[1] and an equal number of counsellors chosen from each, in order that the larger towns might have, in proportion to the number of their citizens, a greater number of counsellors, and be able, as is equitable, to contribute more votes. For the power and, therefore, the right of a dominion is to be estimated by the number of its citizens; and I do not believe that any fitter means can be devised for maintaining this equality between citizens, who are all by nature so constituted, that everyone wishes to be attributed to his own stock, and be distinguished by race from the rest.

19. Furthermore, in the state of nature, there is nothing which any man can less claim for himself, and make his own, than the soil, and whatever so adheres to the soil, that he cannot hide it anywhere, nor carry it whither he pleases. The soil, therefore, and whatever adheres to it in the way we have mentioned, must be quite common property of the commonwealth—that is, of all those who, by their united force, can vindicate their claim to it, or of him to whom all have given authority to vindicate his claim. And therefore the soil, and all that adheres to it, ought to have a value with the citizens proportionate to the necessity there is, that they may be able to set their feet thereon, and defend their common right or liberty. But in the eighth section of this chapter we have shown the advantages that the commonwealth must necessarily derive hence.

20. In order that the citizens may be as far as possible equal, which is of the first necessity in a commonwealth, none but the descendants of a king are to be thought noble. But if all the descendants of kings were allowed to marry wives, or beget children, they would grow, in process of time, to a very large number, and would be, not only burdensome, but also a cause of very great fear, to king and all. For men who have too much leisure generally meditate crime. And hence it is that kings are, on account of their nobles, very much induced to make war, because kings surrounded with nobles find more quiet and safety in war than in peace. But I pass by this as notorious enough,

[1] Chap. VI. Secs. 11, 15, 16.

and also the points which I have mentioned in Secs. 15-27 of the last chapter. For the main points have been proved in this chapter, and the rest are self-evident.

21. That the judges ought to be too numerous for a large proportion of them to be accessible to the bribes of a private man, and that they should not vote openly, but secretly, and that they deserve payment for their time, is known to everyone.[1] But they everywhere have by custom a yearly salary; and so they make no great haste to determine suits, and there is often no end to trials. Next, where confiscations accrue to the king, there frequently in trials not truth nor right, but the greatness of a man's riches is regarded. Informers are ever at work, and everyone who has money is snatched as a prey, which evils, though grievous and intolerable, are excused by the necessity of warfare, and continue even in time of peace. But the avarice of judges that are appointed but for two or three years at most is moderated by fear of their successors, not to mention, again, that they can have no fixed property, but must lend their money at interest to their fellow-citizens. And so they are forced rather to consult their welfare than to plot against them, especially if the judges themselves, as we have said, are numerous.

22. But we have said, that no military pay is to be voted.[2] For the chief reward of military service is liberty. For in the state of nature everyone strives, for bare liberty's sake, to defend himself to the utmost of his power, and expects no other reward of warlike virtue but his own independence. But, in the civil state, all the citizens together are to be considered as a man in the state of nature; and, therefore, when all fight on behalf of that state, all are defending themselves, and engaged on their own business. But counsellors, judges, magistrates, and the like, are engaged more on others' business than on their own; and so it is but fair to pay them for their time. Besides, in war, there can be no greater or more honourable inducement to victory than the idea of liberty. But if, on the contrary, a certain portion of the citizens be designated as soldiers, on which account it will be necessary to award them a fixed pay,

---

[1] Chap. VI. Secs. 27, 28.   [2] Chap. VI. Sec. 31.

the king will, of necessity, distinguish them above the rest
(as we showed, Sec. 12)—that is, will distinguish men who
are acquainted only with the arts of war, and, in time of
peace, from excess of leisure, become debauched, and,
finally, from poverty, meditate nothing but rapine, civil
discord, and wars. And so we can affirm, that a monarchy
of this sort is, in fact, a state of war, and in it only the
soldiery enjoy liberty, but the rest are slaves.

23. Our remarks about the admission of foreigners
(Chap. VI. Sec. 32) I believe to be obvious. Besides, no
one can doubt that the king's blood-relations should be at
a distance from him, and occupied, not by warlike, but by
peaceful business, whence they may get credit and the
dominion quiet. Though even this has not seemed a sufficient precaution to the Turkish despots, who, therefore,
make a point of slaughtering all their brothers. And no
wonder: for the more absolutely the right of dominion has
been conferred on one man, the more easily, as we showed
by an instance (Sec. 14), it can be transferred from one to
another. But that in such a monarchy, as we here suppose, in which, I mean, there is not one mercenary soldier,
the plan we have mentioned provides sufficiently for the
king's safety, is not to be doubted.

24. Nor can anyone hesitate about what we have said in
the thirty-fourth and thirty-fifth sections of the last
chapter. But that the king must not marry a foreigner [1]
is easily proved. For not to mention that two commonwealths, although united by a treaty, are yet in a state of
hostility (Chap. III. Sec. 14), it is very much to be avoided
that war should be stirred up, on account of the king's
domestic affairs, both because disputes and dissensions
arise peculiarly from an alliance founded on marriage, and
because questions between two commonwealths are mostly
settled by war. Of this we read a fatal instance in Scripture. For after the death of Solomon, who had married
the king of Egypt's daughter, his son Rehoboam waged a
most disastrous war with Shishak, king of the Egyptians,
who utterly subdued him. [2] Moreover, the marriage of
Lewis XIV., king of France with the daughter of Philip IV.

---

[1] Chap. VI. Sec. 36.   [2] 1 Kings xiv. 25 ; 2 Chron. xii.

was the seed of a fresh war.[1] And, besides these, very many instances may be read in history.

25. The form of the dominion ought to be kept one and the same, and, consequently, there should be but one king, and that of the same sex, and the dominion should be indivisible.[2] But as to my saying that the king's eldest son should succeed his father by right, or (if there be no issue) the nearest to him in blood, it is clear as well from Chap. VI. Sec. 13, as because the election of the king made by the multitude should, if possible, last for ever. Otherwise it will necessarily happen, that the supreme authority of the dominion will frequently pass to the multitude, which is an extreme and, therefore, exceedingly dangerous change. But those who, from the fact that the king is master of the dominion, and holds it by absolute right, infer that he can hand it over to whom he pleases, and that, therefore, the king's son is by right heir to the dominion, are greatly mistaken. For the king's will has so long the force of law, as he holds the sword of the commonwealth ; for the right of dominion is limited by power only. Therefore, a king may indeed abdicate, but cannot hand the dominion over to another, unless with the concurrence of the multitude or its stronger part. And that this may be more clearly understood, we must remark, that children are heirs to their parents, not by natural, but by civil law. For by the power of the commonwealth alone is anyone master of definite property. And, therefore, by the same power or right, whereby the will of any man concerning his property is held good, by the same also his will remains good after his own death, as long as the commonwealth endures. And this is the reason, why everyone in the civil state maintains after death the same right as he had in his lifetime, because, as we said, it is not by his own power, but by that of the commonwealth, which is everlasting, that he can decide anything about his property. But the king's case is quite different. For the king's will is the civil law itself, and the king the commonwealth itself. Therefore, by the death of the king, the commonwealth is in a manner

---

[1] The war between France and Spain, terminated by the first peace of Aix-la-Chapelle, 1665.

[2] Chap. VI. Sec. 37.

dead, and the civil state naturally returns to the state of nature, and consequently the supreme authority to the multitude, which can, therefore, lawfully lay down new and abolish old laws. And so it appears that no man succeeds the king by right, but him whom the multitude wills to be successor, or in a theocracy, such as the commonwealth of the Hebrews once was, him whom God has chosen by a prophet. We might likewise infer this from the fact that the king's sword, or right, is in reality the will of the multitude itself, or its stronger part; or else from the fact, that men endowed with reason never so utterly abdicate their right, that they cease to be men, and are accounted as sheep. But to pursue this further is unnecessary.

26. But the right of religion, or of worshipping God, no man can transfer to another. However, we have treated of this point at length in the last chapters of our Theologico-Political Treatise, which it is superfluous to repeat here. And herewith I claim to have reasoned out the foundations of the best monarchy, though briefly, yet with sufficient clearness. But their mutual interdependence, or, in other words, the proportions of my dominion, anyone will easily remark, who will be at the pains to observe them as a whole with some attention. It remains only to warn the reader, that I am here conceiving of that monarchy, which is instituted by a free multitude, for which alone these foundations can serve. For a multitude that has grown used to another form of dominion will not be able without great danger of overthrow to pluck up the accepted foundations of the whole dominion, and change its entire fabric.

27. And what we have written will, perhaps, be received with derision by those who limit to the populace only the vices which are inherent in all mortals; and use such phrases as, "the mob, if it is not frightened, inspires no little fear," and "the populace is either a humble slave, or a haughty master," and "it has no truth or judgment," etc. But all have one common nature. Only we are deceived by power and refinement. Whence it comes that when two do the same thing we say, "this man may do it with impunity, that man may not;" not because the deed,

but because the doer is different. Haughtiness is a property of rulers. Men are haughty, but by reason of an
appointment for a year; how much more then nobles, that
have their honours eternal! But their arrogance is glossed
over with importance, luxury, profusion, and a kind of
harmony of vices, and a certain cultivated folly, and
elegant villany, so that vices, each of which looked at
separately is foul and vile, because it is then most conspicuous, appear to the inexperienced and untaught honourable and becoming. "The mob, too, if it is not frightened,
inspires no little fear;" yes, for liberty and slavery are
not easily mingled. Lastly, as for the populace being
devoid of truth and judgment, that is nothing wonderful,
since the chief business of the dominion is transacted behind its back, and it can but make conjectures from the
little, which cannot be hidden. For it is an uncommon
virtue to suspend one's judgment. So it is supreme folly
to wish to transact everything behind the backs of the
citizens, and to expect that they will not judge ill of the
same, and will not give everything an unfavourable interpretation. For if the populace could moderate itself, and
suspend its judgment about things with which it is imperfectly acquainted, or judge rightly of things by the
little it knows already, it would surely be more fit to
govern, than to be governed. But, as we said, all have
the same nature. All grow haughty with rule, and cause
fear if they do not feel it, and everywhere truth is
generally transgressed by enemies or guilty people; especially where one or a few have mastery, and have respect
in trials not to justice or truth, but to amount of wealth.

28. Besides, paid soldiers, that are accustomed to military
discipline, and can support cold and hunger, are likely to
despise a crowd of citizens as very inferior for storming
towns or fighting pitched battles. But that my dominion
is, therefore, more unhappy or less durable, no one of
sound mind will affirm. But, on the contrary, everyone
that judges things fairly will admit, that that dominion is
the most durable of all, which can content itself with preserving what it has got, without coveting what belongs to
others, and strives, therefore, most eagerly by every means
to avoid war and preserve peace.

29. But I admit that the counsels of such a dominion can hardly be concealed. But everyone will also admit with me that it is far better for the right counsels of a dominion to be known to its enemies, than for the evil secrets of tyrants to be concealed from the citizens. They who can treat secretly of the affairs of a dominion have it absolutely under their authority, and, as they plot against the enemy in time of war, so do they against the citizens in time of peace. Now that this secrecy is often serviceable to a dominion, no one can deny; but that without it the said dominion cannot subsist, no one will ever prove. But, on the contrary, to entrust affairs of state absolutely to any man is quite incompatible with the maintenance of liberty; and so it is folly to choose to avoid a small loss by means of the greatest of evils. But the perpetual refrain of those who lust after absolute dominion is, that it is to the essential interest of the commonwealth that its business be secretly transacted, and other like pretences, which end in the more hateful a slavery, the more they are clothed with a show of utility.

30. Lastly, although no dominion, as far as I know, has ever been founded on all the conditions we have mentioned, yet from experience itself we shall be able to prove that this form of monarchy is the best, if we consider the causes of the preservation and overthrow of any dominion that is not barbarous. But this I could not do without greatly wearying the reader. However, I cannot pass over in silence one instance, that seems worth remembering: I mean the dominion of the Arragonese, who showed a singular loyalty towards their kings, and with equal constancy preserved unbroken the constitution of the kingdom. For as soon as they had cast off the slavish yoke of the Moors, they resolved to choose themselves a king, but on what conditions they could not quite make up their minds, and they therefore determined to consult the sovereign pontiff of Rome. He, who in this matter certainly bore himself as Christ's vicar, blamed them for so obstinately wishing to choose a king, unwarned by the example of the Hebrews. However, if they would not change their minds, then he advised them not to choose a king, without first instituting customs equitable and suitable to the national genius, and

above all he would have them create some supreme council, to balance the king's power like the ephors of the Lacedæmonians, and to have absolute right to determine the disputes, which might arise between the king and the citizens. So then, following this advice, they established the laws, which seemed to them most equitable, of which the supreme interpreter, and therefore supreme judge, was to be, not the king, but the council, which they call the Seventeen, and whose president has the title of Justice.[1] This Justice then, and the Seventeen, who are chosen for life, not by vote but by lot, have the absolute right of revising and annulling all sentences passed upon any citizen by other courts, civil or ecclesiastical, or by the king himself, so that every citizen had the right to summon the king himself before this council. Moreover, they once had the right of electing and deposing the king. But after the lapse of many years the king, Don Pedro, who is called the Dagger, by canvassing, bribery, promises, and every sort of practice, at length procured the revocation of this right. And as soon as he gained his point, he cut off, or, as I would sooner believe, wounded his hand before them all, saying, that not without the loss of royal blood could subjects be allowed to choose their king.[2] Yet he effected this change, but upon this condition, " That the subjects have had and shall have the right of taking arms against any violence whatever, whereby any may wish to enter upon the dominion to their hurt, nay, against the king himself, or the prince, his heir, if he thus encroach." By which condition they certainly rather rectified than abolished that right. For, as we have shown (Chap. IV. Secs. 5, 6), a king can be deprived of the power of ruling, not by the civil law, but by the law of war, in other words the subjects may resist his violence with violence. Besides this condition they stipulated others, which do not concern our

[1] See Hallam's " History of the Middle Ages," Chap. IV., for the constitutional history of Arragon. Hallam calls the Justiza the Justiciary, but the literal translation, Justice, seems warranted by our own English use of the word to designate certain judges.

[2] Hallam says, that the king merely cut the obnoxious Privilege of Union, which he describes rather differently, through with his sword. The Privilege of Union was so utterly " eradicated from the records of the kingdom, that its precise words have never been recovered."

present design. Having by these customs given themselves
a constitution to the mind of all, they continued for an incredible length of time unharmed, the king's loyalty towards his subjects being as great as theirs towards him.
But after that the kingdom fell by inheritance to Ferdinand of Castile, who first had the surname of Catholic;
this liberty of the Arragonese began to displease the
Castilians, who therefore ceased not to urge Ferdinand to
abolish these rights.   But he, not yet being accustomed to
absolute dominion, dared make no such attempt, but re-
plied thus to his counsellors: that (not to mention that he
had received the kingdom of Arragon on those terms, which
they knew, and had most solemnly sworn to observe the
same, and that it was inhuman to break his word) he was
of opinion, that his kingdom would be stable, as long as its
safety was as much to the subjects' as to the king's interest, so that neither the king should outweigh the subjects,
nor yet the subjects the king ; for that if either party were
too powerful, the weaker would not only try to recover its
former equality, but in vexation at its injury to retaliate
upon the other, whence would follow the ruin of either or
both.   Which very wise language I could not enough
wonder at, had it proceeded from a king accustomed to
command not freemen but slaves.   Accordingly the Arragonese retained their liberties after the time of Ferdinand,
though no longer by right but by the favour of their too
powerful kings, until the reign of Philip II., who oppressed
them with better luck, but no less cruelty, than he did the
United Provinces.   And although Philip III. is supposed
to have restored everything to its former position, yet the
Arragonese, partly from eagerness to flatter the powerful
(for it is folly to kick against the pricks), partly from
terror, have kept nothing but the specious names and
empty forms of liberty.

31. We conclude, therefore, that the multitude may
preserve under a king an ample enough liberty; if it con-
trive that the king's power be determined by the sole
power, and preserved by the defence of the multitude
itself.   And this was the single rule which I followed in
laying the foundations of monarchy.

CHAPTER VIII.

OF ARISTOCRACY.

So far of monarchy. But now we will say, on what plan an aristocracy is to be framed, so that it may be lasting. We have defined an aristocratic dominion as that, which is held not by one man, but by certain persons chosen out of the multitude, whom we shall henceforth call patricians. I say expressly, "that which is held by certain persons chosen." For the chief difference between this and a democracy is, that the right of governing depends in an aristocracy on election only, but in a democracy for the most part on some right either congenital or acquired by fortune (as we shall explain in its place); and therefore, although in any dominion the entire multitude be received into the number of the patricians, provided that right of theirs is not inherited, and does not descend by some law to others, the dominion will for all that be quite an aristocracy, because none are received into the number of the patricians save by express election. But if these chosen persons were but two, each of them will try to be more powerful than the other, and from the too great power of each, the dominion will easily be split into two factions; and in like manner into three, four, or five factions, if three, four, or five persons were put into possession of it. But the factions will be the weaker, the more there are to whom the dominion was delegated. And hence it follows, that to secure the stability of an aristocracy, it is necessary to consider the proportionate size of the actual dominion, in order to determine the minimum number of patricians.

2. Let it be supposed, then, that for a dominion of moderate size it suffices to be allowed a hundred of the best men, and that upon them has been conferred the supreme authority of the dominion, and that they have consequently the right to elect their patrician colleagues, when any of

the number die. These men will certainly endeavour to secure their succession to their children or next in blood. And thus the supreme authority of the dominion will always be with those, whom fortune has made children or kinsmen to patricians. And, as out of a hundred men who rise to office by fortune, hardly three are found that excel in knowledge and counsel, it will thus come to pass, that the authority of the dominion will rest, not with a hundred, but only with two or three who excel by vigour of mind, and who will easily draw to themselves everything, and each of them, as is the wont of human greed, will be able to prepare the way to a monarchy. And so, if we make a right calculation, it is necessary, that the supreme authority of a dominion, whose size requires at least a hundred first-rate men, should be conferred on not less than five thousand. For by this proportion it will never fail, but a hundred shall be found excelling in mental vigour, that is, on the hypothesis that, out of fifty that seek and obtain office, one will always be found not less than first-rate, besides others that imitate the virtues of the first-rate, and are therefore worthy to rule.

3. The patricians are most commonly citizens of one city, which is the head of the whole dominion, so that the commonwealth or republic has its name from it, as once that of Rome, and now those of Venice, Genoa, etc. But the republic of the Dutch has its name from an entire province, whence it arises, that the subjects of this dominion enjoy a greater liberty. Now, before we can determine the foundations on which this aristocratic dominion ought to rest, we must observe a very great difference, which exists between the dominion which is conferred on one man and that which is conferred on a sufficiently large council. For, in the first place, the power of one man is (as we said, Chap. VI. Sec. 5) very inadequate to support the entire dominion; but this no one, without manifest absurdity, can affirm of a sufficiently large council. For, in declaring the council to be sufficiently large, one at the same time denies, that it is inadequate to support the dominion. A king, therefore, is altogether in need of counsellors, but a council like this is not so in the least. In the second place, kings are mortal, but councils are everlasting. And so the power

of the dominion which has once been transferred to a large enough council never reverts to the multitude. But this is otherwise in a monarchy, as we showed (Chap. VII. Sec. 25). Thirdly, a king's dominion is often on sufferance, whether from his minority, sickness, or old age, or from other causes; but the power of a council of this kind, on the contrary, remains always one and the same. In the fourth place, one man's will is very fluctuating and inconstant; and, therefore, in a monarchy, all law is, indeed, the explicit will of the king (as we said, Chap. VII. Sec. 1), but not every will of the king ought to be law; but this cannot be said of the will of a sufficiently numerous council. For since the council itself, as we have just shown, needs no counsellors, its every explicit will ought to be law. And hence we conclude, that the dominion conferred upon a large enough council is absolute, or approaches nearest to the absolute. For if there be any absolute dominion, it is, in fact, that which is held by an entire multitude.

4. Yet in so far as this aristocratic dominion never (as has just been shown) reverts to the multitude, and there is under it no consultation with the multitude, but, without qualification, every will of the council is law, it must be considered as quite absolute, and therefore its foundations ought to rest only on the will and judgment of the said council, and not on the watchfulness of the multitude, since the latter is excluded from giving its advice or its vote. The reason, then, why in practice aristocracy is not absolute, is that the multitude is a cause of fear to the rulers, and therefore succeeds in retaining for itself some liberty, which it asserts and holds as its own, if not by an express law, yet on a tacit understanding.

5. And thus it is manifest that this kind of dominion will be in the best possible condition, if its institutions are such that it most nearly approaches the absolute—that is, that the multitude is as little as possible a cause of fear, and retains no liberty, but such as must necessarily be assigned it by the law of the dominion itself, and is therefore not so much a right of the multitude as of the whole dominion, asserted and maintained by the aristocrats only as their own. For thus practice agrees best with theory, as appears from the last section, and is also self-evident.

For we cannot doubt that the dominion rests the less with the patricians, the more rights the commons assert for themselves, such as those which the corporations of artisans in Lower Germany, commonly called Guilds, generally possess.

6. But the commons need not apprehend any danger of a hateful slavery from this form of dominion, merely because it is conferred on the council absolutely. For the will of so large a council cannot be so much determined by lust as by reason; because men are drawn asunder by an evil passion, and cannot be guided, as it were, by one mind, except so far as they desire things honourable, or that have at least an honourable appearance.

7. In determining, then, the foundations of an aristocracy, it is above all to be observed, that they should rest on the sole will and power of the supreme council, so that it may be as independent as possible, and be in no danger from the multitude. In order to determine these foundations, which are to rest, I say, upon the sole will and power of the council, let us see what foundations of peace are peculiar to monarchy, and unsuited to this form of dominion. For if we substitute for these equivalent foundations fit for an aristocracy, and leave the rest, as they are already laid, we shall have removed without doubt every cause of seditions; or, at least, this kind of dominion will be no less safe than the monarchical, but, on the contrary, so much the more so, and of so much better a condition, as, without danger to peace and liberty, it approaches nearer than monarchy to the absolute (Secs. 3, 6). For the greater the right of the supreme authority, the more the form of dominion agrees with the dictate of reason (Chap. III. Sec. 5[1]), and, therefore, the fitter it is to maintain peace and liberty. Let us run through, therefore, the points we stated in our sixth chapter, beginning with the ninth section, that we may reject what is unfit for this kind of dominion, and see what agrees with it.

8. That it is necessary, in the first place, to found and fortify one or more cities, no one can doubt. But that city is above all to be fortified, which is the head of the whole

---

[1] Ought not this reference to be to Chap. III. Sec. 6 ?

dominion, and also those that are on its frontiers. For that which is the head of the whole dominion, and has the supreme right, ought to be more powerful than the rest. But under this kind of dominion it is quite unnecessary to divide all the inhabitants into clans.

9. As for the military, since under this dominion equality is not to be looked for among all, but between the patricians only, and, in particular, the power of the patricians is greater than that of the commons, it is certain that it makes no difference to the laws or fundamental principles of this dominion, that the military be formed of others besides subjects.[1] But it *is* of the first importance that no one be admitted into the number of the patricians, that has not a proper knowledge of the art of war. But for the subjects to be excluded, as some would have it, from military service, is surely folly. For besides that the military pay given to subjects remains within the realm, whereas, on the contrary, what is paid to a foreign soldiery is altogether lost, the greatest strength of the dominion is also thereby weakened. For it is certain that those fight with peculiar valour who fight for altar and hearth. Whence, also, it is manifest that those are no less wrong, who lay down that military commanders, tribunes, centurions, etc., should be chosen from among the patricians only. For with what courage will those soldiers fight who are deprived of all hope of gaining glory and advancement? But, on the other hand, to establish a law forbidding the patricians to hire foreign soldiers when circumstances require it, whether to defend themselves, and suppress seditions, or for any other reason, besides being inconsiderate, would also be repugnant to the supreme right of the patricians, concerning which see Secs. 3, 4, 5 of this chapter. But the general of a single army, or of the entire military, is to be chosen but in time of war, and among the patricians only, and is to hold the command for a year at most, without power of being continued therein, or afterwards reappointed. For this law, necessary as it is under a monarchy, is so above all under this kind of dominion. For although it is much easier, as we have said above, to transfer the dominion

----

[1] Cf. Chap. VI. Sec. 10.

from one man to another than from a free council to one
man ; yet it does often happen, that patricians are subdued
by their own generals, and that to the much greater harm
of the commonwealth.   For when a monarch is removed,
it is but a change of tyrant, not of the form of dominion ;
but, under an aristocracy, this cannot happen, without an
upsetting of the form of dominion, and a slaughter of the
greatest men.   Of which thing Rome has offered the most
mournful examples.   But our reason for saying that, under
a monarchy, the militia should serve without pay, is here
inapplicable.   For since the subjects are excluded from
giving their advice or votes, they are to be reckoned as
foreigners, and are, therefore, to be hired for service on no
worse terms than foreigners.   And there is in this case no
danger of their being distinguished above the rest by the
patricians : nay, further, to avoid the partial judgment
which everyone is apt to form of his own exploits, it is
wiser for the patricians to assign a fixed payment to the
soldiers for their service.

10. Furthermore, for this same reason, that all but the
patricians are foreigners, it cannot be without danger to
the whole dominion, that the lands and houses and the
whole soil should remain public property, and be let to the
inhabitants at a yearly rent.   For the subjects having no
part in the dominion would easily, in bad times, all forsake
their cities, if they could carry where they pleased what
goods they possess.   And, therefore, lands and farms are
not to be let, but sold to the subjects, yet on condition that
they pay every year an aliquot part of the year's produce,
etc., as is done in Holland.

11. These points considered, I proceed to the foundations
on which the supreme council should rest and be established. We have shown (Sec. 2) that, in a moderate-sized
dominion, this council ought to have about five thousand
members.   And so we must look for means of preventing
the dominion from gradually getting into fewer hands, and
of insuring, on the contrary, that the number of members
be increased in proportion to the growth of the dominion
itself ; and, next, that between the patricians, equality be
as far as possible maintained ; and, further, that there may
be speed and expedition in their counsels, and that they

tend to the general good; and, lastly, that the power of the patricians or council exceed the power of the multitude, yet so that the multitude suffer no harm thereby.

12. But jealousy causes a great difficulty in maintaining our first point. For men are, as we have said, by nature enemies, so that however they be associated, and bound together by laws, they still retain their nature. And hence I think it is, that democracies change into aristocracies, and these at length into monarchies. For I am fully persuaded that most aristocracies were formerly democracies. For when a given multitude, in search of fresh territories, has found and cultivated them, it retains, as a whole, its equal right of dominion, because no man gives dominion to another spontaneously. But although every one of them thinks it fair, that he should have the same right against another that that other has against him, he yet thinks it unfair, that the foreigners that join them should have equal right in the dominion with themselves, who sought it by their own toil, and won it at the price of their own blood. And this not even the foreigners themselves deny, for, of course, they migrate thither, not to hold dominion, but for the benefit of their own private business, and are quite satisfied if they are but allowed the liberty of transacting that business in safety. But meanwhile the multitude is augmented by the influx of foreigners, who gradually acquire the national manners, until at last they are distinguished by no other difference than that of incapacity to get office; and while their number daily increases, that of the citizens, on the contrary, is by many causes diminished. For families often die out, and some persons are disqualified for their crimes, and a great many are driven by domestic poverty to neglect affairs of state, and meanwhile the more powerful aim at nothing else, but to govern alone; and thus the dominion is gradually limited to a few, and at length by faction to one. And here we might add other causes that destroy dominions of this sort; but as they are well known, I pass them by, and proceed now to state the laws by which this dominion, of which we are treating, ought to be maintained.

13. The primary law of this dominion ought to be that which determines the proportionate numbers of patricians

and multitude. For a proportion (Sec. 1) ought to be maintained between the multitude and the patricians, so that with the increase of the former the number of the latter should be raised. And this proportion (in accordance with our remarks in the second section) ought to be about fifty to one, that is, the inequality between the members of each should never be greater. For (Sec. 1) without destroying the form of dominion, the number of patricians may be greater than the number of the multitude. But there is no danger except in the smallness of their number. But how it is to be provided that this law be kept unbroken, I will presently show in its own place.

14. Patricians, in some places, are chosen only out of particular families. But it is ruinous to lay this down expressly by law. For not to mention that families often die out, and that the other families can never be excluded without disgrace, it is also repugnant to the form of this dominion, that the dignity of patrician should be hereditary (Sec. 1). But on this system a dominion seems rather a democracy, such as we have described in Sec. 12, that is in the hands of very few citizens. But, on the other hand, to provide against the patricians choosing their own sons and kinsmen, and thereby against the right of dominion remaining in particular families, is impossible, and indeed absurd, as I shall show (Sec. 39). But provided that they hold that right by no express law, and that the rest (I mean, such as are born within the dominion, and use the vulgar tongue, and have not a foreign wife, and are not infamous, nor servants, nor earning their living by any servile trade, among which are to be reckoned those of a wine-merchant, or brewer) are not excluded, the form of the dominion will, notwithstanding, be retained, and it will be possible to maintain the proportion between the patricians and the multitude.

15. But if it be further by law appointed that no young men be chosen, it will never happen that a few families hold the right of government in their hands. And, therefore, be it by law appointed, that no man that has not reached his thirtieth year be put on the list of candidates.

16. Thirdly, it is next to be ordained, that all the

patricians must be assembled at certain fixed times in a particular part of the city, and that whoever does not attend the council, unless he be hindered by illness or some public business, shall be fined some considerable amount. For, were it otherwise, most of them would neglect the public, for the sake of their own private affairs.

17. Let this council's functions be to pass and repeal laws, and to choose their patrician colleagues, and all the ministers of the dominion. For he, that has supreme right, as we have decided that this council has, cannot give to anyone authority to pass and repeal laws, without at the same time abdicating his own right, and transferring it to him, to whom he gives that power. For he, that has but for one day only authority to pass and repeal laws, is able to change the entire form of the dominion. But one can, without forfeiting one's supreme right, temporarily entrust to others the daily business of dominion to be administered according to the established laws. Furthermore, if the ministers of dominion were chosen by any other but this council, then its members would be more properly called wards than patricians.

18. Hence some are accustomed to create for the council a ruler or prince, either for life, as the Venetians, or for a time, as the Genoese; but yet with such great precautions, as make it clear enough, that it is not done without great risk. And assuredly we cannot doubt but that the dominion thereby approaches the monarchical form, and as far as we can conjecture from their histories, it was done for no other reason, than that before the institution of these councils they had lived under a ruler, or doge, as under a king. And so the creation of a ruler is a necessary requisite indeed for the particular nation, but not for the aristocratic dominion considered in itself.

19. But, inasmuch as the supreme authority of this dominion rests with this council as a whole, not with every individual member of it (for otherwise it would be but the gathering of an undisciplined mob), it is, therefore, necessary that all the patricians be so bound by the laws as to form, as it were, one body governed by one mind. But the laws by themselves alone are weak and easily broken, when their vindicators are the very persons who

are able to transgress them, and the only ones who are to take warning by the punishment, and must punish their colleagues in order by fear of the same punishment to restrain their own desire : for all this involves a great absurdity. And, therefore, means must be sought to preserve order in this supreme council and keep unbroken the constitution of the dominion, so that yet the greatest possible equality may exist between patricians.

20. But since, from a single ruler or prince, able also to vote in the debates, there must necessarily arise a great inequality, especially on account of the power, which must of necessity be granted him, in order to enable him to discharge his duty in safety ; therefore, if we consider the whole matter aright, nothing can be devised more useful to the general welfare than the institution of another council of certain patricians subordinate to the supreme council, whose only duty should be to see that the constitution, as far as it concerns the councils and ministers of the dominion, be kept unbroken, and who should, therefore, have authority to summon to judgment and, in conformity with established law, to condemn any delinquent who, as a minister of the dominion, has transgressed the laws concerning his office. And these patricians we shall hereafter call syndics.

21. And they are to be chosen for life. For, were they to be chosen for a time, so that they should afterwards be eligible for other offices in the dominion, we should fall into the very absurdity which we have just pointed out in the nineteenth section. But lest they should become quite haughty by very long rule, none are to be elected to this office, but those who have reached their sixtieth year or more, and have discharged the duties of senator, of which below.

22. Of these, too, we shall easily determine the number, if we consider that these syndics stand to the patricians in the same relation as the whole body of patricians together does to the multitude, which they cannot govern, if they are fewer than a proper number. And, therefore, the number of the syndics should be to that of patricians as their number is to that of the multitude, that is (Sec. 13), as one to fifty.

23. Moreover, that this council may discharge its func-

tions in security, some portion of the soldiery must be assigned to it, and be subject to its orders.

24. The syndics and other ministers of state are to have no salary, but such emoluments, that they cannot maladminster affairs of state without great loss to themselves. For we cannot doubt that it is fair, that the ministers of this kind of dominion should be awarded a recompense for their time, since the commons are the majority in this dominion, and the patricians look after their safety, while they themselves have no trouble with affairs of state, but only with their own private ones. But since, on the other hand, no man (Chap. VII. Sec. 4) defends another's cause, save in so far as he thereby hopes to establish his own interest, things must, of necessity, be so ordered that the ministers, who have charge of affairs of state, should most pursue their own interest, when they are most watchful for the general good.

25. To the syndics then, whose duty, as we said, it is to see that the constitution is kept unbroken, the following emoluments are to be awarded: namely, that every householder that inhabits any place in the dominion, be bound to pay every year a coin of small value, say a quarter of an ounce of silver, to the syndics, that thus they may know the number of inhabitants, and so observe what proportion of them the patricians constitute; and next that every new patrician on his election must pay the syndics some large sum, for instance, twenty or twenty-five pounds of silver. Moreover, that money, in which the absent patricians (I mean those who have failed to attend the meeting of the council) are condemned, is also to be awarded to the syndics; and a part, too, of the goods of defaulting ministers, who are bound to abide their judgment, and who are fined a certain sum of money, or have their goods confiscated, should be devoted to them, not to all indeed, but to those only who sit daily, and whose duty it is to summon the council of syndics, concerning whom see Sec. 28. But, in order that the council of syndics may always be maintained at its full number, before all other business in the supreme council, when it is assembled at the usual time, inquiry is to be made about this. Which, if the syndics neglect, let it then devolve upon the presi-

dent of the senate (concerning which we shall soon have occasion to speak), to admonish the supreme council on this head, to demand of the president of the syndics the reason of his silence, and to inquire what is the supreme council's opinion in the matter. But if the president of the senate is likewise silent, let the case be taken up by the president of the supreme court of justice, or if he too is silent by some other patrician, and let him demand an explanation of their silence from the presidents of the senate and the court of justice, as well as from the president of the syndics. Lastly, that that law, whereby young men are excluded, may likewise be strictly observed, it is to be appointed that all who have reached the thirtieth year of their age, and who are not by express law excluded, are to have their names inscribed on a list, in presence of the syndics, and to receive from them, at a fixed price, some sign of the honour conferred on them, namely, that they may be allowed to wear a particular ornament only permitted to them, to distinguish them and make them to be had in honour by the rest; and, at the same time, be it ordained, that in elections none may nominate as patrician anyone whose name is not inscribed on the general list, and that under a heavy penalty. And, further, let no one be allowed to refuse the burden of a duty or office, which he is chosen to bear. Lastly, that all the absolutely fundamental laws of the dominion may be everlasting, it must be ordained that if anyone in the supreme council raise a question about any fundamental law, as of prolonging the command of any general of an army, or of diminishing the number of patricians, or the like, he is guilty of treason, and not only is he to be condemned to death, and his goods confiscated, but some sign of his punishment is to remain visible in public for an eternal memorial of the event. But for the confirming of the other general rights of the dominion, it is enough, if it be only ordained, that no law can be repealed nor new law passed, unless first the college of syndics, and then three-fourths or four-fifths of the supreme council agree thereto.

26. Let the right also of summoning the supreme council and proposing the matters to be decided in it, rest with the syndics, and let them likewise be given the first place in

the council, but without the right to vote. But before they take their seats, they must swear by the safety of that supreme council and by the public liberty, that they will strive with the utmost zeal to preserve unbroken the ancient laws. and to consult the general good. After which let them through their secretary open in order the subjects of discussion.

27. But that all the patricians may have equal authority in making decrees and electing the ministers of the dominion, and that speed and expedition in all matters may be possible, the order observed by the Venetians is altogether to be approved, for they appoint by lot a certain number of the council to name the ministers, and when these have named in order the candidates for office, every patrician signifies by ballot his opinion, approving or rejecting the candidate in question, so that it is not afterwards known, who voted in this or that sense. Whereby it is contrived, not only that the authority of all the patricians in the decision is equal, and that business is quickly despatched, but also, that everyone has absolute liberty (which is of the first necessity in councils) to give his opinion without danger of unpopularity.

28. But in the councils of syndics and the other councils, the same order is to be observed, that voting is to be by ballot. But the right of convoking the council of syndics and of proposing the matters to be decided in the same ought to belong to their president, who is to sit every day with ten or more other syndics, to hear the complaints and secret accusations of the commons against the ministers, and to look after the accusers, if circumstances require, and to summon the supreme council even before the appointed time, if any of them judge that there is danger in the delay. Now this president and those who meet with him every day are to be appointed by the supreme council and out of the number of syndics, not indeed for life, but for six months, and they must not have their term renewed but after the lapse of three or four years. And these, as we said above, are to be awarded the goods that are confiscated and the pecuniary fines, or some part of them. The remaining points which concern the syndics we will mention in their proper places.

29. The second council, which is subordinate to the supreme one, we will call the senate, and let its duty be to transact public business, for instance, to publish the laws of the dominion, to order the fortifications of the cities according to law, to confer military commissions, to impose taxes on the subjects and apply the same, to answer foreign embassies, and decide where embassies are to be sent. But let the actual appointment of ambassadors be the duty of the supreme council. For it is of the greatest consequence to see that no patrician be called to any office in the dominion but by the supreme council itself, lest the patricians themselves should try to curry favour with the senate. Secondly, all matters are to be referred to the supreme council, which in any way alter the existing state of things, as the deciding on peace and war. Wherefore, that the senate's decrees concerning peace and war may be valid, they must be confirmed by the supreme council. And therefore I should say, that it belonged to the supreme council only, not to the senate, to impose new taxes.

30. In determining the number of senators these points are to be taken into consideration: first, that all the patricians should have an equal hope of gaining senatorial rank; secondly, that notwithstanding the same senators, whose time (for which they were elected) is elapsed, may be continued after a short interval, that so the dominion may always be governed by skilled and experienced men; and lastly, that among the senators many may be found illustrious for wisdom and virtue. But to secure all these conditions, there can be no other means devised, than that it should be by law appointed, that no one who has not reached his fiftieth year, be received into the number of senators, and that four hundred, that is about a twelfth part of the patricians, be appointed for a year, and that two years after that year has elapsed, the same be capable of re-appointment. For in this manner about a twelfth part of the patricians will be constantly engaged in the duty of senator, with only short intervening periods; and this number surely, together with that made up by the syndics, will be little less than the number of patricians that have attained their fiftieth year. And so all the patricians will always have a great hope of gaining the rank

of senator or syndic, and yet notwithstanding, the same patricians, at only short intervals, will always hold senatorial rank, and (according to what we said, Sec. 2) there will never be wanting in the senate distinguished men, excelling in counsel and skill.   And because this law cannot be broken without exciting great jealousy on the part of many patricians, it needs no other safeguard for its constant validity, than that every patrician who has reached the age we mentioned, should offer the proof thereof to the syndics, who shall put his name on the list of candidates for the senatorial duties, and read the name before the supreme council, so that he may occupy, with the rest of the same rank, a place set apart in this supreme council for his fellows, next to the place of the senators.

31. The emoluments of the senators should be of such a kind, that their profit is greater from peace than from war.   And therefore let there be awarded to them a hundredth or a fiftieth part of the merchandise exported abroad from the dominion, or imported into it from abroad. For we cannot doubt, that by this means they will, as far as they can, preserve peace, and never desire to protract war.   And from this duty not even the senators themselves, if any of them are merchants, ought to be exempt ; for such an immunity cannot be granted without great risk to trade, as I think no one is ignorant.   Nay, on the contrary, it must be by law ordained, that no senator or ex-senator may fill any military post; and further, that no one may be declared general or prætor, which officers we said (Sec. 9) were to be only appointed in time of war, whose father or grandfather is a senator, or has held the dignity of senator within two years.   Which laws we cannot doubt, that the patricians outside the senate will defend with all their might : and so it will be the case, that the senators will always have more profit from peace than from war, and will, therefore, never advise war, except the utmost need of the dominion compels them.   But it may be objected to us, that on this system, if, that is, syndics and senators are to be allowed so great profits, an aristocracy will be as burdensome to the subjects as any monarchy. But not to mention that royal courts require larger expenditure, and are yet not provided in order to secure peace,

and that peace can never be bought too dear; it is to be
added, first, that all that under a monarchy is conferred on
one or a few, is here conferred upon very many.   Next
kings and their ministers do not bear the burden of the
dominion with the subjects, but under this form of dominion it is just the reverse; for the patricians, who are
always chosen from the rich, bear the largest share of the
weight of the commonwealth.   Lastly, the burdens of a
monarchy spring not so much from its king's expenditure,
as from its secret policy.   For those burdens of a dominion,
that are imposed on the citizens in order to secure peace
and liberty, great though they be, are yet supported and
lightened by the usefulness of peace.   What nation ever
had to pay so many and so heavy taxes as the Dutch?   Yet
it not only has not been exhausted, but, on the contrary,
has been so mighty by its wealth, that all envied its good
fortune.   If therefore the burdens of a monarchy were imposed for the sake of peace, they would not oppress the
citizens; but, as I have said, it is from the secret policy of
that sort of dominion, that the subjects faint under their
lord; that is, because the virtue of kings counts for more
in time of war than in time of peace, and because they, who
would reign by themselves, ought above all to try and have
their subjects poor; not to mention other things, which
that most prudent Dutchman V. H.[1] formerly remarked,
because they do not concern my design, which is only to
describe the best state of every kind of dominion.

32. Of the syndics chosen by the supreme council, some
should sit in the senate, but without the right of voting,
so that they may see whether the laws concerning that
assembly be duly observed, and may have the supreme
council convoked, when anything is to be referred to it
from the senate.   For the supreme right of convoking this
council, and proposing to it subjects of discussion, is, as we
have already said, with the syndics.   But before the votes
of the contemporaries of the senators be taken, the pre-

[1] "This V. H. is Pieter de la Court (1618-85), an eminent publicist,
who wrote under the initials D. C. (De la Court), V. H. (Van den Hove,
the Dutch equivalent).   He was a friend of John de Witt, and opposed
to the party of the Statholders."—POLLOCK'S *Life and Philosophy of
Spinoza*, towards end of Chap. X.

sident of the senate for the time being shall explain the
state of affairs, and what the senate's own opinion is on the
matter in question, and why; after which the votes shall
be collected in the accustomed order.

33. The entire senate ought not to meet every day, but,
like all great councils, at a certain fixed time. But as in
the mean time the business of the dominion must be
executed, it is, therefore, necessary that some part of the
senators be chosen, who, on the dismissal of the senate,
shall supply its place, and whose duty it shall be to summon
the senate itself, when need is; to execute its orders about
affairs of state; to read letters written to the senate and
supreme council; and, lastly, to consult about the matters
to be proposed in the senate. But that all these points,
and the order of this assembly, as a whole, may be more
easily conceived, I will describe the whole matter more
precisely.

34. The senators who, as we have said already, are to be
chosen for a year, are to be divided into four or six series,
of which let the first have the first seat in the senate for
the first three or two months in the year; and at the ex-
piration of this time, let the second series take the place of
the first, and so on, observing their turns, so that that
series which was first in the first months may be last in
the second period. Furthermore, there are to be appointed
as many presidents as there are series, and the same
number of vice-presidents to fill their places when required—that is, two are to be chosen out of every series,
one to be its president, the other its vice-president. And
let the president of the first series preside in the senate
also, for the first months; or, in his absence, let his vice-
president fill his place; and so on with the rest, observing
the same order as above. Next, out of the first series,
some are to be chosen by vote or lot to fill the place of the
senate, when it is dismissed, in conjunction with the president and vice-president of the same series; and that, for the
same space of time, as the said series occupies the first place
in the senate; and thus, when that time is past, as many
are again to be chosen out of the second series, by vote or
lot, to fill, in conjunction with their president and vice-
president, the place of the first series, and supply the lack

of a senate; and so on with the rest. And there is no need that the election of these men—I mean those that I have said are to be chosen for periods of three or two months, by vote or lot—should be made by the supreme council. For the reason which we gave in the twenty-ninth section is not here applicable, much less the reason stated in the seventeenth. It suffices, then, that they be elected by the senate and the syndics present at its meeting.

35. But of these persons we cannot so precisely ascertain the number. However, this is certain, that they must be too numerous to be easily susceptible of corruption. For though they can by themselves determine nothing concerning affairs of state, yet they can delay the senate, or, what would be worst of all, delude it by putting forward matters of no importance, and keeping back those that are of greater—not to mention that, if they were too few, the absence of one or two might delay public business. But as, on the contrary, these consuls are for that very reason appointed, because great councils cannot devote themselves every day to public business, a remedy must be looked for necessarily here, and their inadequacy of number be made up for by the shortness of their term of office. And thus, if only thirteen or so be chosen for two or three months, they will be too many to be corrupted in this short period. And for this cause, also, did I recommend that their successors should by no means be appointed, except at the very time when they do succeed, and the others go away.

36. We have said, that it is also their duty, when any, though few, of them think it needful, to convoke the senate, to put before it the matters to be decided, to dismiss it, and to execute its orders about public business. But I will now briefly state the order in which this ought to be done, so that business may not be long protracted by useless questions. Let, then, the consuls consult about the matter to be proposed in the senate, and what is required to be done; and, if they are all of one mind about it, then let them convoke the senate, and, having duly explained the question, let them set forth what their opinion is, and, without waiting for another's opinion, collect the votes in their order. But if the consuls support more than one opinion,

then, in the senate, that opinion is first to be stated on the question proposed, which was supported by the larger number of consuls. And if the same is not approved by the majority of senate and consuls, but the waverers and opponents together are in a majority, which is to be determined by ballot, as we have already mentioned, then let them set forth the second opinion, which had fewer votes than the former among the consuls, and so on with the rest. But if none be approved by a majority of the whole senate, the senate is to be adjourned to the next day, or for a short time, that the consuls meanwhile may see, if they can find other means, that may give more satisfaction. But if they do not succeed in finding other means, or if the majority of the senate refuses to approve such as they have found, then the opinion of every senator is to be heard; and if the majority of the senate also refuses to support any of these, then the votes are to be taken again on every opinion, and not only the affirmative votes, as hitherto, but the doubtful and negative are to be counted. And if the affirmative prove more numerous than the doubtful or negative, then that opinion is to hold good; but, on the contrary, to be lost, if the negative prove more numerous than the doubtful or affirmative. But if on every opinion there is a greater number of doubters than of voters for and against, then let the council of syndics join the senate, and vote with the senators, with only affirmative and negative votes, omitting those that signify a hesitating mind. And the same order is to be observed about matters referred by the senate to the supreme council. So much for the senate.

37. As for the court of justice or bench, it cannot rest upon the same foundations as that which exists under a monarch, as we described it in Chap. VI. Secs. 26, and following. For (Sec. 14) it agrees not with the foundations of our present dominion, that any account be made of families or clans. And there must be a further difference, because judges chosen from the patricians only might indeed be restrained by the fear of their patrician successors, from pronouncing any unjust judgment against any of the patricians, and, perhaps, would hardly have the courage to punish them after their deserts; but they

would, on the other hand, dare everything against the
commons, and daily carry off the rich among them for a
prey. I know that the plan of the Genoese is therefore
approved by many, for they choose their judges not among
the patricians, but among foreigners. But this seems to
me, considering the matter in the abstract, absurdly ordained, that foreigners and not patricians should be called
in to interpret the laws. For what are judges but interpreters of the laws? And I am therefore persuaded that
herein also the Genoese have had regard rather to the
genius of their own race, than to the very nature of this
kind of dominion. We must, therefore, by considering the
matter in the abstract, devise the means which best agree
with the form of this government.

38. But as far as regards the number of the judges, the
theory of this constitution requires no peculiar number ;
but as under monarchical dominion, so under this, it suffices
that they be too numerous to be corrupted by a private
man. For their duty is but to provide against one private
person doing wrong to another, and therefore to decide disputes between private persons, as well patricians as commons, and to exact penalties from delinquents, and even
from patricians, syndics, and senators, as far as they have
offended against the laws, whereby all are bound. But
disputes that may arise between cities that are subject to
the dominion, are to be decided in the supreme council.

39. Furthermore the principle regulating the time, for
which the judges should be appointed, is the same in both
dominions, and also the principle of a certain part of them
retiring every year; and, lastly, although it is not necessary for every one of them to be of a different family, yet
it is necessary that two related by blood should not sit on
the same bench together. And this last point is to be observed also in the other councils, except the supreme one, in
which it is enough, if it be only provided by law that in
elections no man may nominate a relation, nor vote upon
his nomination by another, and also that two relations may
not draw lots from the urn for the nomination of any
minister of the dominion. This, I say, is sufficient in a
council that is composed of so large a number of men, and
has no special profits assigned to it. And so utterly un-

harmed will the dominion be in this quarter, that it is absurd to pass a law excluding from the supreme council the relations of all the patricians, as we said in the four-teenth section. But that it is absurd is manifest. For that law could not be instituted by the patricians them-selves, without their thereby all absolutely abdicating their own right, and therefore not the patricians themselves but the commons would defend this law, which is directly con-trary to what we proved in Secs. 5 and 6. But that law of the dominion, whereby it is ordained that the same uniform proportion be maintained between the numbers of the patricians and the multitude, chiefly contemplates this end of preserving the patricians' right and power, that is, pro-vides against their becoming too few to be able to govern the multitude.

40. But the judges are to be chosen by the supreme council out of the patricians only, that is (Sec. 17) out of the actual authors of the laws, and the judgments they pass, as well in civil as criminal cases, shall be valid, if they were pronounced in due course of justice and without partiality; into which matter the syndics shall be by law authorized to inquire, and to judge and determine thereof.

41. The judges' emoluments ought to be the same, as we mentioned in the twenty-ninth section of the sixth chapter; namely, that they receive from the losing party upon every judgment which they pass in civil cases, an aliquot part of the whole sum at stake. But as to their sentences in criminal cases, let there be here this difference only, that the goods which they confiscate, and every fine whereby lesser crimes are punished, be assigned to them-selves only, yet on this condition, that they may never compel anyone to confess by torture, and thus, precaution enough will be taken against their being unfair to the commons, and through fear too lenient to the patricians. For besides that this fear is tempered by avarice itself, and that veiled under the specious name of justice, they are also numerous, and vote, not openly, but by ballot, so that a man may be indignant at losing his case, but can have no reason to impute it to a particular person. Moreover the fear of the syndics will restrain them from pronouncing an inequitable, or at least absurd sentence, or from acting

any of them treacherously, besides that in so large a number of judges there will always be one or two, that the unfair stand in awe of. Lastly, as far as the commons are concerned, they also will be adequately secured if they are allowed to appeal to the syndics, who, as I have said, are by law authorized to inquire, judge, and determine about the conduct of the judges. For it is certain that the syndics will not be able to escape the hatred of the patricians, and on the other hand, will always be most popular with the commons, whose applause they will try as far as they can to bid for. To which end, opportunity being given them, they will not fail to reverse sentences pronounced against the laws of the court, and to examine any judge, and to punish those that are partial, for nothing moves the hearts of a multitude more than this. Nor is it an objection, but, on the contrary, an advantage, that such examples can but rarely occur. For not to mention that that commonwealth is ill ordered where examples are daily made of criminals (as we showed Chap. V. Sec. 2), those events must surely be very rare that are most renowned by fame.

42. Those who are sent as governors to cities and provinces ought to be chosen out of the rank of senators, because it is the duty of senators to look after the fortifications of cities, the treasury, the military, etc. But those, who were sent to somewhat distant regions, would be unable to attend the senate, and, therefore, those only are to be summoned from the senate itself, who are destined to cities founded on their native soil ; but those whom they wish to send to places more remote are to be chosen out of those, whose age is consistent with senatorial rank. But not even thus do I think that the peace of the dominion will be sufficiently provided for, that is, if the neighbouring cities are altogether denied the right of vote, unless they are so weak, that they can be openly set at naught, which cannot surely be supposed. And so it is necessary, that the neighbouring cities be granted the right of citizenship, and that from every one of them twenty, or thirty, or forty chosen citizens (for the number should vary with the size of the city) be enrolled among the patricians, out of whom three, four, or five ought to be yearly elected to be of the senate, and one for life to be a syndic. And let

those who are of the senate be sent with their syndic, to govern the city out of which they were chosen.

43. Moreover, judges are to be established in every city, chosen out of the patricians of that city.　But of these I think it unnecessary to treat at length, because they concern not the foundations of this sort of dominion in particular.

44. In every council the secretaries and other officials of this kind, as they have not the right of voting, should be chosen from the commons.　But as these, by their long practice of business, are the most conversant with the affairs to be transacted, it often arises that more deference than right is shown to their advice, and that the state of the whole dominion depends chiefly on their guidance: which thing has been fatal to the Dutch.　For this cannot happen without exciting the jealousy of many of the noblest.　And surely we cannot doubt, that a senate, whose wisdom is derived from the advice, not of senators, but of officials, will be most frequented by the sluggish, and the condition of this sort of dominion will be little better than that of a monarchy directed by a few counsellors of the king.　(See Chap. VI. Secs. 5-7).　However, to this evil the dominion will be more or less liable, according as it was well or ill founded.　For the liberty of a dominion is never defended without risk, if it has not firm enough foundations; and, to avoid that risk, patricians choose from the commons ambitious ministers, who are slaughtered as victims to appease the wrath of those, who are plotting against liberty.　But where liberty has firm enough foundations, there the patricians themselves vie for the honour of defending it, and are anxious that prudence in the conduct of affairs should flow from their own advice only ; and in laying the foundations of this dominion we have studied above all these two points, namely, to exclude the commons from giving advice as much as from giving votes (Secs. 3, 4), and, therefore, to place the whole authority of the dominion with the whole body of patricians, but its exercise with the syndics and senate, and, lastly, the right of convoking the senate, and treating of matters affecting the common welfare with consuls chosen from the senate itself. But, if it is further ordained that the secretary, whether in

the senate or in other councils, be appointed for four or
five years at most, and have attached to him an assistant-
secretary appointed for the same period, to bear part of
the work during that time, or that the senate have not
one, but several secretaries, employed one in one depart-
ment, and another in another, the power of the officials
will never become of any consequence.

45. Treasurers are likewise to be chosen from the commons, and are to be bound to submit the treasury accounts
to the syndics as well as to the senate.

46. Matters concerning religion we have set forth at
sufficient length in our Theologico-Political Treatise. Yet
certain points we then omitted, of which it was not there
the place to treat; for instance, that all the patricians
must be of the same religion, that is, of that most simple
and general religion, which in that treatise we described.
For it is above all to be avoided, that the patricians themselves should be divided into sects, and show favour, some
to this, and others to that, and thence become mastered by
superstition, and try to deprive the subjects of the liberty
of speaking out their opinions. In the second place, though
everyone is to be given liberty to speak out his opinion,
yet great conventicles are to be forbidden. And, therefore,
those that are attached to another religion are, indeed, to
be allowed to build as many temples as they please; yet
these are to be small, and limited to a certain standard of
size, and on sites at some little distance one from another.
But it is very important, that the temples consecrated to
the national religion should be large and costly, and that
only patricians or senators should be allowed to administer its principal rites, and thus that patricians only
be suffered to baptize, celebrate marriages, and lay on
hands, and that in general they be recognized as the
priests of the temples and the champions and interpreters
of the national religion. But, for preaching, and to
manage the church treasury and its daily business, let
some persons be chosen from the commons by the senate
itself, to be, as it were, the senate's deputies, and, therefore, bound to render it account of everything.

47. And these are points that concern the foundations
of this sort of dominion; to which I will add some few

others less essential indeed, but yet of great importance. Namely, that the patricians, when they walk, should be distinguished by some special garment, or dress, and be saluted by some special title; and that every man of the commons should give way to them; and that, if any patrician has lost his property by some unavoidable misfortune, he should be restored to his old condition at the public expense; but if, on the contrary, it be proved that he has spent the same in presents, ostentation, gaming, debauchery, &c., or that he is insolvent, he must lose his dignity, and be held unworthy of every honour and office. For he, that cannot govern himself and his own private affairs, will much less be able to advise on public affairs.

48. Those, whom the law compels to take an oath, will be much more cautious of perjury, if they are bidden to swear by the country's safety and liberty and by the supreme council, than if they are told to swear by God. For he who swears by God, gives as surety some private advantage to himself, whereof he is judge; but he, who by his oath gives as surety his country's liberty and safety, swears by what is the common advantage of all, whereof he is not judge, and if he perjures himself, thereby declares·that he is his country's enemy.

49. Academies, that are founded at the public expense, are instituted not so much to cultivate men's natural abilities as to restrain them. But in a free commonwealth arts and sciences will be best cultivated to the full, if everyone that asks leave is allowed to teach publicly, and that at his own cost and risk. But these and the like points I reserve for another place.[1] For here I determined to treat only such matters as concern an aristocratic dominion only.

---

[1] This promise is not kept by the author, no doubt owing to his not living to finish the work.

CHAPTER IX.

OF ARISTOCRACY.   CONTINUATION.

HITHERTO we have considered an aristocracy, so far as it takes its name from one city, which is the head of the whole dominion. It is now time to treat of that, which is in the hands of more than one city, and which I think preferable to the former. But that we may notice its difference and its superiority, we will pass in review the foundations of dominion, one by one, rejecting those foundations, which are unsuited to the present kind, and laying in their place others for it to rest upon.

2. The cities, then, which enjoy the right of citizenship, must be so built and fortified, that, on the one hand, each city by itself may be unable to subsist without the rest, and that yet, on the other hand, it cannot desert the rest without great harm to the whole dominion. For thus they will always remain united. But cities, which are so constituted, that they can neither maintain themselves, nor be dangerous to the rest, are clearly not independent, but absolutely subject to the rest.

3. But the contents of the ninth and tenth sections of the last chapter are deduced from the general nature of aristocracy, as are also the proportion between the numbers of the patricians and the multitude, and the proper age and condition of those that are to be made patricians; so that on these points no difference can arise, whether the dominion be in the hands of one or more cities. But the supreme council must here be on a different footing. For if any city of the dominion were assigned for the meeting of this supreme council, it would in reality be the head of the dominion; and, therefore, either they would have to take turns, or a place would have to be assigned for this council, that has not the right of citizenship, and belongs

equally to all. But either alternative is as difficult to effect, as it is easy to state; I mean, either that so many thousands of men should have to go often outside their cities, or that they should have to assemble sometimes in one place, sometimes in another.

4. But that we may conclude aright what should be done in this matter, and on what plan the councils of this dominion ought to be formed, from its own very nature and condition, these points are to be considered; namely, that every city has so much more right than a private man, as it excels him in power (Chap. II. Sec. 4), and consequently that every city of this dominion has as much right within its walls, or the limits of its jurisdiction, as it has power; and, in the next place, that all the cities are mutually associated and united, not as under a treaty, but as forming one dominion, yet so that every city has so much more right as against the dominion than the others, as it exceeds the others in power. For he who seeks equality between unequals, seeks an absurdity. Citizens, indeed, are rightly esteemed equal, because the power of each, compared with that of the whole dominion, is of no account. But each city's power constitutes a large part of the power of the dominion itself, and so much the larger, as the city itself is greater. And, therefore, the cities cannot all be held equal. But, as the power of each, so also its right should be estimated by its greatness. The bonds, however, by which they should be bound into one dominion, are above all a senate and a court of justice (Chap. IV. Sec. 1). But how by these bonds they are all to be so united, that each of them may yet remain, as far as possible, independent, I will here briefly show.

5. I suppose then, that the patricians of every city, who, according to its size, should be more, or fewer (Sec. 3), have supreme right over their own city, and that, in that city's supreme council, they have supreme authority to fortify the city and enlarge its walls, to impose taxes, to pass and repeal laws, and, in general, to do everything which they judge necessary to their city's preservation and increase. But to manage the common business of the dominion, a senate is to be created on just the same footing as we described in the last chapter, so that there be

between this senate and the former no difference, except
that this has also authority to decide the disputes, which
may arise between cities.   For in this dominion, of which
no city is head, it cannot be done by the supreme council.
(See Chap. VI. Sec. 38.)

6. But, in this dominion, the supreme council is not to
be called together, unless there is need to alter the form of
the dominion itself, or on some difficult business, to which
the senators shall think themselves unequal; and so it will
very rarely happen, that all the patricians are summoned
to council.   For we have said (Chap. VIII. Sec. 17), that
the supreme council's function is to pass and repeal laws,
and to choose the ministers of the dominion. But the laws,
or general constitution of the whole dominion, ought not to
be changed as soon as instituted.   If, however, time and
occasion suggest the institution of some new law or the
change of one already ordained, the question may first be
discussed in the senate, and after the agreement of the
senate in the matter, then let envoys next be sent to the
cities by the senate itself, to inform the patricians of every
city of the opinion of the senate, and lastly, if the majority
of the cities follow that opinion, it shall then remain good,
but otherwise be of no effect.   And this same order may
be observed in choosing the generals of the army and the
ambassadors to be sent to other realms, as also about
decrees concerning the making of war or accepting conditions of peace.   But in choosing the other public officials,
since (as we showed in Sec. 4) every city, as far as can be,
ought to remain independent, and to have as much more
right than the others in the dominion, as it exceeds them
in power, the following order must necessarily be observed.
The senators are to be chosen by the patricians of each
city; that is, the patricians of one city are to elect in their
own council a fixed number of senators from their colleagues of their own city, which number is to be to that of
the patricians of that city as one to twelve (Chap. VIII.
Sec. 30); and they are to designate whom they will to be
of the first, second, third, or other series; and in like
manner the patricians of the other cities, in proportion to
their number, are to choose more or fewer senators, and
distribute them among the series, into a certain number of

which we have said the senate is to be divided. (Chap. VIII. Sec. 34.) By which means it will result, that in every series of senators there will be found senators of every city, more or fewer, according to its size. But the presidents and vice-presidents of the series, being fewer in number than the cities, are to be chosen by lot by the senate out of the consuls, who are to be appointed first. The same order is to be maintained in appointing the supreme judges of the dominion, namely, that the patricians of every city are to elect from their colleagues in proportion to their number more or fewer judges. And so it will be the case, that every city in choosing officials will be as independent as possible, and that each, in proportion to its power, will have the more right alike in the senate and the court of justice; supposing, that is, that the order observed by senate and court in deciding public affairs, and settling disputes is such in all respects, as we have described it in the thirty-third and thirty-fourth sections of the last chapter.[1]

7. Next, the commanders of battalions and military tribunes are also to be chosen from the patricians. For as it is fair, that every city in proportion to its size should be bound to levy a certain number of soldiers for the general safety of the whole dominion, it is also fair, that from the patricians of every city in proportion to the number of regiments, which they are bound to maintain, they may appoint so many tribunes, captains, ensigns, etc., as are needed to discipline that part of the military, which they supply to the dominion.

8. No taxes are to be imposed by the senate on the subjects; but to meet the expenditure, which by decree of the senate is necessary to carry on public business, not the subjects, but the cities themselves are to be called to assessment by the senate, so that every city, in proportion to its size, should pay a larger or smaller share of the expense. And this share indeed is to be exacted by the patricians of every city from their own citizens in what way they please, either by compelling them to an assessment, or, as is much fairer, by imposing taxes on them.

---

[1] So the text: but the court of justice is not described till the thirty-seventh and following sections of Chap. VIII.

9. Further, although all the cities of this dominion are not maritime, nor the senators summoned from the maritime cities only, yet may the same emoluments be awarded to the senators, as we mentioned in the thirty-first section of the last chapter. To which end it will be possible to devise means, varying with the composition of the dominion, to link the cities to one another more closely. But the other points concerning the senate and the court of justice and the whole dominion in general, which I delivered in the last chapter, are to be applied to this dominion also. And so we see, that in a dominion which is in the hands of several cities, it will not be necessary to assign a fixed time or place for assembling the supreme council. But for the senate and court of justice a place is to be appointed in a village, or in a city, that has not the right of voting. But I return to those points, which concern the cities taken by themselves.

10. The order to be observed by the supreme council of a single city, in choosing officials of the dominion and of the city, and in making decrees, should be the same that I have delivered in the twenty-seventh and thirty-sixth sections of the last chapter. For the policy is the same here as it was there. Next a council of syndics is to be formed, subordinate to the council of the city, and having the same relation to it as the council of syndics of the last chapter had to the council of the entire dominion, and let its functions within the limits of the city be also the same, and let it enjoy the same emoluments. But if a city, and consequently the number of its patricians be so small that it cannot create more than one syndic or two, which two are not enough to make a council, then the supreme council of the city is to appoint judges to assist the syndics in trials according to the matter at issue, or else the dispute must be referred to the supreme council of syndics. For from every city some also out of the syndics are to be sent to the place where the senate sits, to see that the constitution of the whole dominion is preserved unbroken, and they are to sit in the senate without the right of voting.

11. The consuls of the cities are likewise to be chosen by the patricians of their city, and are to constitute a sort of senate for it. But their number I cannot determine,

nor yet do I think it necessary, since the city's business of great importance is transacted by its supreme council, and matters concerning the whole dominion by the great senate. But if they be few, it will be necessary that they give their votes in their council openly, and not by ballot, as in large councils. For in small councils, when votes are given secretly, by a little extra cunning one can easily detect the author of every vote, and in many ways deceive the less attentive.

12. Besides, in every city judges are to be appointed by its supreme council, from whose sentence, however, let everyone but an openly convicted criminal or confessed debtor have a right of appeal to the supreme court of justice of the dominion. But this need not be pursued further.

13. It remains, therefore, to speak of the cities which are not independent. If these were founded in an actual province or district of the dominion, and their inhabitants are of the same nation and language, they ought of necessity, like villages, to be esteemed parts of the neighbouring cities, so that each of them should be under the government of this or that independent city. And the reason of this is, that the patricians are chosen by the supreme council, not of the dominion, but of every city, and in every city are more or fewer, according to the number of inhabitants within the limits of its jurisdiction (Sec. 5). And so it is necessary, that the multitude of the city, which is not independent, be referred to the census of another which is independent, and depend upon the latter's government. But cities captured by right of war, and annexed to the dominion, are either to be esteemed associates in the dominion, and though conquered put under an obligation by that benefit, or else colonies to enjoy the right of citizenship are to be sent thither, and the natives removed elsewhere or utterly destroyed,

14. And these are the things, which touch the foundations of the dominion. But that its condition is better than that of the aristocracy, which is called after one city only, I conclude from this, namely, that the patricians of every city, after the manner of human desire, will be eager to keep, and if possible increase their right, both in their city and in the senate; and therefore will try, as far as

possible, to attract the multitude to themselves, and consequently to make a stir in the dominion by good deeds
rather than by fear, and to increase their own number; because the more numerous they are, the more senators they
will choose out of their own council (Sec. 6), and hence the
more right (Sec. 6) they will possess in the dominion. Nor
is it an objection, that while every city is consulting its
own interest and suspecting the rest, they more often
quarrel among themselves, and waste time in disputing.
For if, while the Romans are debating, Saguntum is lost:[1]
on the other hand, while a few are deciding everything in
conformity with their own passions only, liberty and the
general good are lost.   For men's natural abilities are too
dull to see through everything at once; but by consulting,
listening, and debating, they grow more acute, and while
they are trying all means, they at last discover those
which they want, which all approve, but no one would
have thought of in the first instance. But if anyone retorts,
that the dominion of the Dutch has not long endured
without a count or one to fill his place, let him have this
reply, that the Dutch thought, that to maintain their liberty
it was enough to abandon their count, and to behead the
body of their dominion, but never thought of remoulding
it, and left its limbs, just as they had been first constituted, so that the county of Holland has remained without a count, like a headless body, and the actual dominion
has lasted on without the name.   And so it is no wonder
that most of its subjects have not known, with whom the
authority of the dominion lay.   And even had this been
otherwise, yet those who actually held dominion were far
too few to govern the multitude and suppress their powerful adversaries.   Whence it has come to pass, that the
latter have often been able to plot against them with impunity, and at last to overthrow them. And so the sudden
overthrow of the said republic[2] has not arisen from a
useless waste of time in debates, but from the misformed
state of the said dominion and the fewness of its rulers.

---

[1] Livy, "Hist.," Bk. xxi. Chaps. VI. and following.
[2] A.D. 1672.   William Henry, Prince of Orange, afterwards William
III. of England, was made Statholder by a popular insurrection, consequent on the invasion of the French.

15. This aristocracy in the hands of several cities is also preferable to the other, because it is not necessary, as in the first described, to provide against its whole supreme council being overpowered by a sudden attack, since (Sec. 9) no time or place is appointed for its meeting. Moreover, powerful citizens in this dominion are less to be feared. For where several cities enjoy liberty, it is not enough for him, who is making ready his way to dominion, to seize one city, in order to hold dominion over the rest. And, lastly, liberty under this dominion is common to more. For where one city reigns alone, there the advantage of the rest is only so far considered, as suits that reigning city.

CHAPTER X.

OF ARISTOCRACY. CONCLUSION.

1.

HAVING explained and made proof of the foundations of both kinds of aristocracy, it remains to inquire whether by reason of any fault they are liable to be dissolved or changed into another form. The primary cause, by which dominions of this kind are dissolved, is that, which that most acute Florentine[1] observes in his "Discourses on Livy " (Bk. iii. Chap. I.), namely, that like a human body, " a dominion has daily added to it something that at some time or other needs to be remedied." And so, he says, it is necessary for something occasionally to occur, to bring back the dominion to that first principle, on which it was in the beginning established. And if this does not take place within the necessary time, its blemishes will go on increasing, till they cannot be removed, but with the dominion itself. And this restoration, he says, may either happen accidentally, or by the design and forethought of the laws or of a man of extraordinary virtue. And we cannot doubt, that this matter is of the greatest importance, and that, where provision has not been made against this inconvenience, the dominion will not be able to endure by its own excellence, but only by good fortune ; and on the other hand that, where a proper remedy has been applied to this evil, it will not be possible for it to fall by its own fault, but only by some inevitable fate, as we shall presently show more clearly. The first remedy, that suggested itself for this evil, was to appoint every five years a supreme dictator for one or two months, who should have the right to inquire, decide, and make ordinances concerning the acts of the senators and of every official, and

---

[1] Machiavelli.

thereby to bring back the dominion to its first principle. But he who studies to avoid the inconveniences, to which a dominion is liable, must apply remedies that suit its nature, and can be derived from its own foundations; otherwise in his wish to avoid Charybdis he falls upon Scylla. It is, indeed, true that all, as well rulers as ruled, ought to be restrained by fear of punishment or loss, so that they may not do wrong with impunity or even advantage; but, on the other hand, it is certain, that if this fear becomes common to good and bad men alike, the dominion must be in the utmost danger. Now as the authority of a dictator is absolute, it cannot fail to be a terror to all, especially if, as is here required, he were appointed at a stated time, because in that case every ambitious man would pursue this office with the utmost energy; and it is certain that in time of peace virtue is thought less of than wealth, so that the more haughty a man he is, the more easily he will get office. And this perhaps is why the Romans used to make a dictator at no fixed time, but under pressure of some accidental necessity. Though for all that, to quote Cicero's words, "the tumour of a dictator was displeasing to the good."[1] And to be sure, as this authority of a dictator is quite royal, it is impossible for the dominion to change into a monarchy without great peril to the republic, although it happen for ever so short a time. Furthermore, if no fixed time were appointed for creating a dictator, no notice would be paid to the interval between one dictator and another, which is the very thing that we said was most to be observed; and the whole thing would be exceedingly vague, and therefore easily neglected. Unless, then, this authority of a dictator be eternal and fixed, and therefore impossible to be conferred on one man without destroying the form of dominion, the dictatorial authority itself, and consequently the safety and preservation of the republic will be very uncertain.

2. But, on the other hand, we cannot doubt (Chap. VI. Sec. 3), that, if without destroying the form of dominion, the sword of the dictator might be permanent, and only

---

[1] Cic. ad Quint. Grat. iii. 8, 4. The better reading is "rumour," not "tumour." "The good" in such a passage means the aristocratic party.

terrible to the wicked, evils will never grow to such a pitch, that they cannot be eradicated or amended. In order, therefore, to secure all these conditions, we have said, that there is to be a council of syndics subordinate to the supreme council, to the end that the sword of the dictator should be permanent in the hands not of any natural person, but of a civil person, whose members are too numerous to divide the dominion amongst themselves (Chap. IX. Secs. 1, 2), or to combine in any wickedness. To which is to be added, that they are forbidden to fill any other office in the dominion, that they are not the paymasters of the soldiery, and, lastly, that they are of an age to prefer actual security to things new and perilous. Wherefore the dominion is in no danger from them, and consequently they cannot, and in fact will not be a terror to the good, but only to the wicked. For as they are less powerful to accomplish criminal designs, so are they more so to restrain wickedness. For, not to mention that they can resist it in its beginnings (since the council lasts for ever), they are also sufficiently numerous to dare to accuse and condemn this or that influential man without fear of his enmity; especially as they vote by ballot, and the sentence is pronounced in the name of the entire council.

3. But the tribunes of the commons at Rome were likewise regularly appointed; but they were too weak to restrain the power of a Scipio, and had besides to submit to the senate their plans for the public welfare,[1] which also frequently eluded them, by contriving that the one whom the senators were least afraid of should be most popular with the commons. Besides which, the tribunes' authority was supported against the patricians by the favour of the commons. and whenever they convoked the commons, it looked as if they were raising a sedition rather than assembling a council. Which inconveniences have certainly no place in the dominion which we have described in the last two chapters.

4. However, this authority of the syndics will only be

---

[1] Not by law, except before B.C. 287 and in the interval between the dictatorship of Sulla and the consulship of Pompey and Crassus. But in the golden age of the republic the senate in fact controlled the tribunes.

able to secure the preservation of the form of the dominion, and thus to prevent the laws from being broken, or anyone from gaining by transgressing; but will by no means suffice to prevent the growth of vices, which cannot be forbidden by law, such as those into which men fall from excess of leisure, and from which the ruin of a dominion not uncommonly follows. For men in time of peace lay aside fear, and gradually from being fierce savages become civilized or humane, and from being humane become soft and sluggish, and seek to excel one another not in virtue, but in ostentation and luxury. And hence they begin to put off their native manners and to put on foreign ones, that is, to become slaves.

5. To avoid these evils many have tried to establish sumptuary laws; but in vain. For all laws which can be broken without any injury to another, are counted but a laughing-stock, and are so far from bridling the desires and lusts of men, that on the contrary they stimulate them. For "we are ever eager for forbidden fruit, and desire what is denied."[1] Nor do idle men ever lack ability to elude the laws which are instituted about things, which cannot absolutely be forbidden, as banquets, plays, ornaments, and the like, of which only the excess is bad; and that is to be judged according to the individual's fortune, so that it cannot be determined by any general law.

6. I conclude, therefore, that the common vices of peace, of which we are here speaking, are never to be directly, but indirectly forbidden; that is, by laying such foundations of dominion, that the result may be, that the majority, I do not say are anxious to live wisely (for that is impossible), but are guided by those passions whence the republic has most advantage. And therefore the chief point to be studied is, that the rich may be, if not thrifty, yet avaricious. For there is no doubt, that, if this passion of avarice, which is general and lasting, be encouraged by the desire of glory, most people would set their chief affection upon increasing their property without disgrace, in order to acquire honours, while avoiding extreme infamy. If then we examine the foundations of both kinds of aristocracy

---

[1] Ovid, "Amores," III. iv. 17.

which I have explained in the last two chapters, we shall see, that this very result follows from them. For the number of rulers in both is so large, that most of the rich have access to government and to the offices of the dominion open to them.

7. But if it be further ordained (as we said, Chap. VIII. Sec. 47), that patricians who are insolvent be deposed from patrician rank, and that those who have lost their property by misfortune be restored to their former position, there is no doubt that all will try their best to keep their property. Moreover, they will never desire foreign costumes, nor disdain their native ones, if it is by law appointed, that patricians and candidates for office should be distinguished by a special robe, concerning which see Chap. VIII. Secs. 25, 47. And besides these, other means may be devised in every dominion agreeable to the nature of its situation and the national genius, and herein it is above all to be studied, that the subjects may do their duty rather spontaneously than under pressure of the law.

8. For a dominion, that looks no farther than to lead men by fear, will be rather free from vices, than possessed of virtue. But men are so to be led, that they may think that they are not led, but living after their own mind, and according to their free decision; and so that they are restrained only by love of liberty, desire to increase their property, and hope of gaining the honours of the dominion. But effigies, triumphs, and other incitements to virtue, are signs rather of slavery than liberty. For rewards of virtue are granted to slaves, not freemen. I admit, indeed, that men are very much stimulated by these incitements; but, as in the first instance, they are awarded to great men, so afterwards, with the growth of envy, they are granted to cowards and men swollen with the extent of their wealth, to the great indignation of all good men. Secondly, those, who boast of their ancestors' effigies and triumphs, think they are wronged, if they are not preferred to others. Lastly, not to mention other objections, it is certain that equality, which once cast off the general liberty is lost, can by no means be maintained, from the time that peculiar honours are by public law decreed to any man renowned for his virtue.

9. After which premisses, let us now see whether do-minions of this kind can be destroyed by any cause to which blame attaches. But if any dominion can be ever-lasting, that will necessarily be so, whose constitution being once rightly instituted remains unbroken. For the constitu-tion is the soul of a dominion. Therefore, if it is preserved, so is the dominion. But a constitution cannot remain un-conquered, unless it is defended alike by reason and common human passion : otherwise, if it relies only on the help of reason, it is certainly weak and easily overcome. Now since the fundamental constitution of both kinds of aristocracy has been shown to agree with reason and com-mon human passion, we can therefore assert that these, if any kinds of dominion, will be eternal, in other words, that they cannot be destroyed by any cause to which blame attaches, but only by some inevitable fate.

10. But it may still be objected to us, that, although the constitution of dominion above set forth is defended by reason and common human passion, yet for all that it may at some time be overpowered. For there is no passion, that is not sometimes overpowered. by a stronger contrary one; for we frequently see the fear of death overpowered by the greed for another's property. Men, who are running away in panic fear from the enemy, can be stopped by the fear of nothing else, but throw themselves into rivers, or rush into fire, to escape the enemy's steel. In whatever degree, there-fore, a commonwealth is rightly ordered, and its laws well made; yet in the extreme difficulties of a dominion, when all, as sometimes happens, are seized by a sort of panic terror, all, without regard to the future or the laws, approve only that which their actual fear suggests, all turn towards the man who is renowned for his victories, and set him free from the laws, and (establishing thereby the worst of pre-cedents), continue him in command, and entrust to his fidelity all affairs of state : and this was, in fact, the cause of the destruction of the Roman dominion, But to answer this objection, I say, first, that in a rightly constituted republic such terror does not arise but from a due cause. And so such terror and consequent confusion can be attri-buted to no cause avoidable by human foresight. In the next place, it is to be observed, that in a republic such as

we have above described, it is impossible (Chap. VIII. Secs. 9, 25) for this or that man so to distinguish himself by the report of his virtue, as to turn towards himself the attention of all, but he must have many rivals favoured by others. And so, although from terror there arise some confusion in the republic, yet no one will be able to elude the law and declare the election of anyone to an illegal military command, without its being immediately disputed by other candidates; and to settle the dispute, it will, in the end, be necessary to have recourse to the constitution ordained once for all, and approved by all, and to order the affairs of the dominion according to the existing laws. I may therefore absolutely assert, that as the aristocracy, which is in the hands of one city only, so especially that which is in the hands of several, is everlasting, or, in other words, can be dissolved or changed into another form by no internal cause.

CHAPTER XI.

OF DEMOCRACY.

1.

I PASS, at length, to the third and perfectly absolute dominion, which we call democracy. The difference between this and aristocracy consists, we have said, chiefly in this, that in an aristocracy it depends on the supreme council's will and free choice only, that this or that man is made a patrician, so that no one has the right to vote or fill public offices by inheritance, and that no one can by right demand this right, as is the case in the dominion, whereof we are now treating. For all, who are born of citizen parents, or on the soil of the country, or who have deserved well of the republic, or have accomplished any other conditions upon which the law grants to a man right of citizenship; they all, I say, have a right to demand for themselves the right to vote in the supreme council and to fill public offices, nor can they be refused it, but for crime or infamy.

2. If, then, it is by a law appointed, that the elder men only, who have reached a certain year of their age, or the first-born only, as soon as their age allows, or those who contribute to the republic a certain sum of money, shall have the right of voting in the supreme council and managing the business of the dominion; then, although on this system the result might be, that the supreme council would be composed of fewer citizens than that of the aristocracy of which we treated above, yet, for all that, dominions of this kind should be called democracies, because in them the citizens, who are destined to manage affairs of state, are not chosen as the best by the supreme council, but are destined to it by a law. And although for this reason dominions of this kind, that is, where not the best, but those who happen by chance to be rich, or who are born

eldest, are destined to govern, are thought inferior to an
aristocracy; yet, if we reflect on the practice or general
condition of mankind, the result in both cases will come to
the same thing.   For patricians will always think those
the best, who are rich, or related to themselves in blood, or
allied by friendship.   And, indeed, if such were the nature
of patricians, that they were free from all passion, and
guided by mere zeal for the public welfare in choosing their
patrician colleagues, no dominion could be compared with
aristocracy.   But experience itself teaches us only too well,
that things pass in quite a contrary manner, above all, in
oligarchies, where the will of the patricians, from the absence
of rivals, is most free from the law.   For there the patricians intentionally keep away the best men from the council,
and seek for themselves such colleagues in it, as hang upon
their words, so that in such a dominion things are in a
much more unhappy condition, because the choice of patricians depends entirely upon the arbitrary will of a few,
which is free or unrestrained by any law.   But I return to
my subject.

3. From what has been said in the last section, it is
manifest that we can conceive of various kinds of democracy.   But my intention is not to treat of every kind, but
of that only, "wherein all, without exception, who owe allegiance to the laws of the country only, and are further
independent and of respectable life, have the right of voting
in the supreme council and of filling the offices of the dominion."   I say expressly, "who owe allegiance to the
laws of the country only,' to exclude foreigners, who are
treated as being under another's dominion.   I added,
besides, "who are independent," except in so far as they
are under allegiance to the laws of the dominion, to exclude
women and slaves, who are under the authority of men and
masters, and also children and wards, as long as they are
under the authority of parents and guardians.   I said,
lastly, "and of respectable life," to exclude, above all, those
that are infamous from crime, or some disgraceful means
of livelihood.

4. But, perhaps, someone will ask, whether women are
under men's authority by nature or institution?   For if it
has been by mere institution, then we had no reason com-

pelling us to exclude women from government. But if we consult experience itself, we shall find that the origin of it is in their weakness. For there has never been a case of men and women reigning together, but wherever on the earth men are found, there we see that men rule, and women are ruled, and that on this plan, both sexes live in harmony. But on the other hand, the Amazons, who are reported to have held rule of old, did not suffer men to stop in their country, but reared only their female children, killing the males to whom they gave birth.[1] But if by nature women were equal to men, and were equally distinguished by force of character and ability, in which human power and therefore human right chiefly consist; surely among nations so many and different some would be found, where both sexes rule alike, and others, where men are ruled by women, and so brought up, that they can make less use of their abilities. And since this is nowhere the case, one may assert with perfect propriety, that women have not by nature equal right with men: but that they necessarily give way to men, and that thus it cannot happen, that both sexes should rule alike, much less that men should be ruled by women. But if we further reflect upon human passions, how men, in fact, generally love women merely from the passion of lust, and esteem their cleverness and wisdom in proportion to the excellence of their beauty, and also how very ill-disposed men are to suffer the women they love to show any sort of favour to others, and other facts of this kind, we shall easily see that men and women cannot rule alike without great hurt to peace. But of this enough.

---

[1] Justin, Histories, ii. 4.

BIBLIOGRAPHICAL NOTE
By Francesco Cordasco, Ph.D.

This list enumerates the most important books on Spinoza and will provide a working bibliography.

BIBLIOGRAPHY: The titles listed in WORKS and in BIO-GRAPHICAL & CRITICAL STUDIES all contain bibliographical details. The most valuable bibliography is that furnished by the catalogue of the library of the late Professor Abraham Wolf; cf. "Private Libraries", *London Times Literary Supplement* (September 30, 1939), p. 568.

TRANSLATIONS: Besides the Elwes translations other English translations include those of H. White and A. H. Stirling (*Ethics*, 1899) and of A. Wolf (*Treatise on God, Man, and his Well-Being*, 1910). Professor Wolf undertook a translation of the complete works but this was never, completed (*Works of Spinoza*, 1928—). French translations were made by E. Saisset (3 vols., 1861), and by Ch. Appuhn (4 vols., 1904, etc.); the best German translations are by B. Auerbach (2 vols., 1871), and that one edited by C. Gebhardt (3 vols., 1914-22).

WORKS: The best edition of the works is *Spinoza Opera* edited by C. Gebhardt (4 vols., Heidelberg, 1926), but great value will still be found in the older editions of Paulus (1802); Gfrörer (1830); Bruder (1843-1846); Van Vloten and Land (1882).

BIOGRAPHICAL & CRITICAL STUDIES: D. Camerer, *Die Lehre Spinozas* (1877); F. Pollock, *Spinoza: His Life and Philosophy* (1880, rep. 1899, 1911); J. Martineau, *Study of*

Spinoza (1882, rep. 1883, 1895). J. Caird, *Spinoza* (1888, rep. 1901); K. O. Meinsma, *Spinoza und en zijn Kring* (1896, German translation, 1909); J. Freudenthal, *Die Lebensgeschichte Spinozas in Quellenschriften* (1899); H. H. Joachim, *Study of the Ethics of Spinoza* (1901); R. A. Duff, *Spinoza's Ethical and Political Philosophy* (1903); J. Freudenthal, *Das Leben Spinozas* (1904, rep. 1927); K. Fischer, *Spinoza* (5th edition, 1909); A. Wolf, *Spinoza* (1910); E. Dunin-Borkowski, *Der Junge de Spinoza* (1910); V. Delbos, *Le Problème moral dans la philosophie de Spinoza* (1916); L. Brunschvicg, *Spinoza et ses Contemporains* (1923); L. Roth, *Spinoza, Descartes and Maimonides* (1924); J. A. Gunn, *Benedick Spinoza* (1925); A. Wolf, ed., *The Oldest Biography of Spinoza* (1927); R. McKeon, *The Philosophy of Spinoza* (1928); L. Roth, *Spinoza* (1929); H. Sérouya, *Spinoza, sa vie et sa philosophie* (1933); W. Bernald, *The Philosophy of Spinoza* (1934); G. Roverelli, *Il pensiero spinoziano nell' idealismo moderno* (1934); H. A. Wolfson, *The Philosophy of Spinoza* (1934); P. Siwek, *Spinoza et le panthéisme religieux* (1937); D. Bidney, *The Psychology and ethics of Spinoza* (1940); R. Kayser, *Spinoza* (1946); J. Sikkes, *Spinoza, leer en leven* (1946).

SOCIETY PUBLICATIONS: The *New York Spinoza Society* has published the texts of addresses presented to it. The *Chronicon Spinozanum* (1921—) and the *Bibliotheca Spinozana* (1922—), both edited by C. Gebhardt, were suspended during the second world war. An important Dutch Spinoza Society issued a catalogue of its library in 1871 (A. van der Linde, *Benedictus Spinoza: bibliographie,* Gravenhage, 1871) which lists 445 titles.